The Principal Navigations, Voyages, Traffiques and Discoveries of the English Nation — Volume 08; Asia, Part I

Richard Hakluyt

Alpha Editions

This edition published in 2024

ISBN 9789362511911

Design and Setting By
Alpha Editions
www.alphaedis.com
Email - info@alphaedis.com

As per information held with us this book is in Public Domain.
This book is a reproduction of an important historical work.
Alpha Editions uses the best technology to reproduce historical work
in the same manner it was first published to preserve its original nature.
Any marks or number seen are left intentionally to preserve.

Contents

VOL. VIII.	- 1 -
ASIA. PART I.	- 2 -
OF THE ENGLISH NATION IN ASIA.	- 3 -
DEDICATIO LIBRI.	- 52 -
CAPVT. 1.	- 53 -
CAPVT. 2.	- 56 -
CAPVT. 3.	- 58 -
CAPVT. 4.	- 66 -
CAPVT. 5.	- 68 -
CAPVT. 6.	- 69 -
CAPVT. 7.	- 70 -
CAPVT. 8.	- 72 -
CAPVT. 9.	- 73 -
CAPVT. 10.	- 74 -
CAPUT. 11.	- 75 -
CAPVT. 12.	- 77 -
CAPVT. 13.	- 100 -
CAPVT. 14.	- 101 -
CAPVT. 15.	- 104 -
CAPVT. 16.	- 105 -
CAPVT. 17.	- 107 -
CAPVT. 18.	- 109 -
CAPVT. 19.	- 110 -
CAPVT. 20.	- 112 -

CAPVT. 21.	- 114 -
CAPVT 22.	- 116 -
CAPVT. 23.	- 118 -
MANDEVILLE'S VOYAGES	- 142 -
PART II.	- 143 -
CAPVT. 24.	- 144 -
CAPVT. 25.	- 145 -
CAPVT. 26.	- 146 -
CAPVT. 27.	- 148 -
CAPVT. 28.	- 150 -
CAPVT. 29.	- 152 -
CAPVT. 30.	- 188 -
CAPVT. 31.	- 190 -
CAPVT. 32.	- 191 -
CAPVT. 33.	- 192 -
CAPVT. 34.	- 203 -
CAPVT. 35.	- 208 -
CAPVT. 36.	- 211 -
CAPVT. 37.	- 215 -

VOL. VIII.

ASIA. PART I.

Navigations, Voyages, Traffiques, and Discoueries

OF THE ENGLISH NATION IN ASIA.

The life and trauailes of Pelagius borne in Wales.

Pelagius Cambrius ex ea Britanniæ parte oriundus, famati illius Collegij Bannochorensis a Cestria non procul, præpositus, erat, in quo Christianorum philosophorum duo millia ac centum, ad plebis in Christo commoditatem militabant, manuum suarum laboribus, iuxta Pauli doctrinam victitantes. Post quam plures exhibitos, pro Christiana Repub. labores, vir eruditione insignis, et tum Græcè, tum Latinè peritus, vt Tertullianus alter, quorundam Clericorum lacessitus iniurijs, grauatim tulit, ac tandem a fide defecit.

Peragratis igitur deinceps Gallijs, in Aegyptum, et Syriam aliásque orientis Regiones demum peruenit. Vbi ex earum partium Monacho præsul ordinatus, sui nominis hæresim fabricabat: asserens hominem sine peccato nasci, ac solo voluntatis imperio sine gratia saluari posse, vt ita nefarius baptismum ac fidem tolleret. Cum his et consimilibus impostricis doctrinæ fæcibus in patriam suam reuersus, omnem illam Regionem, Iuliano et Cælestino Pseudoepiscopis fautoribus, conspurcabat. Verum ante lapsum suum studia tractabat honestissima, vt post Gennadium, Bedam, et Honorium alij ferunt authores, composuítque multos libros ad Christianam vtilitatem. At postquam est Hereticus publicatus, multo plures edidit hæresi succurrentes, et ex diametro cum vera pietate pugnantes, vnde erat a suis Britannis in exilium pulsus, vt in Epistola ad Martinum 5. Valdenus habet. Claruit anno post Christum incarnatum, 390. sub Maximo Britannorum Rege.

The same in English.

Pelagius, borne in that part of Britaine which is called Wales, was head or gouernour of the famous Colledge of Bangor, not farre from Chester, wherein liued a Societie of 2100. Diuines, or Students of Christian philosophie, applying themselues to the profite of the Christian people, and liuing by the labours of their owne hands, according to Pauls doctrine. He was a man excellently learned, and skilfull both in the Greeke and Latine tongues, and as it were another Tertullian; after his long and great trauailes for the good of the Christian common wealth, seeing himselfe abused, and iniuriously dealt withall by some of the Clergie of that time, he tooke the matter so grieuously, that at the last he relapsed from the faith.

Whereupon he left Wales, and went into France, and hauing gone through France, [Footnote: He is said to have resided long at Rome, only leaving on the capture of that city by the Gottis.] hee went therehence into Egypt, Syria, and other Countries of the East, and being made Priest by a certaine Monke of those partes, he there hatched his heresie, which according to his name was called the heresie of the Pelagians: which was, that manne was borne without sinne, and might be saued by the power of his owne will without grace, that so the miserable man might take away faith and baptisme. With this and the like dregges of false doctrine, he returned againe into Wales, and there by the meanes of the two false Prelates Iulian and Celestine, who fauoured his heresie, hee infected the whole Countrey with it. But before his fall and Apostasie from the faith, he exercised himselfe in the best studies, as Gennadius, Beda, Honorius, and other authors doe report of him, and wrote many bookes seruing not a litle to Christian vtilitie: but being once fallen into his heresie, hee wrote many more erroneous bookes, then he did before honest, and sincere: whereupon, at the last his owne Countreymen banished him, as Walden testifieth in his Epistle to Pope Martine the fift. He flourished in the yere after the Incarnation, 390. Maximus being then King of Britaine.

* * * * *

A testimonie of the sending of Sighelmus Bishop of Shirburne, by King Alphred, vnto Saint Thomas of India in the yeare of our Lord 883, recorded by William of Malmesburie, in his second booke and fourth Chapter de gestis regum Anglorum.

Eleemosynis intentus priuilegia ecclesiarum, sicut pater statuerat, roborauit; et trans mare Romam, et ad sanctum Thomam in Indiam multa munera misit. Legatus in hoc missus Sighelmus Shirburnensis Episcopus cum magna prosperitate, quod quiuis hoc seculo miretur, Indiam penetrauit; inde rediens exoticos splendores gemmarum, et liquores aromatum, quorum illa humus ferax est, reportauit.

The same in English.

King Alphred being addicted to giving of almes, confirmed the priuileges of Churches as his father had determined; and sent also many giftes beyond the seas vnto Rome, and vnto S. Thomas of India. His messenger in this businesse was Sighelmus bishop of Schirburne; [Footnote: Sherborne, in Dorsetshire, where an abbey was founded in 700.] who with great prosperitie (which is a matter to be wondered at in this our age) trauailed thorough India, and returning home brought with him many strange and precious vnions and costly spyces, such as that countrey plentifully yeeldeth.

* * * * *

A second testimony of the foresaid Sighelmus his voyage vnto Saint Thomas of India &c. out of William of Malmesburie his second booke de gestis pontificum Anglorum, cap. de episcopis Schireburnensibus, Salisburiensibus, Wiltunensibus.

Sighelmus trans mare, causa eleemosynarum regis, et etiam ad Sanctam Thomam in Indiam missus mira prosperitate, quod quiuis in hoc seculo miretur, Indiam penetrauit; indequè rediens exotici generis gemmas, quarum illa humus ferax est, reportauit. Nonnullæ illarum adhuc in ecclesiæ monumentis visuntur.

The same in English.

Sighelmus being for the performance of the kings almes sent beyond the seas, and trauailing vnto S. Thomas of India, very prosperously (which a man would woonder at in this age) passed through the sayde countrey of India, and returning home brought with him diuers strange and precious stones, such as that climate affourdeth. Many of which stones are as yet extant in the monuments of the Church.

* * * * *

The trauailes of Andrew Whiteman aliás Leucander, Centur. 11. [Footnote: This is misprinted "Centur. 2" in the original edition, but as Ramsey Abbey (in Huntingdonshire) was only founded by Ailwin the Saxon, A.D. 969-74, the 11th Century is probably meant, as further on Whiteman is said to have flourished in 1020. Ramsey is so called from *Ram's Ey*, an island in the fens.]

Andræas Leucander aliás Whiteman (iuxta Lelandum) Monachus, & Abbas Ramesiensis Coenobij tertius fuit. Hic bonis artibus studio quodam incredibili noctes atque dies inuigilabat, et operæ præcium ingens inde retulit. Accessit præterea et ardens quoddam desiderium, ea proprijs et apertis oculis videndi loca in quibus Seruator Christus redemptionis nostræ mysteria omnia consummauit, quorum prius sola nomina ex scripturarum lectione nouerat: vnde et sacram Hierosolymorum vrbem miraculorum, prædicationis, ac passionis eius testem inuisit, atque domum rediens factus est Abbas. Claruisse fertur anno nati Seruatoris, 1020 sub Canuto Dano.

The same in English.

Andrew Leucander otherwise called Whiteman (as Leland reporteth) was by profession a Monke, and the third Abbat of the Abbey of Ramsie: he was exceedingly giuen to the studie of good artes, taking paines therein day and night, and profited greatly thereby. And amonst all other things, he had an incredible desire to see those places with his eyes, wherein Christ our Sauiour performed and wrought all the mysteries of our redemption, the names of which places he onely knew before by the reading of the Scriptures. Whereupon he began his iourney, and went to Ierusalem a witnesse of the miracles, preaching, and passion of Christ, and being againe returned into his countrey, he was made the aforesayd Abbat. He flourished in the yeere of Christ 1020. under Canutus the Dane.

* * * * *

The voyages of Swanus one of the sonnes of Earl Godwin vnto Ierusalem, Anno
   Dom. 1052, recorded by William of Malmsburie lib. 2. de gestis regum Anglorum, Capite 13.

Swanus peruersi ingenij et infidi in regem, multoties a patre et fratre Haroldo desciuit: et pirata factus, prædis maritimis virtutes maiorum polluit. Postremò pro conscientia Brunonis cognati interempti, et (vt quidam dicunt) fratris Ierosolimam abijt: indeque rediens, a Saracenis circumuentus, et ad mortem cæsus est.

The same in English.

Swanus being of a peruerse disposition, and faithlesse to the king, often times disagreed with his father and his brother Harold: and afterwards proouing a pirate, he stained the vertues of his ancestours with his robberies vpon the seas. Last of all, being guilty vnto himselfe of the murther of his kinseman Bruno, and (as some do report) of his owne brother, he trauailed vnto Ierusalem: and in his returne home, being taken by the Saracens, was beaten, and wounded vnto death.

* * * * *

A voyage of three Ambassadours, who in the time of K. Edward the Confessor, and about the yere of our Lord 1056, were sent vnto Constantinople, and from thence vnto Ephesus, together with the occasion of their sending, &c. recorded by William of Malmesburie, lib. 2. de gestis regum Anglorum, capite 13.

Die sancti paschatis ad mensam apud Westmonasterium assederat, diademate fastigatus, et optimatum turma circumuallatus. Cumque alij longam quadragesimæ inediam recentibus cibis compensantes, acriter comederent, ille a terrenis reuocato animo, diuinum quiddam speculatus, mentes conuiuantium permouit ampliorem perfusus in risum: nulloque causam lætitiæ perquirere præsumente, tunc quidem ita tacitum donec edendi satietas obsonijs finem imposuit. Sed remotis mensis, cum in triclinio regalibus exueretur, tres optimates eum prosequuti, quorum vnus erat comes Haroldus, secundus abbas, tertius episcopus, familiaritatis ausu interrogant quid riserat: mirum omnibus nec immeritò videri, quarè in tanta serenitate diei et negòtij, tacentibus cæteris, scurrilem cachinnum ejecerit. Stupenda (inquit) vidi, nec ideo sine causa risi. Tum illi, vt moris est humani ingenij, sciscitari et quærere causam ardentiùs, vt supplicibus dignantèr rem impertiatur. Ille multùm cunctatus tandem instantibus mira respondit: septem dormientes in monte Cælio requiescere iam ducentis annis in dextro iacentes latere: sed tunc in hora ipsa risus sui, latus inuertisse sinistrum: futurum vt septuaginta quatuor annis ita iaceant: dirum nimirum miseris mortalibus omen. Nam omnia ventura in his septuaginta quatuor annis, quæ dominus circa finem mundi prædixit discipulis suis: gentem contra gentem surrecturam, et regnum aduersus regnum, terræmotus per loca, pestilentiam et famem, terrores de coelo et signa magna, regnorum mutationes, gentilium in Christianos bella, item Christicolarum in paganos victorias. Talia mirantibus inculcans passionem septem dormientium, et habitudines corporum singulorum, quas nulla docet litera, ita promptè disseruit: ac si cum eis quotidiano victitaret contubernio. His auditis, comes militem, episcopus clericum, abbas monachum, ad veritatem verborum exsculpendam, Manicheti Constantinopolitano imperatori misere, adiectis regis sui literis et muneribus. Eos ille benignè secum habitos episcopo Ephesi destinauit, epistola pariter, quam sacram vocant, comitante: vt ostenderentur legatis regis Angliæ septem dormientium marturiales exuuiæ. Factúmque est vt vaticinium regis Edwardi Græcis omnibus comprobatum, qui se a patribus accepisse iurarent, super dextrum illos latus quiescere: sed post introitum Anglorum in speluncam, veritatem peregrinæ prophetiæ contubernalibus suis prædicarunt. Nec moram festinatio malorum fecit, quin Agareni, et Arabes, et Turci, alienæ scilicèt a Christo gentes, Syriam, et Lyciam, et minorem Asiam omnino, et maioris multas vrbes, inter quas et Ephesum, ipsam etiam Hierosolymam depopulati, super Christianos inuaderent.

The same in English.

Vpon Easter day king Edward the Confessor being crowned with his kingly diademe, and accompanied with diuers of his nobles, sate at dinner in his pallace at Westminster. And when others, after their long abstinence in the Lent, refreshed themselues with dainty meats, and fed thereupon very earnestly, he lifting vp his mind from earthly matters and meditating on heauenly visions (to the great admiration of those which were present) brake forth into an exceeding laughter: and no man presuming to enquire the cause of his mirth, they all kept silence til dinner was ended. But after dinner as he was in his bedchamber putting off his solemne roabes, three of his Nobles to wit earle Harold, an Abbot, and a Bishop, being more familiar with him then the residue followed him in and bouldly asked him what was the occasion of his laughter: for it seemed very strange vnto them all, what should moue him at so solemne a time and assembly, while others kept silence, to laugh so excessively. I saw (quoth he) admirable things, and therefore laughed I not without occasion. Then they (as it is the common guise of all men) demaunded and enquired the cause more earnestly, humbly beseeching faith that hee would vouchsafe to impart that secret vnto them. Whereupon musing a long while vnto himself, at length he told them wonderfull things: namely that seuen Sleepers had rested in mount Cælius two hundred yeeres, lying upon their right sides but in the very houre of his laughter, that they turned themselues on their left sides; and that they should continue so lying for the space of 74. yeeres after; being a dismal signe of future calamitie vnto mankinde. For all things should come to passe within these 74. yeeres, which, as our Sauiour Christ foretold vnto his disciples, were to be fulfilled about the ende of the world: namely that nation should rise against nation, and kingdome against kingdome, and that there should bee in many places earthquakes, pestilence, and famine, terrible apparitions in the heauens, and great signes, together with alterations of kingdomes, warres of infidels against the Christians, and victories of the Christians against the infidels. And as they wondered at these relations, he declared vnto them the passion of the seuen Sleepers, with the proportion and shape of cache of their bodies (which things, no man liuing had as then committed vnto writing) and that so plainely and distinctly, as if he had conuersed a long time in their company. Hereupon the earle sent a knight, the bishop a clearke, the Abbot a monke vnto Maniches the Emperour of Constantinople, with the letters and gifts of their King. Who giuing them friendly entertainment, sent them ouer vnto the bishop of Ephesus; and wrote his letters vnto him giuing him charge, that the English Ambassadours might be admitted to see the true, and material habiliments of the seuen Sleepers. And it came to passe that King Edwards vision was approued by all the Greeks, who protested they were aduertised by their fathers, that the foresaid seuen Sleepers had alwayes before that time rested vpon their right sides; but after the Englishmen were entered into the caue, those Sleepers confirmed the trueth of the outlandish prophesie, vnto their countreymen. Neither were the calamities foretold, any long time delayed: for the Aragens, Arabians, Turkes and other vnbeleeuing nations inuading the Christians, harried and spoiled Syria, Lycia, the lesser Asia, and many cities of Asia the greater, and amongst the rest Ephesus, yea, and Ierusalem also.

* * * * *

The voyage of Alured bishop of Worcester vnto Ierusalem, an. 1058. Recorded by Roger Houeden in parte priore Annalium, fol. 255. linea 15.

[Sidenote: A.D. 1058] Aluredus Wigorniensis Episcopus ecclesiam, quam in ciuitate, Glauorna à fundamentis constraxerat, in honore principis Apostolorum Petri honorificè dedicauit: et posteà regis licentia Wolstanum

Wigorniensem Monachum à se ordinatum Abbatum constituit ibidem. Dein præsulatu dimisso Wiltoniensis ecclesiæ, qui sibi ad regendum commissus fuerat, et Hermanno, cujus suprà mentionem fecimus, reddito, mare transijt, et per Hungarian profectus est Hierosolymam, &c.

The same in English.

In the yere of our Lord 1058. Alured bishop of Worcester, very solemnly dedicated a Church (which himselfe had founded and built in the citie of Gloucester) vnto the honour of S. Peter the chiefe Apostle:[Footnote: This is Gloucester Cathedral, the crypt, the chapels surrounding the choir, and the lower part of the nave being the portions built by Alured that are still extant.] and afterward by the kings permission ordained Wolstan a Monke of Worcester of his owne choice, to be Abbate in the same place. And then having left his Bishopricke which was committed vnto him ouer the Church of Wilton, and having resigned the same vnto Hermannus aboue mentioned, passed ouer the seas, and trauailed through Hungarie vnto Ierusalem, &c.

* * * * *

The voyage of Ingulphus Abbat of Croiland vnto Ierusalem, performed (according to Florentius Wigorniensis) in the yeere of our Lord, 1064, and described by the said Ingulphus himselfe about the conclusion of his briefe Historie.

[Sidenote: A.D. 1064] Ego Ingulphus humilis minister Sancti Guthlaci Monasterijque sui Croilandensis, natus in Anglia, et a parentibus Anglicis, quippè vrbis pulcherrimæ Londoniarum, pro literis addiscendis in teneriore setate constitutus, primum Westmonasterio, postmodum Oxoniensi studio traditus eram. Cúmque in Aristotele arripiendo supra multo coætaneos meos profecissem, etiam Rhetoricam Tullij primam et secundam talo tenus induebam. Factus ergo adolescentior, fastidiens parentum meorum exiguitatem, paternos lares relinquere, et palatia regum aut principum affectans, mollibus vestiri, pomposisque lacinijs amiciri indies ardentius appetebam. [Sidenote: A.D. 1051] Et eccè, inclytus nunc rex noster Angliæ, tunc adhunc comes Normanniæ Wilhelmus ad colloquium tunc regis Angliæ Edwardi cognati sui, cum grandi ministrantium comitatu Londonias aduentabat, Quibus citius insertus, ingerens me vbíque ad omnia emergentia negotia peragenda, cum prosperè plurima perfecissem, in breui agnitus Ilustrissimo comiti et astrictissimè adamatus, cum ipso Normanniam enauigabam. Factus ibidem scriba eius, pro libito totam comitis curiam, ad nonnullorum inuidiam regebam; quosque volui humiliabam, et quos volui exaltabam. Cumque iuuenili calore impulsus in tam celso statu supra meos natales consistere tæderem, quin semper ad altiora conscendere, instabili animo, ac nimium prurienti affectu, ad erubescentiam ambitiosus auidissimè desiderarem: [Sidenote: A.D. 1064. According to Florentius Wegorniensis.] nuntiatur per vniuersam Normanniam plurimos archiepiscopos imperij cum nonnullis alijs terræ principibus velle pro merito animarum suanim more peregrinoram cum debita deuotione Hierosolymam proficisci. De familia ergo comitis domini nostri plurimi tam milites quàm clerici, quorum primus et præcipuus ego eram, cum licentia, et domini nostri comitis beneuolentia, in dictum iter nos omnes accinximus: et Alemanniam petentes, equites triginta numero et ampliùs domino Maguntino coniuncti sumus. Parati namque omnes ad viam, et cum dominis episcopis connumerati septem milia, pertranseuntes prosperè multa terrarum spatia, tandem Constantinopolim peruenimus. Vbi Alexium Imperatorem eius adorantes Agiosophiam vidimus, et infinita sanctuaria osculati sumus. Diuertentes inde per Lyciam in manus Arabicorum latrorium incidimus; euis ceratique de infinitis pecunijs, cum mortibus multorum, et maxima vitæ nostræ periculo vix euadentes, tandem desideratissimam ciuitatem Hierosolymam læto introitu tenebamus. Ab ipso tunc patriarcha Sophronio nomine, viro veneranda canitie honestissimo ac sanctissimo, grandi cymbalorum tonitru, et luminarium immenso fulgore suscepti, ad diuinissimam ecclesiam sanctissimi sepulchri, tam Syrorum, quàm Latinornm solenni processione deducti sumus. Ibi quot preces inorauimus, quot lachrymas infleuimus, quot suspiria inspirauimus, solus eius inhabitator nouit D. noster Iesus Christus. Ab ipso itaque gloriosissimo sepulchro Christi ad alia sanctuaria ciuitatis inuisenda circumducti, infinitam summam sanctarum ecclesiarum, et oratorioram, quæ Achim Soldanus dudum destruxerat, oculis lachrymosis vidimus. Et omnibus ruinis sanctissimæ ciuitatis, tam extra, quàm intra; numerosis lachrymis intimo affectu compassi, ad quorundam restaurationem datis non paucis pecunijs, exire in patriam et sacratissimo Iordane intingi, vniuersáque Chrtsti vestigia osculari, desiderantissima deuotione suspirabamus. Sed Arabum latrunculi qui omnem viam obseruabant, longiùs a ciuitate euagari, sua rabiosa multitudine innumera non sinebant. Vere igitur accidente, stolus nauium Ianuensium in porta Ioppensi applicuit. In quibus, cum sua mercimonia Christiani mercatores per ciuitates maritimas commutassent, et sancta loca similitèr adorassent, ascendentes omnes maria nos commisimus. Et iactati fluctibus et procellis innumeris tandem Brundusium, et prospero itinere per Apulium Romam petentes, sanctorum Apostolorum Petri et Pauli limina, et copiosissima sanctorum martyrum monumenta per omnes stationes osculati sumus. Indè archiepiscopi, cæterique principes imperij Alemanniam per dextram repetentes, nos versus Franciam ad sinistram declinantes cum inenarribilibus et gratijs et osculis ab inuicem discessimus. Et tandem de triginta equitibus, qui de Normannia pingues exiuimus, vix viginti pauperes peregrini, et omnes pedites, macie multa attenuati, reuersi sumus.

The same in English.

I Ingulphus [Footnote: This Abbot, or pretended Abbot of Croyland (whose name is attached to a work once highly valued, professing to be a history of the Abbey of Croyland from 626 to 1089, but which, is now believed to be a monkish fabrication of a much later age), is said by himself to have been, on his return from the Holy Land, appointed prior of the Abbey of Fontenelle, in Normandy, and on William becoming King of England, Abbot of Croyland. He was believed to have died in 1109.] an humble seruant of reuerend Guthlac and of his monastery of Croiland, borne in England, and of English parents, at the beautifull citie of London, was in my youth for the attaining of good letters, placed first at Westminster, and afterward sent to the Vniuersitie of Oxford. And hauing excelled diuers of mine equals in learning of Aristotle, I inured my selfe somewhat vnto the first and second Rhethorique of Tullie. And as I grew in age, disdayning my parents meane estate, and forsaking mine owne natiue soyle, I affected the Courts of kings and princes, and was desirous to be clad in silke, and to weare braue and costly attire. [Sidenote: A.D. 1051] And loe, at the same time William our souereigne king now, but then Erle of Normandie, with a great troup of followers and attendants came vnto London, to conferre with king Edward the Confessour his kinsman. Into whose company intruding my selfe, and proffering my seruice for the performance of any speedy or weightie affayres, in short time, after I had done many things with good successe, I was knowen and most entirely beloued by the victorious Erle himselfe, and with him I sayled into Normandie. And there being made his secretarie, I gouerned the Erles Court (albeit with the enuie of some) as my selfe pleased, yea whom I would I abased, and preferred whom I thought good. When as therefore, being carried with a youthful heat and lustie humour, I began to be wearie euen of this place, wherein I was aduanced so high aboue my parentage, and with an inconstant minde, and affection too too ambitious, most vehemently aspired at all occasions to climbe higher: there went a report throughout all Normandie, that diuers Archbishops of the Empire, and secular princes were desirous for their soules health, and for deuotion sake, to goe on pilgrimage to Ierusalem. Wherefore out of the family of our lorde the Earle, sundry of vs, both gentlemen and clerkes (principall of whom was myselfe) with the licence and good will of our sayd lord the earle, sped vs on that voiage, and trauailing thirtie horses of vs into high Germanie, we ioyned our selues vnto the Archbishop of Mentz. And being with the companies of the Bishop seuen thousand persons sufficiently prouided for such an expedition, we passed prosperously through many prouinces, and at length attained vnto Constantinople. Where doing reuerence vnto the Emperor Alexius, we sawe the Church of Sancta Sophia, and kissed diuers sacred reliques. Departing thence through Lycia, we fell into the hands of the Arabian theeues: and after we had beene robbed of infinite summes of money, and had lost many of our people, hardly escaping with extreame danger of our liues, at length we ioyfully entered into the most wished citie of Ierusalem. Where we wer receiued by the most reuerend, aged, and holy patriarke Sophronius, with great melodie of cymbals and with torch-light, and were accompanied vnto the most diuine Church of our Sauiour his sepulchre with a solemne procession aswell of Syrians as of Latines. Here, how many prayers we vttered, what abundance of teares we shed, what deepe sighs we breathed foorth, our Lord Iesus Christ onely knoweth. Wherefore being conducted from the most glorious sepulchre of Christ to visite other sacred monuments of the citie, we saw with weeping eyes a great number of holy Churches and oratories, which Achim the Souldan of Egypt had lately destroyed. And so hauing bewailed with sadde teares, and most sorowful and bleeding affections, all the ruines of that most holy city both within and without, and hauing bestowed money for the reedifying of some, we desired with most ardent deuotion to go forth into the countrey, to wash our selues in the most sacred riuer of Iordan, and to kisse all the steppes of Christ. Howbeit the theeuish Arabians lurking vpon euery way, would not suffer vs to trauell farre from the city, by reason of their huge and furious multitudes. Wherefore about the spring there arriued at the port of Ioppa a fleet of ships from Genoa. In which fleet (when the Christian merchants had exchanged all their wares at the coast townes, and had likewise visited the holy places) wee all of vs embarked committing ourselues to the seas: and being tossed with many stormes and tempests, at length wee arriued at Brundusium: and so with a prosperous iourney trauelling thorow Apulia towards Rome, we there visited the habitations of the holy apostles Peter and Paul, and did reuerence vnto diuers monuments of holy martyrs in all places thorowout the city. From thence the archbishops and other princes of the empire trauelling towards the right hand for Alemain, and we declining towards the left hand for France, departed asunder, taking our leaues with vnspeakable thankes and courtesies. And so at length, of thirty horsemen which went out of Normandie fat, lusty, and frolique, we returned hither skarse twenty poore pilgrims of vs, being all footmen, and consumed with leannesse to the bare bones.

* * * * *

Diuers of the honourable family of the Beauchamps, with Robert Curtoys sonne of William the Conqueror, made a voyage to Ierusalem 1096. Hol. pag. 22. vol. 2.

Pope Vrbane calling a councell at Clermont in Auuergne, exhorted the Christian princes so earnestly to make a iourney in the Holy land, for the recouery thereof out of the Saracens hands, that the saide great and generall iourney was concluded vpon to be taken in hand, wherein many noble men of Christendome went vnder the leading of Godfrey of Bouillon and others, as in the Chronicles of France, of Germanie, and of the Holy land doeth more plainely appeare. There went also among other diuers noble men foorth of this Realme of England, specially that worthily bare the surname of Beauchampe.

* * * * *

The voyage of Gutuere an English Lady maried to Balduine brother of Godfreide duke of Bouillon, toward Ierusalem about 1097. And the 11. yeere of William Rufus King of England.

The Christian armie of Godfrie of Bouillon passing the citie of Iconium, alias Agogna in the countrey of Licaonia, and from thence by the city of Heraclia, came at length vnto the citie of Marasia, where they encamped, and soiourned there three whole dayes, because of the wife of Balduine brother germane of the duke of Loraigne. Which Lady, being long time vexed with a grieuous maladie, was in extremitie, where at length paying the debt due to nature, she changed this transitorie life, for life eternall; Who, in her life time, was a very worthy and vertuous Lady, borne in England, and descended of most noble parentage named Gutuere; Which, according to her degree, was there most honourably enterred, to the great griefe of all the whole armie. As reporteth William Archbishop of Tyre, lib. 3. cap. 17. hist. belli sacri. The same author in the 10. booke and first chapter of the same historie concerning the same English Lady, writeth further as followeth, Baldwine hauing folowed the warres for a time, gaue his minde to marriage, so that being in England he fell in loue with a very honourable and noble Lady named Gutuere, whom he married and caried with him in that first happy expedition, wherin he accompanied his brethren, the Lords, duke Godfrey and Eustace, persons very commendable in all vertues and of immortall memorie. But he had hard fortune in his iourney, because his foresaid wife, being wearied with a long sicknes finished her life with a happie end neere the citie of Marasia, before the Christian armie came vnto Antioch, where she was honourably buried, as we haue declared before.

* * * * *

Chronicon Hierosolymitanum in lib. 3. cap. 27. maketh also mention of this English Lady which he calleth Godwera in this maner.

Hac in regione Maresch vxor Baldewini nobilissima, quam de regno Angliæ eduxit, diutina corporis molestia aggrauata, et duci Godefrido commendata, vitam exhalauit, sepulta Catholicis obsequijs; cuius nomen erat Godwera.

The same in English.

In this prouince of Maresch the most noble wife of Baldwine, which he caried with him out of England being visited with dayly sicknesses and infirmities of body, and commended to the custody of duke Godfrey, departed out of this life, and was buried after the Christian maner. Her name was Godwera.

* * * * *

The voyage of Edgar the sonne of Edward which was the sonne of Edmund surnamed Ironside, brother vnto K. Edward the confessor, (being accompanied with valiant Robert the sonne of Godwin) vnto Ierusalem, in the yeere of our Lord 1102. Recorded by William of Malmesburie, lib. 3. histo. fol. 58.

[Sidenote: A.D. 1102.] Subsequenti tempore cum Roberto filio Godwini milite audacissimo Edgaras Hierosolymam pertendit Illud fuit tempus quo Turci Baldwinum regem apud Ramas obsederunt: qui cum obsidionis iniuriam ferre nequiret, per medias hostium acies effugit, solius Roberti opera liberatus præeuntis, et euaginato gladio dextra leuaque Turcos cædentis. Sed cum successu ipso truculentior, alacritate nimia procurreret, ensis manu excidit. Ad quem recolligendum cum se inclinasset, omnium incursu oppressus, vinculis palmas dedit. Inde Babyloniam (vt aiunt) ductus, cum Christum abnegare nollet, in medio foro ad signum positus, et sagittis terebratus, martyrium consecrauit. Edgarus amisso milite regressus, multaque beneficia ab Imperatoribus Græcorum, et Alemannorum adeptus (quippè qui etiam eum retinere pro generis amplitudine tentassent) omnia pronatalis soli desiderio spreuit. Quosdam enim profectò fallit amor patriæ vt nihil eis videatur iucundum, nisi consuetum hauserint coelum. Vndè Edgarus fatua cupidine illusus Angliam redijt, vbi (vt superius dixi) diuerso fortunæ ludicro rotatus, nunc remotus et tacitus, canos suos in agro consumit.

The same in English.

Afterward Edgar being sonne vnto the nephewe of Edward the confessour, traueiled with Robert the sonne of Godwin a most valiant knight, vnto Ierusalem. And it was at the same time when the Turkes besieged king Baldwin at Rama: who not being able to endure the straight siege, was by the helpe of Robert especially, going before him, and with his drawen sword making a lane, and slaying the Turkes on his right hande and on his left, deliuered out of that danger, and escaped through the midst of his enemies campe. But vpon his happie successe being more eager and fierce, as he went forward somewhat too hastily, his sworde fell out of his hand. Which as he stouped to take vp, being oppressed with the whole multitude, hee was there taken and bound. From whence (as some say) being carried vnto Babylon or Alcair in Egypt, when he would not renounce Christ, he was tyed vnto a stake in the midst of the market place, and being shot through with arrowes, died a martyr. Edgar hauing lost his knight returned, and being honoured with many rewards both by the Greekish and by the Germaine Emperour (who both of them would right gladly haue entertained him stil for his great nobilitie) contemned all things in respect of his natiue soile. For in very deede some are so inueagled with the loue of their countrey, that nothing can seeme pleasant vnto them, vnlesse they breath in the same aire where they were bred. Wherefore Edgar being misledde with a fond affection, returned into England; and afterward being subiect vnto diuers changes of fortune (as we haue aboue signified) he spendeth [Marginal note: When the author was writing of this history.] now his extreeme old age in an obscure and priuate place of the countrey.

* * * * *

Mention made of one Godericus, a valiant Englishman, who was with his ships in the voyage vnto the Holy land in the second yeere of Baldwine King of Ierusalem, in the third yere of Henry the first of England.

[Chronicon Hierosolymitanum lib. 9. cap. 9.] Verùm de hinc septem diebus euolutis rex ab Assur exiens, nauem quæ dicitur Buza ascendit, et cum eo Godericus pirata de regno Angliæ, ac vexillo hastæ præfixo et elato in aëre ad radios solis vsque, Iaphet cum paucis nauigauit, vt hoc eius signo ciues Christiani recognito, fiduciam vitæ regis haberent, et non facile hostium mínis pauefacti, turpiter diffugium facerent, aut vrbem reddere cogerentur. Sciebat enim eos multum de vita et salute eius desperare, Saraceni autem viso eius signo, et recognito, ea parte quæ vrbem nauigio cingebat illi in galeis viginti et Carinis tredecim, quas vulgo appelant Cazh, occurrerunt, volentes Buzam regis coronare. Sed Dei auxilio vndis maris illis ex aduerso tumescentibus ac reluctantibus, Buza autem regis facili, et agili cursu inter procellas labente, ac volitante, in portu Ioppæ delusis hostibus subitò affuit, sex ex Saracenis in arcu suo in nauicula percussis, ac vulneratis. Intrans itaque ciuitatem dum incolumis omnium pateret oculis, reuixit spiritus cunctorum gementium ei de eius niorte hactenus dolentium, eo quòd caput et rex Christianorum et princeps Hierusalem adhuc viuus et incolumis receptus sit.

The same in English.

But seuen dayes afterward, the King comming out of the towne of Assur entred into a shippe called a Busse, and one Godericke a pirate of the kingdome of England with him, and fastening his banner on the toppe of a speare, and holding it vp aloft in the aire against the beames of the Sunne, sailed vnto Iaphet with a small company; That the Christian Citizens there seeing this his banner, might conceiue hope that the King was yet liuing, and being not easily terrified with the threates of the enemies might shamefully runne away; or be constrained to yeeld vp the citie. For hee knew that they were very much out of hope of his life and safetie. The Saracens seeing and knowing this his banner, that part of them which enuironed the Citie by water made towards him with twentie Gallies and thirteene shippes, which they commonly cal Cazh, seeking to inclose the kings shippe. But, by Gods helpe the billowes of the Sea swelling and raging against them, and the Kings shippe gliding and passing through the waues with an easie and nimble course arriued suddenly in the hauen of Ioppa, the enemies frustrated of their purpose; and sixe of the Saracens were hurt and wounded by shot out of the Kings shippe. So that the King entering into the Citie, and nowe appearing in safetie in all their sightes, the spirits of all them that mourned for him, and vntil then lamented as though hee had bene dead, reuiued, because that the head and King of the Christians, and prince of Ierusalem was yet aliue, and come againe vnto them in perfect health.

* * * * *

Mention made of One Hardine of England one of the chiefest personages, and a leader among other of two hundred saile of ships of Christians that landed at Ioppa in the yeere of our Lord God 1102.

[Chronicon Hierosolymitanum libro 9. cap. 11.] Interea dum hæc obsidio ageretur 200. naues Christianorum nauigio Ioppen appulsæ sunt, vt adorarent in Hierusalem. Horum Bernardus Witrazh de terra Galatiæ, Hardinus de Anglia, Otho de Roges, Hadewerck, vnus de præpotentibus Westfalorum, primi et ductores fuisse referuntur, etc. Erat autem tertia feria Iulij mensis, quando hæ Christianorum copiæ, Deo protegente, huc nauigio angustiatis et obsessis ad opem collatæ sunt. Sarracenorum autem turmæ, videntes quia Christianorum virtus audactur facie ad faciem vicini sibi hospitio proximè iungebatur, media nocte orbi incumbente, amotis tentorijs amplius milliari subtractæ consederunt, dum luce exorta consilium inirent, vtrum Ascalonem redirent, aut ciues Iaphet crebris assultibus vexarent.

The same in English.

Whle the Sarazens continued their siege against Ioppa, two hundred saile of Christian ships arriued at Ioppa, that they might performe their deuotions at Hierusalem. The chiefe men and leaders of these Christians are reported to haue bene: Bernard Witrazh of the land of Galatia, Hardine of England, Otho of Roges, Haderwerck one of the chiefe noblemen of Westphalia, &c. This Christian power through Gods speciall prouision, arriued here for the succour and reliefe of the distressed and besieged Christians in Ioppa, the third day of Iuly, 1102. and in the second yeere of Baldwine king of Ierusalem. Whereupon the multitude of the Sarazens, seeing that the Christian power ioyned themselves boldly, close by them even face to face in a lodging hard by them, the very next night at midnight, remooued their tents, and pitched them more then a mile off, that they might the next morning bee aduised whether they should returne to Ascalon, or by often assaults vexe the citizens of Iaphet.

[Chronicon Hierosolymitanum, eodem libro 9. cap. 12.] continueth this historie of these two hundreth saile of ships, and sheweth how by their prowesse chiefly, the multitude of the Sarazens were in short space vanquished and ouerthrowen: The words are these; Ab ipso verò die tertiæ feriæ dum sic in superbia et elatione suæ multitudinis immobiles Saraceni persisterent, et multis armorum terroribus Christianum populum vexarent, sexta feria appropinquante. Rex Baldwinus in tubis et cornibus a Iaphet egrediens, in manu robusta equitum et peditum virtutem illorum crudeli bello est aggressus, magnis hinc et hinc clamoribus intonantes. Christiani quoque qui nauigio appulsi sunt horribili pariter clamore cum Rege Baldwino, et graui strepitu vociferantes, Babylonios vehementi pugna sunt aggressi, sæuissimis atque mortiferis plagis eos affligentes, donec bello fatigati, et contrà ['vntrà' in source text—KTH] vim non sustinentes fugam versus Ascalonea inierunt. Alij verò ab insecutoribus eripi existimantes, et mari se credentes, intolerabili procellarum fluctuatione absorpti sunt. Et sic ciuitas Ioppe cum habitatoribus suis liberata est; Ceciderunt hac die tria millia Saracenorum Christianorum verò pauci perijsse inuenti sunt.

The same in English.

Yet notwithstanding, after the said third day of Iuly, the Sarazens persisted high minded and insolent, by reason of their great multitude, and much annoied the Christian people with their many forceable and terrible weapons; whereupon, on the sixt day of Iuly early in the morning king Baldwine issued out of Iaphet, his trumpets and cornets yeelding a great and lowd sound, and with a very strong armie as well of horsemen as footemen, who on euery side making great shoutes and outcries, with fierce and sharpe battell set on the maine power of their enemies. The Christians also who arriued in the nauie, rearing great clamours and noyses, with loud voices and shoutings in horrible wise together, with king Baldwine assaulted likewise with strong battell the Babylonians, and afflicted them with most sore and deadly wounds, vntill the Sarazens being wearied with fighting, nor able longer to endure and hold out against the valure of the Christians, fled towards Ascalon. And other of them hoping to escape from them that pursued them, lept into the sea, and were swalowed vp in the waues thereof. And so the citie of Ioppa with the inhabitants thereof were freed of their enemies. There were slaine this day three thousand Sarazens, and but a few of the Christians perished.

* * * * *

A Fleete of Englishmen, Danes, and Flemings, arriued at Ioppa in the Holy land, the seuenth yeere of Baldwine the second king of Hierusalem. Written in the beginning of the tenth booke of the Chronicle of Hierusalem, in the 8. yeere of Henry the first of England.

Chap: 1.

At the same time also in the seuenth yeere of the raigne of Baldwine the Catholike king of Hierusalem, a very great warrelike Fleete of the Catholike nation of England, to the number of about seuen thousand, hauing with them more men of warre of the kingdom of Denmarke, of Flanders and of Antwerpe, arriued with ships which they call Busses, at the hauen of the citie of Iaphet, determining there to make their abode, vntill they hauing obtained the kings licence and safeconduct, might safely worship at Hierusalem. Of which nauie the chiefest and best spoken repairing to the king, spake to him in this maner. Christ preserue the Kings life, and prosper his kingdome from day to day; Wee, being men and souldiours of Christian profession, haue, through the helpe of God, sayled hither through mightie and large seas, from the farre countreys of England, Flanders, and Denmarke, to worship at Ierusalem, and to visit the sepulchre of our Lord. And therefore we are assembled to intreat your clemency touching the matter, that by your fauour and safe conduct we may peaceably goe vp to Ierusalem, and worship there, and so returne.

Chap. 2.

The king fauourably hearing their whole petition, granted vnto them a strong band of men to conduct them, which brought them safely from all assaults and ambushes of the Gentiles by the knowen wayes vnto Ierusalem and all other places of deuotion. After that these pilgrims, and new Christian strangers were brought thither, they offering vnto our Lord their vowes in the temple of the holy sepulchre, returned with great ioy, and without all let vnto Ioppa; where finding the king, they vowed they would assist him in all things, which should seeme good vnto him: who, greatly commending the men, and commanding them to be well entertained with hospitality, answered that he could not on the sudden answere to this point, vntill that after he had called his nobles together, he had consulted with my lord the Patriarch what was most meet and conuenient to be done, and not to trouble in vaine so willing an army. And therefore after a few dayes, calling vnto him my lord the Patriarch, Hugh of Tabaria, Gunfride the keeper and lieutenant of the tower of Dauid, and the other chiefest men of warre, he determined to haue a meeting in the city of Rames, to consult with them what was best to be done.

Chap. 3.

Who, being assembled at the day appointed, and proposing their diuers opinions and iudgements, at length it seemed best vnto the whole company to besiege the city Sagitta, which is also called Sidon, if peradventure, through God's helpe, and by the strength of this new army, by land and sea it might be ouercome. Whereupon all they which were there present and required that this city should be besieged, because it was one of those cities of the Gentiles which continually rebelled, were commended, and admonished of the king euery one to go home, and to furnish themselues with things necessary, and armour for this expedition. Euery one of them departed home; likewise Hugh of Tabaria departed, being a chiefe man of warre against the inuasions of the enemies, which could neuer be wearied day nor night in the countie of the Pagans, in pursuing them with warre and warlike stratagemes all the dayes of his life. Immediatly after this consultation the king sent ambassadours to all the multitude of the English men, requiring them not to remoue their campe nor fleet from the city of Iaphet, but quietly to attend the kings further commandement. The same embassadours also declared vnto the whole army, that the king and all his nobility had determined to besiege and assault the city Sagitta by sea and by land, and that their helpe and forces would there be needfull; and that for this purpose, the king and the patriarch were comming downe vnto the city of Acres and that they were in building of engins, and warlike instruments, to inuade the walles and inhabitants thereof: and that in the meane season they were to remaine at Iaphet, vntill the kings further commandement were knowen. Whereupon they all agreed that it should be so done according to the king's commandement; and answered that they would attend his directions in the Hauen of Iaphet, and would in all points be obedient vnto him vnto the death.

Chap.4.

The king came downe to Acres with the patriarch, and all his family, building, and making there by the space of fortie dayes engins, and many kindes of warlike instruments: and appointing all things to be made perfectly ready, which seemed to be most conuenient for the assaulting of the city. Assoone as this purpose and intent of the king was come vnto the eares of the inhabitants of Sagitta, and that an inuincible power of men of warre was arriued at Iaphet to helpe the king, they were greatly astonied, fearing that by this meanes, they should be consumed and subdued by the king by dint of sword, as other cities, to wit, Cæsaria, Assur, Acres, Cayphas, and Tabaria were vanquished and subdued. And therefore laying their heads together, they promised to the king by secret mediatours, a mighty masse of money of a coyne called Byzantines: and that further they would yeerely pay a great tribute, vpon condition that ceasing to besiege and inuade their city, he would spare their liues. Whereupon these businesses were handled from day to day betweene the king and the citizens, and they sollicited the king for the ransomming both of their city and of their liues, proffering him from time to time more greater gifts. And the king for his part, being carefull and perplexed for the payment of the wages which he ought vnto his souldiers, harkened wholy vnto this offer of money. Howbeit because he feared the Christians, least they should lay it to his charge as a fault, he durst not as yet meddle with the same.

Chap. 5.

In the meane space Hugh of Tabaria being sent for, accompanied with the troupes of two hundred horsemen and foure hundred footmen, inuaded the countrey of the Grosse Carle called Suet, very rich in gold and siluer most abundant in cattle frontering vpon the countrie of the Damascenes, where hee tooke a pray of inestimable riches and cattle, which might haue suffised him for the besiege of Sagitta, whereof he ment to impart liberally to the king, and his companie. This pray being gathered out of sundry places thereabout, and being led away as farre as the citie of Belinas, which they call Cæsaria Philippi, the Turkes which dwelt at Damascus, together with the Saracens inhabitants of the countrie perceiuing this, flocking on all partes together by troupes, pursued Hughes companie to rescue the pray, and passed foorth as farre as the mountaines, ouer which Hughes footemen did driue the pray. There beganne a great skirmish of both partes, the one side made resistance to keepe the pray, the other indeuoured with all their might to recouer it, vntill at length the Turkes and Saracens preuailing, the pray was rescued and brought back againe: which Hugh and his troupes of horsemen, suddenly vnderstanding, which were on the side of the mountaines, incontinently rid backe vpon the spurre, among the straight and craggie rockes, skirmishing with the enemies, and succouring their footemen, but as it chanced they fought vnfortunately. For Hugh, being vnarmed, and immediatly rushing into the middest of all dangers, and after his woonted manner inuading and wounding the infidels, being behinde with an arrowe shot through the backe which pierced thorough his liuer and brest, he gaue vp the ghost in the handes of his owne people. Hereupon the troupes of the Gentiles being returned with the recouered pray, and being deuided through the secret and hard passages of the craggie hilles, the souldiers brought the dead bodie of Hugh, which they had put in a litter, into the citie of Nazareth, which is by the mount Thaber, where with great mourning and lamentation, so worthie a prince, and valiant champion was honourably and Catholikely interred. The brother of the said Hugh named Gerrard, the same time lay sicke of a grieuous disease. Which hearing of the death of his brother, his sicknesse of his body increasing more vehemently through griefe, he also deceased within eight dayes after, and was buried by his brother, after Christian maner.

Chap. 6.

After the lamentable burials of these so famous Princes, the King, taking occasion of the death of these principall men of his armie, agreed, making none priuie thereto, to receiue the money which was offered him for his differing off the siege of the citie of Sagitta, yet dissembling to make peace, with the Saracens, but that he ment to go through with the worke, that he had begunne. Whereupon sending a message vnto Iaphet, hee aduised the English souldiers to come downe to Acres with their fleete, and to conferre and consult with him touching the besieging and assaulting of the citie of Sagitta, which rising immediatly vpon the kings commaundement, and foorthwith hoysing vp the sayles of their shippes aloft with pendants and stremers of purple, and diuerse other glorious colours, with their flagges of scarlet colour and silke, came thither, and casting their ancres, rode hard by the citie. The king the next day calling vnto him such as were priuie and acquainted with his dealings, opened his griefe vnto the chiefe Captaines of the English men and Danes, touching the slaughter of Hugh, and the death of his brother, and what great confidence he reposed in them concerning these warres: and that nowe therefore they being departed and dead, he must of necessity differre the besieging of Sagitta, and for this time dismisse the armie assembled. This resolution of the king being spred among the people, the armie was dissolued, and the Englishmen, Danes and Flemings, with sailes and oares going aboard their fleete, saluted ['saulted' in source text—KTH] the king, and returned home vnto their natiue countries.

* * * * *

The trauailes of one Athelard an Englishman, recorded by master Bale Centur. 12.

Athelardus Bathoniensis Coenobij monachus, naturalium rerum mysteria, et causas omnes, diligentiâ tam vndecunque exquisitâ perscrutatus est, vt cum aliquibus veteris seculi philosophis non indignè conferri possit. Hic olim spectatæ indolis Adolescens, vt virente adhuc ætate iuuenile ingenium foecundaret, atque ad res magnas pararet relicta dulci patria longinquas petijt regiones. Cum verò Ægyptum et Arabiam peragrans, plura inuenisset, quæ eius desiderabat animus, cum magno laborum, ac literarum lucro in Angliam tum demùm reuertebatur. Claruit anno virginei partus, 1130. Henrico primo regnante.

The same in English.

Athelard a Monke of the Abbie of Bathe was so diligent a searcher of the secrets, and causes of naturall things, that he deserueth worthely to be compared with some of the auncient Philosophers. This man although young, yet being of a good wit, and being desirous to increase and enrich the same with the best things, and to prepare himselfe as it were for greater matters, left his Countrey for a time, and trauailed into forreine Regions. He went through Egypt, and Arabia, and found out many things which he desired to his owne priuate contentment, and the profite of good letters generally, and so being satisfied, returned againe into his Countrey: he flourished in the yeere 1130. Henry the first being then king of England.

* * * * *

The life and trauailes of one William of Tyre, an Englishman. Centur. 12.

[Sidenote: Hic etiam Guilielmus Tyrensis claruit sub Henrico primo.] Guilielmus, Ecclesiæ Dominici sepulchri Hierosolymæ Regularium Canonicorum prior, natione Anglicus vir vita et moribus commendabilis, Anno Dom. 1128. postquam Tyrorum Ciuitas fidei Christianæ restituta est a Guimundo Hierosolymorum patriarcha, eidem vrbi primus Archiepiscopus præficiebatur. Est autem Tyrus ciuitas antiquissima, Phoeniciæ vniuersæ Metropolis, quæ inter Syriæ protuincias, et bonorum omnium penè commoditate, et incolarum frequentia primum semper obtinuit locum: post conscripta quædam opuscula, et Epistolas, ad Dominum migrauit, An. Christi 1130. quum duobus tantum sedisset annis, et in Tyrensi Ecclesia sepelitur.

The same in English.

William the Prior of the Canons Regular in the Church of Ierusalem, called the Lords Sepulchre, was an Englishman borne, and of a vertuous and good behauiour. After that the Citie of Tyre was restored againe to the Christian faith, Guimunde the Patriarke of Ierusalem made him the first Archbishop of Tyre, in the yeere 1128. Which Tyre is a very ancient Citie, the Metropolis of all Phoenicia, and hath bene accompted the chiefest Prouince of Syria, both for fruitful commodities and multitude of inhabitants. This William hauing in his life written many Bookes and Epistles, died at last in the yeere 1130. hauing bene Archbishop the space of two yeeres, and was buried in the Church of Tyre.

* * * * *

The trauailes of Robertus Ketenensis.

Robertus Ketenensis natione et cognomine Anglus, degustatis primum per Anglorum gymnasia humanarum artium elementis literarijs, vltramarinas statim visitare prouincias in animo constituit: Peragratis ergò Gallijs, Italia, Dalmatia, et Græcia, tum demum peruenit in Asiam, vbi non paruo labore, ac vitæ suæ periculo inter Saracenos truculentissimum hominum genus, Arabicam linguam ad amussim didicit In Hispaniam postea nauigio traductus, circa fluuium Hiberum Astrologicæ artis studio, cum Hermanno quodam Dalmata, magni sui itineris comite se totum dedit. [Sidenote: Claruit sub Stephano.] Clarutt anno seruatoris nostri, 1143 Stephano regnante, et Pampilonæ sepelitur.

The same in English.

This Robert Ketenensis was called an Englishman by surname, as he was by birth: who after some time spent in the foundations of humanitie, and in the elements of good Artes in the Vniuersities of England, determined to trauaile to the partes beyond sea: and so trauailed through France, Italie, Dalmatia, and Greece, and came at last into Asia, where he liued in great danger of his life among the cruell Saracens, but yet learned perfectly the Arabian tongue. Afterwardes he returned by sea into Spaine, and there about the riuer Iberus, gaue him selfe wholy to the studie of Astrologie, with one Hermannus a Dalmatian, who had accompanied him in his long voyage. He flourished in the yeere 1143. Steuen being then king of England, and was buried at Pampilona.

* * * * *

A voyage of certaine English men vnder the conduct of Lewes king of France vnto the Holy land.

[Sidenote: 1147. Tempore regis Stephani.] Tantæ expeditionis explicito apparatu vterque princeps iter arripuit, et exercitu separtito. Imperator enim Conradus præcedebat itinere aliquot dierum, cum Italorum, Germanorum, aliarúmque gentium amplissimis copijs. Rex vero Lodouicus sequebatur Francorum, Flandrensium, Normannorum, Britonum, Anglorum, Burgundionum, Prouincialium, Aquitanorum, equestri simul et pedestri agmine comitatus. Gulielmus Neobrigensis, fol. 371.

The same in English.

Both the princes prouision being made for so great an expedition, they seuering their armies, entered on their iourney. For the Emperour Conradus went before, certaine dayes iourney, with very great power of Italians, Germans, and other countreys. And king Lewes followed after accompanied with a band of horsemen and footmen of French men, Fiemmings, Normans, Britons, Englishmen, Burgundions, men of Prouence, and Gascoins.

* * * * *

The voyage of Iohn Lacy to Ieirusalem.

[Sidenote: 1173.] Anno Domini 1172 fundata fuit abbatia de Stanlaw per dominum; Iohannem Lacy Constabularium Cestriæ et dominum de Halton, qui obijt in Terra sancta anno sequenti: qui fuit vicessimus annus regni regis Henrici secundi.

The same in English.

In the yere of our Lord 1172 was founded the abbey of Stanlaw by the lord Iohn Lacy Constable of Chester, and lord of Halton, who deceased in the Holy land the yere following: which was in the twentieth yere of king Henry the second.

* * * * *

The voyage of William Mandeuile to Ierusalem.

[Sidenote: 1177.] William Mandeuile earle of Essex, with diuers English lords and knights, went to the Holy land in the 24 yere of Henry the second. Holinshed pag. 101.

* * * * *

A great supply of money to the Holy land by Henry the 2.

The same yeere King Henry the second being at Waltham, assigned an aide to the maintenance of the Christian souldiers in the Holy lande, That is to wit, two and fortie thousand marks of siluer, and fiue hundred marks of golde. Matth. Paris and Holins. pag. 105.

* * * * *

A letter written from Manuel the Emperour of Constantinople, vnto Henrie the second King of England, Anno Dom. 1177. wherein mention is made that certaine of King Henries Noble men and subjects were present with the sayd Emperour in a battell of his against the Soldan of Iconium. Recorded by Roger Houeden, in Annalium parte posteriore, in regno Hen. 2. fol. 316, et 317.

Eodem anno Manuel Constantinopolitanus imperator, habito prælio campestri cum Soltano Iconij et illo devicto, in hac forma scripsit Domino regi Angliæ.

Manuel in Christo deo Porphyrogenitus, diuinitus coronatus, sublimis, potens, excelsus, semper Augustus, et moderator Romanorum, Comnenus, Henrico nobilissimo regi Angliæ, charissimo amico suo, salutem et omne bonum. Cum imperium nostrum necessarium reputet notificare tibi, vt dilecto amico suo, de omnibus quæ sibi obueniunt; ideò et de his quæ nunc acciderunt ei, opportunum iudicauit declarare tuæ voluntati. Igitur a principio coronationis nostræ imperium nostrum aduersus dei inimicos Persas nostrum odium in corde nutriuit, dum cerneret illos in Christianos gloriari, eleuatique in nomen dei, et Christianorum dominari regionibus.

Quo circa et alio quidem tempore indifferentèr inuasit eos, et prout deus ei concessit, sic et fecit. Et quæ ab ipso frequenter patrata sunt ad contritionem ipsorum et perditionem, imperium nostrum credit nobilitatem tuam non latere. Quoniam autem et nunc maximum exercitum contra eos ducere proposuit, et bellum contra omnem Persidem mouere, quia res cogebat. Et non vt voluit multum aliquem apparatum fecit, sicut ei visum est. Veruntamen prout tempus dabat et rerum status, potentèr eos inuasit. Collegit ergo circa se imperium nostrum potentias suas: sed quia carpenta ducebat armorum, et machinarum, et aliorum instrumentorum conferentium ciuitatem expugnationibus, pondera portantia: idcircò nequaquam cum festinatione iter suum agere poterat. Ampliùs autem dum adhuc propriam regionem peragraret, antequam barbarorum aliquis aduersus nos militaret in bellis aduersarius, ægritudo difficillima fluxus ventris invasit nos, qui diffusus per agmina imperij nostri pertransibat, depopulando et interimendo multos, omni pugnatore grauior. Et hoc malum inualescens maximè nos contriuit. Ex quo verò fines Turcorum inuasimus, bella quidem primum frequentia concrepabant, et agmina Turcorum cum exercitibus imperij nostri vndique dimicabant. Sed Dei gratia ex toto à nostris in fugam vertebantur barbari. Post verò vbi ei qui illic adjacet angustiæ loci, quæ à Persis nominatur Cibrilcimam, propinquauimus, tot Persarum turmæ peditum et equitum, quorum pleræque ab interioribus partibus Persidis occurrerant in adiutorium contribulium suorum, exercitui nostro superuenerunt, quot penè nostrorum excederent numerum. Exercitu itaque imperii nostri propter viæ omnino angustiam et difficultatem, vsque ad decem milliaria extenso; et cum neque qui præibant possent postremos defendere, neque versa vice rursus postremi possent præeuntes inuare, non mediocritèr ab inuicem hos distare accidit. Sanè primæ cohortes permultùm ab acie imperij nostri diuidebantur, postremarum oblitæ, illas non præstolantes. Quoniam igitur Turcorum agmina ex iam factis prælijs cognouerant, non conforre sibi à fronte nobis repugnare, loci angustiam bonum subuentorem cum inuenissent, posteriora statuerunt inuadere agmina, quod et fecerunt. Arctissimo igitur vbique loco existente, instabant barbari vndique, à dextris et a sinistris, et aliundè dimicantes, et tela super nos quasi imbres descendentia interimebant viros et equos complures. Ad hæc itaque imperium nostrum vbi malum superabundabat, reputans secum oportunum iudicabat retrò expectare, atque illos qui illic erant adiuuare, expectando vtiquè contra infinita illa Persarum agmina bellum sustinuit. Quanta quidem, dum ab his circundaretur, patrauerit, non opus est ad tempus sermonibus pertexere, ab illis autem qui interfuerunt, forsitan discet de his tua nobilitas. Inter hæc autem existente imperio nostro, et omne belli grauamen in tantum sustinente, postremæ cohortes vniuersæ Gnecorum et Latinorum, et reliquorum omnium generum conglobatæ, quæ iaciebantur ab inimicis tela non sustinentes, impactione vtuntur, et ita violentèr ferebantur, dùm ad adiacentem ibi collem quasi ad propugnaculum festinarent: sed precedentes impellunt nolentes. Multo autem eleuato paluere, ac perturbante oculos, et neminem permittente videre quæ circa pedes erant, in præcipitium quod aderat profundissimæ vallis alius super alium homines et equi sic incontinentè portati corruerunt, quòd alij alios conculcantes ab inuicem interemerunt non ex gregarijs tantum, sed ex clarissimis et intimis nostris consanguineis. Quis enim inhibere poterat tantæ multitudinis importabilem impulsum? At verò imperium nostrum tot et tantis confertum barbáris saucians, sauciatúmque, adeò vt non modicam in eos moueret perturbationem, obstupentes perseuerant iam ipsius, et non remittebatur, benè iuuante deo, campum obtinuit. Neque locum illum scandere aduersarios permisit, in quo dimicauit cum barbaris. Nec quidem equum suum illorum timore incitauit, celerius aliquando ponere vestigia. Sed congregando omnia agmina sua, et de morte eripiendo ea, collocauit circa se: et sic primes attigit, et ordinatim proficiscens ad exercitus suos accessit. Ex tunc igitur videns Soltanus, quòd post tanta quæ acciderant exercitibus nostris, imperium nostrum, sicut oportunum erat, rem huiusmodi dispensauit, vt ipsum rursùm inuaderet: mittens supplicauit imperio nostro, et deprecatorijs vsus est sermonibus, et requisiuit pacem illius, promittens omnem imperij nostri adimplere voluntatem, et seruitium suum contra omnem hominem dare, et omnes qui in regno suo tenebantur captiuos absoluere, et esse ex toto voluntatis nostræ. Ibidem ergo per duos dies integros, in omni potestate morati sumtis, et cognito quòd nihil poterat fieri contra ciuitatem Iconij, perditis testudinibus et machins bellicis, eo quòd boues cecidissent a telis in modo pluuiæ iactis, qui eas trahebant: Simul autem eo quòd et vniuersa animalia nostra irruente in illa difficillima ægritudine laborabant, suscepit Soltani depræcationem et foedera et iuramenta peracta sub vexillis nostris, et pacem suam ei dedit. Inde ingressum imperium nostrum in regionem suam regreditur, tribulationem habens non mediocrem super his quos perdidit corisanguineis, maximas tamen Deo gratias agens, qui per suam bonitaiem et nunc Ipsum honorauit: Gratum autem habuimus, quòd quosdam nobilitatis tuæ principes accidit interesse nobiscum, qui narrabunt de omnibus quæ acciderant, tuæ voluntati seriem. Cæterum autem, licèt contristati simus propter illos qui ceciderunt: oportunum tamen duximus, de omnibus quæ; acciderant, declarare tibi, vt dilecto amico nostro, et vt permultùm coniuncto imperio nostro, per puerorum nostrorum intimam consanguinitatem. Vale. Data mense Nouembris, indictione tertia.

The same in English.

In the yeere 1177, Manuel the emperour of Constantinople hauing fought a field with the Soldan of Iconium, and vanquished him, wrote vnto Henry the second king of England in maner following.

Manuel Comnenus in Christ the euerliuing God a faithful emperour, descended of the linage of Porphyrie, crowned by Gods grace, high, puissant, mighty, alwayes most souereign, and gouernour of the Romans; vnto Henry the most famous king of England, his most deare friend, greeting and all good successe. Whereas our imperiall highnesse thinketh it expedient to aduertise you our welbeloued friend of all our affaires: We thought it not amisse to signifie vnto your, royal Maiestie certaine exploits at this present atchieued by vs. From the beginning therefore of our inauguration our imperiall highnes hath mainteined most deadly feod and hostility against Gods enemies the Persians, seeing them so to triumph ouer Christians, to exalt themselues against the Name of God, and to vsurpe ouer Christian kingdomes. For which cause our imperial highnesse hath in some sort encountered them heretofore, and did as it pleased God to giue vs grace. And we suppose that your Maiestie is not ignorant, what our imperiall highnesse hath often performed for their ruine and subversion. For euen now, being vrged thereunto, we haue determined to leade a mighty army against them, and to wage warre against all Persia. And albeit our forces be not so great as we could wish they were, yet haue we according to the time, and the present state of things strongly inuaded them. Wherefore our Maiestie imperiall hath gathered our armies together: but because we had in our armie sundry carts laden with armour, engines and other instruments for the assault of cities, to an exceeding weight we could not make any great speed in our iourney. Moreouer while our imperiall highnesse was yet marching in our owne dominions, before any barbarous enemy had fought against vs: our people were visited with the most grieuous disease of the fluxe, which being dispersed in our troups destroyed and slew great numbers, more then the sword of the enemy would haue done, which mischiefe so preuailing, did woonderfully abate our forces. But after we had inuaded the Turkish frontiers, we had at the first very often and hot skirmishes, and the Turks came swarming to fight against our imperiall troups. Howbeit by Gods assistance those miscreants were altogether scattered and put to flight by our souldiers. But as we approched vnto that strait passage which is called by the Persians Cibrilcimam, so many bands of Persian footemen and horsemen (most whereof came from the innermost parts of Persia, to succour their Allies) encountred our army, as were almost superiour vnto vs in number. Wherefore the army of our Imperiall highnesse, by reason of the straightnesse and difficultie of the way, being stretched ten miles in length; and the first not being able to helpe the last, nor yet contrarywise the last to rescue the first, it came to passe that they were very farre distant asunder.

And in very deed the foremost troupes were much separated from the guard of our imperiall person, who forgetting their fellowes behind, would not stay any whit for them. Because therefore the Turkish bands knew full well by their former conflicts that it was bootlesse for them to assaile the forefront of our battell, and perceiuing the narownesse of the place to be a great aduantage, they determined to set vpon our rereward, and did so. Wherefore our passage being very straight, and the infidels assayling vs vpon the right hand and vpon the left, and on all sides, and discharging their weapons as thicke as hailestones against vs, slew diuers of our men and horses. Hereupon, the slaughter of our people still encreasing, our maiestie imperiall deemed it requisite to stay behind, and to succour our bands in the rereward, and so expecting them we sustained the fierce encounter of many thousand Persians. What exploits our Imperiall person atchieued in the same skirmish, I hold it needlesse at this time to recount: your maiestie may perhaps vnderstand more of this matter by them which were there present Howbeit our Imperiall highnesse being in the middest of this conflict, and enduring the fight with so great danger, all our hindermost troups, both Greekes, Latines, and other nations, retiring themselues close together, and not being able to suffer the violence of their enemies weapons, pressed on so hard, and were caried with such maine force, that hastening to ascend the next hill for their better safegard, they vrged on them which went before, whether they would or no. Wherevpon, much dust being raised, which stopped our eyes and vtterly depriued vs of sight, and our men and horses pressing so sore one vpon the necke of another, plunged themselues on the sudden into such a steepe and dangerous valley, that treading one vpon another, they quelled to death not onely a multitude of the common souldiours, but diuers most honourable personages, and some of our neere kinsmen. For who could restraine the irresistable throng of so huge a multitude? Howbeit our Imperiall highnesse being enuironed with such swarmes of Infidels, and giuing and receiuing wounds (insomuch that the miscreants were greatly dismaied at our constancie) we gaue not ouer, but by Gods assistance wonne the field. Neither did we permit the enemie to ascend vnto that place, from whence we skirmished with him. Neither yet spurred wee on our horse any faster for all their assaults. But marshalling air our troupes together, and deliuering them out of danger, we disposed them about our Imperial person; and so we ouertooke the foremost, and marched in good order with our whole army. Nowe the Soldan perceiuing that notwithstanding the great damages which we had sustained, our Imperial hignes prouided to giue him a fresh encounter, humbly submitting himselfe vnto vs, and vsing submissive speaches, made suite to haue peace at our hands, and promised to fulfill the pleasure of our maiestie Imperiall, to doe vs seruice against all commers, to release all our subiects which were captiues in his realme, and to rest wholy at our commaund. [Sidenote: The citie of Iconium intended to haue bene besieged.] Here therefore we remained two dayes with great authoritie; and considering that wee could attempt nought against the citie of Iconium, hauing lost all our warrelike engines, both for defence and for batterie, for that the oxen which drew them were slaine with the enemies weapons, falling as thicke as hailestones: and also for because all our beasts in a maner were most grieuously diseased; our maiestie Imperial accepted of the Soldans petition, league, and oath being made and taken vnder our ensignes, and granted our peace vnto him. Then returned we into our owne dominions, being greatly grieued for the losse of our deere kinsmen, and yeelding vnto God most humble thanks, who of his goodnesse had euen now giuen vs the victory. [Sidenote: Certaine noblemen of the king of England were with the Emperor in his battell against the Soldan of Iconium.] We are right glad likewise that some of your maiesties princes and nobles accompanied vs in this action, who are able to report vnto you all things which haue happened. And albeit we were exceedingly grieued for the losse of our people; yet thought it we expedient to signifie vnto you the successe of our affaires, as vnto our welbeloued friend, and one who is very neerely allied vnto our highnesse Imperial, by reason of the consanguitie of our children Farewell. Giuen in the moneth of Nouember, and vpon the tenth Indiction.

* * * * *

The life and trauailes of Baldwinus Deuonius, sometime Archbishop of Canterbury.

Baldwinus Deuonius, tenui loco Excestrire natus, vir ore facundus, exactus Philosophus, et de omne studiorum genus per illos dies aptissimus inueniebatur. Scholarum rector primùm erat, tum postea Archidiaconus, eruditione ac sapientia in omni negotio celebris: fuit præterea Cisterciensis Monachus, et Abbas Fordensis Coenobij, magnus suorum testimatione, ar vniuiersæ eorum societati quasi Antesignanus: fuit deinde Wigorniensis præsul, fuit et mortuo demùm Richardo Cantuariorum Archiepiscopus, ac totius Angliæ Primas. Cui muneri Baldwinus sollicitè inuigilans, egregium se pastorem exhibuit, dominicum semen, quantum patiebatur eius temporis, iniquitas, vbique locorum spargens. Richardus Anglorum rex, acceptis tunc regni insignijs, summo studio classem, ac omnia ad Hierosolymitanum bellum gerendum necessaria parauit. Secutus est illico regem in Syriam, et Palestinam vsque Baldwinus, vt esset in tam Sancto (vt ipse putabat) itinere laborum, dolorum, ac periculorum particeps. Præfuit Cantuariensi Ecclesiæ ferè 6 annis, et Richardum regem in Syriam secutus, anno Salutis nostræ 1190. Tyri vitam finiuit, vbi et sepultus est.

The same in English.

Baldwine a Deuonshire man borne in Exceter of mean parentage, was a very eloquent man, an exact Philosopher, and in those dayes very excellent in all kind of studies. He was first of all a Schoolemaster: afterwards he became an Archdeacon, very famous for his learning and wisedom in all his doings. He was also a Cistercian Monke and Abbot of Foord Monasterie, and the chiefe of all those that were of his order: he grew after this to be bishop of Worcester, and at last after the death of Archb. Richard he was promoted and made Archbishop of Canterbury, and Primate of all England. In the discharge of which place he being very vigilant, shewed, himself a worthy Pastor, sowing the seed of Gods word in euery place as farre foorth as the iniquitie of that time permitted. In his time king Richard with all indeauour prepared a Fleet and all things necessary for waging of warre against the Infidels at Ierasalem, taking with him the standerd and ensignes of the kingdome. This Baldwine eftsoones folowed the king into Syria and Palestina, as one desirous to be partaker of his trauailes, paines, and perils in so holy a voyage. Hee was Archbishop of Canterburie almost sixe yeres: but hauing followed the king into Syria, in the yeere 1190. he died at Tyre, where he was also buried.

* * * * *

An annotation concerning the trauailes of the sayd Baldwirie, taken out of Giraldus Cambrensis, in his Itinerarium Cambrise, lib, a. Cap. 14. Fol 229.

Inter primos Thomæ Becketi successor hic secundus, audita saluatoris et salutiferæ Crucis iniuria nostris (proh dolor) diebus per Saladinum irrogata, cruce signatus, in eiusdem obsequijs, tam remotis finibus quàm propinquis, prædicationis officiunm viriliter assumpsit. Et postmodùm iter accipiens, nauigióque fungens apud Marsiliam, transcurso tandem pelagi profundo, in portu Tyrensi incolumis applicuit: et inde ad exercitum nostrum obsidentem pariter et obsessum Aconem transiuit: vbi multos ex nostris inueniens, et ferè cunctos principum defectu, in summa desolatlone iam positos, et desperatione, alios quidem longa expectatione fatigatos, alios fame et inopia grauiter afflictos, quosdam verò aëris, inclementia distemperatos, diem foelicitèr in terra sacra clausurus extremum, singulos pro posse vinculo charitatis amplectens, sumptibus et impensis, verbis, et vitæ mentis confirmauit.

The same in English.

This Baldwine being the second successor vnto Thomas Becket, after he had heard the wrong which was done to our Sauiour, and the signe of the Crosse by Saladin the Sultan of Egypt, taking vpon him the Lords Character, he couragiously perfourmd his office of preaching in the obedience thereof, as well in farre distant Countreis as at home. And afterwards taking his iourney and imbarking himselfe at Marseils, hauing at length passed the Leuant sea, he arriued safely in the Hauen of Tyrus, and from thence went ouer to Achon vnto our armie, besieging the Towne, and yet (as it were) besieged it selfe: where finding many of our Countreymen, and almost all men remaining in wonderfull pensiuenesse and despaire, through the withdrawing of the Princes, some of them tyred with long expectation, others grieuously afflicted with hunger and pouertie, and others distempered with the heate of the weather, being ready happily to ende his dayes in the Holy land, embracing euery one according to his abilitie in the bond of loue, he ayded them at his costes and charges, and strengthened them with his wordes and good examples of life.

* * * * *

A note drawen out of a very ancient booke remaining in the hands of the right worshipfull M. Thomas Tilney Esquire, touching Sir Frederike Tilney his ancestor, knighted at Acon in the Holy land for his valour, by K. Richard the first, as foloweth.

Pertinuit iste liber prius Frederico Tilney de Boston, in comitatu Lincolniæ militi facto apud Acon in terra Iudeæ anno Regis Richardi primi tertio. Vir erat iste magnæ staturæ et potens in corpore: qui cum partibus suis dormit apud Tirrington iuxta villam sui nominis Tilney in Mershland. Cuius altitudo in salua custodia permanet ibidem vsque in hunc diem. Et post eius obitum sexdecem militibus eius nominis Tilney hæreditas illa successiuè obuenit, quorum vnus post alium semper habitabat apud Boston prædictum; dum fratris senioris hæreditas hæredi generali deuoluta est, quæ nupta est Iohanni duci Norfolciæ. Eorum miles vltimus fuit Philippus Tilney nuper de Shelleigh in Comitatu Suffolciæ, pater et genitor Thomæ Tilney de Hadleigh in Comitatu prædicto Armigeri, cut modò attinet iste liber. Anno ætatis suæ 64, Anno Domini 1556.

The same in English.

This booke pertained in times past vnto Sir Frederick Tilney of Boston in the Countie of Lincolne, who was knighted at Acon in the land of Iurie, in the third yeere of the reigne of king Richard the first. This knight was of a tall stature, and strong of body, who resteth interred with his forefathers at Tirrington, neere vnto a towne in Marshland called by his owne name Tilney. The iust height of this knight is there kept in safe custody vntill this very day. Also, after this mans decease, the inheritance of his landes fell successively vnto sixteene sundry knights called all by the name of Tilney, who dwelt alwayes, one after another, at the towne of Boston aforesayd, vntill such time as the possessions of the elder brother fell vnto an heire general, which was maried vnto Iohn duke of Northfolke. The last knight of that name was sir Philip Tilney late of Shelleigh in the Countie of Suffolke, predecessor and father vnto Thomas Tilney of Hadleigh in the

Countie aforesayd Esquire, vnto whom the said booke of late appertained. In the yeere of his age 64 and in the yeere of our Lord, 1556.

* * * * *

The trauailes of one Richard surnaræd Canonicus.

Richardus Canonicus ad Trinitatis fanum Londini Regularis, ab ipsa pueritia, bonarum artium literas impense amauit, excoluit, ac didicit. Qui ex continuo labore atque exercitatione longa, talis tandem euasit orator, et Poeta, quales ea ætas rarissimos nutriebat. Ob id Richardo Anglorum tunc Regi charus, longam cum eo peregrinationem in Palæstinam ac Syriam, dum expugnaret Turcas, suscepit. Vnde in Angliam tum demum reuersus, omnia quæ presens vidit in vrbibus, agris, ac militum castris, fideli narratione, tam carmine, quam prosa descripsit. Neque interim omisit eiusdem Regis mores, et formam, per omnia corporis lineamenta designare, addiditque præclaro suo open hoc aptissimum pro titulo nomen, scilicet, Itinerarium Regis Richardi. Claruit anno redemptionis nostne 1200 sub Ioanne Anglorimi Rege.

The same in English.

Richard surnamed Canonicus an obseruant Frier of Trinitie Church in London, was in great loue with the studies of good Artes, and tooke paines in them and learned them. And at last by his continuall endeauour and long exercise therein, he grewe to bee such an Oratour and Poet, as fewe were in that age liuing, by reason whereof hee grew in fauour with Richard then King of England, and vndertooke that long voyage with him into Palestina and Syria against the Turkes. From whence being returned againe into England, hee faithfully described both in Verse and Prose all such things, as hee had seene in the Cities, fieldes and tentes of the souldiours, where hee was present, and omitted not to note the behauiour, forme, and proportion of body in the foresayd king, giuing to his notable worke this most apt name for the title, The Iournall of King Richard. He flourished in the yeere of our Redemption 1200. vnder Iohn king of England.

* * * * *

The large contribution to the succour of the Holy land, made by king Iohn king of England, in the third yeere of his reigne 1201. Matth. Paris and Holinsh. pag. 164.

At the same time also the Kings of France and England gaue large money towards the maintenance of the army which at this present went foorth vnder the leading of the earle of Flanders and other, to warre against the enemies of the Christian faith at the instance of pope Innocent. There was furthermore granted vnto them the fortieth part of all the reuenues belonging vnto ecclesiastical persons, towards the ayd of the Christians then being in the Holy and: and all such aswel of the nobility, as other of the weaker sort, which had taken vpon them the crosse, and secretly layed it downe were compelled eftsoones to receiue it now againe.

* * * * *

The trauailes of Hubert Walter bishop of Sarisburie.

Hubertus Walterus Sarisburiensis Episcopus, vir probus, ingenioque ac pietate clarus, inter præcipuos vnus eorum erat, qui post Richardum regem expugnandorum Saracenorum gratia in Syriam proficiscebantur. Cum ex Palæstina rediens, audiret in Sicilia, quod idem Richardus in inimicorum manus incidisset, omisso itinere incoepto, ad eum cursim diuertebat: Quem et ille statim in Angliam misit, vt illic regij Senatus authoritate, indicto pro eius redemptione tributo pecuniam colligeret quod et industrius fecit ac regem liberauit. Inde Cantuariorum Archiepiscopus factus, post eius mortem Ioanni illius fratri ac successori paria fidelitatis officia præstitit. Longa enim oratione toti Anglorum nationi persuasit, quod vir prouidus, præstans, fortis, genere nobilissimus, et imperio dignissimus esset: quo salutatus a populo fuit, atque in regem coronatus. Composuit quædam opuscula, et ex immenso animi dolore demum obijsse fertur, Anno salutis humanæ 1205. cum sedisset annos 11. Menses octo, et dies sex. Quum vidisset ex intestinis odijs, omnia in transmarinis regionibus pessùm ire, regnante Ioanne.

The same in English.

Hubert Walter bishop of Sarisburie, a vertuous man, and famous for his good wit and piety, was one of the chiefest of them that followed king Richard into Syria going against the Saracens. As he returned from Palæstina and came in his iourney into Sicilia, he there heard of the ill fortune of the king being fallen into his enemies handes, and thereupon leauing his iourney homewards, he went presently and in all haste to the place where the king was captiued, whom the king immediatly vpon his comming sent into England, that by the authority of the councell, a tribute might be collected for his redemption: which this Hubert performed with great diligence, and deliuered the king. After this he was made Archbishop of Canterburie, and after the death of King Richard he shewed the like dueties of fidelitie and trust to his brother Iohn that succeeded him. For by a long oration he perswaded the whole nation of the English men, that he was a very circumspect man, vertuous, valiant, borne of noble parentage, and most woorthy of the crowne. Whereupon he was so receiued of all the people and crowned king. He wrote certaine books, and died at the last with very great griefe of minde, in the yeere 1205, hauing beene archbishop the space of 11 yeres 8 moneths and six dayes, by reason of the ciuil discords abroad, whereby all things went topsie turuy, and in the reigne of king Iohn.

* * * * *

The trauailes of Robert Curson.

Robertus Curson ex nobili quodam Anglorum ortus genere, disciplinis tum prophanis, tum sacris studiosus incubuit, idque (quantum ex coniecturis colligo) in celebratissima Oxonij Academia. Præstantissimis illic institutoribus vsus, ex summa circa ingenuas artes industria, et assiduo literarum labore, famam sibi inter suos celeberrimam comparauit. Ampliora deinde meditatus Parisiorum Lutetiam, atque Romam ipsam petijt, illic Theologus Doctor, hic verò Cardinalis effectus. Vnde vterque Matthæus Parisius, ac Westmonasterius, hoc de ipso testimonium adferunt: hic libro 2. ille 8. suorum Chronicorum. Anno Domini 1218 (inquiunt) in captione Damiatæ Ægypti vrbis, sub Ioanne Brenno Hierosolymorum rege, fuit cum Pelagio Albanensi Magister Robertus de Curson, Anglus, Clericus celeberrimus, genere nobilis, ac Romanæ Ecclesiæ Cardinalis, etc. Bostonus Buriensis in sua Catalogo Cursonum aliquos libros composuisse narrat. Claruit anno superius numerato per prædictos testes in Anglia regnante Henrico tertio Ioannis regis filio: fuitque hic diebus Honorij tertij Romani pontificis in Angliam, Bostono teste, legatus.

The same in English.

Robert Curson descended of a noble family of England, vsed great diligence aswell in prophane as in diuine studies in the famous Vniuersitie of Oxford (as I coniecture.) He had there the best scholemasters that were to be gotten, and was most industrious, in the arts and continual exercises of learning: by meanes whereof he grew to be of great renowne where he liued. Afterward thinking of greater matters he went to Paris, and thence to Rome it selfe, and at Paris he proceeded doctor of Diuinity, at Rome he was made cardinall: whereupon both Matthew Paris and Matthew of Westminster produce this testimony of him, the one in his second booke, the other in his eight booke of Chronicles. In the yere of our Lord (say they) 1218, at the taking of Damiata a city of Egypt vnder Iohn Brenne king of Ierusalem, M. Robert Curson an English man, a most famous clearke of noble parentage, and cardinall of the church of Rome, was there with Pelagius Albanensis, &c. Boston of Burie in Suffolke in his catalogue reporteth, that he wrote diuers books. He flourished in the yeere aforesayd by the witnesses aforesayd. Henry the third sonne of king Iohn being then king of England: and by the further testimony of Boston, this Curson was legate into England in the dayes of Honorius the third, bishop of Rome.

* * * * *

The voyage of Ranulph earle of Chester, of Saer Quincy earle of Winchester,
William de Albanie earle of Arundel, with diuers other noble men to the Holy land, in the second yere of King Henry the third. Matth. Paris. Holensh. pag. 202.

In the yeere 1218, Ranulph earle of Chester was sent into the Holy land by king Henry the third with a goodly company of souldiers and men of warre, to ayde the Christians there against the Infidels, which at the same time had besieged the city of Damiata in Egypt. In which enterprise the valiancy of the same earle after his comming thither was to his great praise most apparent There went with him in that iourney Saer de Quincy earle of Winchester, William de Albanie earle of Arundel, besides diuers barons, as the lord Robert fitz Walter, Iohn constable of Chester, William de Harecourt, and Oliuer fitz Roy sonne to the king of England, and diuers others.

* * * * *

The voyage of Henry Bohun and Saer Quincy to the Holy land.

This yere, being the sixt yere of Henry the third, deceased Henry de Bohun earle of Hereford, and Saer de Quincy earle of Winchester, in their journey which they made to the Holy land. Matth. Paris. Holensh. pag. 202. col. 2.

* * * * *

The trauailes of Ranulph Glanuile earle of Chester.

Ranulphus Glanuile Cestriæ Comes, vir nobilissimi generis, et vtroque iure eruditus, in albo illustrium virorum à me meritò ponendus venit. Ita probè omnes adolescentiæ suæ annos legibus tum humanis tum diuinis consecrauit, vt non prius in hominem pet ætatem euaserit, quàm nomen decúsque ab insigni eruditione sibi comparauerit. Cum profecti essent Francorum Heroes Ptolemaidem, inito cum Ioanne Brenno Hierosolymorum rege concilio, Damiatam Ægypti vrbem obsidendam constituebant, anno salutis humanæ 1218. Misit illùc Henricus rex, ab Honorio 3 Rom. Pontifice rogatus, cum magna armatorum manu Ranulphum, ad rem Christianum iuuandam. Cuius virtus, Polydoro teste, in eo bello miris omnium laudibus celebrata fuit. Quo confecto negotio, Ranulphus in patriam reuersus, scripsit, De legibus Angliæ librum vnum. Fertur præterea, et alia quædam scripsisse, sed tempus edax rerum, ea nobis abstulit. Claruit anno à Seruatoris nostri natiuitate 1230 confectus senio, dum Henricus tertius sub Antichristi tyrannide in Anglia regnaret.

The same in English.

Ranulph Granuile earle of Chester, a man of a very noble house, and learned in both the Lawes, deserues of deutie to be here placed by me in the catalogue of woorthy and notable men. He applied so well all the yeeres of his youth to the study of humane and diuine Lawes, that he came not so soone to the age of a man, as he had purchased to himselfe by reason of his singular learning, renowme and honour. When the noble men of France went to Ptolomais, vpon the counsell of Iohn Brenne king of Ierusalem, they resolued to besiege Damiata a city of Egypt, in the yeere 1218. And then Henry the king vpon the motion of Honorius the third, bishop of Rome, sent thither this earle Ranulph with a great power of armed souldiers, to further the enterprise of the Christians: whose valure in that warre (by the testimonie of Polidor Virgil) was marueilously commended of all men. After the end of which businesse, he being returned into his countrey, wrote a booke of the lawes of England. It is also reported that he wrote other books, but time the destroyer of many memorials, hath taken them from vs. He flourished in the yeere after the natiuity of Christ 1230, being very aged, and in the reigne of K. Henry the third.

* * * * *

The voyage of Petrus de Rupibus bishop, of Winchester, to Ierusalem in the yere of grace 1231, and the 15 of Henry the third.

Anno gratis 1231, mense verò Iulio, Petrus Wintoniensis episcopus, completo in terra sancta iam fere per quinquennium magnifice peregrinationis voto, reuersus est in Angliam, Kalendis Augusti; et Wintoniam veniens, susceptus est cum processione solenni in sua ecclesia cathedrali.

The same in English.

In the yere of grace 1231, and in the moneth of Iuly, Peter bishop of Winchester hauing spent almost fiue whole yeres in fulfilling his vow of pilgrimage in the Holy land with great pompe, returned into England, about the Kalends of August, and coming unto Winchester was received with solemne procession into his cathedrall church.

* * * * *

The honourable and prosperous voyage of Richard earle of Cornewall, brother to king Henry the third, accompanied with William Longespee earle of Sarisburie, and many other noble men into Syria.

In the 24 yere of king Henry the third, Richard earle of Cornwall the kings brother, with a navy of ships sailed into Syria, where in the warres against the Saracens he greatly advanced the part of the Christians. There went over with him the earle of Sarisburie, William Longspee, and William

Basset, John Beauchampe, Geoffrey de Lucie, John Neuel, Geoffrey Beauchampe, Peter de Brense, and William Furniuall.

Simon Montfort earle of Leicester went ouer also the same time; but whereas the earle of Cornwall tooke the sea at Marseils, the earle of Leicester passed thorow Italy, and tooke shipping at Brindize in Apulia: and with him went these persons of name, Thomas de Furniual with his brother Gerard de Furniuall, Hugh Wake, Almerike de S. Aumond, Wiscard Ledet, Punchard de Dewin, and William de Dewin that were brethren, Gerald Pesmes, Fouke de Baugie, and Peter de Chauntenay.

Shortly after also Iohn earle of Albemarle, William Fortis, and Peter de Mallow a Poictouin, men for their valiancy greatly renowmed, went thither, leading with them a great number of Christian souldiors, Matth. Paris. Matth. West Holensh. pag. 225. col. 2.

* * * * *

The voyage of William Longespee [Marginal note:—Or, Longsword.] Earle of Sarisburie into Asia, in the yeere 1248, and in the 32 yeere of the reigne of Henry the third, king of England.

Lewis the French king being recovered of his sicknesse which he fell into, in the yeere 1234, vowed thereupon for a free will sacrifice to God, that he (if the Councell of his realme would suffer him) would in his owne person visit the Holy land: which matter was opened and debated in the Parliament of France held in the yeere 1247. Where at length it was concluded, that the king according to his vow should take his journey into Asia, and the time thereof was also prefixed, which should be after the feast of S. John Baptist the next yeere ensuing.

At which time William Longespee a worthie warrior, with the bishop of Worcester and certaine other great men in the Realme of England (mooved with the example of the Frenchmen) prepared themselves likewise to the same journey.

It fell out in this enterprise, that about the beginning of October, the French king assaulted and tooke Damiata, being the principall fort or hold of the Saracens in all Egypt, Anno 1249, and having fortified the Citie with an able garrison left with the Duke of Burgundies he remooved his tents from thence to goe Eastward. In whose armie followed William Longespee, accompanied with a piked number of English warriors retaining unto him. But such was the disdaine of the Frenchmen against this William Longespee and the Englishmen that they could not abide them, but flouted them after an opprobrious maner with English tailes, insomuch that the French king himselfe had much adoe to keepe peace betweene them.

The originall cause of this grudge betweene them began thus. [Sidenote: A fort won by the Englishmen] There was not farre from Alexandria in Egypt a strong fort or castle replenished with great Ladies and rich treasure of the Saracens: which hold it chanced the sayd William Longespee with his company of English soldiers to get, more by politique dexteritie then by open force of armes, wherewith, he and his retinue were greatly enriched. When the Frenchmen had knowledge hereof (they not being made priuie hereto) began to conceive an heart burning against the English souldiers, and could not speake well of them after that.

[Sidenote: A rich bootie also gotten by the Englishmen.] It hapned againe not long after that the sayd William had intelligence of a company of rich merchants among the Saracens going to a certaine Faire about the parts of Alexandria, having their camels, asses and mules, richly loden with silkes, precious jewels, spices, gold and silver, with cart loades of other wares, beside victuall and other furniture, whereof the souldiers then stood in great need: he having secret knowledge hereof, gathered all the power of Englishmen unto him that he could, and so by night falling vpon the merchants, some he slew with their guides and conducters, some he tooke, some hee put to flight: the carts with the driuers, and with the oxen, camels, asses and mules, with the whole cariage and victuals he tooke and brought with him, losing in all the skirmish but one souldier and eight of his seruitors: of whom notwithstanding some he brought home wounded to be cured.

[Sidenote: The iniurie of the Frenchmen to our English.] This being knowen in the Campe, foorth came the Frenchmen which all this while loytered in their pauilions, and meeting this cariage by the way, tooke all the foresayd praie whole to themselues, rating the said William and the Englishmen for aduenturing and issuing out of the Campe without leaue or knowledge of their Generall, contrary to the discipline of warre. William said againe he had done nothing but he would answere to it, whose purpose was to haue the spoyle deuided to the behoofe of the whole armie.

[Sidenote: Will. Longspee iustly forsaketh the French king.] When this would not serue, hee being sore grieued in his minde so cowardly to be spoyled of that which he so aduenturously had trauailed for, went to the King to complaine: But when no reason nor complaint would serue by reason of the proude Earle of Artoys the Kings brother, which vpon spight and disdaine stood agaynst him, he bidding the King forewell sayd hee would serue him no longer: and so William de Longespee with the rest of his company breaking from the French hoste went to Achon. Vpon whose departure the earle of Artoys sayd, Now is the army of French men well rid of these tailed people, which words spoken in great despight were ill taken of many good men that heard them.

But not long after, when the keeper of Cayro & Babylonia, bearing a good mind to the Christian religion, and being offended also with the Souldan, promised to deliuer the same to the French king, instructing him what course was best for him to take to accomplish it, the king hereupon in all haste sent for William Longespee, promising him a full redress of all his iniuries before receiued: who at the kings request came to him againe, and so ioyned with the French power.

After this, it happened that the French king passing with his armie towardes Cayro aforesayd, came to the great riuer Nilus, on the further part whereof the Soldan had pitched himselfe to withstand his comming ouer: there was at this time a Saracen lately conuerted to Christ, seruing the earle Robert the French kings brother, who told him of the absence of the Soldan from his tents, and of a shallow foord in the riuer where they might easily passe ouer. Whereupon the sayd earle Robert and the Master of the Temple with a great power, esteemed to the third part of the army issued ouer the riuer, after whom followed W. Longspee with his band of English souldiers. These being ioyned together on the other side of the water, encountred the same day with the Saracens remaining in the tents and put them to the worst. Which victory being gotten, the French earle surprised with pride and triumph, as though hee had conquered the whole earth, would needs forward, diuiding himselfe from the maine hoste, thinking to winne the spurres alone. To whom certain sage men of the Temple, giuing him contrary counsell, aduised him not to do so, but rather to returne and take their whole company with them, and so should they be more sure against all deceits and dangers, which might be layed priuily for them. The maner of that people (they sayd) they better knew, and had more experience thereof then he: alledging moreouer their wearied bodies, their tired horses, their famished souldiers, and the insufficiency also of their number, which was not able to withstand the multitude of the enemies, especially at this present brunt, in which the aduersaries did well see the whole state of their dominion now to consist either in winning all or losing all.

Which when the proud earle did heare, being inflated with no lesse arrogancy then ignorance, with opprobrious taunts reuiled them, calling them cowardly dastards, and betrayers of the whole countrey, obiecting vnto them the common report of many, which sayd, that the land of the holy crosse might soone be woon to Christendome, were it not for rebellious Templaries, with the Hospitalaries, and their followers.

To these contumelious rebukes, when the master of the Temple answered againe for him and his fellowes, bidding him display his ensigne when he would, and where he durst, they were as ready to follow him, as he to goe before them. Then began William de Longespe the worthy knight to speake, desiring the earle to giue eare to those men of experience, who had better knowledge of those countreyes and people then he had, commending also their counsell to be discreet and wholesome, and so turning to the master of the Temple, began with gentle wordes to mittigate him likewise. The knight had not halfe ended his talke, when the Earle taking his wordes out of his mouth, began to fume and sweare, crying out of those cowardly Englishmen with tailes: What a pure armie (sayd he) should we haue here, if these tailes and tailed people were purged from it, with other like words of villany, and much disdaine: [Sidenote: The worthy answere of William Longspe to Earle Robert.] whereunto the English knight answering againe, well, Earle Robert (said he) wheresoeuer you dare set your foote, my step shall go as farre as yours, and (as I beleeue) we goe this day where you shall not dare to come neere the taile of my horse, as in deede in the euent it prooued true: for Earle Robert would needes set forward, weening to get all the glory to himselfe before the comming of the hoste, and first inuaded a litle village or castle, which was not farre off, called Mansor. The countrey Boores and Pagans in the villages, seeing the Christians comming, ranne out with such a maine cry and shout, that it came to the Soldans hearing, who was neerer then our men did thinke. In the meane time, the Christians inuading and entring into the munition [Footnote: Fortification.] incircumspectly, were pelted and pashed [Footnote: "That can be cut with any iron, or pashed with mighty stones." CHAPMAN *Iliad*, xiii., 297.] with stones by them which stood aboue, whereby a great number of our men were lost, and the armie sore maymed, and almost in despaire.

Then immediatly vpon the same, commeth the Soldan with all his maine power, which seeing the Christian armie to be deuided, and the brother separated from the brother, had that which he long wished for, and so inclosing them round about, that none should escape, had with them a cruell fight.

Then the earle beganne to repent him of his heady rashnes, but it was too late, who then seeing William the English knight doughtily fighting in the chiefe brunt of the enemies, cried vnto him most cowardly to flie, seeing God (saith he) doth fight against vs: To whom the Knight answering againe, God forbid (sayth he) that my fathers sonne should runne away from the face of a Saracene. [Sidenote: The cowardly flight of Earle Robert.] The Earle then turning his horse, fled away, thinking to auoid by the swiftnes of his horse, and so taking the riuer Thafnis, oppressed with harnesse, was there sunken and drowned.

Thus the Earle being gone, the Frenchmen began to dispaire and scatter. [Sidenote: The valiant ende of William Longespe.] Then William de Longespe bearing all the force of the enemies, stoode against them as long as he could, wounding and slaying many a Saracen, till at length his horse being killed, and his legges maymed, he could no longer stande, who yet notwithstanding as he was downe, mangled their feete and legges, and did the Saracens much sorrow, till at last after many blowes and wounds, being stoned of the Saracens, he yeelded his life. And after the death of him, the Saracens setting vpon the residue of the armie, whom they had compassed on euery side, deuoured and destroyed them all, insomuch that scarce one man remained aliue, sauing two Templaries, one Hospitaler, and one poore rascall souldier, which brought tidings hereof to the King.

And thus by the imprudent and foolish hardines of that French Earle, the Frenchmen were discomfited, and that valiant English Knight ouermatched, to the griefe of all Christian people, the glory of the Saracens, and the vtter destruction and ruine of the whole French armie, as afterwards it appeared.

* * * * *

The Voyage of Prince Edward the sonne of king Henry the third into Asia, in the yeere 1270.

About the yeere of our Lord, 1267. Octobonus the Popes Legate being in England, prince Edward the sonne of king Henry, and other Noble men of England tooke vpon them the crosse vpon S. Iohn Baptists day, by the sayd Legates hands at Northampton, to the reliefe of the Holy land, and the subuersion of the enemies of the crosse of Christ. For which purpose, and for the better furnishing of the prince towards the iourney, there was granted him a subsidie throughout all the realme, and in the moneth of May, in the yeere of our Lord 1270. he began to set forward.

At Michælmas following he with his company came to Eguemortes, which is from Marsilia eight leagues Westward, and there taking ship againe (hauing a mery and prosperous wind) within ten dayes arriued at Tunez, where he was with great ioy welcommed, and entertained of the Christian princes that there were to this purpose assembled, as of Philip the French King, whose father Lodouicus died a litle before, of Carolus the king of Sicilia, and the two kings of Nauarre and Arragon, and as this lord Edward came thither for his father the king of England, thither came also Henry the sonne of the king of Almaine for his father, who at his returne from the voyage was slaine in a chappell at Viterbium.

When prince Edward demanded of these kings and princes what was to be done, they answered him againe and sayd, the prince of this citie and the prouince adioyning to the same hath bene accustomed to pay tribute vnto the king of Sicily euery yere: and now for that the same hath bene for the space of seuen yeeres vnpaied and more, therefore we thought good to make invasion vpon him. But the king knowing the same tribute to be but iustly demaunded, hath now according to our owne desire satisfied for the time past, and also paid his tribute before hand.

Then sayd he, My Lords, what is this to the purpose? are we not here all assembled, and haue taken vpon vs the Lords Character to fight against the infidels and enemies of Christ? What meane you then to conclude a peace with them? God forbid we should do so, for now the land is plaine and hard, so that we may approch to the holy city of Ierusalem. Then said they, now haue we made a league with them, neither is it lawful for vs to breake the same. But let vs returne againe to Sicilia, and when the winter is past we may well take shipping to Acra. But this counsel nothing at all liked him, neither did he shew himselfe wel pleased therewith: but after hee had made them a princely banket, he went into his closet or priuy chamber from amongst them, neither would be partaker of any of that wicked money which they had taken. They notwithstanding continuing their purpose, at the next mery wind tooke shipping, and for want of ships left 200. of their men a shore, crying out, and pitiously lamenting for the peril and hazard of death that they were in: wherewith prince Edward being somewhat mooued to compassion: came backe againe to the land, and receiued and stowed them in his owne ships, being the last that went aboord.

Within seuen dayes after, they arriued in the kingdom of Sicilia, ouer agaynst the Citie Trapes, [Footnote: Trapani, N.E. of Marsala.] casting their ankers a league from thence within the sea, for that their shippes were of great burden, and throughly fraught: and from the hauen of the city they sent out barges and boates to receiue and bring such of the Nobilitie to land as would, but their horses for the most part, and all their armour they kept still within boord.

At length towards the euening the sea began to be rough, and increased to a great tempest and a mightie: insomuch that their ships were beaten one against anothers sides, and drowned. There was of them at that tempest lying at anker more then 120. with all their armour and munition, with innumerable soules besides, and that wicked money also which they had taken before, likewise perished, and was lost.

But the tempest hurt not so much as one ship of prince Edwards, who had in number 13. nor yet had one man lost thereby, for that (as it may be presupposed) he consented not to the wicked counsell of the rest.

When in the morning the princes and kings came to the sea side, and saw all their ships drowned, and saw their men and horses in great number cast vpon the land drowned, they had full heauie hearts, as well they might, for of all their ships and mariners, which were in number 1500. besides the common souldiers, there was no more saued then the manners of one onely ship, and they in this wise.

There was in that ship a good and wise Matrone, a Countesse or an Erles wife, who perceiuing the tempest to grow, and fearing her selfe, called to her the M. of the ship, and asked him whether in attempting to the shoare it were not possible to saue themselues: he answered, that to saue the ship it was impossible: howbeit the men that were therein by Gods helpe he doubted not. Then sayd the countesse, for the ship force no whit, saue the soules therein, and haue to thee double the value of the shippe: who immediatly hoising the sailes with all force, ran the shippe aground so neere the shore as was possible, so that with the vehemency of the weather and force he came withall, he brast the ship and saued all that was within the same, as he had shewed, and sayd before.

Then the kings and princes (altering their purpose after this so great a shipwracke) returned home againe euery one vnto their owne lands: onely Edward, the sonne of the king of England, remained behinde with his men and ships, which the Lord had saued and preserued.

[Sidenote: The arriual of Prince Edward at Acra.] Then prince Edward renouating his purpose, tooke shipping againe, and within fifteene daies after Easter arriued he at Acra, and went a land, taking with him a thousand of the best souldiers and most expert, and taried there a whole moneth, refreshing both his men and horses, and that in this space he might learne and know the secrets of the land. [Sidenote: Nazareth taken by the prince.] After this he tooke with him sixe or seuen thousand souldiers, and marched forward twenty miles from Acra, and tooke Nazareth, and those that he found there he slew, and afterward returned againe to Acra. But their enemies following after them, thinking to haue set vpon them at some streit or other advantage, were espied by the prince, and returning againe vpon them gaue a charge, and slew many of them, and the rest they put to flight.

[Sidenote: A victorie against the Saracens wherein 1000 of them are slaine.] After this, about Midsummer, when the prince had vnderstanding that the Saracens began to gather at Cakow which was forty miles from Acra, he marching thither, set vpon them very earely in the morning, and slew of them more then a thousand, the rest he put to flight, and tooke rich spoiles, marching forward till they came to a castle named Castrum peregrinorum, situate vpon the sea coast, and taried there that night, and the next day they returned againe toward Acra.

In the meane season the king of Ierusalem sent vnto the noble men of Cyprus, desiring them to come with speed to ayd the Christians, but they would not come, saying they would keepe their owne land, and go no further. [Sidenote: The Princes of Cyprus acknowledge obedience to the kings of England.] Then prince Edward sent vnto them, desiring that at his request they would come and ioyne in ayd with him: who immediatly thereupon came vnto him with great preparation and furniture for the warres, saying, that at his commandement they were bound to do no lesse, for that his predecessors were sometimes the gouernors of that their land, and that they ought alwayes to shew their fidelity to the kings of England.

Then the Christians being herewith animated, made a third voyage or road, and came as farre as the fort called Vincula sancti Petri, and to S. Georgius, and when they had slain certaine there, not finding any to make resistance against them, they retired againe from whence they came: when thus the fame of prince Edward grew amongst his enemies, and that they began to stand in doubt of him, they deuised among themselues how by some pollicy they might circumuent him, and betray him. Whereupon the prince and admirall of Ioppa sent vnto him, faining himselfe vnder great deceit willing to become a Christian, and that he would draw with him a great number besides, so that they might be honorably entertained and vsed of the Christians. This talke pleased the prince well, and perswaded him to finish the thing he had so well begun by writing againe, who also by the same messenger sent and wrote backe vnto him diuers times about the same matter, whereby no mistrust should spring.

This messenger (sayth mine author) was one ex caute nutritis, one of the stony hearted, that neither feared God nor dreaded death.

The fift time when this messenger came, and was of the princes seruants searched according to the maner and custome what weapon and armour he had about him, as also his purse, that not so much as a knife could be seene about him, he was had vp into the princes chamber, and after his reuerence done, he pulled out certaine letters, which he deliuered the prince from his lord, as he had done others before. This was about eight dayes after Whitsuntide, vpon a Tuesday, somewhat before night, at which time the prince was layed vpon his bed bare headed, in his ierkin for the great heat and intemperature of the weather.

When the prince had read the letters, it appeared by them, that vpon the Saturday next following, his lord would be there ready to accomplish all that he had written and promised. The report of these newes by the prince to the standers by, liked them well, who drew somewhat backe to consult thereof amongst themselues. [Sidenote: Prince Edward traiterously wounded.] In the meane time, the messenger kneeling, and making his obeisance to the prince (questioning further with him) put his hand to his belt, as though he would haue pulled out some secret letters, and suddenly he pulled out an enuenomed knife, thinking to haue stroken the prince in the belly therewith as he lay: but the prince lifting vp his hand to defend the blow, was striken a great wound into the arme, and being about to fetch another stroke at him, the prince againe with his foot tooke him such a blow, that he feld him to the ground: with that the prince gate him by the hand, and with such violence wrasted the knife from him, that he hurt himselfe therewith on the forehead, and immediately thrust the same into belly of the messenger and striker, and slew him.

The princes seruants being in the next chamber not farre off, hearing the busling, came with great haste running in, and finding the messenger lying dead in the floore, one of them tooke vp a stoole, and beat out his brains: whereat the prince was wroth for that he stroke a dead man, and one that was killed before.

But the rumour of this accident, as it was strange, so it went soone thorowout all the Court, and from thence among the common people, for which they were very heauy, and greatly discouraged. To him came also the Captaine of the Temple, and brought him a costly and precious drinke against poison, least the venime of the knife should penetrate the liuely blood, and in blaming wise sayd vnto him: did I not tell your Grace before of the deceit and subtilty of this people? Notwithstanding, said he, let your Grace take a good heart, you shall not die of this wound, my life for yours. But straight way the Surgions and Physicians were sent for, and the prince was dressed, and within few dayes after, the wound began to putrifie, and the flesh to looke dead and blacke: wherupon they that were about the prince began to mutter among themselues, and were very sad and heauy.

Which thing, he himself perceiuing, said vnto them: why mutter you thus among your selues? what see you in me, can I not be healed? tell me the trueth, be ye not afrayd. Whereupon one sayd vnto him, and it like your Grace you may be healed, we mistrust not, but yet it will be very painfull for you to suffer. May suffering (sayd he againe) restore health? yea sayth the other, on paine of losing my head. Then sayd the prince, I commit my selfe vnto you, doe with me what you thinke good.

Then sayd one of the Physicians, is there any of your Nobles in whom your Grace reposeth special trust? to whom the prince answered Yea, naming certeine of the Noble men that stood about him. Then sayd the Physician to the two, whom the prince first named, the Lord Edmund, [Marginal note: The lord Edmond was the prince his brother.] and the lord Iohn Voisie, And doe you also faithfully loue your Lord and prince? Who answered both, Yea vndoubtedly. Then sayth he, take you away this gentlewoman and lady (meaning his wife) and let her not see her lord and husband, till such time as I will you thereunto. Whereupon they tooke her from the princes presence, crying out, and wringing her hands. Then sayd they vnto her, Be you contented good Lady and Madame, it is better that one woman should weepe a little while, then that all the realme of England should weepe a great season.

Then on the morrow they cut out all the dead and inuenimed flesh out of the princes arme, and threw it from them, and sayd vnto him: how cheereth your Grace, we promise you within these fifteene dayes you shall shew your selfe abroad (if God permit) vpon your horsebacke, whole and well as euer you were. And according to the promise he made the prince, it came to passe, to the no little comfort and admiration of all his subiects.

When the great Souldan heard hereof, and that the prince was yet aliue, he could scarsely beleeue the same, and sending vnto him three of his Nobles and Princes, excused himselfe by them, calling his God to witnesse that the same was done neither by him nor his consent. Which princes and messengers standing aloofe off from the kings sonne, worshipping him, fell flat vpon the ground: you (sayd the prince) do reuerence me, but yet you loue me not. But they vnderstood him not, because he spake in English vnto them, speaking by an Interpreter: neuerthelesse he honourably entertained them, and sent them away in peace.

Thus when prince Edward had beene eighteene moneths in Acra, he tooke shipping about the Assumption of our Lady, as we call it, returning homeward, and after seuen weekes he arriued in Sicilia at Trapes, and from thence trauailed thorow the middes of Apulia, till he came to Rome, where he was of the Pope honorably entertained.

From thence he came into France, whose fame and noble prowesse was there much bruted among the common people, and enuied of the Nobility, especially of the Earle of Chalons, who thought to haue intrapped him and his company, as may appeare in the story: but Prince Edward continued foorth his iourney to Paris, and was there of the French king honourably entertained: and after certaine dayes he went thence into Gascoine, where he taried till that he heard of the death of the king his father, at which time he came home, and was crowned king of England, in the yere of our Lord 1274.

* * * * *

The trauaile of Robert Turneham.

Robertus Turneham Franciscanus, Theologiæ professor insignis, Lynnæ celebri Irenorum ad ripas Isidis emporio, collegio suorum fratrum magnificè præfuit. Edwardus Princeps, cognomento Longus, Henrici tertij filius, bellicam expeditionem contra Saracenos Assyriam incolentes, anno Dom. 1268. parabat. Ad quam profectionem quæsitus quoque Orator vehemens, qui plebis in causa religionis animos excitaret, Turnehamus principi visus vel dignissimus est, qui munus hoc obiret. Sic tanquam signifer constitutus Assyrios vna cum Anglico exercitu petijt, ac suum non sine laude præstitit officiuin. Claruit anno salutiferi partus, 1280. varia componens, sub eodem Edwardo eius nominis primo post Conquestum.

The same in English.

Robert Turneham Franciscan, a notable professor of Diuinitie, was with great dignitie Prior of the Colledge of his Order in the famous Mart Towne of Lynne, situate vpon the riuer of Isis in Norfolke. Prince Edward surnamed the Long, the sonne of Henrie the third, prepared his warlike voyage against the Saracens dwelling in Syria, in the yeere of our Lord, 1268. For the which expedition some earnest preacher was sought to stirre vp the peoples minds in the cause of religion. And this Turneham seemed to the Prince most worthy to performe that office: so that he being appointed as it were a standard bearer, went into Syria with the English army, and performed his duety with good commendation. He flourished in the yeere of Christ 1280, setting forth diuers workes vnder the same King Edward the first of that name after the Conquest.

* * * * *

The life of Syr Iohn Mandeuill Knight, written by Master Bale.

Ioannes Mandeuil, vir equestris ordinis, ex fano Albini oriundus, ita à teneris vt aiunt, vnguiculis literarum studijs assueuerat, vt in illis bonam foelicitatis suæ partem poneret. Nam generis sui stemmata illustra, nulli vsui futura ducebat, nisi illa clariora doctis artibus redderet. Quare cum animum Euangelica lectione ritè instituisset, transtulit sua studia ad rem Medicam, artem imprimis liberali ingenio dignam. Sed inter alia, ingens quædam cupido videndi Africam, et Asiam, vastioris orbis partes, eius animum inuaserat. Comparato igitur amplo viatico, peregrè profectus est, anno à Christo nato, 1332. et domum tanquam alter Vlysses, post 34. annos rediens, à paucissimis quidem cognitus fuit. Interim Scythiam, Armeniam, Maiorem et Minorem, Aegyptum, vtramque Lybiam, Arabiam, Syriam, Mediam, Mesopotamiam, Persiam, Chaldæam, Græciam, Illyrium, Tartariam, et alia spaciosi orbis regna, laborioso itinere visitauit. Denique linguarum cognitione præditus, ne tot ac tantarum rerum varietates, et miracula quæ oculatus testis viderat, memoriæque mandauerat, obliuione premerentur, in tribus linguis, Anglica, Gallica, et Latina, graphicè scripsit Itinerarium 33. annorum. Reuersus in Angliam, ac visis sui seculi malis, vir pius dicebat, nostris temporibus iam verius quàm olim dici potest, virtus cessat, Ecclesia calcatur, Clerus errat, dæmon regnat, simonia dominatur, etc. Leodij tandem obijt, anno Domini 1372. die 17. Nouembris, apud Guilielmitas sepultus.

The same in English.

Iohn Mandeuil Knight, borne in the towne of S. Albons, was so well giuen to the studie of learning from his childhood, that he seemed to plant a good part of his felicitie in the same: for he supposed that the honour of his birth would nothing auaile him, except he could render the same more honourable by his knowledge in good letters. Hauing therefore well grounded himselfe in religion by reading the Scriptures, he applied his studies to the arte of Physicke, a profession worthy a noble wit: but amongst other things, he was rauished with a mightie desire to see the greater partes of the world, as Asia, and Africa. Hauing therefore prouided all things necessarie for his iourney he departed from his countrey in the yeere of Christ, 1332, and as another Vlysses returned home, after the space of 34. yeeres, and was then knowen to a very fewe. In the time of his trauaile he was in Scythia, the greater and lesse Armenia, Egypt, both Lybias, Arabia, Syria, Media, Mesopotamia, Persia, Chaldæa, Greece, Illyrium, Tartarie, and diuers other kingdomes of the world: and hauing gotten by this meanes the knowledge of the languages, least so many and great varieties, and things miraculous, whereof himselfe had bene an eie witnes, should perish in obliuion, he committed his whole trauell of 33. yeeres to writing in three diuers tongues, English, French and Latine. Being arriued againe in England, and hauing seene the wickednes of that age, he gaue out this speach. In our time (sayd he) it may be spoken more truely then of olde, that vertue is gone, the Church is vnder foote, the Clergie is in errour, the deuill raigneth, and Simonie beareth the sway, &c.

He died at Leege, in the yeere 1311. the 17. day of Nouember, being there buried in the Abbie of the Order of the Guilielmites.

* * * * *

The Tombe and Epitaph of Sir Iohn Mandeuil, in the citie of Leege, spoken of by Ortelius, in his booke called Itinerarium Belgiæ, in this sort.

[Sidenote: Fol. 15, 16.] Magna et populosa Leodij suburbia, ad collium radices, in quorum iugis multa sunt, et pulcherrima monasteria, inter quæ magnificum illud, ac nobile D. Laurentio dicatum, ab Raginardo Episcopo. Est in hac quoque regione, vel suburbijs Leodij, Guilielmitarum Coenobium, in quo Epitaphium hoc Ioannis à Mandeuille, excepimus.

[Sidenote: Epitaphìum.] Hic iacet vir nobilis, D. Ioannes de Mandeuille, aliter dictus ad Barbam, Miles, Dominus de Campdi, natus de Anglia, Medicinæ professor, deuotissimus, orator, et bonorum largissimus pauperibus erogator, qui toto quasi orbe lustrato, Leodij diem vitæ suæ clausit extremum. Anno Dom. 1371. Mensis Nouembris, Die 17.

Hæc in lapide: in quo cælata viri armati imago, Leonem calcantis, barba bifurcata, ad caput manus benedicens, et vernacula hæc verba: Vos qui paseis sor mi, pour l'amour deix proïes por mi. Clipeus erat vacuus, in quo olim fuisse dicebant laminam æream, et eius in ea itidem cælata insignia, Leonem videlicet argenteum, cui ad pectus lunula rubea in campo cæruleo, quem Limbus ambiret denticulatus ex auro. Eius nobis ostendebant, et cultros, ephipiáque, et calcaria quibus vsum fuisse asserebant, in peragrando toto ferè terrarum orbe, vt clariùs testatur eius Itinerarium, quod typis etiam excusum passim habetur.

* * * * *

Tabvla Præsentis Libri Ioannes Mandevil, singvla per ordinem capitula, et in eorum quolibet quid agitur, notificat euidenter.

Capvt. 1 Commendatio breuis terræ Hierosolymltanæ.

2 Iter ab Anglia tam per terras quàm per aquas, vsque in Constantinopolim.

3 De vrbe Constantinopoli, et reliquijs ibidem contentis.

4 Via tam per terras quàm per aquas, à Constantinopoli vsque Acharon, vel Acon.

5 Via à Francia et Flandria, per solas terras vsque in Hierusalem.

6 Via de Cypro vel de Hierusalem, vsque in Babyloniam Egypti.

7 De Pallatio Soldani, et nominibus præteritorum Soldanorum.

8 De Campo Balsami in Egypto.

9 De Nilo fluuio, et Egypti territorio.

10 De conductu Soldani.

11 De Monasterio Sinay.

12 Iter per desertum Sinay, vsque in Iudeam.

13 De ciuitate Bethleem, et semita, vsque in Ierusalem.

14 De Ecclesia gloriosi sepulchri Domini in vrbe Ierusalem.

15 De tribus alijs Ecclesiis, et specialiter de Templo Domini.

16 De pluribus locis sacris extra vrbem.

17 De sacris locis extra muros ciuitatis.

18 De alijs locis notabilibus.

19 De Nazareth et Samaria.

20 De Territorio Galileæ et Samariæ.

21 De secta detestabili Sarracenorum.

22 De vita Mahometi.

23 De colloquio Authoris cum Soldano.

24 Persuasio ad non credentes terrarum diuersitates per orbem terræ.

25 De Armenia, et Persia.

26 De Ethiopia et diamantibus, ac de infima et media India.

27 De foresto piperis.

28 De Ecclesia beati Thomæ Apostoli.

29 De quibusdam meridionalibus insulis, et farina et melle.

30 De Regno Cynocephalorum, et alijs Insulis.

31 De multis alijs insulis Meridionalibus.

32 De bona regione Mangi.

33 De Pygmeis, et itinere vsque prouinciam Cathay.

34 De pallacio Imperatoris magni Chan.

35 De quatuor solemnitatibus, quas magnus Chan celebrat in Anno.

36 De præstigijs in festo, et de comitatu Imperatoris.

37 Qua de causa dicitur magnus Chan.

38 De territorio Cathay, et moribus Tartarorum.

39 De sepultura Imperatoris magni Chan, et de creatione successoris.

40 De multis regionibus Imperio Tartariæ subiectis.

41 De magnificentia Imperatoris Indiæ.

42 De frequentia Palatij, et comitatu Imperatoris præsbiteri Ioannis.

43 De quisbusdam miris per Regiones Imperij Indiæ.

44 De loco et dispositione Vallis infaustæ.

45 De quibusdam alijs admirandis, per Indorum insulas.

46 De periculis et tormentis in valle infausta.

47 De Bragmannorum insulis, et aliorum.

48 Aliquíd de loco Paradisi terrestris per auditum.

49 In reuertendo de Regnis Cassam, et Riboth, de Diuite Epulone, vel consimili.

50 De compositione huius tractatus in Ciuitate Leodiensi.

Liber Præsens, Cvivs Avthor est Ioannes Mandevil militaris ordinis, agit de diuersis patrijs, Regionibus, Prouincijs, et insulis, Turcia, Armenia maiore et minore, Ægypto, Lybia bassa et alta, Syria, Arabia, Persia, Chaldæa, Tartaria, India, et de infinitis insulis, Ciuitatibus, villis, castris, et locis, quæ gentes, legum, morum, ac rituum inhabitant diuersorum.

DEDICATIO LIBRI.

Principi excellentissimo, præ cunctis mortalibus præcipuè venerando, Domino Edwardo eius nominis tertio, diuina prouidentia Francorum et Anglorum Regi Serenissimo, Hiberniæ Domino, Aquitainiæ Duci, mari ac eius insulis occidentalibus dominanti, Christianorum encomio et ornatui, vniuersorumque arma gerentium Tutori, ac Probitatis et strenuitatis exemplo, principi quoque inuicto, mirabilis Alexandri Sequaci, ac vniuerso orbi tremendo, cum reuerentia non qua decet, cum ad talem, et tantam reuerentiam minùs sufficientes extiterint, sed qua paruitas, et possibilitas mittentis ac offerentis se extendunt, contenta tradantur.

Pars prima, continens Capita 23.

CAPVT. 1.

Commendatio breuis terræ Hierosolimitanæ.

Cum terra Hierosolimitana, terra promissionis filiorum Dei, dignior cunctis mundi terris sit habenda multis ex causis, et præcipuè illâ, quod Deus conditor coeli et mundi, ipsam tanti dignatus fuit æstimare, vt in eo proprinm filium saluatorem mundi, Christum exhibuerit generi humano per incarnationem ex intemerata Virgine, et per eius conuersationem humillimam in eadem, ac per dolorosam mortis suæ consummationem ibidem, átque indè per eius admirandam resurrectionem, ac ascensionem in coelum, et postremò quia creditur illic in fine seculi reuersurus, et omnia iudicaturus: certum est, quòd ab omnibus qui Christiano nomine à Christo dicuntur, sit tanquam à suis proprijs hæredibus diligenda, et pro cuiúsque potestate ac modulo honoranda. [Sidenote: Loquitur secundum tempora in quibus vixit.] A principibus quidem, et potentibus vt ipsam conentur de infidelium manibus recuperare, qui eam iam pridem à nobis, nostris exigentibus meritis, abstulerunt, et per annos heu plurimos possederunt: a mediocribus antem et valentibus, vt per peregrinationem deuotam loca tam pia, et vestigia Christi ac discipolorum tam Sancta, principaliter in remissionem visitent delictorum. Ab impotentibus verò, et impeditis, quatenus supradictos vel hortentur, vel in aliquo modo iuuent, seu certè fideles fondant orationes. Verum quia iam nostris temporibus verius quàm olim dici potest,

> Virtus, Ecclesia, Clerus, dæmon, symonia,
> Cessat, calcatur, errat, regnat, dominatur,

ecce iusto Dei iudicio, credita est terra tam inclyta, et sacrosancta impiorum manibus Saracenorum, quod non est absque dolore pijs mentibus audiendum, et recolendum. EGO Ioannes Mandeuill militaris ordinis saltem gerens nomen, natus et educatus in terra Angliæ, in villa sancti Albani, ducebar in Adolescentia mea tali inspiratione, vt quamuis non per potentiam, nec per vires proprias possem præfatam terram suis hæredibus recuperare, irem tamen per aliquod temporis spacium peregrinari ibidem, et salutarem aliquantulum de propinquo. [Sidenote: Ioannis Mandiuilli peregrinatio, per tres et triginta annos continuata.] Vnde in anno ab Incarnatione Domini 1322. imposui me nauigationi Marsiliensis maris et vsque in hoc temporis, Anni 1355. scilicet, per 33. annos in transmarinis partibus mansi, peregrinatus sum, ambulaui, et circuiui multas, ac diuersas patrias, regiones, prouincias, et insulas, Turciam, Armeniam maiorem, et minorem, Ægyptum, Lybiam bassam et altam, Syriam, Arabiam, Persiam,

Chaldeam, Æthiopiæ partem magnam, Tartariam, Amazoniam, Indiam minorem, et mediam, ac partem magnam de maiori, et in istis, et circum istas regiones, multas insulas, Ciuitates, vrbes, castra, villas, et loca, vbi habitant variæ gentes, aspectuum, morum, legum, ac rituum, diuersorum: Attamen quia summo desiderio in terra promissionis eram, ipsam diligentius per loca vestigiorum filij Dei perlustrare curaui, et diutius in illa steti. Quapropter et in hac prima parte huius operis iter tam peregrinandi, quam nauigandi, à partibus Angliæ ad ipsam describo, et loca notabiliter sancta, quæ intra eandem sunt breuiter commemoro et diligenter, quatenus peregrinis tam in itinere quam in prouentione valeat hæc descriptio in aliquo deseruire.

The English Version. [Footnote: This English version (for the variations from the Latin are so great that it cannot be called a *translation*) was published in 1725 from a MS. of the end of the 14th or beginning of the 15th century, in the Cottonian Library, marked Titus. C. xvi.

Instead of being divided into 50 chapters like the Latin, it contains only 33, but I have thought it best to make it correspond as nearly with the Latin as possible, merely indicating where the various chapters begin in the English version. From the last paragraph of the introductory chapter, it would seem that the English version was written by Mandeville himself.—E. G.]

[Sidenote: The Prologue] For als moche as the Lond bezonde the See, that is to seye, the Holy Lond, that men callen the Lond of Promyssioun, or of Beheste, passynge alle othere Londes, is the most worthi Lond, most excellent, and Lady and Sovereyn of alle othere Londes, and is blessed and halewed of the precyous Body and Blood of oure Lord Jesu Crist; in the whiche Lond it lykede him to take Flesche and Blood of the Virgyne Marie, to envyrone that holy Lond with his blessede Feet; and there he wolde of his blessednesse enoumbre him in the seyd blessed and gloriouse Virgine Marie, and become Man, and worche many Myracles, and preche and teche the Feythe and the Lawe of Cristene Men unto his Children; and there it lykede him to suffre many Reprevinges and Scornes for us; and he that was Kyng of Hevene, of Eyr, of Erthe, of See and of alle thinges that ben conteyned in hem, wolde alle only ben cleped Kyng of that Lond, whan he seyde, "*Rex sum Judeorum,*" that is to seyne, "I am Kyng of Jewes;" and that Lond he chees before alle other. Londes, as the beste and most worthi Lond, and the most vertouse lond of alle the world: For it is the herte and the myddes of all the world; wytnessynge the philosophere, that seythe thus; "*Vertus rerum in medio consistit:*" That is to seye, "The vertue of thinges is in the myddes;" and in that Lond he wolde lede his lyf, and suffre passioun and dethe of Jewes, for us; for to bye and to delyvere us from peynes of helle, and from dethe withouten ende; the whiche was ordeyned for us, for the synne of oure formere fader Adam, and for oure owne synnes also: for as for himself, he hadde non evylle deserved: For he thoughte nevere evylle ne dyd evylle: And he that was kyng of glorie and of joye myghten best in that place suffre dethe; because he ches in that lond, rathere than in ony othere, there to suffre his passioun and his dethe: For he that wil pupplische ony thing to make it openly knowen, he wil make it to ben cryed and pronounced, in the myddel place of a town; so that the thing that is proclamed and pronounced, may evenly strecche to alle parties: Righte so, he that was formyour of alle the world, wolde suffre for us at Jerusalem; that is the myddes of the world; to that ende and entent, that his passioun and his dethe, that was pupplischt there, myghte ben knowen evenly to alle the parties of the world. See now how dere he boughte man, that he made after his owne ymage, and how dere he azen boghte us, for the grete love that he hadde to us; and we nevere deserved it to him. For more precyous catelle ne gretter ransoum, ne myghte he put for us, than his blessede body, his precyous blood, and his holy lyf, that he thralled for us; and alle he offred for us, that nevere did synne. A dere God, what love hadde he to his subjettes, whan he that nevere trespaced, wolde for trespassours suffre dethe! Righte wel oughte us for to love and worschipe, to drede and serven suche a Lord; and to worschipe and preyse suche an holy lond, that broughte forthe suche fruyt, thorghe the whiche every man is saved, but it be his owne defaute. Wel may that lond be called delytable and a fructuous lond, that was bebledd [Footnote: Coloured with blood] and moysted with the precyouse blode of oure Lord Jesu Crist; the whiche is the same lond, that oure lord behighten us in heritage. And in that lond he wolde dye, as seised, for to leve it to us his children. Wherfore every gode Cristene man, that is of powere, and hathe whereof, scholde peynen him with all his strengthe for to conquere oure righte heritage, and chacen out alle the mysbeleevynge men. For wee ben clept cristene men, aftre Crist our Fadre. And zif wee ben righte children of Crist, we oughte for to chalenge the heritage, that oure Fadre lafte us, and do it out of hethene mennes hondes. But nowe pryde, covetyse and envye han so enflawmed the hertes of lordes of the world, that thei are more besy for to disherite here neyghbores, more than for to chalenge or to conquere here righte heritage before seyd. And the comoun peple, that wolde putte here bodyes and here catelle, for to conquere oure heritage, thei may not don it withouten the lordes. For a semblee of peple withouten a cheventeyn, [Footnote: Chieftain.] or a chief lord, is as a flock of scheep withouten a schepperde; the whiche departeth and desparpleth, [Footnote: Disperseth.] and wyten never whidre to go. But wolde God, that the temporel lordes and all worldly lordes weren at gode accord, and with the comen peple woulden taken this holy viage over the see. Thanne I trowe wel, that within a lytyl tyme, our righte heritage before seyd scholde be reconsyled and put in the hondes of the right heires of Jesu Crist.

And for als moche as it is longe tyme passed, that there was no generalle passage ne vyage over the see; and many men desiren for to here speke of the holy lond, and han thereof great solace and comfort; I John Maundevylle, Knyght, alle be it I be not worthi, that was born in Englond, in the town of Scynt Albones, passed the see in the zeer of our Lord Jesu Crist MCCCXXII, in the day of Seynt Michelle; and hidre [Footnote: There.] to have ben longe tyme over the see, and have seyn and gon thorghe manye dyverse londes, and many provynces and Kingdomes and iles, and have passed thorghe Tartarye, Percye, Ermonye [Footnote: Armenia.] the litylle and the grete; thorghe Lybye, Caldee, and a gret partie of Ethiope; thorghe Amazoyne, Inde the lasse and the more, a gret partie; and thorghe out many othere iles, that ben abouten Inde; where dwellen many dyverse folkes, and of dyverse manneres and lawes, and of dyverse schappes of men. Of which londes and iles, I schall speake more pleynly hereaftre. And I schall devise zou sum partie of thinges that there ben, whan time schalle ben, aftre it may best come to my mynde; and specially for hem, that wylle and are in purpos for to visite the holy citee of Jerusalem, and the holy places that are thereaboute. And I schalle telle the weye, that thei schulle holden thidre. For I have often tymes passed and ryden the way, with gode companye of many lordes: God be thonked.

And zee schulle undirstonde, that I have put this boke out of Latyn into Frensche, and translated it azen out of Frensche into Englyssche, that every man of my nacioun may undirstonde it. But lordes and knyghtes and othere noble and worthi men, that conne Latyn but litylle, and han ben bezonde the see, knowen and undirstonden, zif I erre in devisynge, for forzetynge, [Footnote: Forgetting.] or elles; that thei mowe redresse it and amende it. For thinges passed out of longe tyme from a mannes mynde or from his syght, turnen sone into forzetynge: Because that mynde of man ne may not ben comprehended ne witheholden, for the freeltee of mankynde.

To teche zou the Weye out of Englond to Constantinoble.

[Sidenote: Cap I.] In the name of God Glorious and Allemyghty. He that wil passe over the see, to go to the city of Jerusalem, he may go by many wayes, bothe on see and londe, aftre the contree that hee cometh fro; manye of hem comen to on ende. But troweth not that I wil telle zou alle the townes and cytees and castelles, that men schulle go by; for than scholde I make to longe a tale; but alle only summe contrees and most princypalle stedes, that men schulle gone thorgh, to gon the righte way.

CAPVT. 2.

Iter ab Anglia tam per terras quam per aquas vsque in Constantinopolim.

Qui de Hybernia, Anglia, Scotia, Noruegia, aut Gallia, iter arripit ad partes Hierosolymitanas potest saltem vsque ad Imperialem Greciæ Ciuitatem Constantinopolim eligere sibi modum proficiscendi, siue per terras, siue per aquas. Et si peregrinando eligit transigere viam, tendat per Coloniam Agrippinam, et sic per Almaniam in Hungariam ad Montlusant Ciuitatem, sedem Regni Hungariæ. [Sidenote: Regis Hungariæ olim potentia.] Et est Rex Hungariæ multum potens istis temporibus. Nam tenet et Sclauoniam, et magnam partem Regni Comannorum, et Hungariam, et partem Regni Russiæ. Oportet vt peregrinus in finibus Hungariæ transeat magnum Danubij flumen, et vadat in Belgradum; Hoc flumen oritur inter Montana Almaniæ, et currens versus Orientem, recipit in se 40. flumina antequam finiatur in mare. De Belgrade intratur terra Bulgariæ, et transitur per Pontem petrinum fluuij Marroy, et per terram Pyncenars, et tunc intratur Græcia, in Ciuitates, Sternes, Asmopape, et Andrinopolis, et sic in Constantinopolim, vbi communiter est sedes Imperatoris Greciæ. Qui autem viam eligit per aquas versus Constantinopolim nauigare, accipiat sibi portum, prout voluerit, propinquum siue remotum, Marsiliæ, Pisi, Ianuæ, Venetijs, Romæ, Neapoli, vel alibi: sicque transeat Tusciam, Campaniam, Italiam, Corsicam, Sardiniam, vsque in Siciliam, quæ diuiditur ab Italia per brachiam maris non magnum. [Sidenote: Mons ætna.] In Sicilia est mons Ætna iugiter ardens, qui ibidem apellatur Mons Gibelle, et præter illum habentur ibi loca Golthan vbi sunt septem leucæ quasi semper ignem spirantes: secundum diuersitatem colorum harum flammarum estimant. [Sidenote: Aeolides insulæ.] Incolæ annum fertilem fore, vel sterilem, siccum vel humidum, calidum, vel frigidum: hæc loca vocant caminos Infernales, et à finibus Italiæ vsque ad ista loca sunt 25. miliaria. [Sidenote: Temperes Siciliæ Insulæ.] Sunt autem in Sicilia aliqua Pomeria in quibus inueniuntur frondes, flores, et fructus per totum annum, etiam, in profunda hyeme. Regnum Siciliæ est bona, et grandis insula habens in circuitu ferè leucas 300. [Sidenote: Leuca Lombardica. Quid sit dieta.] Et ne quis eret, vel de facili reprehendat quoties scribo leucam, intelligendum est de leuca Lombardica, quæ aliquantò maior est Geometrica; et quoties pono numerum, sub intelligatur fere, vel circiter, siue citra, et dietam intendo ponere, de 10. Lombardicis leucis: Geometrica autem leuca describitur, vt notum est, per hos versus.

>Quinque pedes passum faciunt, passus quoque centum
>Viginti quínque stadium, si millia des que
Octo facis stadia, duplicatum dat tibi leuca.

[Sidenote: Portus Greciæ.] Postquam itáque peregrinus se credidit Deo et mari, si prospera sibi fuerit nauigatio, non ascendet in terram, donec intret aliquem portum Greciæ, scilicet, Myrroyt, Valonæ, Durase, siue alium prout Diuinæ placuerit uoluntati, et exhinc ibit Constantinopolim prædictam, quaæ olim Bysantium, vel Vesaton dicebatur. Hic autem notandum est, quòd a portu Venetie, vsque ad Constantinopolim directè per mare octingentæ leucæ et 80. communiter computantur ibi contentæ.

The English Version.

First, zif a man come from the west syde of the world, as Engelond, Irelond, Wales, Skotlond or Norwaye; he may, zif that he wole, go thorge Almayne, and thorge the kyngdom of Hungarye, that marchethe to the lond of Polayne, and to the lond of Pannonye, and so to Slesie. And the Kyng of Hungarye is a gret lord and a myghty, and holdeth grete lordschippes and meche lond in his hond. For he holdeth the kyngdom of Hungarie, Solavonye and of Comanye a gret part, and of Bulgarie, that men clepen the lond of Bougiers, and of the Reme of Roussye a gret partie, whereof he hathe made a Duchee, that lasteth unto the lond of Nyflan, and marchethe to Pruysse. And men gon thorghe the lond of this lord, thorghe a cytee that is clept Cypron, and by the castelle of Neaseburghe, and be the evylle town, that sytt toward the ende of Hungarye. And there passe men the ryvere of Danubee. This ryvere of Danubee is a fulle gret ryvere; and it gothe into Almayne, undre the hilles of Lombardye: and it receiveth into him 40 othere ryveres; and it rennethe thorghe Hungarie and thorghe Greece and thorghe Traachie, and it entreth into the see, toward the est, so rudely and so scharply, that the watre of the see is fressche and holdethe his swetnesse 20 myle within the see.

And aftre gon men to Belgrave, and entren into the lond of Bourgres; [Footnote: Bulgaria.] and there passe men a brigge of ston, that is upon the ryver of Marrok. [Footnote: The river Maros.] And men passen thorghe the lond of Pyncemartz, and comen to Greece to the cytee of Nye, and to the cytee of Fynepape, and aftre to the cytee of Dandrenoble, [Footnote: Adrianople.] and aftre to Constantynoble, that was wont to be clept Bezanzon.

CAPVT. 3.

De vrbe Constantinopoli, et reltquijs ibidem contentis.

Constantinopolis pulchra est Ciuitas, et nobilis, triangularis in forma, firmitérque murata, cuius duæ partes includuntur mari Hellesponto, quòd plurimi modò appellant brachium sancti Georgij, et aliqui Buke, Troia vetus. Versus locum vbi hoc brachium exit de mari est late terræ planities, in quâ antiquitus stetit Troia Ciuitas de qua apud Poetas mira leguntur sed nunc valdè modica apparent vestigia Ciuitatis. In Constantinopoli habentur multa mirabilia, ac insuper multæ sanctorum venerandæ relliquæi, ac super omnia, preciosissimi Crux Christi, seu maior pars illius, et tunica inconsutilis, cum spongia et arandine, et vno clauorum, et dimidia parte coronæ spineæ, cuius altera medietas seruatur in Capetla Regis Franciæ, Parisijs. Nam et ego indignus ditigenter pluribus vicibus respexi partem vtrámque: dabatur quóque mihi de illa Parisijs vnica spina, quam vsque nunc preciose conseruo, et est ipsa spina non lignea sed uelut de iuncis marinis rigîda, et pungitiua. [Sidenote: Eclesia sanctæ Sophiæ] Ecclesia Constantinopolitana in honorem sanctæ Sophiæ, id est, ineffabilis Dei sapientiæ dedicato dicitur, et nobilissima vniuersarum mundi Ecclesiarum, tam in schemate artificiosi operis, quàm in seruatis ibi sacrosanctis Relliquijs: [Sidenote: Regina Helena Britanna] nam et continet corpus sancte Annæ matris nostræ Dominæ translatum illuc per Reginam Helenam ab Hierosolymis: et corpus S. Lucæ Euangelistæ translatum de Bethania Iudeæ; Et Corpus beati Ioannis Chrysostomi ipsius Ciuitatis Episcopi, cum multis atlijs reliquijs preciosis; quoniam est ibi vas grande cum huiusmodi reliquijs velut marmoreum de Petra Enhydros; quod iugiter de seipso desudans aquam semel, in anno inuenitur suo sudore repletum. [Sidenote: Imago Iustiniani.] Ante hanc Ecclesiam, super columnam marmoream habetur de ære aurato opere fuscrio, magna imago Iustiniani quondam Imperatoris super equum sedentis, fuit autem primitus in manu imaginis fabricata sphæra rotunda, quæ iam diu è manu sua sibi cecidit, in signum quòd Imperator muliarum terraram dominium perdidit. Námque solebat esse Dominus, Romanorum Græcorum, Asiæ, Syriæ, Iudeæ, Ægypti, Arabiæ, et Persiæ, at nunc solum retinet Greciam, cum aliquibus terris Greciæ adiacentibus, sicut Calistrum, Cholchos, Ortigo, Tylbriam, Minos, Flexon, Melos, Carpates, Lemnon, Thraciam, et Macedoniam totam: Súntque sub eo Caypoplij, et alti Pyntenardi, ac maxima pars Commannorum. Porrò imago tenet manum eleuatam et extentam in orientem, velut in signum cominationis ad Orientales infideles. De prædicta terra Thraciæ fuit Philosophus Aristoteles oriundus in Ciuitate Stageres, et est ibi in loco tumba eius velut altare, vbi et singulis annis certo die celebratur à populo festum illius, ac si fuisset sanctus. Temporibus ergò magnorum consiliorum conueniunt illuc sapientes terræ, reputantes sibi per inspirationem immitti consilium optimum de agendis. Item ad diuisionem Thraciæ et Macedoniæ sunt duo mirabiliter alti montes, vnus Olympus, alter Athos, cuius vltimi vmbra oríente sole apparet ad 76. miliaria, vsque in insulam Lemnon. In horum cacumine montium ventus non currit, nec aer mouetur, quod frequentèr probatum est per ingenium Astronomorum, qui quandóque ascendentes scripserunt, literas in puluere, quas sequenti anno inuenerunt quasi recentèr scriptas, et quia est ibi purus aer sine mixtione elementi aquæ necesse est vt ascendentes habeant secum spongias aquæ plenas pro adhelitus respiratione: In prædicta autem sanctæ sophiæ Ecclesia, (sicut ibidem dicitur,) voluit olim quidam Imperator corpus cuiusdam sui defuncti sepelire cognati: cuius cum foderetur sepulchrum, ventum est ad mausoleum antiquum in quo super incineratum corpus iacebat discus auri puri, et erat sculptum in eo literis Græcis, Hebraicis, et Latinis sic. Iesus Christus nascetur de Virgine, et ego credo in eum. Et erat simul inscripta data defuncti secundum modum illius temporis quæ continebat duo millia annorum ante incarnationem ipsius Christi de Maria Virgine. Seruatur quóque hodierno tempore eadem patina in Thesaurario eiusdem Ecclesiæ, et dicitur illud corpus fuisse Hermetis sapientis. Omnes quidem, terrarum, regionum et insularum homines, qui isti Greco obediunt Imperatori sunt Christiani, et baptizati, tamen variant singuli in aliquo articulo fidem suam a nostra vera fide Catholica, et diuersificant in multis suos ritus à ritibus Romanæ Ecclesiæ, quia iamdiu omiserunt obedire Pontifici Romano, dicentes, quoniam beatus Petrus Apostolus habuit sedem in Antiochia, quamuis passus fuit in Roma: [Sidenote: Patriarchæ Antiocheni authoritas.] Idcirco patriarcha Antiochenus habet in illis Orientalibus partibus similem potestatem, quàm Pontifex Romanus in istis Occidentalibus. Imperator etiam Constantinopolitanus creat eorum patriarcham, et instituit pro sua voluntate Archiepiscopos, et Episcopos, et confert dignitates, et beneficia, similiter inuenta occasione destituit, deponit, et priuat.

The English Version.

And there dwellethe comounly the Emperour of Greece. And there is the most fayr chirche and the most noble of alle the world: and it is of Seynt Sophie. And before that chirche is the ymage of Justynyan the Emperour, covered with gold, and he sytt upon an hors y crowned. And he was wont to holden a round appelle of gold in his hond: but it is fallen out thereof. And men seyn there, that it is a tokene, that the Emperour hathe y lost a gret partie of his londes, and of his lordschipes: for he was wont to be Emperour of Romayne and of Grece, of alle Asye the lesse, and of the lond of Surrye, of the lond of Judee, in the whiche is Jerusalem, and of the lond of Egypt, of Percye, of Arabye. But he hathe lost alle, but Grece; and that lond he holt alle only. And men wolden many tymes put the appulle into the ymages hond azen, but it wil not holde it. This appulle betokenethe the lordschipe, that he hadde over alle the worlde, that is round. And the tother hond he lifteth up azenst the est, in tokene to manace the mysdoeres. This ymage stont upon a pylere of marble at Constantynoble.

Of the Crosse and the Croune of oure Lord Jesu Crist.

[Sidenote: Cap. II.] At Costantynoble is the cros of our Lord Jesu Crist, and his cote withouten semes, that is clept *tunica inconsutilis*, and the spounge, and the reed, of the whiche the Jewes zaven oure Lord eyselle [Footnote: Vinegar] and galle, in the cros. And there is on of the nayles, that Crist was naylled with on the cros. And some men trowen, that half the cros, that Crist was don on, be in Cipres, in an abbey of monkes, that men callen the Hille of the Holy Cros; but it is not so: for that cros, that is in Cypre, is the cros, in the whiche Dysmas the gode theef was honged onne. But alle men knowen not that; and that is evylle y don. For profyte of the offrynge, thei seye, that it is the cros of oure Lord Jesu Crist. And zee schulle undrestonde, that the cros of oure Lord was made of 4 manere of trees, as it is conteyned in this vers,

In cruce fit palma, cedrus, cypressus, oliva.

For that pece, that went upright fro the erthe to the heved, [Footnote: Head.] was of cypresse; and the pece, that wente overthwart, to the whiche his honds wern nayled, was of palme; and the stock, that stode within the erthe, in the whiche was made the morteys, was of cedre; and the table aboven his heved, that was a fote and an half long, on the whiche the title was writen, in Ebreu, Grece and Latyn, that was of olyve. And the Jewes maden the cros of theise 4 manere of trees: for thei trowed that oure Lord Jesu Crist scholde han honged on the cros, als longe as the cros myghten laste. And therfore made thei the foot of the cros of cedre. For cedre may not, in erthe ne in watre, rote. And therfore thei wolde, that it scholde have lasted longe. For thei trowed, that the body of Crist scholde have stonken; therfore thei made that pece, that went from the erthe upward, of cypres: for it is welle smellynge; so that the smelle of his body scholde not greve men, that wenten forby. And the overhwart pece was of palme: for in the Olde Testament, it was ordyned, that whan on overcomen, he scholde be crowned with palme: and for thei trowed, that thei hadden the victorye of Crist Jesus, therfore made thei the overthwart pece of palme. [Footnote: The reference is to the Olympic Games.] And the table of the tytle, thei maden of olyve; for olyve betokenethe pes. And the storye of Noe wytnessethe, whan that the culver [Footnote: Dove. Anglo-Saxon, *Cuifra*.] broughte the braunche of olyve, that betokened pes made betwene God and man. And so trowed the Jewes for to have pes, when Crist was ded: for thei seyd, that he made discord and strif amonges hem. And zee schulle undirstonde, that oure Lord was y naylled on the cros lyggynge; and therfore he suffred the more peyne. And the Cristene men, that dwellen bezond the see, in Grece, seyn that the tree of the cros, that we callen cypresse, was of that tree, that Adam ete the appulle of: and that fynde thei writen. And thei seyn also, that here Scripture seythe, that Adam was seek, [Footnote: Sick] and seyed to his sone Sethe, that he scholde go to the Aungelle, that kepte paradys, that he wolde senden hym oyle of mercy, for to anoynte with his membres, that be myghte have hele. And Sethe wente. But the aungelle wolde not late him come in; but seyd to him, that he myghte not have of the oyle of mercy. But he toke him three greynes of the same tree, that his fadre eet the appelle offe; and bad him, als sone as his fadre was ded, that he scholde putte theise three greynes undre his tonge, and grave him so: and he dide. And of theise three greynes sprang a tree, as the aungelle seyde, that it scholde, and bere a fruyt, thorghe the whiche fruyt Adam scholde be saved. And whan Sethe cam azen, he fonde his fadre nere ded. And whan he was ded he did with the greynes, as the aungelle bad him; of the whiche sprongen three trees, of the whiche the cros was made, that bare gode froyt and blessed, oure Lord Jesu Crist; thorghe whom, Adam and alle that comen of him, scholde be saved and delyvered from drede of dethe withouten ende, but it be here own defaute. This holy cros had the Jewes hydde in the erthe, undre a roche of the Mownt of Calvarie; and it lay there 200 zeer and more, into the tyme that Seynt Elyne, that was modre to Constantyn the Emperour of Rome. And sche was doughtre of Kyng Cool born in Colchestre, that was Kyng of Engelond, that was clept thanne, Brytayne the more; the whiche the Emperour Constance wedded to his wyf, for here bewtee, and gat upon hire Constantyn, that was aftre Emperour of Rome.

And zee schulle undirstonde, that the cros of oure Lord was eyght cubytes long, and the overthwart piece was of lengthe thre cubytes and an half. And a partie of the crowne of oure Lord, wherwith he was crowned, and on of the nayles, and the spere heed, and many other relikes ben in France, in the kinges chapelle. And the crowne lythe in a vesselle of cristalle richely dyghte. For a kyng of Fraunce boughte theise relikes somtyme of the Jewes; to whom the Emperour had leyde hem to wedde, for a gret summe of sylvre. And zif alle it be so, that men seyn, that this croune is of thornes, zee schulle undirstonde, that it was of jonkes of the see, that is to sey, rushes of the see, that prykken als scharpely as thornes. For I have seen and beholden many tymes that of Parys and that of Costantynoble: for thei were bothe on, made of russches of the see. But men han departed hem in two parties: of the whiche, o part is at Parys, and the other part is at Costantynoble. And I have on of tho precyouse thornes, that semethe licke a white thorn; and that was zoven to me for gret specyaltee. For there are many of hem broken and fallen into the vesselle, that the croune lythe in: for thei breken for dryenesse, whan men meven hem, to schewen hem to grete lords, that comen thidre.

And zee schalle undirstonde, that oure Lord Jesu, in that nyghte that he was taken, he was y lad in to a gardyn; and there he was first examyned righte scharply; and there the Jewes scorned him, and maden him a crowne of the braunches of albespyne, that is white thorn, that grew in that same gardyn, and setten it on his heved, so faste and so sore, that the blood ran down be many places of his visage, and of his necke, and of his schuldres. And therfore hathe white thorn many vertues: for he that berethe a braunche on him thereoffe, no thondre ne no maner of tempest may dere him; ne in the hows, that it is inne, may non evylle gost entre ne come unto the place that it is inne. And in that same gardyn, Seynt Petre denyed our Lord thryes.

Aftreward was oure Lord lad forthe before the bisschoppes and the maystres of the lawe, in to another gardyn of Anne; and there also he was examyned, repreved, and scorned, and crouned eft with a whyte thorn, that men clepethe barbarynes, that grew in that gardyn, and that hathe also manye vertues. And aftreward he was lad in to a gardyn of Cayphas, and there he was crouned with eglentier. And aftre he was lad in to the chambre of Pylate, and there he was examynd and crouned. And the Jewes setten him in a chayere and cladde him in a mantelle; and there made thei the croune of jonkes of the see; and there thei kneled to him, and skornede him, seyenge, *Ave, Rex Judeorum*, that is to seye, *Heyl, Kyng of Jewes*. And of this croune, half is at Parys, and the other half at Costantynoble. And this croune had Crist on his heved, whan he was don upon the cros: and therfore oughte men to worschipe it and holde it more worthi than ony of the othere.

And the spere schaft hathe the Emperour of Almayne: but the heved is at Parys. And natheles the Emperour of Costantynoble seythe that he hathe the
spere heed: and I have often tyme seen it; but it is grettere than that at Parys.

Of the Cytee of Costantynoble, and of the Feithe of Grekis.

[Sidenote: Cap. III.] At Costantynoble lyethe Seynte Anne oure Ladyes modre, whom Seynte Elyne dede brynge fro Jerusalem. And there lyethe also the body of Iohn Crisostome, that was Erchebisschopp of Costantynoble. And there lythe also Seynt Luke the Evaungelist: for his bones werein broughte from Bethanye, where he was beryed. And many other relikes ben there. And there is the vesselle of ston, as it were of marbelle, that men clepen enydros, that evermore droppeth watre, and fillethe himself everiche zeer, til that it go over above, withouten that that men take fro withinne.

Costantynoble is a fulle fayr cytee, and a gode and a wel walled, and it is three cornered. And there is an arm of the see Hellespont: and sum men callen it the mouthe of Costantynoble; and sum men callen it the brace of Seynt George: and that arm closethe the two partes of the cytee. And upward to the see, upon the watre, was wont to be the grete cytee of Troye, in a fulle fayr playn: but that cytee was destroyed by hem of Grece, and lytylle apperethe there of, be cause it so longe sithe it was destroyed.

Abouten Grece there ben many iles, as Calistre,[Footnote: Calliste, one of the Cyclades.] Calcas, [Footnote: Colchos.] Critige, [Footnote: Cerigo.] Tesbria, [Footnote: Resorio.] Mynea, [Footnote: Mynia is a town in the Island of Amorgos.] Flaxon, [Footnote: Flexos.] Melo, [Footnote: Milo.] Carpate, [Footnote: Carpathos, probably.] and Lempne. [Footnote:

Lemnos.] And in this ile is the Mount Athos, [Footnote: Athos is on the main land, on a promontory S.E. of Solonica.] that passeth the cloudes. And there ben many dyvers langages and many contreys, that ben obedyent to the Emperour; that is to seyn Turcople, Pyneynard, Cornange, and manye othere, at Trachye, [Footnote: Thrace.] and Macedoigne, of the whiche Alisandre was kyng. In this contree was Aristotle born, in a cytee that men clepen Stragera, a lytil fro the cytee of Trachaye. And at Stragera lythe Aristotle; and there is an awtier upon his toumbe: and there maken men grete festes of hym every zeer, as thoughe he were a seynt. And at his awtier, thei holden here grete conseilles and here assembleez: and thei hopen, that thorghe inspiracioun of God and of him, thei schulle have the better conseille. In this contree ben righte hyghe hilles, toward the ende of Macedonye. And there is a gret hille, that men clepen Olympus, [Footnote: The altitude is 9753 feet.] that departeth Macedonye and Trachye: and it is so highe, that it passeth the cloudes. And there is another hille, that is clept Athos, [Footnote: It is only 6678 feet. This is the old Greek verse: [Greek: Athoos kaluptei pleura lemnias boos.]] that is so highe, that the schadewe of hym rechethe to Lempne, that is an ile; and it is 76 myle betwene. And aboven at the cop of the hille is the eir so cleer, that men may fynde no wynd there. And therefore may no best lyve there; and so is the eyr drye. And men seye in theise contrees, that philosophres som tyme wenten upon theise hilles, and helden to here nose a spounge moysted with watre, for to have eyr; for the eyr above was so drye. And aboven, in the dust and in the powder of the hilles, thei wroot lettres and figures with hire fingres: and at the zeres end thei comen azen, and founden the same lettres and figures, the whiche thei hadde writen the zeer before, withouten ony defaute. And therfore it semethe wel, that theise hilles passen the clowdes and joynen to the pure eyr.

At Constantynoble is the palays of the Emperour, righte fair and wel dyghte: and therein is a fair place for justynges, or for other pleyes and desportes. And it is made with stages and hath degrees aboute, that every man may wel se, and non greve other. And undre theise stages ben stables wel y vowted [Footnote: Vaulted.] for the Emperours hors; and alle the pileres ben of Marbelle. And with in the chirche of Seynt Sophie, an emperour somtyme wolde have biryed the body of his fadre, whan he was ded; and as thei maden the grave, thei founden a body in the erthe, and upon the body lay a fyn plate of gold; and there on was writen, in Ebreu, Grece and Latyn, lettres that seyden thus, *Jesu Cristus nascetur de Virgine Maria, et ego credo in eum*. That is to seyne, *Jesu Crist schalle be born of the Virgyne Marie, and I trowe in hym*. And the date whan it was leyd in the erthe, was 2000 zeer before oure Lord was born. And zet is the plate of gold in the thresorye of the chirche. And men seyn, that it was Hermogene the wise man.

And zif alle it so be, that men of Grece ben Cristene, zit they varien from our feithe. For thei seyn, that the Holy Gost may not come of the Sone; but alle only of the Fadir. And thei are not obedyent to the Chirche of Rome, ne to the Pope. And thei seyn, that here patriark hathe as meche power over the see as the Pope hathe on this syde the see. And therefore Pope Johne the 22'd sende letters to hem, how Christene feithe scholde ben alle on; and that thei scholde ben obedyent to the Pope, that is Goddis vacrie [Footnote: Vicar.] on erthe; to whom God zaf his pleyn power, for to bynde and to assoille: and therfore thei scholde ben obedyent to him. And thei senten azen dyverse answeres; and amonges other, thei seyden thus: *Potentiam tuam summam, circa tuos subjectos firmiter credimus. Superbiam tuam summam tolerare non possumus. Avaritiam tuam summam satiare non intendimus. Dominus tecum: quia Dominus nobiscum est.* That is to seye: *We trowe wel, that thi power is gret upon thi subgettes. We mai not suffre thi high pryde. We ben not in purpos to fulfille thi gret covetyse. Lord be with thi: for oure Lord is with us. Fare welle.* And other answere myghte he not have of hem. And also thei make here sacrement of the awteer of therf [Footnote: Unleavened. *Anglo-Saxon*, þeorf ('peorf' in source text—KTH)] bred: for oure Lord made it of suche bred, whan he made his mawndee. [Footnote: Last Supper.] And on the Scherethors [Footnote: Shrove Thursday.] day make thei here therf bred, in tokene of the mawndee, and dryen it at the sonne, and kepen it alle the zeer, and zeven it to seke men, in stede of Goddis body. And thei make but on unxioun, whan thei christene children. And thei annoynte not the seke men. And thei saye, that there nys no purgatorie, and the soules schulle not have nouther joye ne peyne, tille the day of doom. And thei seye, that fornicatioun is no synne dedly, but a thing that is kyndely: and the men and women scholde not wedde but ones; and whoso weddethe oftere than ones, here children ben bastardis and geten in synne. And here prestis also ben wedded. And thei saye also, that usure is no dedly synne. And they sellen benefices of Holy Chirche: and so don men in others places: God amende it, whan his wille is. And that is gret sclaundre. [Footnote: Scandal.] For now is symonye kyng crouned in Holy Chirche: God amende it for his mercy. And thei seyn, that in Lentone, men schulle nor faste, ne synge masse; but on the Satreday and on the Sonday. And thei faste not on the Satreday, no tyme of the zeer, but it be Cristemasse even on Estre even. And thei suffre not the Latines to syngen at here awteres: and zif thei done, be ony aventure, anon thei wasschen the awteer with holy watre. And thei seyn, that there scholde be but o masse seyd at on awtier, upon o day. And thei seye also, that oure Lord ne eet nevere mete: but he made tokene etyng. And also thei seye, that wee synne dedly, in schavynge oure berdes. For the berd is tokene of a man, and zifte of oure Lord. And thei seye, that wee synne dedly, in etynge of bestes, that weren forboden in the Old Testament, and of the olde lawe; as swyn, hares, and othere bestes, that chewen not here code. And thei seyn, that wee synnen, when wee eten flessche on the dayes before Assche Wednesday, and of that wee eten flessche the Wednesday, and egges and chese upon the Frydayes. And thei accursen alle tho, that absteynen hem to eten flessche the Satreday. Also the Emperour of Costantynoble makethe the patriarke, the erchebysschoppes and bisschoppes; and zevethe dygnytees and the benefices of chirches, and deprivethe hem that ben worthy, whan he fyndethe ony cause. And so is the lord bothe temperelle and spirituelle, in his contree, And zif zee wil wite [Footnote: Know.] of here A, B, C, what lettres thei ben, here zee may seen hem, with the names, that thei clepen hem there amonges them.

Alpha, Betha, Gamma, Deltha, Epsilon, Zeta, Eta, Theta, Iota, Kappa, Lambda, My,Ny, Xi, Omicron, Pi, Rho, Sigma, Tau, Upsilon, Phi, Chi, Psi, Omega. [Greek letters removed for pain-text edition—KTH]

And alle be it that theise thinges touchen not to o way, nevertheles thei touchen to that, that I have hight zou, to schewe zou a partie of custumes and maneres, and dyversitees of contrees. And for this is the first contree that is discordant in feythe and in beleeve, and variethe from our feythe, on this half the see, therefore I have sett it here, that zee may knowe the dyversitee that is betwene our feythe and theires. For many men han gret lykynge to here speke of straunge thinges of dyverse contreyes.

CAPVT. 4.

Via tam per terras quam per aquas à Constantinopoli vsque Acharon. [Marginal note: Vel Achon.]

A Constantinopoli qui voluerit ire pedes, transibit statim nauigio Brachium Sancti Georgij quod satis est strictum, ibíque ad Ruphinal quod est forte castrum, inde ad Puluereal, et hinc ad castrum Synopulum. Ex tunc intrat Cappadociam, terram latam sed plenam altis montibus, deinde Turciam ad portum Theueron, et ad Ciuitatem ita dictam, nunc munitam firmis turribus, ac muris, per quam transit fluuius Reglay. Postea transitur sub Alpibus Noyremont, et per valles de Mallenbrinis in districto Rupium, ac per villam Doronarum, et alias villas adiacentes fluuijs Reglay, et Granconiæ, sícque peruenitur ad Antiochiam minorem super Reglay, quæ vocatur nobilior Ciuitas Syriæ: Notandum autem quòd Regnum olim dictum Syria, modò communiter vocatur Suria. [Sidenote: Antiochia.] Ista verò Antiochia, est magna, pulchra, ac firma, licet quandóque maior, pulchrior, ac firmior fuerit. Tunc autem transitur per Ciuitates Laonsam, Gibellam, Tortusiam, Toruplam, et Berythum super mare vbi sanctus Georgius fertur occidisse Draconem. Hinc pergitur in Ciuitatem nunc dictam Acon, quondam Ptolomaidem, antiquitùs Acharon, quæ tempore quo eam vltimò Christiani tenebant circa annum incarntionis Domini 1280. erat Ciuitas valdè fortis, sed modò apparent eius magnæ ruinæ. Porrò a

Constantinopoli poterit peregrinus faciliùs versus Hierosolymorum partes per mare nauigare quam per terras peregrinare prædictas, si deus illi propitius fuerit, et mare fidem conseruauerit. [Sidenote: Sio.] Qui ergò a Constantinopoli iter transire nauigando disponit, tendat ad Ciuitatem [Marginal Note: Vel Smyrnam.] Myrnam vbi nunc ossa Sancti Nicholai venerantur, et sic procedendo per multa maritima loca veniet ad Insulam Sio vbi crescit gummi mastix lucidum: Inde ad Insulam Pathmos Sancti Ioannis Euangelistæ, et ad Ephesum vbi idem noscitur sepultus: hanc totam minorem Asiam tenent nunc pessimi Turci, et eam appellant minorem Turciam. Post Ephesum nauigatur per plures Insulas vsque Pataram Ciuitatem, vndè oriundus fuit beatus Nicholaus, ac per Myrrheam vbi stetit Ephesus, vbi nascuntur fortia vina valdè, deinde ad Insulam Cretæ, hinc Coos postea Lango, vndè Hypocrates Medicus dicitur natus: [Sidenote: Rhodus Insula.] tuncque ad grandem Insulam Rhodum; et sciendum quod a Constantinopoli vsque Rhodum, per mare dicuntur ducentæ octuaginta leucæ. Hanc insulam totam tenent, et gubernant Christiani Hospitalarij nunc temporis, quæ quondam Colosse dicebatur: nam et multi Saracenorum adhuc eam sic appellant, vnde et Epistola, quam beatus Paulus ad habitatores huius Insulæ scripsit, intitulabatur ad Colossenses. Ab hoc loco nauigando in Cyprum, aspicitur absorptio Ciuitatis Sathaliæ, quæ sicut olim Sodoma dicitur perijsse, propter vnicum crimen contra naturam a quodam Iuuene petulante commissum. [Sidenote: Cyprus Insula.] Sciendum quod a Rhodo ad Cyprum feruntur plenè quingentæ quinquaginta leucæ: Cyprus magna, et pulchra est Insula habens Archiepiscopatum, cum quinque Episcopatibus suffraganeis: Illuc Famagosta, est vnus de principalibus portibus mundi, in quo ferè omnium mercatores conueniunt nationum, tam Christianorum, quam multorum Paganorom, et similiter apud portum Limechon. Est ibi et Abbatia ordinis sancti Benedicti, in monte sanctæ Crucis, vbi dicitur saluati latronis seruari crux, qui in eadem cruce audiuit à Christo, Hodiè mecum eris in Paradiso. [Sidenote: Fortis Cyprí vina.] Corpus etiam sancti Hylarionis seruatur ibi, in castro Damers quod Rex Cypri facit diligentissimè custodiri: Vltrà modum fortia vina nascuntur in Cypro, quæ primo rubra, post annum albescunt, et quo vetustiora, eo albiora ac magis odorifera, ac fortia efficiuntur. Vlteriùs paucissimæ villæ, aut Ciuitates sunt Christianorum, sed ferè omnia Saraceni possident infideles: et proh dolor, ab Anno 1200. incarnationis Domini aut circa, pacificè tenuerunt. [Sidenote: Ioppa, vel Iaffe.] Qui autem a Cypro prospere legit spacia maris, poterit in duobus naturalibus diebus peruenire in portum Ioppæ, qui Iaffe nunc nuncupatur, et proximus est a Ireusalem, distans 16, tantum leucas, hoc est dieta cum dimidia. [Sidenote: Portus Tyri, alias Sur.] Et sciendum quod circa medium, inter Cyprum, et Iaffe est portus Tyri quondam munitissimæ Ciuitatis, hanc dum vltimo Saraceni à Christianis ceperunt turpissimè destruxerunt, custodientes iam curiosè portum, timore

Christianorum. Iste portus non vocatur modo Tyrus, sed Sur. Nam et ab illa parte est ibi introitus terræ Suriæ. Ante istam Ciuitatem Tyrum habetur quidam lapis, super quem dominus noster Iesus Christus sedendo suis discipulis vel populis prædicauit. Vnde, et Christiani olim super hunc locum construxerunt Ecclesiam in nomine Saluatoris. Peregrinus vero qui ab hoc loco vult peregrinari, morosè sciat, quod ad octo leucas à Tyro in orientem est Sarepta Sydoniorum, vbi olim Elias Propheta filium viduæ suscitauit a morte. Itemque sciat, quod à Tyro in vnica dieta pergere potest in Achon, siue Acharon supra scripta. [Sidenote: Achon, olim Acharon. Mons Carmeli.] Circa Acon versùs mare, ad 120. stadia, quorum 16. leucam constituunt, est mons Carmeli, vbi morabatur præfatus Elias, et super alium montem Villa Saffra vbi sanctus Iacobus, et Ioannes germani Apostoli nascebantur, et in quorum natiuitatis loco pulchra habetur Ecclesia. [Sidenote: Fossa Beleon.] Item propè Acon ad ripam dictam Beleon, est fossa multum vtilis, et mirabilis quæ dicitur fossa Mennon, hæc est rotunda circumferentia, cuius diameter continet prope 100. cubitos, plena alba et resplendente arena, et mundi ex qua conficitur mundum et perlucidum vitrum. Pro hac arena venitur per aquas, et per terras, et exportatur manibus et vehiculis propè et procul, et quantumcúnque de die exhauritur, repleta manè altero reperitur: Et est in fossa ventus grandis et iugis, qui mirabiliter arenam commouere videtur. Si quis autem vitrum de hac arena factum in fossa reponeret, conuerteretur iterum in arenam, et qui imponeret frustum metalli, verteretur in vitrum: nonnulli reputant hanc fossam esse spiraculum maris arenosi, de quo mari aliquid locuturus sum in sequentibus. Ab Acon via versus Jerusalem bifurcatur: nam qui tenet vnum latus potest ire secus Iordanem fluuium, in Ciuitatem Damascum, qui verò aliud, ibit in tribus aut quatuor dietis Gazam, de qua olim fortis Samson asportauit nocte fores portarum: deinde in Cæsaream Philippi, et Ascalonem, et Ioppam portum supradictum, Hincque in Rama, et Castellum Emaus, et sic in Ierusalem vrbem sacrosanctam.

CAPVT. 5.

Via à Francia aut Flandria per solas terras vsque Ierusalem.

Itineribus, quæ per terras, et per mare a nostris partibus ducunt in terram promissionis descriptis, restat breuiter dicendum de alia via, per quam omnino mare transeundum non est, videlicet per Almaniam, per Bohemiam, per Prussiam, et hinc per terram Paganorum regni Lituaniæ, et sic per longam, et pessimam terram primæ Tartariæ vsque in Indiam: Dico autem Tartariæ primæ, quoniam de hac exijt primus Imperator totius Tartariæ, qui semper vocatur Grand Can, quo vix maiorem mundus habet terrenum Dominum, excepto Imperatore superioris Indiæ, de quibus in secunda et tertia huius tractatus partibus, aliquanto est diffusius narrandum. Cuncti principes huius primæ Tartariæ, quorum summus semper vocatur

Bachu, et moratur in Ciuitate Horda, [Marginal note: Horda est multitudo riuens in agris.] reddunt Imperatore Grand Can, magna tributa. [Sidenote: Mores Tartarorum.] Est autem hæc prima Tartaria terra misera et sabulosa, et infructuosa: hoc enim scio, quòd per aliquod tempus steti in ea, et perambulaui Insulas, regiones, et terras circumiacentes, scilicet, Russiæ, Inflau, Craco, Latton, Restau, et alias nonnullas: crescunt námque in ista Tartaria modica blada, pauca vina, et fructuum, ac frugum parua copia, exceptis herbis pro pastu Bestiarum, quarum ibi est abundantia: nam carnibus illarum vescuntur pro omnibus cibarijs, ius earum sorbentes, et pro potu bibentes lac de omni genere bestiarum. Quin etiam pauperiores manducant canes, lupos, catos, ratos, talpas, ac mures, ac huiusmodi bestiolas omnes: sed nec aliquis Princeps aut prælatus comedit vltra semel in die, et hoc parcè, vel parcissimè: et sunt homines valdè immundi, quia non nisi benè diuites vtuntur mappis, linteaminibus, aut lineis indumentis: sed nec habent copiam lignorum, vnde et fimum boum, ac omnium bestiarum desiccatum ad solem accipiunt pro ignis materia, vbi se calefaciunt, et coquendo coquunt. Aestiuo tempore, cadunt ibi frequenter tempestates, tonitruorum, fulminum, et grandinum, quibus domus, arbores, bestiæ, et homines, comburuntur, euelluntur, et occiduntur. Nam et quandoque subrepentè oritur ibi calor immoderatus, et improuiso frigus immoderatum. Deníque cum terra illa, se multum inclinet ad polum Septentrionalem, fortius ibi gelare solet, et frequentius, ac diutius quàm ad partes nostras, vnde et quasi omnes habent ibi stupas, in quibus manducant, et operantur. [Sidenote: Hyeme præcipue iter faciunt per terram.] Nec valet à nostris partibus ingredi ad illam nisi tempore gelicidij, quod ad introitum eius sunt tres dictæ, de via molli, aquatica, et profunda, in qua dum viator putaret se stare securum, profunderetur in lutum ad tibias, ad genua, ad femora vel ad renes: hoc ergo sciendum quòd paucissimi tendunt per hanc viam in terram promissionis: Nam iter est graue, distortum, longum, et periculosum sicut audistis, imò periculosius quàm scribo.

CAPVT. 6.

Via de Cypro vel Ierusalem vsque in Babyloniam Ægypti.

Descripto sicut potui triplicitèr itinere in terram sanctam, restat videre de duabus alijs vijs, quæ incidentèr solent contingere peregrinis: Multi námque illorum ex speciali deuotione desiderant visitare ossa beatissimæ Virginis Catharinæ in monte Sinay: [Sidenote: Babylonia Aegypti.] Cum igitur ipsis sit necessarius Soldani Babyloniæ conductus eo quod Imperator sit, et dominus omnium illarum terrarum, quidam postquam perueniunt in Cyprum tendunt primò in Babyloniam Ægypti, pro impetrando conductu securo, átque indè pergentes in Sinay vadunt in Ierusalem. Quidam verò postquam perfecerunt peregrinationem Hierosolymitanam, pergunt per terras ad Soldanum pro conductu, et tum in Sinay, propter quòd vtramque viam breuiter describo. [Sidenote: Damiata portus Aegypti.] De Cypro in Ægyptum itur per mare relinquendo Hierosolymorum terram ad manum sinistram, et accipitur primus portus Ægypti, dictus Damiata: ibi quondam fuit Ciuitas valdè munita, sed quod Christiani illam, primi et altera vice ceperunt, Sarraceni vltimò destruxerunt, et aliam remotius à mari eiusdem nominis Ciuitatem ædificauerunt: [Sidenote: Alexandria.] Hinc venitur in portum Alexandriæ Ægypti, quæ est Ciuitas magna, pulchra, et fortis valde, sed ábsque aquis potabilibus. Adducit tamen sibi per longos ductus aquam Nili fluminis in cisternis ad potandum. Alexandria nobilis, 30. stadia habet longitudinis decémque in latum. In ea restant adhuc plures Ecclesiæ à tempore Christianorum, sed Sarraceni non sustinentes picturas Sanctorum omnes parietes albauerunt. De Alexandria per terras venitur in Babyloniam Ægypti, quæ etiam fundata iacet supra prædictum Nilum fluuium: Dicitur autem hæc Babylonia minor ad differentiam magnæ Babyloniæ, siue Babel, vbi Deus linguas confudit olim, quæ tendendo inter Orientem et Septentrionem distat ab ista dietas circiter 40. nec est sub potestate Soldani, sed Imperatoris Persarum, qui illam tenet in homagio ab Imperatore Cathay, dicto, Grand Can. [Sidenote: Cayr ciuitas.] Hæc autem Babylonia Ægypti est Ciuitas grandis et fortis, tamen valdè prope eam est alia maior dicta Cayr, in qua vt sæpiùs residet Soldanus, quanquam Babylonia nomen per seculum diffusius est cognitum: Altera autem via peregrinorum de Hierosolymis pro conducta tendentium ad Soldanum talis esse potest. [Sidenote: Abilech desertum.] Primò tendant de Ierusalem in suprà dictam Gazam Palestinorum, inde ad Castellum Dayre, átque ex tunc exitur de terra Syriæ, et intratur à superiori parte in desertum longum arenosum, et sterile, propè ad septem dietas, quod lingua eorum vocatur Abilech; tamen per illud inueniantur plura hospitia, vbi haberi possunt ad victum nccessaria. Et qui in eundo rectum iter tenet, veniet in Ciuitatem dictam, Balbes, quæ est ad finem Regni Halapiæ: Sícque expleto Deserto, intratur terra Ægypti, quam ipsi Canopat vocant, et aliqui Mersur, átque ex tunc in Babyloniam, et Cayr, præfatam: In ista verò Babylonia habetur pulchra Ecclesia Mariæ virginis, in loco vbi morabatur cum filio suo, et Ioseph tempore suæ fugæ, et creditur ibi contineri corpus Virginis Barbaræ.

CAPVT. 7.

De Pallatio Soldani, ac numero, et nominibus præteritorum Soldanorum.

Cayr ciuitas Imperialis et Regalis est valdè munita, et grandis, decorata sede propria Sarracenorum Regní, vbi dominus eorum Soldanus communiter residere solet, in suo Calahelick, id est, castro forti, et lato, ac in euecta rupe statuto. Siquidem Soldanus eorum lingua sonat nomen similis maiestatis, quo nos in Latino dicimus Cæsarem, aut Imperatorem. Pro custodia huius Castri sunt ibidem omni tempore morantes sex millia personarum, et pro, seruiendo, dum ibi residet, ipsi Soldano, qui omnes de Curia eadem accipiunt necessaria, et donatiua. Iste Imperator Soldanus, est Rex, Dominúsque quinque Regnoram magnorum: Canopat, hoc est, Ægypti: totius Iudeæ, sicut olim Dauid, et Salomon; Halapiæ, in terra Machsyriæ, cuius ciuitas Damascus olim erat principalis; Arabiæ, quod est regnum valdè protensum, et cum his possidet dominatus omnium Caliphorum: ad quod sciendum, quòd quaundóque fuerunt tres Caliphorum dominatus: Ex quibus primus Caliphus qui dicebatur Chaldæorum, et Arabum, cuius erat sedes in Ciuitate Baldac. Alter Barbarorum et Affricorum, cuius erat sedes in Maroco super Mare Hispaniæ. Tertius Aegypti: [Sidenote: Caliphus quid sit.] Est autem Caliphus inter eos, velut inter nos Imperator, et Papa simul, scilicet, Dominus temporalium et spiritualium. [Sidenote: Series Soldanorum Aegypti.] Exactis igitur Caliphis circa annum incarnationis Christi 1150, primus Soldanorum fuit nominatus Saracon: secundus filius eius, Saladin, qui anno 1190. cum Turcis totam ferè terram promissionis abstulit à Christianis. Et sub quo Richardus Rex Angliæ cum alijs principibus Christianis custodiebat passum Rupium, ne ille sicut proposuerat transire, profecisset vltra. Tertius Melachsala, à quo sanctus Ludouicus rex Franciæ captiuabatur in bello. Quartus Turquenna, qui Regem prædictum redemi dimisit pro pecunia. Quintus Meleth. Sextus Melethemes. Septimus Melec dayr, sub quo Edwardus Rex Angliæ intrauit cum nostris Syriam, damnificans plurimum Sarracenos. [Sidenote: Edwardus princeps Angliæ, Regis Hen. 3. filius.] Octauus Melec salle. Nonus Elphi, qui Anno Incarnationis Domini 1289. destruxit in illis partibus enormiter Christianos, et penitus omnes inde fugauit, atque recepit Tripolim Ciuitatem. Decimus Melethasseras: hic cepit Anno Domini 1291. in octaua paschæ Accharon, fugatis vel occisis ex ea omnibus Christianis. Exinde amissis succedentium nominibus, sextus decimus dicebatur vel dicitur Melec Mandibron: sub isto steti ego per aliquod tempus stipendiarius in guerris suis contra Bedones, qui ei tunc temporis rebellabant. Horum etiam mores, et continentiam populorum, in sequentibus declarabo: sicut veraciter fateri possum, ipse ad filiam cuiusdam sui Principis me obtulit vxorare, et magnis dotari possessionibus, dummodò Christianitati resignassem: Eúmque dimisi Soldanum, quando de partibus illis recessi. [Sidenote: Potentia Soldani Aegypti.] Soldanus præter homines ad sua castra seruanda deputatos, potest educere quoties velit in exercitum de hominibus de ipsius stipendijs viuentibus et ad eius iugitèr mandata paratis, 20. millia armatorum, ex sola Ægypto: Et ex Syria, et Turcia, et alijs terris, 50. millia exceptis ruralibus, et Ciuitatem comitatibus, qui sunt velut innumerabiles. Miles quidem stipendiarius recipit de Curia pro anni Tempore 121. aureos, et sub tali stipendio seruit cum tribus equis et vno Camelo. Quadringenti vel Quingenti horum militum ordinati sunt sub vno rectore, que vocatur Admirabilis: Et ille solus recipit de curia tantum, sicut omnes sibi subditi: Notandum quod nunquam extraneus Nuncius ire permittitur ad Soldanum nisi auratis indutus vestibus, vel panno Tartarico aut camoleoto ad modum nobilium Sarracenorum: [Sidenote: Reuerentia exhibita Soldano.] et oportet vt vbicunque primum nuncius Soldanum aspiciat, siue ad fenestras, siue alibi, vt cadat ad genua, vel protinus osculetur terram, quia talem reuerentiam facere, signum est quòd ille desiderat ei loqui. Quamdiu autem tales loquuntur sibi, aut literas ostendunt, circumstant Apparitores extensis brachijs leuatos tenentes mucrones, gladios, gezas, et mackas ad feriendum, et occidendum, si quid dictum vel nunciatum fuerit, quod Imperatori displiceat, quam citò ille signauerit trucidari. Veruntamen sciendum est quòd nullius hominis personaliter ab ipso quidquam petentis consueuit repellere preces rationabiles, et contra eorum leges aut mores non venientes. Porrò ego in Curia manens, vidi circa Soldanum vnum venerabilem, et expertum medicum, de nostris partibus oriundum: [Marginal note: Cuius nomen erat M. Ioannes ad Barbam.] solet namque circa se retinere diuersarum medicos nationum, et quos nominandæ audierit esse famæ: Nos tamen rarò inuicem conuenimus ad colloquium, eò quòd meum seruitium cum suo modicum congruebat: longo autem posteà tempore, et ab illo loco remotè, videlicet in Leodij ciuitate, composui hortatu et adiutorio eiusdem venerabilis viri hunc tractatum, sicut in fine operis totius enarrabo. Itémque in Cayr ciuitate ducuntur ad forum communitur tam viri quàm mulieres aliarum legum, et nationum venales, et ad modum bestiaram venduntur pro pecunia ad seruiendum in suis artificijs. [Sidenote: Mos oua furnis fouendi.] Habetur quoque ibi domus plena furnis paruis, in quibus per custodes domus tam hyeme quàm æstate fouentur oua gallinarum, anatum, aucarum, et columbarum, vsque ad procreationem suorum pullorum, et hijs intendunt, pro certo pretio accipiendo à mulierculis illic oua ferentibus.

CAPVT. 8.

De Campo Balsami in Egypto.

[Sidenote: Balsamum.] Extra hanc ciuitatem Cayr, est Campus seu ager Balsami: circa quod sciendum, quòd optimum totius mundi Balsamum in magno crescit Indiæ deserto, vbi Alexander Magnus dicitur quondam locutus fuisse arboribus Solis et Lunæ, de quo in sequentibus aliquid est scribendum. Illo itaque Indiæ Balsamo duntaxat excepto, non est liquor in vniuerso orbe, qui huic creditur comparari. Has arbores seu arbusta Balsami fecit quondam quidam de Caliphis Aegypti de loco Engaddi inter mare mortuum, et Ierico, vbi Domino volente excreuerat, eradicari, et in argo prædicto plantari: est tamen hoc mirandum, quod vbicuncque alibi siue prope, siue remote plantantur, quamuis fortè virent, et exurgant, non tamen fructificant. Et è contrario apparet hoc miraculosum, quod in hoc agro Cayr non se permittant coli per Sarracenos, sed solummodò per Christianos, vel aliter non fructificarent: Et dicunt ipsi Sarraceni hoc sæpius se tentasse: sunt autem arbusta trium vel quatuor pedem altitudinis, velut vsque ad renes hominis, et lignum eorum aspiciendum, sicut vitis syluestris. Folia non marcescunt, quin prius marcescant fructus, cernitur ad formam Cubebæ, et gummi eorum est Balsamum. Ipsi appellant arbores Enochkalse, fructum Abebifau, et liquorum gribalse. Extrahitur verò gummi de arbusculis per hunc modem: De lapide acuto, vel de osse fracto dant scissuras per cortices in ligno, et ex vulneribus Balsamum lachrymatur, quod in vasculis suscipiunt, cauentes quout possunt, ne quid de illo labatur in terram: Nam se de ferro, vel alio metallo fieret incissura, liquor Balsami corrumperetur à sua virtute. [Sidenote: Virtutes veri Balsami.] Veri Balsami virtutes sunt magnæ quidem, et innumerosæ: nam vix aliquis mortalium scire potuit omnes, quamuis inter Physicos quinquaginta scribantur. Raro vtique Sarraceni vendunt Christianis purum et verum Balsamum, quin priùs commisceant, et falsificant sicut ego ipse frequenter vidi. Nam aliqui tertiam, seu quartam partem immiscent terrebynthinæ. [Sidenote: Sophisticationes Balsami.] Alii ramusculos arbustarum, et fructus eorum coquunt in oleo, quod vendunt pro Balsamo: et quidam (quod pessimam est) nil Balsami habentes, distillant oleum, per clauos gariophillos, et spicum nardum, et similes odoriferas species, hoc pro Balsamo exponentes, atque aliis pluribus modis deludunt ementes. [Sidenote: Probatio veri Balsami.] Sed et Mercatores inuicem nonnunquam sophisticant altera vice: probatio autem veri Balsaml potest haberi pluribus modis, quorum aliquos hic describo. Est enim Citrini coloris, valdè clarum, et purum, et fortissimum in odoris fragrantia: si ergò apparet alterius quàm Citrini coloris sciatur non simplicis, sed cuiuscunque commixtæ substantiæ, vel ita spissum, vt non possit fluere, scitote sophisticatum. Item si posueris modicum veri Balsami in manus palma, non poteris sustinere eam linialiter in feruore splendentis Solis ad spacium recitandæ Dominicæ orationis. Item si in clara flamma ignis vel candeliæ cereæ miseris punctum cultelli cum gutta puri Balsami, ipsa gutta de facilè comburetur. Item si in scutella munda cum puro lacte caprino posueris modicum veri Balsami, statim, miscebit se, et vnietur cum lacte, ìta vt Balsamum non cognoscetur. Item è contrà, si posueris verum Balsamum cum aqua Lympida, nunquam miscebit se aquæ, etiamsi aquam moueris vehementer, imò Balsamum semper tendit ad fundum vasis, nam est in sui quanitate valdè ponderosam, et iuxta quod minùs ponderosum inueneris, ampliùs falsificatum noueris.

CAPVT. 9.

De Nile fluuio, et Aegypti territorio.

Nilus suprà dictus fluuius Aegypti appellatus est alio nomine Gyon, cuius origo est à Paradiso terrestri. Hic venit currens per deserta Indiæ Maioris, hincque per meatus subterraneos transit plures terras: exiens sub Monte Aloth, inter Indiam et Aethiopiam, et Mauritaniam intra deserta Aegypti, irrigans totam longitudinem Aegypti vsque ad Alexandriam, ibíque se perdit in mare. [Sidenote: Inundatio Nilo.] Sole intrante signum Cancri omni anno hoc est, ad quindenam ante Festum Natiuitatis Ioannis Baptistæ incipit paulatim fluuius crescere, et inundare, quousque sol intret Virginem, quod est circa Festum Laurentij, atque ex tunc decrescere, et minui, donec Sole veniente in Lybram intra suos alueos se conseruet: Dúmque per inundationem nimis effluit, damnificat terræ culturas, et fit Charistia in Aegypto. [Sidenote: Raro in Aegyptio pluuia.] Et similiter dum parum exundat, ingruit esuries, quoniam in Aegypto rarissimè pluit, aut apparent nubes, quoniam si quandoque pluerit in æstate, terra muribus adimpleur. [Sidenote: Nubia.] Terra Aegypti continet in longitudine dietas quindecim, in latitudine ferè tres, et habet triginta dietas deserti: à finibus Aegypti vsque Nubiam, duodecim sunt dietæ. Hi Nubij sunt Christiani, sed nigri, velut Aethiopes, vel Mauri.

[Sidenote: Phoenix visa a Mandeuillo.] Phoenix auis, de qua dicitur, quod semper vnica sit in mundo, viuens per annos quingentos, quæ et seipsam comburit, ac de cineribus eius, siue per naturam, siue per miraculum alia creatur, hæc interdum apparet in Aegypto, et sicut mihi monstrabatur, vidi duabus vicibus. Modicum est maior Aquila, cristam in capite maiorem pauonis, collum habens croceum, dorsum Indicum, alas purpureas, caudam duobus coloribus, per transuersum croceo et rubeo regulatam, qui singuli colores sunt ad splendorem Solis delectabiliter videntibus resplendentes. In Aegypto multæ habentur arbores sexcies aut septies in anno fructificantes, ibique frequenter inueniuntur in terra Smaragdi, et circa oram Nili alij lapides pretiosi. [Sidenote: Mecha.] A Babylonia Aegypti, vsque ad ciuitatem Meccam, (quam Pagani ibidem appellant Iacrib, et est in magnis desertis Arabiæ) sunt triginta duæ dietæ. In ea veneratur detestandum cadauer Machon siue Machometi honorabiliter et reuerenter in Templo eius, quod ibi vocatur Musket, de cuius vita aliquid infrà narrabo. Per prædicta itaque apparet, quod Imperator Sarracenorum Soldanus Babyloniæ, valdè potens est Dominus.

CAPVT. 10.

De couductu Soldani, et via vsque in Sinay.

Priùs dictum est de reuerentia Soldani, quandò ad ipsum intratur exhibenda. Sciendum ergò, cum ab eo petitur securus conductus, nemini denegare consueuit, sed datur petentibus communiter sigillum eius, in appenditione absque literis: hoc sigillum, pro vexillo in virga aut hasta dum peregrini ferunt, omnes Sarraceni videntes illud flexis genibus in terram se reuerenter inclinant, et portantibus omnem exhibent humanitatem. Verumtamen satis maior fit reuerentia literis Soldani sigillatis, quod et Admirabiles, et quicunque alij Domini, quando eis monstrantur, antequam recipiant, se multùm inclinant: Deinde ambabus manibus eas capientes ponunt super propria capita, posteà osculantur, et tandem legunt inclinati cum magna veneratione, quibus semel aut bis perlectis, offerunt se promptos ad explendum quicquid ibi iubetur, ac insuper exhibent deferenti, quicquid possint commodi, vel honoris: sed talem conductum per literas Soldani vix quisquam peregrinorum accipit, qui non in Curia illius stetit, vel notitiam apud illum habuerit. [Sidenote: Literæ Soldani in gratiam Mandeuilli concessæ.] Ego autem habui in recessu meo, in quibus etiam continebatur ad omnes sibi subiectos speciale mandatum, vt me permitterent intrare, et respicere singula loca, pro meæ placito voluntatis, et mihi exponerent quorumcunque locorum mysteria distinctè et absque vllo velamine veritatis, ac me cum omni sodalitate mea benignè reciperent, et in cunctis rationalibus audirent, requisiti autem si necesse foret de ciuitate conducerent in ciuitatem. Habito itaque peregrinis conductu, ad Montem Sinay potest à Cayr vnam duarum incipere semitarum, vsque vallem Helim, vbi adhuc sunt duodecim fontes aquarum. Nam vna viarum est, vt pertranseat passagium maris rubri, non longè ab eodem loco, vbi olim populus Israel Duce Mose, Deo iubente, siccis pedibus transiit idem mare. [Sidenote: Ratio, cur Rubrum mare sic appellatur.] Quod quidem, licèt aqua sit satis clara, dicitur ibi Rubrum propter lapillos, et arenas subrufi coloris: et continet ibi nunc temporis passus maris in latitudine ferè sex leucas. Transmissoque mari, ibit super hanc longè ab oris eiusdem per dietas quatuor, atque ex tunc relinquens mare, tendit per deserta sex aut septem dierum, vsque in vallem præfatam. Alia est autem via, vt de Babylonia intret Dyrcen deserta, tendens ad quendam fontem, quem dicitur Moses [Marginal note: Vel Maus.] fecisse: et hinc ad riuulum Marach, qui quondam, Mose imponente lignum, ab amaritudine dulcescebat, et sic tandem in premissam vallem perueniant. Et restat via grandis dietæ ad Montem Sinay ab hac valle. Nam à Babylonia vsque in Sinay, æstimatur esse via duodecim dictarum, quamuis nonnulli citius perueniunt. Hoc verè sciendum, neminem peregrinorum per hæc deserta sine ductore posse tendere, cui notæ sunt viæ, sed nec equi valent transire, præcipuè quòd non inuenirent in desertis quid bibere. [Sidenote: Abstinentia Camelorum ab aquis.] Aliquo tamen modo transitur per Camelos, eò quòd se continere possunt de potu duobus aut tribus diebus: Et oportet vt itinerantes ferant secum per viam necessaria ad victum proprium, et Camelorum, nisi quòd interdum fortè Cameli aliquid sibi abrodere possunt circa cortices arbustorum, et folia ramusculorum.

CAPUT. 11.

De Monasterio Sinay, et reliquijs beatæ Catherinæ.

Mons Sinay appellatur ibi desertum Syn: quasi in radice montis istius habetur Coenobium Monachorum pergrande, cuius clausura in circuitu est firmata muris altis, et portis ferreis, pro metu bestiarum deserti. Hi Monachi sunt Arabes, et Græci, et in magno conuentu multum Deo deuoti: viuunt in magna abstinentia, vtentes simplicibus cibariis, de lotis et dactylis, et huiusmodi, nec vinum potantes, festis acceptis. Illic in Ecclesia Beatæ Virginis et matris Catherinæ semper lampades plurimæ sunt ardentes, nam habetur ibi plena copia olei oliuarum. A posteriori parte magni altaris monstratur locus, vbi Moysi apparuit Dominus in rubo ardente, ipsum rubum adhuc seruans, quem dum monachi intrant, semper se discalceant gratia illias verbi, quo Deus iussit Moysi ibidem, Solue calciamentum de pedibus tuis, locus enim in quo stas, terra sancta est: hunc locum appellant Bezeleel, id est, vmbra Dei. Et propè altare tribus gradibus in altitudine, habetur capsa, seu Tumba Alabastri, sanctissima continens ossa Virginis. Christiani qui ibidem morantur, cum magna reuerentia aduenientibus peregrinis, à Monachorum prælato, seu ab alio in hoc instituto, excipiuntur. Is quodam instrumento argenteo consueuit ossa defricare, siue linire, vt ex iis exeat modicum olei, velut parumper sudoris, quod tamen non apparet in colore sui tanquam olei seu Balsami, sed aliquantulum pluris magnitudinis. Et ex isto traditur interdum aliquid petentibus peregrinis, sed parùm, quia nec multùm exudat. Ostendere solent et caput ipsius Catherinæ cum inuolumento sanguinolento, et multas prætereà sanctas, et venerabiles reliquias, quæ omnia intuitus sum diligentur et sæpè, oculis indignis. Habent quoque in ista Ecclesia propriam Lampadem quilibet Monachorum, quæ imminente illius discessu lumen per diuinum miraculum variat vel extinguit. [Sidenote: Monarchorum sophismata.] Ego etiam curiosius super vno dubio quod priùs audieram, plures interrogationes feci ab aliquibus Monachorum, vtrum scilicet prælato eorum decedente semper successor per diuinum signum eligetetur: et vix tandem ab eis recepi responsum, quòd per vnum istorum miraculorum habetur successor, videlicet in missa sepulturæ defuncti omnibus Monachorum lampadibus extinctis, illius sola Dei nutu reaccenditur, quem fieri vult prælatum, vel de coelo inuenitur missus breuiculus super altare, inscriptum habens nomen prælati futuri. Intra hanc Ecclesiam nunquam musca, vel aranea, aut huiusmodi immundi vermiculi nascuntur, quod similiter per diuinum accidit miraculum: nam antè replebatur Ecclesia talibus immunditiis, et totus conuentus recederet ad construendum Ecclesiam in alio loco. Et ecce Dei genetrix virgo beata eis visibiliter obuiauit, iubens reuerti, et dicens nunquam Ecclesiam similibus infestari. In cuius obuiationis loco in ascensu procliuo huius montis per multos gradus construxerunt Ecclesiam, ædificium excellens, in honorem eiusdem virginis. Et alibuantò altius, per eiusdem montis ascensum est vetus Capella, quam vocant Eliæ Prophetæ, et locum specialiter appellant Horeb. A cuius latere in montis appendentia colitur vinea, quam nominant Iosuæ scophis, de qua quidam putare volunt, quod Sanctus Ioannes Euangelista eam primò plantauit. In superiori verò montis vertice, est

Capella, quam dicunt Moysis, et illic rupis seruans adhuc corporis eius formam impressam dum se abscondit, viritus dominum respicere in facie. Locus quoque ibi ostenditur, in quo Deus tradidit ei decem mandata, siue legem proprio digito scriptam, et sub rupe cauerna in qua mansit ieiunus diebus 40. Ab hoc monte qui vocatur Mosi, restat via producta ad quartam Leucæ, vsque in montem qui dicitur Sanctæ Catherinæ per vallem speciosam, ac multùm frigidam. Circa eius medium habetur Ecclesia, nomine 40. Martyrum constructa, vbi interdum veniunt Monachi cantare missam: Hic mons est satis altior Monte Moysis, in cuius vertice Angeli Dei piè creduntur attulisse, et sepeliisse corpus sanctissimæ Martyris Catherinæ cum inuolumento capitis suprà dicto. Attamen in ipso certo sepulturæ loco, licèt quandoque stetit Capella, modò non est habitaculum, sed modicus aceruus petrarum. Notandum, quòd vterque horum montium potest vocari mons Sinay, eo quod totus circumiacens locus deserti Sin appellatur. Sur desertum inter mare Rubrum, et solitudinem Sinay. Desertum Sur idem Scriptura quod et Cades. Visitatis igitur à peregrinis his sacrosanctis memorijs, et valefacto Monachis, recommendant se eorum orationibus, et meritis: tuncque solet aliquid victualium offerri peregrinis, pro inchoanda via deserti Syriæ versus Ierusalem. Et sicut dixi de priori deserto, sic nec istud securè est peragrandum absque Drogemijs; id est, semitarum ductoribus, propter vastitudinem deserti.

CAPVT. 12.

Iter a deserto Sinay vsque ad Iudeam.

Per istud latum et longum desertum, moratur vel potius vagata maxima multitudo malorum, et incompositorum hominum, qui non manent in domibus, sed sub pellium tabernaculis, quemadmodum et olim filij Israel in eodem deserto ambulauerunt, quoniam aquæ non manent ibi diu in locis certis: et ideò mutant tabernacula sequentes aquas: non colunt terras, raro manducant panem, sed tantùm carnes bestiarum deserti quas venantur, coquentes super petras calefactas ad Solem: fortes sunt et feroces, et velut desperati de vita propria non curantes, qui licèt non habeant arma præter lanceam, et tarchiam, et caput grandi albo linteolo inuolutum, tamen non verentur exercere guerras, et inire proelia contra Dominum suum Soldanum: nam et ego stipendiarius in expeditione Soldani contra eos sæpius fui. Isti sunt quidem Arabes, sed notiori nomine appellantur Bedoyns et Acopars, et quamuis plurima mala agunt per desertum, raro tamen nocent peregrinis beatæ Virginis Catharinæ. [Sidenote: Ioannes Mandeuil militans contra Arabes. Beersheba.] Itaque peregrinus qui debitum tenuit iter, veniat à finibus deserti in primam ciuitatem Iudeæ, quæ dicitur Berseba: est vicus grandis Hebron inde miliario vergens ad Austrum: Hieronymus. Notandum, Theros Mons Dei in regione Maglaw iuxta Montem. Notandum similiter, Arabiam in deserto esse, cui iungitur Mons et desertum Sarracenorum, quod vocatur Phaaran. Mihi autem videtur, quod dupliei nomine, nupe Mons Sinay, nunc Oreb vocatur. Hieronymus. Phaaran nunc oppidum trans Oreb, iam iunctum Sarracenis, qui in solitudine vagi pererrant. Hos interfecerunt filij Israel, cùm de Monte Sinay castra mouissent. Est ergo, vt dixi, trans Jordanem contra Australem plagam, et distat ab Helyn, contra Orientem, itinere dierum trium. In deserto autem Phaaran, Scriptura commemorat habitasse Ismaelem, vade et Ismaelitæ, qui nunc Sarraceni. Legimus quoque Chederlaomer percussisse eos qui erant in deserto Phaaran quod nunc dicitur Ascalon, et circa eam Regio Palestinorum. Hieronymus. Hæc Bersheba erat bona et spectabilis, vltimo tempore Christianorum, et adhuc ibi restant nonnullæ Ecclesiæ.

[Sidenote: Ciuitas Hebron.] Hinc ad Leucas duas venitur in ciuitatem Hebron, et Hebron ab Helyn distat ad Meridianam plagani millibus circiter 39. de qua legitur, quòd primis temporibus fuerit habitatio maximorum Gigantium, Regúmque, posteà Dauidis. In hac est illa spelunca duplex, quæ seruat ossa sanctorum Patriarcharum, Abrahæ, Isaac, et Jacob, Saræ, et Rebeccæ, consistitque ad radicem montis, et habetur super istam cum propugnaculis ad modum castri constructa pulchra Ecclesia. Sarraceni appellant istam speluncam Kariackaba, custodienies locum diligenter ac reuerenter propter honorem Patriarcharum, et non permittentes quenquam Christianorum aut Iudæorum ingredi, nisi ostenderit super hæc specialem gratiam à Soldano. Nam ipsi communiter reputant tam Christianos quàm Iudaeos pro canibus, et quando despectiuè eos volunt appellare, dicunt Kylp, id est, canis.

[Sidenote: Vallis Mambræ Quercus arida.] Ab Hebron incipit vallis Mambræ, quæ protenditur ferè vsque Ierusalem: haud remotè ad Hebron est mons Mambre, et in ipso monte arbor quercus aridæ quæ pro antiquitate sui, speciale sibi nomen meruit in mundo vniuerso, vt vocetur arbor sicca: Sarraceni autem eam dicunt Dirp: hæc creditur stetisse ante tempora Abrahæ, tamen quidam volunt putare à mundi initio, virens donec passionis Christi tempore siccaretur. Hoc autem certum est haberi eam ob omnibus nationibus in venerationem.

[Sidenote: Gambil species Aromatis] In quodam loco præfatæ vallis est planicies, vbi per plures fossas effodiunt homines Gambil, quod comeditur loco specierum aromaticarum, et per villas defertur venale, sed et hoc audiui, quòd nulla ibi fossa ita valet exhauriri, si dimittatur per annum, quin inueniatur de prædicta Gambil impleta.

Ad duas leucas de Hebron, monstratur sepultura Loth filii fratris Abraham. Item de ciuitate Hebron per quinque leucas amoeni itineris, hoc est in medio die, venitur in Bethleem Iudeæ. [Sidenote: Kiriath Arbe.] Notandum, Arbe, id est, quatuor, primum dicum de eo quod ibi tres Patriarchæ

Abraham, Isac, et Iacob sepulti sunt, et Adam magnus, vt in Iudæorum libro scriptum est, licet eum quidam conditum in loco Caluariæ suspicentur. Corruptè in nostris codicibus Arboth scribitur, alibi erat arbor cùm in Hebræis legatur Arbe, hæc est autem eadem Hebron olim Metropolis Philistinorum, ab vno filiorum Caleb sortita vocabulum.

The English Version.

Of the Weye fro Costantynoble to Jerusalem. Of Seynt John the Evaungelist; and of Ypocras Daughter, transformed from a Woman to a Dragoun.

[Sidenote: Cap. IV] Now returne I azen, for to teche zou the way from Costantynoble to Jerusalem. He that wol thorghe Turkye, he gothe toward the cytee of Nyke, and passethe thorghe the gate of Chienetout, and alle weyes men seen before hem the hille of Chienetout, that is righte highe: and it is a myle, and an half from Nyke. And whoso will go be watre, be the brace of Seynt George, and by the see, where Seynt Nycholas lyethe, and toward many other places: first men gothe to an ile, that is clept Sylo. [Footnote: Chios] In that ile growethe mastyck on smale trees: and out of hem comethe gomme, as it were of plombtrees or of cherietrees. And aftre gon men thorghe the ile of Pathmos, and there wrot Seynt John the Evaungelist the Apocalips. And zee schulle undrestonde, that Seynt Johne was of age 32 zeer, whan oure Lord suffred his passioun; and aftre his passioun, he lyvede 67 zeer, and in the 100th zeer of his age he dyede. From Pathmos men gone unto Ephesim, a fair citee and nyghe to the see. And there dyede Seynte Johne and was buryed behynde the highe awtiere, in a toumbe. And there is a fair chirche. For Cristene men weren wont to holden that place alweyes. And in the tombe of Seynt John is noughte but manna, that is clept aungeles mete. For his body was translated into paradys. And Turkes holden now alle that place, and the citee and the chirche. And alle Asie the lesse is y cleped Turkye. And zee schulle undrestonde, that Seynt Johne leet [Footnote: Let.] make his grave there in his lyf, and leyd himself there inne alle quyk. And therefore somme men seyn, that he dyed noughte, but that he restethe there till the day of doom. And forsothe there is a great marveyle: for men may see there the erthe of the tombe apertly many tymes steren and meven, [Footnote: Stir and move.] as there wern quykke thinges undre.

And from Ephesim men gon throghe many iles in the see, unto the cytee of Paterane, [Footnote: Patera.] where Seynt Nicholas was born, and so to Martha, [Footnote: Myra.] where he was chosen to ben bisschoppe; and there growethe right gode wyn and strong; and that men callen wyn of Martha. And from thens gone men to the ile of Crete, that the Emperour zaf somtyme to Janeweys. [Footnote: The Genoese.] And thanne passen men thorghe the isles of Colos and of Lango; [Footnote: Cos.] of the whiche iles Ypocras [Footnote: Hippocrates.] was lord offe. And some men seyn, that in the ile of Lango is zit the doughtre of Ypocras, in forme and lykeness of a gret dragoun, that is a hundred fadme of lengthe, as men seyn: for I have not seen hire. And thei of the isles callen hire, lady of the lond. And sche lyethe in an olde castelle, in a cave, and schewethe twyes or thryes in the zeer. And sche dothe none harm to no man, but zif men don hire harm. And sche was thus chaunged and transformed, from a fair damysele, into lyknesse of a dragoun, be a goddesse, that was clept Deane. [Footnote: Diana.] And men seyn, that sche schalle so endure in that forme of a dragoun, unto the tyme that a knyghte come, that is so hardy, that dar come to hire and kiss hire on the mouthe: and then schall sche turne azen to hire own kynde, and ben a woman azen: but aftre that sche schalle not liven longe. And it is not long siththen, that a knyghte of the Rodes, that was hardy and doughty in armes, seyde that he wole kyssen hire. And whan he was upon his coursere, and wente to the castelle, and entred into the cave, the dragoun lifte up hire hed azenst him. And whan the knyghte saw hire in that forme so hidous and so horrible, he fleyghe awey. And the dragoun bare the knyghte upon a roche, mawgre his hede; and from that roche, sche caste him in to the see: and so was lost bothe hors and man. And also a zonge man, that wiste not of the dragoun, wente out of a schipp, and wente thorghe the ile, til that he come to the castelle, and cam in to the cave; and wente so longe, til that he fond a chambre, and there he saughe a damysele, that kembed hire hede, and lokede in a myrour: and sche hadde meche tresoure abouten hire: and he trowed, that sche hadde ben a comoun woman, that dwelled there to resceyve men to folye. And he abode, tille the damysele saughe the schadewe of him in the myrour. And sche turned hire toward him, and asked hym, what he wolde. And he seyde, he wolde ben hire limman or paramour. And sche asked him, zif that he were a knyghte. And he seyde, nay. And then sche seyde, that he myghte not ben hire lemman: but sche bad him gon azen unto his fellowes, and make him knyghte, and come azen upon the morwe, and sche scholde come out of the cave before him; and thanne come and kysse hire on the mowthe, and have no drede; for I schalle do the no maner harm, alle be it that thou see me in lyknesse of a dragoun. For thoughe thou see me hidouse and horrible to loken onne, I do the to wytene, [Footnote: Know.] that it is made be enchauntement. For withouten doubte, I am non other than thou seest now, a woman; and therfore drede the noughte. And zif thou kysse me, thou schalt have alle this tresoure, and be my lord, and lord also of alle that ile. And he departed fro hire and wente to his felowes to schippe, and leet make him knyghte, and cam azen upon the morwe, for to kysse this damysele. And whan he saughe hire comen out of the cave, in forme of a dragoun, so hidouse and so horrible, he hadde so grete drede, that he fleyghe azen to the schippe; and sche folewed him. And whan sche saughe, that he turned not azen, sche began to crye, as a thing that hadde meche sorwe: and thanne sche turned azen, in to hire cave; and anon the knyghte dyede. And siththen hidrewards, myghte no knyghte se hire, but that he dyede anon. But whan a knyghte comethe, that is so hardy to kisse hire, he schalle not dye; but he schalle turne the damysele in to hire righte forme and kyndely schapp, and he schal be lord of alle the contreyes and iles aboveseyd.

And from thens men comen to the Ile of Rodes, the whiche ile Hospitaleres holden and governen; and that token thei sumtyme from the Emperour: and it was wont to be clept Collos; and so callen it the Turks zit. And Seynt Poul, in his Epistles, writeth to hem of that Ile, *ad Colossenses*. [Footnote: The truth is the Epistle was written to the Church of Collosæ in Phrygia Major.] This ile is nyghe 800 myle from Costantynoble.

And from this ile of Rodes, men gon to Cipre, where bethe many vynes, that first bene rede, and aftre o zeer, thei becomen white: and theise wynes that ben most white, ben most clere and best of smelle. And men passen be that way, be a place that was wont to ben a gret cytee and a gret lond: and the cytee was clept Cathaillye: the which cytee and lond was lost thorghe folye of a zonge man. For he had a fayr damysele, that he loved wel, to his paramour; and sche dyed sodeynly, and was don in a tombe of marble: and for the grete lust, that he had to hire, he wente in the nyghte unto hire tombe and opened it, and went in and lay be hire, and wente his way. And whan it came to the ende of nine monethes, there com a voys to him, and seyde, Go to the tombe of that woman, and open it and beholde what thou hast begotten on hîre: and if thou lette to go, thou schalt have a gret harm. And he zede [Footnote: Went.] and opened the tombe; and there fleyghe out an eddere righte hidous to see; the whiche als swythe fleighe aboute the cytee and the contree; and sone after the cytee sank downe. And there ben manye perilouse passages.

Fro Rodes to Cypre ben 500 myle and more. But men may gon to Cypre, and come not at Rodes. Cypre is righte a gode ile and a fayr and a gret, and it hathe 4 princypalle cytees within him. And there is an erchebysshoppe at Nichosie, and 4 othere byschoppes in that lond. And at Famagost is on of the princypalle havenes of the see, that is in the world: and there arryven Cristene men and Sarazynes and men of alle naciouns. In Cipre is the hille of the Holy Cros; and there is an abbeye of monkis blake; and there is the cros of Dismas the gode theef, as I have seyd before. And summe men trowen, that there is half the crosse of oure Lord: but it is not so: and thei don evylle, that make men to beleeve so. In Cipre lythe Seynt Zenomyne: of whom men of that contree maken gret solempnytee. And in the Castelle of Amours lythe the body of Seynt Hyllarie: and men kepen it right worschipfully. And besyde Famagost was Seynt Barnabee the apostle born. In Cipre men hunten with papyonns, that ben lyche lepardes: and thei taken wylde bestes righte welle, and thei ben somdelle [Footnote: Somewhat.] more than lyouns; and thei taken more scharpely the bestes and more delyverly [Footnote: Deliberately.] than don houndes. In Cipre is the manere of lordis and alle othere men, alle to eten on the erthe. For thei make dyches in the erthe alle aboute in the halle, depe to the knee, and thei do pave hem: and whan thei wil ete, thei gon there in and sytten there. And the skylle is, for thei may ben the more fressche: for that lond is meche more hottere than it is here. And at grete festes and for straungeres, thei setten formes and tables, as men don in this contree: but thei had lever sytten in the erthe.

From Cypre, men gon to the lond of Jerusalem be the see: and in a day and in a nyghte, he that hathe gode wynd may come to the haven of Thire [Footnote: Tyre.], that now is clept Surrye. There was somtyme a gret cytee and a gode, of Crystene men: but Sarazins han destroyed it a gret partye; and thei kepe that havene right welle, for drede of Cristene men. Men myghte go more right to that havene, and come not in Cypre: but thei gon gladly to Cypre, to reste hem on the lond, or elles to bye thingis, that thei have nede to here lyvynge. On the see syde, men may fynde many rubyes. And there is the welle, of the whiche Holy Writt spekethe offe, and seythe, *Fons ortorum, et puteus aquarum viventium*: that is to seye, *The welle of gardyns, and the dyche of lyvynge watres*. In this cytee of Thire, seyde the woman to oure Lord, *Beatus venter qui te portavit, et ubera quæ succisti*: that is to seye, *Blessed be the body that she baar, and the pappes that thou sowkedest*. And there oure Lord forzaf the woman of Chananee hire synnes. And before Tyre was wont to be the ston, on the whiche oure Lord sat and prechede: and on that ston was founded the Chirche of Seynt Savyour.

And 8 myle from Tyre, toward the est, upon the see, is the cytee of Sarphen, in Sarept [Footnote: Zarephath.] of Sydonyeus. And there was wont for to dwelle Helye the prophete; and there reysed he Jonas the wydwes sone from dethe to lyf. And 5 myle fro Sarphen is the cytee of Sydon: of the whiche cytee, Dydo was lady, that was Eneas wyf aftre the destruccioun of Troye; and that founded the cytee of Cartage in Affrick, and now is cleped Dydon Sayete. And in the cytee of Tyre regned Agenore the fadre of Dydo. And 16 myles from Sydon is Beruthe. [Footnote: Beyrout.] And from Beruthe to Sardenare is 3 journeys. And from Sardenar is 5 myle to Damask.

And whoso wil go longe tyme on the see, and come nerrer to Jerusalem, he schal go fro Cipre, be see, to the port Jaff. [Footnote: Jaffa.] For that is the nexte havene to Jerusalem. For fro that havene is not but o day journeye and an half to Jerusalem. And the town is called Jaff; for on of the sones of

Noe, that highte Japhet, founded it; and now it is clept Joppe. And zee schulle undrestonde, that it is on of the oldest townes of the world: for it was founded, before Noes flode. And zitt there schewethe in the roche ther, as the irene cheynes were festned, that Andromade, a gret geaunt was bounden with, and put in presoun before Noes flode: of the whiche geaunt is a rib of his syde, that is 40 fote longe. [Footnote: Our author here takes Andromeda for the monster that would have devoured her.]

And whoso wil arryve at the firste port of Thire or Surre, that I have spoken of before, may go be londe, zif he wil, to Jerusalem. And men gothe fro Surre unto the citee of Dacoun [Footnote: St. Jean d'Acre.] in a day. And it was clept somtyme Tholomayde. And it was somtyme a cytee of Cristenemen, fulle fair; but it is now destroyed: and it stont upon the see. And fro Venyse to Akoun, be see, is 2080 myles of Lombardye. And fro Calabre or fro Cecyle to Akoun, be see, is 1300 myles of Lombardye. And the ile of Crete is right in the myd weye. And besyde the cytee of Akoun, toward the see, 120 furlonges on the right syde, toward the southe, is the hylle of Carmelyn, where Helyas the prophete dwellede: and there was first the ordre of Freres Carmes founded. This hille is not right gret, ne fulle highe. And at the fote of this hille was somtyme a gode cytee of Cristene men, that men cleped Cayphas: For Cayphas first founded it: but it is now alle wasted. And on the lift syde of the hille Carmelyn is a town, that men clepen Saffre: and that is sett on another hille. There Seynt James and Seynt Johne were born: and in the worschipe of hem, there is a fair chirche. And fro Tholomayde, that men clepen now Akoun, unto a gret hille, that is clept Scalle of Thires, is 100 furlonges. And besyde the cytee of Akoun renneth a lytille ryvere, that is clept Belon. And there nyghe is the fosse of Mennon, that is alle round: and it is 100 cubytes of largenesse, and it is alle fulle of gravelle, schynynge brighte, of the whiche men maken fair verres [Footnote: Glass.] and clere. And men comen fro fer, by watre in schippes, and be londe with cartes, for to fetten of that gravelle. And thoughe there be nevere so moche taken awey there of, on the day, at Morwe it is as fulle azen as evere it was. And that is a gret mervaille. And there is evermore gret wynd in that fosse, that sterethe everemore the gravelle, and makethe it trouble. And zif ony man do thereinne ony maner metalle, it turnethe anon to glasse. And the glasse, that is made of that grevelle, zif it be don azen in to the gravelle, it turnethe anon in to gravelle as it was first. And therefore somme men seyn, that it was a sweloghe [Footnote: Whirlpool.] of the gravely see.

Also for Akoun aboveseyd gon men forthe 4 journees to the citee of Palestyn, that was of the Philistyenes, that now is clept Gaza, that is a gay cytee and a riche; and it is righte fayr, and fulle of folke, and it is a lytillle fro the see. And from this cytee broughte Sampson the stronge the zates upon an highe lond, whan he was taken in that cytee: and there he slowghe in a paleys the king and hymself, and gret nombre of the beste of the Philistienes, the whiche had put out his eyen, and schaven his hed, and enprisound him, be tresoun of Dalida his paramour. And therefore he made falle upon hem a gret halle, whan thei were at mete. And from thens gon men to the cytee of Cesaire, and so to the Castelle of pylgrymes, and so to Ascolonge, and than to Jaffe, and so to Jerusalem.

Of manye Names of Soudans, and of the Tour of Babiloyn.

[Sidenote: Cap. V.] And whoso wille go be londe thorghe the lond of Babyloyne, where the Sowdan dwellethe comonly, he moste gete grace of him and leve, to go more sikerly [Footnote: Surely.] thorghe tho londes and contrees. And for to go to the mount of Synay, before that men gon Jerusalem, thei schalle go fro Gaza to the castelle of Daire. And after that, men comen out of Surrye, and entren in to wyldernesse, and there the weye is sondy. And that wyldernesse and desert lastethe 8 journeyes. But alleweyes men fynden gode innes, and alle that hem nedethe of vytaylle; And men clepen that wyldernesse Achelleke. And whan a man comethe out of that desert, he entrethe in to Egypt, that men clepen Egypt Canopac: and aftre other langage, men clepen it Morsyn. And there first men fynden a gode toun, that is clept Belethe; and it is at the ende of the kyngdom of Halappee. And from thens men gon to Babyloyne and to Cayre.

At Babyloyne there is a faire chirche of oure lady, where sche dwelled 7 zeer, whan sche fleyghe out of the lond of Judee, for drede of Kyng Heroude. And there lythe the body of Seynt Barbre the Virgine and Martyr. And there duelled Josephe whan he was sold of his bretheren. And there made Nabugodonozor the kyng putte three children in to the forneys of fuyr; for thei weren in the righte trouthe of beleeve: the whiche children men cleped, Ananya, Azaria, Mizælle; as the Psalm of Benedicite seythe. But Nabugodbnozor cleped hem other wise, Sydrak, Misak, and Abdenago: that is to seye, God glorious, God victorious, and God over alle thinges and remes. [Footnote: Realms.] And that was for the myracle, that he soughe Goddes sone go with the children thorghe the fuyr, as he seyde. There duellethe the Soudan in his Calahelyke, (for there is comounly his see) in a fayr castelle strong and gret and wel sett upon a roche. In that castelle duellen alle wey, to kepe it and to serve the Sowdan, mo than 6000 persones, that taken alle here necessaries of the Sowdanes court. I oughte right wel to knowen it; for I duelled with him as Soudyour in his werres a gret while, azen the Bedoynes. And he wolde have maryed me fulle highely, to a gret princes daughtre, zif I wolde han forsaken my lawe and my beleve. But I thanke God, I had no wille to don it, for no thing, that he behighten [Footnote: Promised.] me. And zee schulle undrestonde, that the Soudan is lord of 5 kyngdomes, that he hathe conquered and apropred to him be strengthe: and theise ben the names, the kyngdom of Canapak, that is Egypt; and the kyngdom of Jerusalem, where that David and Salomon were kynges; and the kyngdom of Surrye, of the whiche the cytee of Damasc was chief; and the kyngdom of Alappe, [Footnote: Aleppo.] in the lond of Mathe, and the kyngdom of Arabye, that was to on of the 3 kynges, that made offrying to oure Lord, whan he was born. And many othere londes he holdethe in his hond. And there with alle he holdethe calyffes, that is a fulle gret thing in here langage: and it is als meche to seye as kyng. And there were wont to ben 5 Soudans: but now there is no mo but he of Egypt. And the firste Soudan was Zarocon, that was of Mede, (as was fadre to Sahaladyn) that toke the Califfe of Egypt and sloughe him, and was made Soudan be strengthe. Aftre that was Soudan Sahaladyn, in whoos tyme the Kyng of Englonde, Richarde the firste, with manye othere, kepten the passage, that Sahaladyn ne myghte not passen. Aftre Sahaladyn, regned his sone Boradyn; aftre him his nephewe. Aftre that the Comaynz, that weren in servage in Egypt, felten hem self, that thei weren of gret power, thei chesen hem a Soudain amonges hem: the whiche made him to ben cleped Melethesalan. And in his tyme entred in to the contree, of the kynges of France, Seynt Lowyz, and foughte with him: and the Soudan toke him and enprisound him. And this was slayn of his owne servauntes. And aftre thei chosen an other to be Soudan, that thei cleped Tympieman. And he let delyveren Seynt Lowys out of presoun, for certeyn ransoum. And aftre on theise Comaynz regned, that highte Cachas, and sloughe Tympieman, for to be Soudan: and made him ben cleped Melechemes. And aftre, another that hadde to name Bendochdare, that sloughe Melechemes, for to be Soudan; and cleped himself Melechdare. In his tyme entred the gode Kyng Edward of Englond in Syrye, and dide gret harm to the Sarrazines. And aftre was this Soudan empoysound at Damasce; and his sone thoghte to regne aftre him be heritage, and made him to ben clept Meleschsache. But another, that had to name Elphy, chaced him out of the contree, and made him Soudan. This man toke the cytee of Tripolee and destroyede manye of the Cristene men, the zeer of grace 1289; but he was anon slayn. Aftre that was the sone of Elphy chosen to ben Soldan, and cleped him Mellethasseraff: and he toke the citee of Akoun, and chaced out the Christene men: and this was also empoysond. And than was his brother y made Soudan, and was cleped Melechnasser. And aftre, on that was clept Guytoga, toke him and put him in prisoun, in the Castelle of Mountryvalle; and made him Soudan be strengthe, and cleped him Melechcadelle: and he was of Tartaryne. But the Comaynz chaced him out of the contree, and diden hym meche sorwe; and maden on of hem self Soudan, that hadde to name Lachyn. And he made him to ben clept Melechmanser: the whiche on a day pleyed at the chesse, and his swerd lay besyde him; and so befelle, that on wratthed [Footnote: Provoked.] him, and with his owne propre swerd he was slayn.

And aftre that, thei weren at gret discord, for to make a Soudan. And finally thei accordeden to Melechnasser, that Guytoga had put in prisoun at Mountrivalle. And this regnede longe and governed wisely; so that his eldest sone was chosen aftre him, Melechemader; the whiche his brother leet sle prevyly, for to have the lordschipe, and made him to ben clept Melechmadabron. And he was Soudan, whan I departed fro the contrees. And wyte zee wel, that the Soudan may lede out of Egipt mo than 20000 men of armes. And out of Surrye, and out of Turkye, and out of other contrees, that he holt, he may arrere [Footnote: Raise.—Anglo-Saxon, *Arœran*.] mo than 50000. And alle tho ben at his wages: and thei ben alle weys at him, withouten the folke of his contree, that is withouten nombre. And everyche of hem hath be zere the mountance of 6 score floreynes. But it behovethe, that every of hem holde 3 hors and a cameylle. And be the cytees and be the townes ben amyralles, that han the governance of the peple. On hath to governe 4, and another hath to governe 5, another mo, and another wel mo. And als moche takethe the amyralle be him allone, as alle the other souldyours han undre hym. And therfore whan the Soudan wille avance ony worthi knyghte, he makethe him a amyralle. And whan it is ony derthe, the knyghtes ben right pore, and thanne thei sellen both here hors and here harneys. And the Soudan hath 4 wyfes, on Cristene and 3 Sarazines: of the whiche, on dwellethe at Jerusalem, and another at Damasce, and another at Ascalon. And whan hem lyst, thei remewen to other cytees. And whan the Soudan wille, he may go visite hem. And he hathe as many paramours, as hym lykethe. For he makethe to come before him, the fairest and the nobleste of birthe and the gentylleste damyseles of his contree, and he maketh hem to ben kept and served fulle honourabely, and whan he wole have on to lye withe him, he makethe hem alle to come before him; and he beholdethe in alle, whiche of hem is most to his plesance, and to hire anon he sendethe or castethe a ryng fro his fyngre: And thanne anon sche schalle ben bathed and richely atyred, and anoynted with delicat thinges of swete smelle, and than lad to the Soudanes chambre. And thus he dothe, als often as him list, when he wil have ony of hem. And before the Soudan comethe no strangier, but zif he be clothed in clothe of gold or of Tartarye or of Camaka, in the Sarazines guyse, and as the Sarazines usen. And it behovethe, that anon at the firste sight, that men see the Soudan, be it in wyndowe, or in what place elles, that men knele to him and kysse the erthe: for that is the manere to do reverence to the Soudanne, of hem that speken with him. And whan that messangeres of straunge contrees comen before him, the Meynee of the Soudan, whan the straungeres speken to hym, thei ben aboute the Souldan with swerdes drawen and gysarmez and axes, here armes lift up in highe with the wepenes, for to smyte upon hem, zif thei seye ony woord, that is displeasance to the Soudan. And also, no straungere comethe before him, but that he makethe him sum promys and graunt, of that the straungere asketh resonabely, beso it be not azenst his Lawe. And so don othere prynces bezonden. For thei seyn, that no man schalle come before no prynce, but that he be bettre, and schalle be more gladdere in departynge from his presence, thannie he was at the comynge before hym.

And undirstonde zee, that that Babyloyne that I have spoken offe, where that the Soudan duellethe, is not that gret Babyloyne, where the dyversitee of langages was first made for vengeance, by the myracle of God, when the grete tour of Babel was begonnen to ben made; of the whiche the walles weren 64 furlonges of heighte; that is in the grete desertes of Arabye, upon the weye as men gon toward the kyngdom of Caldee. But it is fulle long, sithe that ony man durste neyhe to the tour; for it is alle deserte and fulle of dragouns and grete serpentes, and fulle of dyverse venymouse bestes alle abouten. That tour, with the cytee, was of 25 myle in cyrcuyt of the walles; as thei of the contree seyn, and as men may demen [Footnote: Judge.] by estymation, aftre that men tellen of the contree. And though it be clept the tour of Babiloyne, zit natheles there were ordeyned with inne many mansiouns and many gret duellynge places, in lengthe and brede: and that tour conteyned gret contree in circuyt: for the tour allone conteyned 10 myle sqware. That tour founded Kyng Nembrothe, that was kyng of that contree: and he was firste kyng of the world. And he leet make an ymage in the lyknesse of his fadre, and constreyned alle his subgettes for to worschipe it. And anon begonnen othere lordes to do the same. And so begonnen the ydoles and symulacres first. The town and the cytee weren fulle wel sett in a fair contree and a playn; that men clepen the contree of Samar: of the whiche the walles of the cytee werein 200 cubytes in heighte, and 50 cubytes in breadthe. And the ryvere of Euphrate ran thorghe out the cytee and aboute the tour also. But Cirus the Kyng of Perse toke from hem the ryvere, and destroyede all the cytee and the tour also. For he departed that ryvere in 360 smale ryveres: because that he had sworn, that he scholde putte the ryvere in suche poynt, that a woman myghte wel passe there, withouten castynge of of hire clothes; for als moche as he hadde lost many worthi men, that trowden to passen that ryvere by swymmynge.

And from Babyloyne, where the Soudan dwellethe, to go right betwene the oryent and the Septemtryon, toward the grete Babyloyne, is 40 journeys to passen be desart. But it is not the grete Babiloyne, in the lond and in the powere of the seyd Soudan; but it is in the power and the lordschipe of Persye. But he holdethe it of the grete Cham, that is the gretteste Emperour and the most sovereyn lord of alle the partes bezonde: and he is lord of the iles of Cathay and of many othere iles, and of a gret partie of Inde. And his lond marchethe unto Prestre Johnes lond; and he holt so moche lond, that he knowethe not the ende. And he is more myghty and grettre lord withoute comparisoun, than is the Soudan. Of his ryalle estate and of his myghte, I schalle speke more plenerly when I schalle speke of the lond and of the contree of Ynde.

Also the cytee of Methone [Footnote: Mecca.] where Machomet lythe, is of the grete desertes of Arabye. And there lithe the body of hym fulle honourabely in here temple, that the Sarazines clepen Muskethe. And it is fro Babyloyne the lesse, where the Soudan duellethe, onto Methon aboveseyd, in to a 32 journeyes. And wytethe wel, that the rewme of Arabye is a fulle gret contree: but there in is over moche dysert. And no man may dwelle there in that desert, for defaute of watre. For that lond is alle gravelly and fulle of sond. And it is drye and nothing fructuous; because that it hathe no moysture: and therefore is there so meche desart. And ziff it hadde ryveres and welles, and the lond also were, as it is in other parties, it scholde ben als fulle of peple and als fulle enhabyted with folk, as in other places. For there is fulle gret multitude of peple, where as the lond is enhabyted. Arabye durethe fro the endes of the reme of Caldee, unto the laste ende of Affryk, and marchethe to the lond of Ydumee, toward the ende of Botron. And in Caldee, the chief cytee is Baldak. [Footnote: Bagdad.] And of Affryk, the chief cytee is Cartage, that Dydo, that was Eneas wyf, founded. The whiche Eneas was of the cytee of Troye, and aftre was Kyng of Itaylle. Mesopotamye strecchethe also unto the Desertes of Arabye; and it is a gret contree. In this contree is the cytee of Araym, where Abrahames fadree duelled, and from whens Abraham departed, be commandement of the aungelle. And of that cytee was Effraym, that was a gret clerk and a gret doctour. And Theophylus was of that cytee also, that oure ladye savede from oure enemye. And Mesopotame durethe fro the ryvere of Eufrates, unto the ryvere of Tygris. For it is betwene tho 2 ryveres. And bezonde the ryvere of Tygre, is Caldee, that is a fulle gret kyngdom. In that Rewyme, at Baldac aboveseyd, was wont to duelle the Calyffeez, that was wont to ben bothe as Emperour and Pope of the Arabyenez; so that he was lord spirituelle and temporelle. And he was successour to Machomete, and of his generatioun; That cytee of Baldak was wont to ben cleped Sutis: [Footnote: Susa.] and Nabugodonozor founded it. And there duelled the holy prophete Daniel; and there he saughe vissiones of Hevene; and there he made the expositioun of dremes. And in old tyme, there were ['wene' in source text—KTH] wont to be 3 Calyffez; and thei dwelleden in the cytee of Baldak aboveseyd.

And at Cayre besides Babyloyne duelled the Calyffee of Egypt. And at Marrok, upon the west see, duelte the Calyffee of Barbaryenes and of Affrycanes. And now is there non of the Calyffeez, ne noughte han ben, sithe the tyme of Sowdan Sahaladyn. For from that tyme hidre, the Sowdan clepethe him self Calyffee. And so han the Calyffeez y lost here name. Also wytethe wel, that Babylone the lesse, where the Soudan duellethe, and at the cytee of Cayr, that is nyghe besyde it, ben grete huge cytees manye and fayr; and that on sytt nyghe that other. Babyloyne sytt upon the ryvere of Gyson, somtyme clept Nyle, that comethe out of Paradys terrestre. That ryvere of Nyle, alle the zeer, whan the sonne entrethe in to the signe of Cancer, it begynnethe to wexe; and it wexethe alle weys, als longe as the sonne is in Cancro, and in the signe of Lyoune. And it wexethe in suche manere, that it is somtyme so gret, that it is 20 cubytes or more of depnesse; and thanne it doth gret harm to the godes, that ben upon the lond. For thanne may no man travaylle to ere [Footnote: Plough.] the londes, for the grete moystness: and therefore is there dere tyme in that contree. And also whan it waxethe lytylle, it is dere tyme in that contree: for defaute of moysture. And whan the sonne is in the signe of Virgo, thanne begynnethe the ryvere for to wane and to decrece lytyl and lytylle; so that whan the sonne is entred into the signe of Libra, thanne thei entren betwene theise ryveres. This ryvere comethe rennynge from Paradys terrestre, betwene the desertes of Ynde; and aftre it smytt unto londe, and rennethe longe tyme many grete contrees undre erthe: and aftre it gothe out undre an highe hille, that men clepen Alothe, that is betwene Ynde and Ethiope, the distance of five monethsjourneyes fro the entree of Ethiope. And aftre it envyronnethe alle Ethiope and Morekane, and gothe alle along fro the Lond of Egipte; unto the cytee of Alisandre, to the ende of Egipte; and there it fallethe into the See. Aboute this ryvere, ben manye briddes and foules, as sikonyes, that thei clepen ibes.

Egypt is a long contree; but it is streyt, that is to seye narow; for thei may not enlargen it toward the desert, for defaute of watre. And the contree is sett along upon the ryvere of Nyle; be als moche as that ryvere may serve be flodes or otherwise, that whanne it flowethe, it may spreden abrood thorghe the contree: so is the contree large of lengthe. For there it reyneth not but litylle in that contree: and for that cause, they have no watre, but zif it be of that flood of that ryvere. And for als moche as it ne reynethe not in that contree, but the eyr is alwey pure and cleer, therfore in that contree ben the gode astronomyeres; for thei fynde there no cloudes, to letten hem. Also the cytee of Cayre is righte gret, and more huge than that of Babyloyne the lesse: and it sytt aboven toward the desert of Syrye, a lytille above the ryvere aboveseyd. In Egipt there ben 2 parties; the Heghte, that is toward Ethiope; and the Lowenesse, that is towardes Arabye. In Egypt is the lond of Ramasses and the lond of Gessen. Egipt is a strong contree: for it hathe manye schrewede havenes, because of the grete Roches, that ben stronge and daungerouse to passe by. And at Egipt, toward the est, is the rede see, that durethe unto the cytee of Coston: and toward the west, is the contree of Lybye, that is a fulle drye lond, and litylle of fruyt: for it is over moche plentee of hete. And that lond is clept Fusthe. And toward the partie

Meridionalle is Ethiope. And toward the Northe is the desart, that durethe unto Syrye: and so is the contree strong on alle sydes. And it is wel a 15 journeyes of lengthe, and more than two so moche of desert: and it is but two journeyes in largenesse. And between Egipt and Nubye, it hathe wel a 12 journees of desert. And men of Nubye ben Cristene: but thei ben blake as the Mowres, for grete hete of the sonne.

In Egipt there ben 5 provynces; that on highte Sahythe, that other highte Demeseer, another Resithe, that is an ile in Nyle, another Alisandre, and another the lond of Damiete. That cytee was wont to be righte strong; but it was twyes wonnen of the Cristene men: and therfore after that the Sarazines beten down the walles. And with the walles and the tour thereof, the Sarazenes maden another cytee more fer from the see, and clepeden it the newe Damyete. So that now no man duellethe at the rathere toun of Damyete. And that cytee of Damyete is on of the havenes of Egypt: and at Alisandre is that other, that is a fulle strong cytee. But there is no watre to drynke, but zif it come be condyt from Nyle, that entrethe in to here cisternes. And who so stopped that watre from hem, thei myghte not endure there. In Egypt there ben but fewe forcelettes or castelles, be cause that the contree is so strong of him self. At the desertes of Egyptes was a worthi man, that was an holy heremyte; and there mette with hym a monstre, (that is to seyne, a monstre is a thing difformed azen kynde both of man or of best or of ony thing elles: and that is cleped a monstre). And this monstre, that mette with this holy heremyte, was as it hadde ben a man, that hadde 2 hornes trenchant on his forehede; and he hadde a body lyk a man, unto the nabele; and benethe he hadde the body lyche a goot. And the heremyte asked him, what he was. And the monstre answerde him, and seyde, he was a dedly creature, suche as God hadde formed, and duelled in tho desertes in purchasynge his Sustynance; and besoughte the heremyte, that he wolde preye God for him, the whiche that cam from Hevene for to saven alle mankynde, and was born of a Mayden, and suffred passioun and dethe, (as we well knowen) be whom we lyven and ben. And zit is the hede with the 2 hornes of that monstre at Alisandre for a Marveyle.

In Egypt is the cytee of Elyople, [Footnote: Heliopolis.] that is to seyne, the cytee of the sonne. In that cytee there is a temple made round, aftre the schappe of the temple of Jerusalem. The prestes of that temple han alle here wrytinges, undre the date of the foul that is clept Fenix: and there is non but on in alle the world. And he comethe to brenne him self upon the awtere of the temple, at the ende of 5 hundred zeer: for so longe he lyvethe. And at the 500 zeers ende, the prestes arrayen here awtere honestly, and putten there upon spices and sulphur vif [Footnote: Live.] and other thinges, that wolen brenne lightly. And than the brid fenix comethe, and brennethe him self to ashes. And the first day next aftre, men fynden in the ashes a worm; and the secunde day next aftre, men fynden a brid quyk and perfyt; and the thridde day next aftre, he fleethe his wey. And so there is no mo briddes of that kynde in alle the world, but it allone. And treuly that is a gret myracle of God. And men may well lykne that bryd unto God; be cause that there nys no God but on; and also, that our Lord aroos fro dethe to lyve, the thridde day. This bryd men seen often tyme, fleen in tho contrees: and he is not mecheles more than an Egle. And he hathe a crest of fedres upon his hed more gret than the poocock hathe; and his nekke is zalowe, aftre colour of an orielle, [Footnote: Golden. From Latin, *Aurea*. Cf. Oriel College, Golden Hall.] that is a ston well schynynge; and his bek is coloured blew, as ynde; [Footnote: Indigo.] and his wenges ben of purple colour, and the Taylle is zelow and red, castynge his taylle azens in travers. And he is a fulle fair brid to loken upon, azenst the sonne: for he schynethe fully gloriously and nobely.

Also in Egypt ben gardyns, than han trees and herbes, the whiche beren frutes 7 tymes in the zeer. And in that lond men fynden many fayre emeraudes and y nowe. And therefore thei ben there grettere cheep. Also whan it reynethe ones in the somer, in the lond of Egipt, thanne is alle the contree fulle of grete myrs. Also at Cayre, that I spak of before, sellen men comounly bothe men and wommen of other lawe, as we don here bestes in the markat. And there is a comoun hows in that cytee, that is alle fulle of smale furneys; and thidre bryngen wommen of the toun here eyren [Footnote: Eggs.] of hennes, of gees and of dokes, for to ben put in to tho furneyses. And thei that kepen that hows covern hem with hete of hors dong, with outen henne, goos or doke or ony other foul; and at the ende of 3 wekes or of a monethe, they comen azen and taken here chickenes and norissche hem and bryngen hem forthe: so that alle the contre is fulle of hem. And so men don there bothe wyntre and somer.

Also in that contree, and in othere also, men fynden longe apples to selle, in hire cesoun: and men clepen hem apples of paradys; and thei ben righte swete and of gode savour. [Footnote: Melons.] And thoghe zee kutte hem in never so many gobettes or parties, overthwart or end longes, evermore zee schulle fynden in the myddes the figure of the Holy Cros of oure Lord Jesu. But thei will roten within 8 days: and for that cause men may not carye of the apples to no fer contrees. And thei han grete leves, of a fote and an half of lengthe: and thei ben covenably large. And men fynden there also the appulle tree of Adam, that han a byte at on of the sydes. And there ben also fyge trees, that baren no leves, but fyges upon the smale braunches; and men clepen hem figes of Pharoon. Also besyde Cayre, withouten that cytee, is the feld where bawme growethe: and it cometh out on smale trees, that ben non hyere than a mannes breek girdle: and thei semen as wode that is of the wylde vyne. And in that feld ben 7 welles, that oure Lord Jesu Crist made with on of his feet, whan he wente to pleyen with other children. That feld is not so well closed, but that men may entren at here owne list. But in that cesonne, that the bawme is growynge, men put there to gode kepynge, that no man dar ben hardy to entre. This bawme growethe in no place, but only there. And thoughe that men bryngen of the plauntes, for to planten in other contrees, thei growen wel and fayre, but thei bryngen forthe no fructuous thing: and the leves of bawme ne fallen noughte. And men kutten the braunches with a scharp flynston or with a scherp bon, [Footnote: Flintstone and bone.] whan men will go to kutte hem: For who so kutte hem with iren, it wolde destroye his vertue and his nature. And the Sarazines clepen the wode Enoch balse; and the fruyt, the whiche is as Quybybes, thei clepen Abebissam; and the lycour, that droppethe fro the braunches, thei clepen Guybalse. And men maken alle weys that bawme to ben tyled [Footnote: Tilled.] of the Cristenemen, or elles it wolde not fructifye; as the Sarazines seyn hem self: for it hathe ben often tyme preved. Men seyn also, that the bawme growethe in Ynde the more, in that desert where the trees of the sonne and of the mone spak to Alisaundre. But I have not seen it. For I have not ben so fer aboven upward: because that there ben to many perilouse passages. And wyte zee wel, that a man oughte to take gode kepe for to bye bawme, but zif he cone knowe it righte wel: for he may righte lyghtely be discoyved. For men sellen a gome, that men clepen turbentyne, in stede of bawme; and thei putten there to a littille bawme for to zeven gode odour. And some putten wax in oyle of the wode of the fruyt of bawme, and seyn that it is bawme: and sume destyllen clowes of gylofre and of spykenard of Spayne and of othere spices, that ben well smellynge; and the lykour that gothe out there of, thei clepe it bawme: and thei wenen, that thei han bawme; and thei have non. For the Sarazines counterfeten it be sotyltee of craft, for to disceyven the Cristene men, as I have sene fulle many a tyme. And after hem, the marchauntis and the apotecaries countrefeten it eftsones, and that it is lasse worthe, and a gret del worse. But zif it lyke zou, I schalle schewe, how zee schulle knowe and preve, to the ende that zee schulle not ben disceyved. First zee schulle wel knowe, that the naturelle bawme is fulle cleer, and of cytrine colour, and stronge smellynge; and zif it be thykke, or reed or blak, it is sophisticate, that is to seyne, contrefeted and made lyke it, for disceyt. And undrestondethe, that zif zee wil putte a litylle bawme in the pawme of zoure hond, azen the sonne, zif it be fyn and gode, zee ne schulle not suffre zoure hand azenst the hete of the sonne. Also takethe a lytille bawme, with the poynt of a knif, and touche it to the fuyr, and zif it brenne, it is a gode signe. Aftre take also a drope of bawme, and put it in to a dissche or in a cuppe with mylk of a goat; and zif it be naturelle bawme, anon it wole take and beclippe the mylk. Or put a drope of bawme in clere watre, in a cuppe of sylver or in a clere bacyn, and stere it wel with the clere watre; and zif that the bawme be fyn and of his owne kynde, the watre schalle nevre trouble: and zif the bawme be sophisticate, that is to seyne countrefeted, the watre schalle become anon trouble: And also zif the bawme be fyn, it schalle falle to the botome of the vesselle, as thoughe it were Quyksylver: For the fyn bawme is more hevy twyes, than is the bawme that is sophisticate and countrefeted. Now I have spoken of Bawme: and now also I schalle speke of an other thing, that is bezonde Babyloyne, above the flode of Nyle, toward the desert, betwene Affrik and Egypt: that is to seyn, of the gerneres [Footnote: Granaries.] of Joseph, that he leet make, for to kepe the greynes for the perile of the dere zeres. And thei ben made of ston, fulle wel made of massones craft: of the whiche two ben merveylouse grete and hye; and the tothere ne ben not so grete. And every gerner hathe a zate, for to entre with inne, a lytille hyghe fro the erthe. For the lond is wasted and fallen, sithe the gerneres were made. And with inne thei ben alle fulle of serpentes. And aboven the gerneres with outen ben many scriptures of dyverse langages. And sum men seyn, that thei ben sepultures of grete lordes, that weren somtyme; but that is not trewe: for alle the comoun rymour and speche is of alle the peple there, bothe and nere, that thei ben the garneres of Joseph. And so fynden thei in here scriptures and in here cronycles. On that other partie, zif thei were sepultures, thei scholden not ben voyd with inne. For zee may well knowe, that tombes and sepultures ne ben not made of suche gretnesse, ne of such highnesse. Wherfore it is not to believe, that thei ben tombes or sepultures. In Egypt also there ben dyverse langages and dyverse lettres, and of other manere condicioun, than there ben in other parties. As I schalle devyse zou, suche as thei ben, and the names how thei clepen hem; to suche entent, that zee mowe knowe the difference of hem and of othere. Athoimis, Bunchi, Chinok, Durain, Eni, Fin, Gomor, Heket, Janny, Karacta, Luzanim, Miche, Naryn, Oldache, Piloh, Quyn, Yron, Sichen, Thola, Urmron, Yph and Yarm, Thoit.

Now will I retourne azen, or I procede ony ferthere, for to declare zou the othere weyes, that drawen toward Babiloyne, where the Soudan him self duellethe, that is at the entree of Egypt; for als moche as mony folk gon thidre first, and aftre that to the Mount Synay, and aftre retournen to Jerusalem, as I have seyd zou here beforn. For thei fulfillen first the more long pilgrymage, and aftre retournen azen be the nexte weyes; because that the more nye weye is the more worthi, and that is Jerusalem. For no other pylgrymage is not lyk, in comparsoun to it. But for to fulle fylle here pilgrymages more esily and more sykerly, men gon first the longer weye. But whoso wil go to Babyloyne be another weye, more schort from the contrees of the west, that I have reherced before; or from other contrees next fro hem; than men gon by Fraunce, be Burgoyne and be Lombardye. It nedethe not to telle zou the names of the cytees, ne of the townes that ben in that Weye: for the weye is comoun, and it is knowen of many naciouns. And there ben many havenes, that men taken the see. Sume men taken the see at Gene, some at Venyce, and passen by the see Adryatyk, that is clept the Goulf of Venyse; that departethe [Footnote: Separates.] Ytaylle and Greece on that syde. And some gon to Naples, some to Rome, and from Rome to Brandys, [Footnote: Brindisi.] and there thei taken the see: and in many othere places, where that havenes ben. And men gon be Tussye, be Champayne, be Calabre, be Appuille, and be the hilles of Ytaylle, Chorisqe, be Sardyne, and be Cycile, that is a gret ile and a gode. In that ile of Cycile there ys a maner of a gardyn, in the whiche ben many dyverse frutes. And the gardyn is alweys grene and florisshing, alle the cesouns of the zeer, als wel in wyntre es in somer. That yle holt in compas aboute 350 Frensche myles. And betwene Cycele and Itaylle there is not but a lytille arm of the see, that men clepen the farde of Mescyne. And Cycile is betwene the See Adryatyk and the See of Lombardye. And fro Cycyle in to Calabre is but 8 myles of Lombardye. And in Cycile there is a manere of serpentes, be the whiche men asseyen and preven, where here children ben bastardis or none, or of lawefulle mariage. For zif thei ben born in righte mariage, the serpentes gon aboute hem, and don hem non harm: and zif thei ben born in Avowtrie, the serpentes byten hem and envenyme hem. And thus manye wedded men preve, zif the children ben here owne. Also in that ile is the Mount Ethna, that men clepen Mount Gybelle; and the Vulcanes that ben evermore brennynge. And ther ben 7 places that brennen and that casten out dyverse flawmes and dyverse colour. And be the chaungynge of tho flawmes, men of that contree knowen, whanne it schalle be derthe or gode tyme, or cold or hoot, or moyst or drye, or in alle othere maneres, how the tyme schalle be governed. And from Itaille unto the Vulcanes nys bat 25 Myle. And men seyn, that the Vulcanes ben weyes of Helle.

Also whoso gothe be Pyse, zif that men list to go that weye, there is an arm of the see, where that men gon to othere havenes in tho marches. And that men passen be the Ile of Greaf, that is at Gene: and aftre arryvethe men in Grece at the havene of the cytee of Myrok, or at the havene of Valone, or at the cytee of Duras: and there is a duk at Duras, or at othere havenes in tho marces: and so men gon to Costantynoble. And aftre gon men be watre to the Ile of Crete, and to the Ile of Rodes, ond so to Cypre, and so to Athens, and fro thens to Costantynoble.

To holde the more righte weye be see, it is wel a 1880 myle of Lombardye. And aftre fro Cipre men gon be see, and leven Jerusalem and alle the contree on the left hond, onto Egypt, and arryven at the cytee of Damyete, that was wont to be fulle strong, and it sytt at the entree of Egypt. And fro Damyete gon men to the cytee of Alizandre, that sytt also upon the see. In that cytee was seynte Kateryne beheded. And there was seynt Mark the

Evangelist martyred and buryed. But the Emperour Leoun made his bones to ben broughte to Venyse. And zit there is at Alizandre a faire chirche, alle white withouten peynture: and so ben alle the othere chirches, that weren of the Cristene men, alle white with inne. For the Panemes and the Sarrazynes madem hem white, for to fordon [Footnote: To destroy.—Anglo-Saxon, *for-don*.] the ymages of seyntes, that weren peynted on the walles. That cytee of Alizandre is wel 30 furlonges in lengthe: but it is but 10 on largenesse. And it is a full noble cytee and a fayr. At that cytee entrethe the ryvere of Nyle in to the see; as I to zou have seyd before. In that ryvere men fynden many precyouse stones, and meche also of lignum aloes: and it is a manere of wode, that comethe out of Paradys terrestre, the whiche is good for manye dyverse medicynes: and it is righte dereworthe. And fro Alizandre men gon to Babyloyne, where the Soudan dwellethe; that sytt also upon the ryvere of Nyle. And this wey is most schort, for to go streyghte unto Babiloyne.

Now schall I seye zou also the weye, that gothe fro Babiloyne to the Mount of Synay, where Seynte Kateryne lythe. He moste passe be the desertes of Arabye; be the whiche descries Moyses ladde the peple of Israel: and thanne passe men be the welle, that Moyses made with his hond in the desertes, whan the people grucched, [Footnote: Grumbled.] for thei fownden no thing to drynke. And than passe men be the welle of Marache, of the whiche the watre was first byttre: but the children of Israel putten there inne a tree; and anon the watre was swete and gode for to drynke. And thanne gon men be desart unto the Vale of Elyn; in the whiche vale be 12 welles: and there ben 72 trees of palme, that beren the dates, the whiche Moyses fond with the children of Israel. And fro that valeye is but a gode journeye to the Mount of Synay.

And whoso wil go be another weye fro Babiloyne, than men gothe be the Rede See, that is an arm of the see occean. And there passed Moyses, with the children of Israel, overthwart the see, alle drye, whan Pharao the Kyng of Egypt chaced hem. And that see is wel a 6 myle of largenesse in bredthe. And in that see was Pharao drowned and alle his hoost, that he ladde. That see is not more reed than another see; but in some place thereof is the gravelle reede: and therfore men clepen it the Rede See. That see reunethe to the endes of Arabye and of Palestyne. That see lastethe more than 4 journeyes. And then gon men be desert unto the Vale of Elyn: and fro thens to the Mount of Synay. And zee may wel undirstonde, that be this desert, no man may go on hors back, be cause that there nys nouther mete for hors ne watre to drynke. And for that cause men passen that desert with camelle. For the camaylle fynt alle wey mete in trees and on busshes, that he fedethe him with. And he may well faste fro drynk 2 dayes or 3: and that may non hors don.

And wyte wel, that from Babiloyne to the Mount Synay is wel a 12 gode journeyes: and some men maken hem more: and some men hasten hem and peynen hem; and therefore thei maken hem lesse. And alle weys fynden men latyneres [Footnote: Men who speak Latin.] to go with hem in the contrees, and ferthere bezonde, in to tyme that men conne [Footnote: Know.] the langage. And it behovethe men to here vitaille with hem, that schalle duren hem in tho desertes, and other necessaries for to lyve by.

And the Mount of Synay is clept the Desert of Syne, that is for to seyne the bussche brennynge: because there Moyses sawghe oure Lord God many tymes, in forme of fuyr brennynge upon that hille; and also in a bussche brennynge; and spak to him. And that was at the foot of the hille. There is an abbeye of monks, wel bylded and wel closed with zates of iren, for drede of the wylde bestes. And the monkes ben Arrabyenes, or men of Greece: and there is a grot covent; and alle thei ben as heremytes; and thei drynken no wyn, but zif it be on principalle festes: and thei ben fulle devoute men, and lyven porely and sympely, with joutes [Footnote: The original note reads 'Gourds', but joutes are actually herbs—KTH.] and with dates: and thei don gret absteynence and penaunce. There is the Chirche of Seynt Kateryne, in the whiche ben manye lampes brennynge. For thei han of oyle of olyves y now, bothe for to brenne in here lampes, and to ete also: and that plentee have thei be the myracle of God. For the ravenes and the crowes and the choughes, and other foules of the contree assemblen hem there every zeer ones, and fleen thider as in pilgrymage: and eyeryche of hem bringethe a braunche of the bayes or of olyve, in here bekes, in stede of offryng, and leven hem there; of the whiche the monkes maken gret plentee of oyle; and this is a gret marvaylle. And sithe that foules, that han no kyndely wytt ne resoun, gon thidre to seche that gloriouse virgyne; wel more oughten men than to seche hire and to worschipen hire. Also behynde the awtier of that chirche is the place where Moyses saughe oure Lord God in a brennynge bussche. And whanne the monkes entren in to that place, thei don of bothe hosen and schoon or botes alweys; be cause that oure Lord seyde to Moyses, *Do of thin hosen and thi schon: for the place that thou stondest on is lond holy and blessed.* And the monkes clepen that place Bezeleel, that is to seyne, the schadew of God. And besyde the highe awtiere, 3 degrees of heighte, is the fertre [Footnote: Bier.] of alabastre, where the bones of Seynte Kateryne lyzn. And the prelate of the monkes schewethe the relykes to the pilgrymes. And with an instrument of sylver, he frothethe the bones; [Footnote: Rubbeth.] and thanne ther gothe out a lytylle oyle, as thoughe it were a maner swetynge, that is nouther lyche to oyle ne to bawme; but it is fulle swete of smelle: And of that thei zeven a litylle to the pilgrymes; for there gothe out but litylle quantitee of the likour. And aftre that thei schewen the heed of Seynte Kateryne, and the clothe that sche was wrapped inne, that is zit alle blody. And in that same clothe so y wrapped, the aungeles beren hire body to the Mount Synay, and there thei buryed hire with it. And thanne thei schewen the bussche, that brenned and wasted nought, in the whiche oure Lord spak to Moyses, and othere relikes y nowe. Also whan the prelate of the abbeye is ded, I have undirstonden, be informacioun, that his lampe quenchethe. And whan thei chesen another prelate, zif he be a gode man and worthi to be prelate, his lampe schal lighte, with the grace of God, withouten touchinge of ony man. For everyche of hem hathe a lampe be him self. And be here lampes thei knowen wel whan ony of hem schalle dye. For whan ony schalle dye, the lyghte begynnethe to chaunge and to wexe dym. And zif he be chosen to ben prelate, and is not worthi, his lampe quenchethe anon. And other men han told me, that he that syngethe the masse for the prelate that is ded, he schalle fynde upon the awtier the name writen of him that schalle be prelate chosen. And so upon a day I asked of the monkes, bothe on and other, how this befelle. But thei wolde not telle me no thing, in to the tyme that I seyde, that thei scholde not hyde the grace, that God did hem; but that thei scholde publissche it, to make the peple to have the more devocioun; and that thei diden synne, to hide Goddis myracle, as me seemed. For the myracles, that God hathe don, and zit dothe every day, ben the wytnesse of his myghte and of his merveylles; as Dayid sethe in the Psaultere; *Mirabilia testimonia tua, Domine*: that is to seyn, *Lord, thi merveyles ben thi wytnesse*. And thanne thei tolde me, bothe on and other, how it befelle fulle many a tyme: but more I myghte not have of hem. In that abbeye ne entrethe not no flye ne todes ne ewtes, ne suche foule venymouse bestes, ne lyzs ne flees, be the myracle of God and of oure lady. For there were wont to ben many suche manere of filthes, that the monkes werein in wille to leve the place and the Abbeye, and weren gon fro thens, upon the mountayne aboven, for to eschewe that place. And oure lady cam to hem, and bad hem tournen azen: and fro this forewardes nevere entred suche filthe in that place amonges hem, ne nevere schalle entre here aftre. Also before the zate is the welle, where Moyses smot the ston, of the whiche the watre cam out plenteously.

Fro that abbeye men gon up the mountayne of Moyses, be many degrees: and there men fynden first a Chirche of oure Lady, where that sche mette the monkes, whan thei fledden awey for the vermyn aboveseyd. And more highe upon that mountayne is the chapelle of Helye the prophete. And that place thei clepen Oreb, where of Holy Writt spekethe. *Et ambulavit in fortisudine cibi illius usque ad Montem Oreb*: that is to seyne, *And he wente in strength of that mete, unto the hille of God, Oreb*. And there nyghe is the vyne that Seynt John the Evaungeliste planted, that men elepen reisins, *staphis*. And a lytille aboven is the Chapelle of Moyses, and the roche where Moyses fleghe to, for drede, when he saughe oure Lord face to face. And in that roche is prented the forme of his body; for he smot so strongly and so harde him self in that roche, that alle his body was dolven with inne, thorghe the myracle of God. And there besyde is the place where oure Lorde toke to Moyses the 10 commandementes of the lawe. And there is the cave undre the roche, where Moyses duelte, whan he fasted 40 dayes and 40 nyghtes. And from that mountayne men passen a gret valeye, for to gon to another mountayne, where Seynt Kateryne was buryed of the aungeles of oure Lord. And in that valey is a chirche of 40 martyres; and there singen the monkes of the abbeye often tyme. And that valey is right cold. And aftre men gon up the mountayne of Seynt Kateryne, that is more highe then the mount of Moyses. And there, where Seynt Kateryne was buryed, is nouther chirche ne chapelle, ne other duellynge place: but there is an heep of stones aboute the place, where the body of hire was put of the aungeles. There was wont to ben a chapelle: but it was casten downe, and zit lyggen the stones there. And alle be it that the collect of Seynte Kateryne seye, that it is the place where oure Lord betaughten the Ten Comandementes to Moyses, and there where the blessed virgyne Seynte Kateryne was buryed; that is to undrestonde, in o contree, or in o place berynge o name. For bothe that on and that othre is clept the Mount of Synay. But there is a grete weye from that on to that othre, and a gret deep valeye betwene hem.

Of the desert bet wen e the chirche of Seynte Kateryne and Jerusalem. Of the drie Tre; and how roses cam first in the world.

[Sidenote: Cap. VI.] Now aftre that men had visited tho holy places, thanne will thei turnen toward Jerusalem. And than wil thei take leve of the monkes, and recommenden hem to here preyeres. And than thei zeven the pilgrimes of here vitaylle, for to passe with the desertes, toward Surrye. And tho desertes duren wel it 13 journeyes. In that desert duellyn manye of Arrabyenes, that men clepen Bedoynes and Ascopardes. And thei ben folke fulle of alle evylle condiciouns. And thei have none houses, but tentes; that thei maken of skynnes of bestes, as of camaylles and of othere bestes, that thei eten; and there benethe thei couchen hem and duellen, in place, where thei may fynden watre, as on the Rede See or elles where For in that desert is fulle gret defaute of watre: and often time it fallethe, that where men fynden watre at o tyme in a place, it faylethe another tyme. And for that skylle, thei make none habitaciouns there. Theise folk, that I speke of, thei tylen not the lond, ne thei laboure noughte; for thei eten no bred, but zif it be ony that dwellen nyghe a gode toun, that gon thidre and eten bred som tyme. And thei rosten here flesche and here fische upon the hote stones azenst the sonne. And thei ben stronge men and wel fyghtynge. And there is so meche multytude of that folk, that thei ben withouten nombre. And thei ne recchen of no thing, ne don not, but chacen afere bestes, to eten hem. And thei recchen no thing of here lif: and therefore thei dowten not the Sowdan, ne non othre prince; but thei dar wel werre with hem, zif thei don ony thing that is grevance to hem. And thei han often tyme werre with the Soudan; and namely, that tyme that I was with him. And thei beren but o scheld and o spere, with outen other armes. And thei wrappen here hedes and here necke with a gret quantytee of white lynnen clothe. And thei ben righte felonouse and foule, and of cursed kynde.

And whan men passen this desert, in comynge toward Jerusalem, thei comen to Bersabee, that was wont to ben a fulle fair town and a delytable of Cristene men: and zit there ben summe of here chirches. In that town dwelled Abraham the patriark, a long tyme. In that toun of Bersabee, founded Bersabee the wife of Sire Urye, the knyghte; on the whiche Kyng David gatt Salomon the wyse, that was king aftre David, upon the 12 kynredes of Jerusalem, and regned 40 zeer. And fro thens gon men to the cytee of Ebron, that is the montance [Footnote: Amount.] of a gode myle. And it was clept somtyme the Vale of Mambree, and sumtyme it was clept the Vale of Teres, because that Adam wepte there, an 100 zeer, for the dethe of Abelle his sone, that Cayn slowghe. Ebron was wont to ben the princypalle cytee of Philistyenes; and there duelleden somtyme the geauntz. And that cytee was also Sacerdotalle, that is to seyne, seyntuarie, of the tribe of Juda: and it was so fre, that men resceyved there alle manere of fugityfes of other places, for here evyl dedis. In Ebron, Josue, Calephe, and here companye comen first to aspyen, how thei myghte wynnen the lond of Beheste. In Ebron regned first Kyng David, 7 zeer and an half: and in Jerusalem he regnede 33 zeer and an half. And in Ebron ben alle the sepultures of the patriarkes, Adam, Abraham, Ysaac, and of Jacob; and of here wyfes, Eve, Sarre, and Rebekke, and of Lya: the whiche sepultures the Sarazines kepen fulle curyously, and han the place in gret reverence, for the holy fadres, the patriarkes, that lyzen there. And thei suffre no Cristene man entre in to that place, but zif it be of specyalle grace of the Soudan. For thei holden Cristen men and Jewes as dogges. And thei seyn, that thei scholde not entre in to so holy place. And men clepen that place, where thei lyzn, double spelunke, or double cave or double dyche; for als meche as that on lyethe above that other. And the Sarazines clepen that place in here langage Karicarba; that is to seyn, the place of patriarkes. And the Jewes clepen that place Arbothe. And in that same place was Abrahames hous: and there he satt and he saughe 3 persones, and worschipte but on; as Holy Writt seyethe, *Tres vidit et unum adoravit*: that is to seyne, *He soughe 3, and worschiped on*: and of tho same resceyved Abraham the aungeles in to his hous. And righte faste by that place is a cave in the roche, where Adam and Eve duelleden, whan thei weren putt out of Paradyse; and there goten thei here children. And in thai same place, was Adam formed and made; aftre that that sum men seyn. For men werein wont for to clepe that place, the feld of Damasce; because that it was in the lordschipe of Damask. And fro thens was he translated in to paradys of delytes, as thei seyn: and aftre that he was dryven out of Paradys, he was there left. And the same day that he was putt in Paradys, the same day he was putt autt: for anon he synned. There begynnethe the Vale of Ebron, that durethe nyghe to Jerusalem. There the Aungelle commaunded Adam, that he scholde duelle with his wyf Eve: of the whiche he gatt Sethe; of whiche tribe, that is to seyn, kynrede, Jesu Crist was born. In that valeye is a feld, where men drawen out of the erthe a thing, that men clepen cambylle: and thei ete it in stede of spice, and thei bere it to selle. And men may not make the hole ne the cave, where it is taken out of the erthe, so depe ne so wyde, but that it is, at the zeres ende, fulle azen up to the sydes, thorgh the grace of God.

And 2 myle from Ebron is the grave of Lothe, that was Abrahames brother. And a lytille fro Ebron is the Mount of Mambre, of the whiche the yaleye takethe his name. And there is a tree of oke, that the Sarazines clepen dirpe, that is of Abrahames tyme, the whiche men clepen the drye tree. And thei seye, that it hathe ben there sithe the beginnynge of the world; and was sumtyme grene, and bare leves, unto the tyme that oure Lord dyede on the cros; and thanne it dryede; and so dyden alle trees, that weren thanne in the World. And summe seyn, be here prophecyes, that a Lord, a prynce of the west syde of the world shalle wynnen the lond of promyssioun, that is the Holy Lond, withe helpe of Cristene men; and he schalle do synge a masse undir that drye tree, and than the tree schalle wexen grene and bere bothe fruyt and leves. And thorghe that myracle manye Sarazines and Jewes schulle be turned to Cristene feythe. And therfore thei don gret worschipe thereto, and kepen it fulle besyly; And alle be it so, that it be drye, natheles zit he berethe gret vertue: for certeynly he that hathe a litille there of upon him, it helethe him of the fallynge evylle: and his hors schalle not ben a foundred: and manye othere vertues it hathe: where fore men holden it fulle precyous.

From Ebron, men gon to Bethelem, in half a day: for it is but 5 myle; and it is fulle fayre weye, be pleynes and wodes fulle deletable.

CAPVT. 13.

De ciuitate Bethleem, et semita vsque in Ierusalem.

Bethleem Ciuitas longa sed parua, firmata est vndique fossatis fortibus: cuius modò habitatores quasi omnos sunt Christiani. In illa ad orientem honesta, et placida habetur Ecclesia: (nescio an aliquam eiusdem quantitatis viderim placentiorem,) extrinsecus habens turres saltaturas, pinnacula, et propugnacula nobili artificio fabricata, et intrinsecus 44. de marmore decoro columnas. Ad principalis autem turris dextram in descensu 16. graduum, est diuersorij locus, vbi ex intacta et benedicta Virgine nascebatur Christus homo Deus. Hic locus est multùm artificiosè operatus marmore, et generosè depictus auro et argento, variòque colore, cui propè ad tres passus est præsepe in quo reclinabatur natus Dominus, ibíque videtur puteus quidam, in quo aliqui putare volunt cecidisse stellam ductricem trium Magorum, post eius peractum officium.

Est etiam ante præsepe Domini, tumba beati Interpretis Hieronymi, et extra Ecclesiam monstratur cathedra, in qua residere solebat. Sub clausura huius ecclesiæ ad dextram, per 18. gradus apparet fossa, quæ dicitur ossium innocentium causa Christi ab Herode impio occisorum. Hinc ad quingentos, vel cítra pedes habetur alia Ecclesia nomine Sancti Nicholai, in quo scilicet loco, post recessum Magorum beata Virgo tempus sui puerperij obseruauit. [Sidenote: Taxat simplicitatem vulgi.] Ibíque monstrantur rubra saxa albis respersa maculis, quòd simpliciores narrant saxis euenisse de abundantia lactis virginis ab vberibus eiecti. In via Bethleem ab Helya miliario contra meridianam plagam iuxta viam quæ ducit Ebron, Christiani de Bethleem colunt circa ciuitatem multam copiam vinearum, ad potum sub ipsorum. [Sidenote: Saraceni non bibunt vinum in manifesto.] Nam Sarraceni non colunt vineas, nec vina vendunt neque in manifesto bibunt, eò quòd liber legis Mahomet, facit super hoc prohibitionem, et interpretatur maledictionem.

[Sidenote: Sanctæ Charitatis.] De Bethleem in Austrum duabus leucis habetur claustrum Sanctæ Charitatis, ibidem suo tempore Abbatissæ. A Bethleem tendendo Ierusalem inuenitur ad dimidiam leucam Ecclesia, in cuius loco Angelus dixit pastoribus, Annuncio vobis gaudium magnum, quod natus est nobis Saluatur qui est Christus Dominus. Est et tumba Rachel Patriarchæ, vbi etiam coaceruata iacent 12. saxa magna, quæ quidam autumant illic tumulasse Iacob, eò quòd Beniamin duodecimus sibi filius nascebatur ibidem. Sícque venitur in Sanctam Ciuitatem Ierusalem. [Sidenote: Bethel] Notandum, Bethel vicus est 12. ab Helya ad dextram euntibus Neapoli, quæ primùm Luza vocabatur. Sed ex eo tempore quo ibat ad Ieroboam, filium Nebat, vituli aurei fabricati sunt, et à decem tribubus adorata, vocata est Bethauen, id est, Domus Idoli, quæ antè vocabatur Domus Dei. Ieronymus. Sed et Ecclesia ædificata est vbi dormiuit Iacob, pergens Mesopotamiam, vbi et ipsi loco Bethel, id est, domus Dei nomen imposuit.

CAPVT. 14.

De Ecclesia gloriosi Sepulchri Domini in vrbe Ierusalem.

Ierusalem cum tota terra prommissionis, est quasi vna de quinque prouincijs vel pluribus, quibus Regnum Syriæ distinguitur. Iungitur autem Iudeæ ad Orientem Regno Arabiæ, ad meridiem Aegypto, ad Occidentem mari mago, et ad Aquilonem Rego Syriæ. Iudeæ terra per diuersa tempora à diuersis possessa fuit nationibus, Cananæorum, Iudæorum, Assyriorum, Persarum, Medorum, Macedonum, Græcorum, Romanorum, Christianorum, Sarracenorum, Barbarorum, Turcorum, and Tartarurum.

Cuius rei causa meritò potest æstimari, quod non sustinuit Deus magnos peccatores longo tempore permanere in terra sibi tam placita, et tam sancta.

[Sidenote: Templum Sepulchri.] Itaque perigrinus veniens in Ierusalem primo expleat suam peregrinationem, ad reuerendum et sacrosanctum Domini nostri Iesu Christi sepulchrum: cuius Ecclesia est in vltima ciuitatis extremitate, ad partem aquilonarem, cum proprio sui ambitus muro ipsi ciuitati adiuncto. Ipsa verò Ecclesia est pulchra et rotundæ formæ cooperta desuper cum tegulis plumbeis, habens in Occidente turrim altam et firmam, in pauimenti Ecclesiæ medio ad figuram dimidij compassi habetur nobili opere Latonico ædificatum paruum Tabernaculum quasi 15. pedum tam longitudinis quàm latitudinis, et altitudinis miro artificio intus extràque compositum, ac multùm diligenter diuersis coloribus ornatum. Hoc itaque in Tabernaculo seu Capella, ad latus dextrum, continetur incomparabilis thesaurus gloriosissimi sepulchri, habentis octo pedes longitudinis, et quinque latitudinis. Et quoniam in toto habitaculo nulla est apertura præter paruum ostium, illustratur accedentibus peregrinis pluribus lampadibus, (quarum ad minus vna coram sepulchro iugiter ardere solet) ingressus.

[Sidenote: Melech Mandybron Soldanus.] Sciendum, quòd ante breue tempus solebat sepulchrum esse ingressis peregrinis accessibile, ad tangendum et osculandum, sed quia multi vel effringebant, vel conabantur sibi effringere aliquid de petra sepulchri, iste Soldanus Melech Mahdybron fecit illud confabricari, vt nec osculari valeat, nec adiri, sed tantummodo intueri, Et ob illam causam in sinistro pariete in altitudine quinque pedum immurari effracturam petræ sepulchri ad quantitatem capitis humani, quod tanquam pro sepulchro ibi ab omnibus veneratur, tangitur, et osculatur.

Dicitur ibi quoque communiter præfatam lampadem coram sepulchro singulis annis in die Sanctæ Parascheues, hora nona extingui, et in media nocte Paschæ sine humano studio reaccendi. [Sidenote: Mandeuillus de hoc dubitat.] Quod (si ita est) euidens diuini beneficij miraculum est. Et quamis id plurimi Christiani simpliciter in magno pietatis merito credant, plerísque tamen est in suspicione. Fortè talia Sarraceni custodes sepulchre fingentes diuulgauerunt, pro augendo emolumenta tributi, quod inde resultaret, seu oblationum quæ dantur.

Singulis autem annis in die coenæ Domini in Parascheue, et in vigilia Paschæ, tribus his diebus manet Tabernaculum hoc apertum continuè, et patet omnibus Christianis gentibus accessus, aliàs verò non per annum sine redditione tributi. Intra Ecclesiam, propè parietem dextrum, est Caluariæ locus, vbi crucifixus pependit Christus Dominus. [Sidenote: Tumba Godefridi de Bollion.] Per gradus ascenditur in hunc locum, et est rupis velut albi coloris, cum aliqua rubedine per loca commixta, habens scissuram, quam dicunt Golgotha, in qua maior pars preciosi sanguinis

Christi dicitur influxisse: vbi et habetur altare constructum, ante quod consistunt tumbæ Godefridi de Bullion, et aliorum Regum Christianorum, qui circa annum incarnationis Domini, 1100. debellauerunt et obtinuerunt sanctam vrbem cum tota patria ex manibus Sarracenorum, et per hoc conquisierunt sibi magnum nomen, vsque in finem sæculi duraturum. [Sidenote: Psal. 74. 12.] Propè ipsius crucifixionis locum continetur literis. Græcis hoc scriptum: [Greek: ho theos basileus hæmon pro aionos eirgasato sotærian en mesoi tæs gæs]. hoc est dicere, Deus Rex noster ante secula operatus est salutem in medio terræ. Item directè in loco, vbi crux sancta stetit cum Christo rupi infixa, habetur hoc exaratum in saxo rupis: [Greek: ho horais esi basis tæs piseos ton kosmon], hoc est, quod vides fundamentum est fidei mundi.

[Sidenote: Iterum taxit ignorantiam vulge. Regina Helena Anglia.] Haud remotè ab hoc Caluariæ monte, habetur et aliud altare, vbi iacet columna flagellationis Domini, cui stant de propinque et ali coælumnæ quatuor de Marmore aquam iugiter resundantes, et (secundum opinionem simplicium) passionem innocentem Christie deflentes. Est sub isto altari crypta, 42. granduum profunda, vbi sancta Helena Regina reperit tres cruces, videlicet Christi, et latronum cum eo crucifixorum, ac etiam clauos crucis Domini in cryptæ pariete.

In medio autem chori huius Ecciesiæ, est locus pauimenti stratus mirè et pulchrè, ad integram compassi figuram vbi depositum corpus Christi de cruce Ioseph ab Aramathia cum suis adiutoribus lauit et condiuit aromatibus. Item infra Ecclesiam à septentrionali parte ostenditur locus, vbi Christus Magdalenæ apparuit post suam resurrectionem, quando eum credidit hortulanum.

[Sidenote: Indorum Capella sive subditorum præsbiteri Ioannis.] A dextro autem latere ad ingressum Ecclesiæ, habentur gradus 18. sub quibus est Capella Indorum, vbi soli peregrini de India per sacerdotes suos cantant iuxta ritum suum Missas, celebràntque diuina. Missam faciunt quidem breuissimam, conficientes in principio verbis debitis sacramentum corporis et sanguinis Christi de pane et vino, ac posteà paucis orationibus additis, totum oratione Dominica concludunt officium. Hoc autem verum est, quod cum maxima attentione, reuerentia, humilitate et deuotione se gerunt et continent diuinis.

[Sidenote: An Ierusalem sit in medio mundi.] Porrò illud, quod quidam peruulgauerunt, aut opinati sunt, Iudæam aut Ierusalem, vel Ecclesiam istam consistere in medio totius mundi, propter prædictam scripturam, (in medio terræ) hoc intelligi non potest localiter ad mensuram corporis terræ: Nam si ad terræ latitudinem, quam æstimant inter duos polos, respiciamus, certum est Iudæam non esse in medio, quod tunc esset sub circulo æquatoris, et esset ibi semper æquinoctium, et vtrumque polorum staret iis in horizonte. Quod vtique non est ita, quod existentibus in Iudæa eleuatur multùm polus arcticus.

Rursus si ad terræ longitudinem spectemus, quæ æstimari potest à Paradiso terrestri, scilicet à digniori et latiori terræ loco, versus eius Nadir, scilicet versus locum sibi in Sphæra terræ oppositum, tunc Iudæa esset ad Antipodes paradisi, quod apparet ita non esse, quod tunc esset viatori de Iudæa ad Paradisum tendentis æqua itineris mensura, siue tenderet versus Orientem, siue versus Occidentem. Sed hoc non est verisimile nec verum, sicut probatum constat per experientiam multorum. Mihi autem videtur, quod præfata Prophetæ scriptura, potest exponi, in medio terræ, id est, circa medium nostri habitabilis, videlicet vt Iudæa sit circa medium inter Paradisum et Antipodes Paradisi, distans tantum ab ipso Paradiso in oriente 96. gradibus, prout ego ipse per viam orientalem tentaui; quanquam de hoc non videtur de facili plena certitudo haberi; eo quòd in longitudine coeli nullæ stellæ manent immobiles, sicut in latitudine manent poli sempèr fixi. Vel potest ita exponi, quòd Dauid qui erat Rex Iudæa, dixit in medio terræ, hoc est, in principali ciuitate terræ suæ Ierusalem, quæ erat ciuitas regalis, siue sacerdotalis terræ Iudeæ: vel fortè spiritus sanctus, qui loquebatur per os prophetæ in hoc verbo vult intelligi non corporeum aut locale, sed totum spirituale, de quo intuitu nihil ad præsens est scribendum,

CAPVT. 15.

De tribus alijs Ecclesijs, et specialiter de templo Domini.

Vltrà duo stadia ab Ecclesia ad Meridiem sancti sepulchri habetur magnum hospitale sancti Ioannis Hierosolymitani, qui caput et fundamentum esse dignoscitur ordinis hospitaliorum modò tententium Rhodum insulam: in quo recipi possunt omnes Christiani perigrini cuiuscunque sint conditionis, seu status, vel dignitatis. Nam Sarraceni pro leui cura anxij rumoris, prohibent ne apud quenquam suorum Christianus pernoctet. Ad sustentationem ædificij huius hospitalis, habentur in eo 124. columnæ marmoreæ, et in parietibus distincti 54. pilarij. Satis propè hunc locum in orientem, est Ecclesia quæ dicitur, de Domina nostra magna: et indè non remotè alia, quæ dicitur nostræ Dominæ latinorum, ædificata super locum, vbi Maria Magdalene, et Maria Cleophæ cum alijs pluribus, dum Christus cruci affigebatur, flebant et dolores lamentabiles exercebant.

Item ab Ecclesia Sancti Sepulchri in orientem ad stadium cum dimidio habetur ædificium mirabile, ac pulchrum valdè, quod templum Domini nominatur, quod constructum est in forma rotunda, cuius circumferentiæ diameter habet 64 cubitos, et altitudo eius 126, et intrinsecus pro sustentatione ædificij, multi pilarij. In medio autem templi est locus altior 14. gradibus, qui et ipse columnis vndíque est stipatus: et secundum quatuor mundi plagas habet templum quatuor introitus per portas Cypressinas artificiosè compositas, nobiliterque sculptas, et excisas. Et ante portam aquilonarem intra templum fontem aquæ mundæ, qui quamuis olim exundabat, tamen nunc minimè fluit. In toto circuitu ædificij extrinsecus est valdè pro atrio latum spacium loci, stratum per totum pauimentum marmoribus. Hoc templum non ducitur stare in eodem loco vbi templum Dei stetit in tempore Christi, quo post resurrectionem a Romanis destructo, istud longo post tempore Adrianus Imperator extruxit, sed non ad formam templi prioris: prædictum tamen excelsum in medio templi locum vocant Iudæi sanctum sanctorum.

Sciatis itàque quòd Sarraceni magnam exhibent huic templo reuerentiam, et honorem sæpius illud discalceati intrantes, et positis genibus deuotè Deum omnipotentem exorantes, nulla enim ibidem habetur imago, sed multæ lampades relucentes. [Sidenote: Literæ Soldani traditæ Mandiuillo.] Neminem Christianorum seu Iudæorum ingredi sinun, templum, reputantes eos indignos ad hoc, et nimium immundos, vndè nisi virtute literarum quas habui a Soldano, nec ego fuissem ingressus. Ingrediens autem cum meis sodalibus deposuimus calciamenta, recogitantes cum multa cordis deuotione, nos magis id facere debere, quàm incredulos Sarrcenos.

Et verè meritò est iste locus in magna reuerentia habendus: dum enim Rex Salomon primum in illo templo per Dei iussionem, et Dauidis patris sui commissionem ædificasset, exorauit præsente cuncto populo Israel, vt quicúnque illic Deum pro iusta causa rogaret audiretur; et Dominus monstrauit exauditionis signum per nebulam de coelo emissam, proùt narrat historia veritatis 3. Regum libro.

Porrò in eo loco vbi statuerat idem Rex ante templum altare holocausti, videlicet extra portam templi occidentalem, habetur et nunc altare, sed non ad instar, nec ad vsum primi: Nam Saraceni, quasi nihil curantes, traxerunt in eo lineos tanquam in astrolabio figentes in linearum centro batellum, ad cuius vmbram per lineas discernuntur diei horæ.

Etiam in hac atrij parte apparent adhuc vestigia portæ speciosæ, vbi Petrus Apostolus, cum Euangelista Ioanne dixit contracto, In nomine Christi Iesu Nazareni surge, et statim consolidabantur illi plantæ.

CAPVT. 16.

De pluribus locis sacris iuxta vrbem.

[Sidenote: Templarij à templo Salomonis dicti.] Viaturo ad dextram satis de propinquo habetur et alia Ecclesia, quæ nunc appellatur schola Salomonis: rursusque ad Meridiem est et aliud templum siue Ecclesia, quæ vocatur Templum Salomonis, quòd olim fuit caput, et fundamentum totius ordinis Templariorum.

[Sidenote: Regina Helena Angla.] A claustro huius templi extrinsecus in Aquilonem habetur decora Ecclesia beatæ Annæ, in cuius loco creditur virgo Maria in eiusdem matris suæ vtero fuisse genita, et concepta, parentunque illius, scilicet, Ioachim et Annæ, tumba saxea monstratur in descensu Ecclesiæ, per 22. gradus, vbi et adhuc patris eius ossa putantur quiescere, sublato inde per reginam Helenam korpore sanctæ Annæ, et recondito (vt prædictum est) in Ecclesia Constantinopoli sanctæ Sophiæ.

[Sidenote: Probatica piscina.] Est et intra hanc Ecclesiam probatica piscina, vbi quondam post motionem Angeli, omnes accedentes primi, a quocúnque languore sanabantur infirmi, quæ tamen nunc temporis ita neglecta iacet, et deformata, vt videtur immunda cistrina. Habetur et ante Ecclesiam arbor grandis, et antiqua, de qua nonnulli fabulantur, quod ad beatæ Mariæ natiuitatem principium accepit, et ortum.

[Sidenote: Mons Sion.] Mons Sion est excelsior locus in vrbe ad cuius radicem, est castrum spectabile constructum per aliquem Soldanorum. In montis autem cacumine videntur multæ sepulturæ regum Indeæ, videlicet Dauid, Salomonis, et quorundam de successoribus suis. Ad introitum montis habetur capella, et in illa lapis monumenti quem Ioseph de Arimathea obuoluit ad ostium sepulchri est valde magnus, et est ibidem aliqua pars columnæ flagellationis, ac pars mensæ super quam Dominus vltimò cænauit cum Apostolis, et instituit noui Testamenti sacramentum sui venerandi corporis, et sanguinis. Sub hac capella ad aliquos gradus monstratur locus eiusdem cænationis, videlicèt cærnaculí magni, et in eo vas, aquarum, in quo Christus lauabat pedes Apostolorum: iuxta quod vas a Gamaliele, et alijs viris timoratis primus sepultus fuit protomartyr Stephanus.

In eo quoque loco intrauit post resurrectionem suam Dominus ianuis clausis ad discipulos dicens pax vobis, et agens alia, quæ plenius Euangelica pandit Historia, ac tandem in die Pentecostes ijsdem spiritum sanctum in linguis igneis misit ibidem. Ab hoc monte Sion versus ciuitatem habetur Ecclesia dedicata sancto saluatori, in quo nunc dicuntur seruari ossa S. Stephani supradicti, et sinistrum brachium S. Ioannis Chrisostomi, cuius corpus vt dictum est requiescit Constantinopoli.

Item ab hoc monte versus Austrum ab opposito plateæ, est pulchra Ecclesia nostræ Dominæ, in cuius loco diu morabatur post ascensionem filij sui, quamius pro parte eiusdem temporis in valle Iosaphat manserit: nam in ista defungebatur, et in illo ab Apostolis honorificè sepulta fuit. [Sidenote: Natatoria Siloe.] Itemque ab hoc monte in vico eundi versus vallem Iosaphat inuenitur fons aquæ dictus Natatoria Siloe, vbi cæcus natus à Christo missus lauabat oculos, et regressus est videns. Et dicunt quidam ibidem sepultrum Isaiam Prophetam.

Porro mons olim dictus Moria de quo loquitur Scriptura sacra est rupis haud longè a supradicto templo Domini in ipsius meredie, in cuius rupis loco excelso velut emenenti sed edito Dominus noster Iesus Christus frequentèr instruebat suos discipulos, et populos, magnáque miracula exhibebat, atque deprehensae mulieri in adulterio omnia peccata dimittebat. [Sidenote: Iohan. 8.]

Ab opposito autem prædicti fontis natatorij habetur imago lapidea, rudi et vetusto opere sculpta, deformitérque detrita, quae manus Absalon nuncupatur, cuius ratio lib. 2. Regum monstratur. Vbi de propè vidi Arborem Sambucum, ad quam vel citrà cuius locum (vt dicitur) Iudas traditor per se suspensus crepuit medius, et diffusa sunt viscera eius.

Præterea à monte Sion versus Meridiem vltrà vallem ad iactum lapidis est locus Aceldema, in quo emptus ager 30. denarijs proditionis est, Et in quo sunt plures sepulturæ peregrinorom, et vestigia cellularum, de quondam illic commorantibus Heremitis.

CAPVT. 17.

De sacris locis extra muros Ciuitatis.

[Sidenote: Vallis Iosaphat.] Extra muros ciuitatis Ierusalem ad plagam orientalem, est vallis Iosaphat contigua, ac si esset fossata muris ipsius ciuitatis, et Ecclesia vbi sanctus Stephanus lapidabatur, et obdormiuit in Domino. Hinc non longè est porta ciuitatis, quæ dicitur aurea, quæ nunc sempèr obfirmata seruatur. Per hanc intrauit Christus sedens asino, et adhuc ostenditur rupis seruare vestigia animalis in tribus aut pluribus sui locis. [Sidenote: Mons Oliuarum. Torrens Cedron.] Statim vltrà vallem Iosaphat aspicitur mons Oliueti, sic dictus à pluribus, quia ibi sunt oliuarum Arbores. In planicie huius vallis decurrit riuulus dictus torrens Cedron, secus quem habetur pulchra, et honorificata Ecclesia sacrosanctæ sepulturæ beatæ, et gloriosæ matris Christi: descenditur autem in Ecclesiam per gradus 44. quòd extrinsecus est vallis inculta per fluxum fortassè torrentis, seu per alios euentus proptèr Antiquitatem temporis. Ibique monstratur sepulchrum eius vacuum. Habentur iuxta sepulchrum duo altaria, sub vno est fons Aquæ quæ putatur exire de vno Paradisi flumine.

Satis propè ab hac Ecclesia ad rupem Gethsemane habetur capella, vbi scilicet Iudæis traditus fuit Christus à Iuda. In ipsa quóque rupe ostendebatur mihi figura impressæ manus ad digitorum extensionem, quo artificiosius humanano studio sculpi non posset, quam referunt Christum sua venerabili manu inclinando ad rupem efficisse dum Iudæi impuras manus ad capiendum iniecerunt in eum. Hic ad iactum lapidis in meridie orauit ['oraiit' in source text—KTH] ad suum patrem, et pro vehementi orationis intentione sanguineum exudauit sudorem: atque ibi non remotè videtur tumba regis Iudeæ Iosaphat, á quo et vallis sibi nomen assumpsit: et credimus in hanc vallem Christum venturum ad nouissimum, et generalissimum iudicium, vbi (Iohele propheta testante) disceptabit de omni actione mortalium. [Sidenote: S. Iacobi sepultura.] Ad tractum sagittæ de hac tumba, est Ecclesia vbi sanctus Iacobus maior Apostolus primo post martyrium fuit sepultus, cuius modo sacrata ossa venerantur Compostellæ in Galizia.

Vltra vallem in supremo montes Oliueti apice discipulus cernentibus, Dominus noster Iesus Christus eleuatis manibus ascendit in coelum, et super eundem locum digna habetur Ecclesia, in qua eiusdem Ascensione tale seruatur in rupe pauimenti indicium, quod sinistri pedis Christi videtur vltimum vestigium.

Hinc satis propè habetur et capella medio montis, vbi Christus sedens prædicauit octo beatitudines, vbi et creditur docuisse discipulos orationem Dominicam, scilicet, Pater noster, &c. Ab eo quoque loco non distat multum Ecclesia beatæ Maaiæ Aegyptiacæ, in qua et eius tumba videtur: et haud procul inde est vicus Bethphage, vbi Christus misit ante passionis suæ tempus duos de discipulis pro asina et pullo eius. In cliuo vero huius montis Oliueti versus ciuitatem, monstratur locus, de quo videns Dominus Ierusalem, fleuit super illam, dicens, quod si cognouisses et tu, &c. [Sidenote: Bethania.] Atque vltrà montem in discensu eius in orientem est villa siue castellum Bethaniæ, distans quasi ad leucam ab vrbe vbi in domo cuiusdam Symonis inuitatu Christus condonauit omnia peccata Mariæ Magdalenæ. Et in ipso castello, quod erat sororis Marthæ, et Mariæ rescuscitauit fratrem earum Lazarum quatriduanum mortuum.

[Sidenote: Ierico.] De Bethania in Ierico sunt 5. leucæ, quæ quondam fuit ciuitas speciosa sed iam est villa modica: ibi Diues Zacchæus ascendit in arborem Sycomorum, vt videret transeuntem Dominum, et restituens fraudata quadraplum, obtinuit peccatorum remissionem omnium.

Item de Bethania ad flumen Iordanis est iter ferè octo leucarum, per montes, ac valles deuios, et desertos. [Sidenote: Christiani Georgici.] Porrò de Bethania in orientem ad 6 leucas venitur in montem magnum, vbi Christus expleto 40. dierum, ac noctium ieiunio temptatus est à diabolo, fuítque in eodem loco quandoque Ecclesia, sed modo habetur ibi quasi coenobium quorundam Christianorum, qui Georgici vocantur. Sciendum enim est, quod vbique intra terram Saracenorum, et similiter multorum Paganorum inueniuntur Christiani dispersi, habitantes sub tributo, qui licet sint baptizati omnes, et beatissimam Trinitatem credentes, diuersificantur tamen nominibus, moribus, ritibus, fide, et opinionibus: ita vt semper vel in multis vel in aliquibus dissentiant à Romanæ Ecclesiæ consuetudinibus.

[Sidenote: Iacobitæ. Syrij. Georgica. Cordelarij. Indi. Nubij. Nestorini. Arriani.] Aliqui námque eorum dicuntur Christiani Iacobitæ: hij errant circa peccatorum remissionem, dicentes, non debere confiteri homini sed soli Deo. Alij Syrij, Isti in fermentato pane conficiunt Sacramentum altaris ritu Græcorum. Alij Indi, Nubij, Nestorini, et Arriani. Præfatus autem mons magnus, vocatur hortus Abrahæ, ex eo quod Abraham patriarcha ibi dicitur commoratus, et currit propè montem riuulus, in cuius aqua vel fonte Deus sal per Helizeum prophetam mitti iussit, vt sanaretur sterilitas, id est, amaritudo aquæ. Nec distat hic mons à Ierico vltra grandem leucam.

CAPVT. 18.

De notabilibus alijs locis, et mari mortuo.

Rursum de ciuitate sanctæ Ierusalem versus Occidentem itinere leucæ, habetur pulchra satis Ecclesia, in loco vbi dicitur creuisse arbor crucis salutiferæ. Arbor excelsa, digno stipite sacra Christi membra tangere. [Sidenote: Nota.] Tenetur istud quidem pro certa veritate: nam et hoc satis testatur constructio tantæ, et talis Ecclesiæ, quamuis multa aliena, et incerta scripta de crucis arbore ferantur per orbem. Hinc ad duas leucas est et alia Ecclesia, vbi obuiauerunt sibi Maria virgo, et Elizabeth eius cognata, et ad saluationem Mariæ Christi baiulæ exultauit Iohannes in vtero Elisabeth grauidæ.

[Sidenote: Emaus Castellum.] De isto quoque ad leucam est Emaus castellum, distans in spacio stadiorum 60. ab Ierusalem, vbi discipuli in coena die resurrectionis Domini cognouerant eum in fractione panis. [Sidenote: Cosdrus Imperator.] Porrò ab Ierusalem ad alium exitum, ad duo stadia videtur spelunca grandis de qua dicitur quod tempore Cosdri Imperatoris Persarum, fuerunt circa Ierusalem 12. mille martyrum occissi, quorum, omnium corpora leo habitans in spelunca congregauit ibidem voluntate diuina, tanquam pro singulorum sepultura obsequiosa.

[Sidenote: Mons Exultationis.] Item ab vrbi ad leucas duas habetur in monte tumba sepulturæ sancti Samuelis prophetæ, qui mons nunc vocatur exultationis vel læticiæ, eò quod peregrinis ab illa parte intrantibus reddit primum sanctæ ciuitatis aspectum. Ab oppido autem Ierico in 30. stadiorum spacio venitur ad Iordauis fluuij locum, vbi beatus Iohannes Baptista Christum sacri baptismatis merebatur tingere lymphis. Et in cuius reuerendi mysterij venerationem habetur ad dimidiam leucam à fluuio ædificium honestæ Ecclesiæ consecratum in nomine eiusdem venerabilis baptistæ ministri. Ab hac Ecclesia de propè vidi domum de qua patiebar mihi narrari, quòd in eodem loco olim fuerit Ieremiæ sancti habitatio prophetæ.

[Sidenote: Iordanis descriptio.] Notandum est. Iordanis fluuius quamuis grandis non sit, bonorum tamen piscium copiam nutrit, ortum accipiens sub monte Libanon ex duobus fontibus, scilicet Ior, et Dan, quæ nomina simul mixta nomen Iordanis efficiunt. Decurrit autem per quendam locum dictum Maron, ac secus stagnum quod diciter Mare Tyberiadis, ac subter montes Gylboe per amoenissima loca, atque in subterraneis meatibus per longum spacium se occultans tandem exit in planitie, quæ dicitur Meldam, id est, forum, quod certis temporibus ibi Nundinæ exercentur, et ad extremum se iactat in mare mortuum.

[Sidenote: Mare mortuum.] Hoc stagnum quod vocatur mare mortuum habet longitudinis 600. ferè stadia, et latitudinis 150. et appropinquat aliqua pars huius maris ad quatuor leucas propè Ierico, videlicet ad latus camporum Engadi, ex quibus (vt supra dictum est) eradicatæ fuerunt abores Balsami, quæ modò sunt in agro Cayr Ægypti. [Sidenote: Nota.] Istud mare dicitur mortuum.

[Sidenote: Cur mare mortuum dicatur.] Primo quidem quòd non viuidè currit, sed est quasi lacus.

Secundò quod amara est eius aqua, et foetidum reddit odorem. Tertio quòd propter eius amaritudinem terra adiacens littori nil viride profert.

Quartò (prout dicitur) si cadat in ea bestia, vel aliud quid viuens, vix poterit plenè mori siue submergi in octo diebus, nec nutrit in se pisces aut quid simile.

Littora quoque sua variant quam sæpè colorem, et sine vlla agitatione ventorum eijcit in quibusdam locis se aqua, extra proprios terminos. Per huiusmodi aquam dicitur Deus pro indicibili vitio Pentapolim submersisse, Sodomam, Gomorram, Adamam, Seboim, et Segor.

Quidam vocant hoc mare lacum Asphaltidis, alij fluuium Dæmonum, aut flumen Putre. Quod autem olim propheta interpretans dixit, montes Gilboe, nec ros nec pluuia veniat super vos, magis spiritualitèr quàm literalitèr videtur intelligendum. [Sidenote: Nota.] Nam ibi crescunt altissimi cedri, et arbores poma ferentes, ad capitis quantitatem humani, ex quibus valdè saporosus fit potus.

Mare istud mortuum determinat fines terræ promissionis, et Arabiæ. Ideoque vltra ipsum mare condidit quondam, vnus successorum Godfridi de Bollion forte et spectabile castrum, ponens illic copiosam Christianorum militiam ad terram promissionis custodiendum. Nunc verò, temporis, est Soldani, et appellatur Caruth, id est mons Regalis. Sub hoc monte est villa dicta Sobal: habitat in illis partibus magna Christianorum multitudo.

CAPVT. 19.

De Nazareth, et Samaria.

Nazareth in prouincia Galileæ in qua nutritus, et de qua cognominatus est Dominus vniuersorum, distans ab Hierosolymis ad tres circiter dietas, erat quondam ciuitas, quæ nunc est dispersa, et rara domorum, quod vix villæ sibi competit nomen: et in loco Annunciationis, vbi Angelus ad Mariam dixit, Aue gratia plena, Dominus tecum, habebatur olim bona Ecclesia, pro qua paruum Saraceni restituerunt habitaculum, in colligendas peregrinorum offerendas.

A Nazareth redeundo per terram Galileæ, transitur per Ramathaym Sophim, vbi nascebatur fidelis Samuel propheta Domini, et per Sylo, vbi locus orationis erat antequam in Ierusalem: et per Sichem magnæ vbertatis vallem, itur in prouinciam Samariæ, vbi habetur et bona ciuitas nunc dicta Neapolts, distans, à sancta vrbe spacio solius dietæ, ac per fontem Iacob, super quem Iesus fatigatus ab itinere colloquebatur Samaritonæ, vbi et apparet ruina destructæ Ecciesiæ quondam illic habitæ. Et est ibi villa adhuc vocata Sychem, et in eo est mausoleum Ioseph patriarchæ filij Iacob: ad cuius ossa visitanda sub deuotione non minus peregrini Iudæi adueniunt, quàm Christiani.

[Sidenote: Samaria nunc Sebaste.] Hinc satis propè est mons Garizin cum vetusto templo orationis Samaritanorum: ex tunc intratur Samaria quæ modò appellatur Sebaste, et est illius principalis ciuitas pronunciæ. In qua fuit primum terræ mandatum corpus beati Ioannis Baptistæ inter sacra corpora Helizæi, et Abdiæ Prophetarum, vt quorum assimilibatur virtutibus in vita, corporibus iungeretur in sepultura. Hæc quoque distat ab Hierosolymis: fortassis a dietas.

[Sidenote: Nota.] Habetur et alius puteus aut fons intra illa montana, quem plerique similiter fontem Iacob appellant, cuius aqua secundum quatuor anni tempora variatur à suo colore, vt sit quandòque clara, quandòque turbida, nunc viridis, et nunc rubra. [Sidenote: Ogerus Dux Danus.] Certum est autem tempore Apostolorum cum Samaria recepisset verbum Dei, illos fuisse conuersos, et baptizatos, in nomine Domini Iesu, et tamen postea per quendam Caliphorum peruersos, Ogerus dux Danorum per Templariorum virtutem rursum subiugauit Christianitati: sicque post plures euentus, et variationes, illi qui nunc sunt Samaritæ, finxerunt sibi hæresim propriam, et ritum ab omnibus nationibus singularem.

[Sidenote: Tegumenti capitis differentia.] Fatentur autem se credere in Deum, qui cuncta creauit: recipiuntque pentateucum scripturæ, cum Psalterio Dauidis, acerrimè contendentes, se solos dilectissimos Dei filios qui etiam pro nobili differentia inuoluunt capita linteo rubeo, Saraceni autem albo, Indi croceo, et Christiani ibi manentes Indico, hoc est, æreo, seu hiacynthino.

Porrò à Nazareth quatuor leucis, est ciuitas olim dicta Naym, in 2. milario Thabor montis contra Meridiem iuxta Endor. Ieronimus. Ante cuius portam resuscitauit Christus defunctum filium vnicum matris suæ, præsentibus duabus turmis hominum copiosorum. Hinc quoque ad leucas duas, est ciuitas Israel, vbi olim morabatur pessima regina Iezabel, quam Dei iudicio equorum vngulis conculcatam, canes ferè vsque ad caluariam comederunt.

CAPVT. 20.

De territorio Gallileæ, et Samariæ, et de villa Sardenay.

Item à Nazareth ad leucæ dimidum, monstrantur in rupe vestigia pedum, quæ dicuntur esse Domini nostri Iesu Christi vbi de manibus Iudæorum, ipsum de alta rupe præcipitare volentium desiluit in istam. De quo saltu quidam intelligunt illud scriptum Euangelicum, Iesus autem transiens per medium illorum ibat.

Ad quatuor autem leucas de Nazareth, est Cana Galileæ, vbi Christus ad vrbanas matris preces, mutauit vndam in vinum optimum.

[Sidenote: Mons Thabor.] Ad distantiam quatuor leucarum à Nazareth, venitur in Thabor, montem spectabilem, vbi transfigurabatur Christus, coram quibusdam suis Apostolis, apparentibus ibidem, Mose, et Helia, prophetis, vocéque dilapsa à magnifica Patris gloria, et videbatur Petro bonum ibi esse: quondam in hoc monte habebatur ciuitas, cum pluribus Ecclesijs; quarum nunc sola restant vestigia, excepto quod ille locus transfigurationis est inhabitatus, qui est Schola Dei nominatus. [Sidenote: Obserueretur.] Notandum. Thabor est in medio Galileæ, campus mira iucunditate sublimis, distans à Diotesaria 3. milliaribus contra Orientem.

Item de Nazareth in tres leucas est villa, seu castrum Zaffara, de quo recolo me supradixisse capite 4. Et inde venitur in Mare Galileæ, quod quamuis dicatur mare, est lacus aquæ dulcis longus.

[Sidenote: Mare Tyberiadis.] Vltra centum 60. forsitan stadia est lacus, bonorum piscium ferax et vber, qui etiam in alio loco sui vocatur mare Tyberiadis, et in alia mare Genezareth, varians sibi nomen, secundum ciuitas, et terras, propinquas. Circa hoc mare Christus frequentèr, et libentèr ambulasse videtur: hic vocauit ad sui discipulatum, Petrum, et Andream, Iacobum, et Ioannem: hic super vndam siccis ambulabat vestigijs, et præcipitem Petrum filium tentantem, verbo increpationis releuat ne mergatur, hic denique rediuiuus à morte repleuit discipulorum rete magnis piscibus 153.

Item in ciuitate Tiberiade, quæ est propè hoc mare habetur in veneratione mensa illius coenæ, quam in Emaus castello Christus cænauit, cum ab oculis commensalium euanuit. Hic de propè monstratur mons ille fertilis, mons ille pinguis, in quo de paucis panibus, et de paucioribus piscibus iussu Christi fuerunt saturati, quinque millia hominum.

Ad initium autem prædicti maris iuxta villam Capernaum habetur fortius castrum totius terræ promissionis, in quo dicitur nata fuisse sancta Anna mater virginis Mariæ.

[Sidenote: Damascus.] Prædictis itaque Christi vestigijs, et terræ sanctæ locis à peregrino cum deuotione cordis et reuerentia debita visitatis, si desiderat reuerti, posit illud facere per Damascum; quæ est ciuitas longa, nobilis, et grandis, ac plena omnium rerum mercimonijs, cum tamen distat à portu maris tribus plenè dietis, per quod spacium itineris, cuncta traijciuntur à suis equis, Dromedarijs, et Camelis: et putatur à plerisque narrantibus fundata in loco vbi Cain protoplaustorum filius Abel fratrem suum occidit.

A Damasco de propinquo est mons Seyr, ciuitas grandis firmata duplicibus muris ac populosa nimis, in qua sunt multi in arte Physica famosi professi. Item à Damasco haud remotè distat castrum satis munitum, et firmum, quod Derces est nominatum. Habent autem in illis, et vlterioribus partibus hunc vsum: si quando castrum ab hostibus fuerit sic obsessum, quòd Dominus eius non possit emittere nuncium amico suo remotè moranti, recipit columbam olim in castro, vel domo amici natam, vel educatam, quam hic sibi per certam prouisionem allatam detinuit incaueatam, et scriptas quas vult literas alligans collo columbæ, dimittit liberam volare, quæ protinus festinat ad focum propriæ natiuitatis. Sicque videtur cognosci in illo castro quid agatur in isto.

[Sidenote: Villa Sardenay.] Cæterum peregrinus à Damasco reuertendo, in quinque leucis venit Sardenay, quæ est villa in alta rupe, cum multis Ecclesijs religiosorum Monachorum, et sanctarum monialium fidei Christianæ. In quarum vna coram maiori altari in tabula lignea erat olim imago beatissimæ virginis Mariæ non sculpta sed depicta in plano spacio. Ex hoc reditur per valles Bokar fertiles et pro pascendis pecorum gregibus exuberantes: et intratur in montana vbi copiositas est fontium qui effluunt impetu de Libano. Ibique decurrit fluuius Sabbatayr, sic dictus quod diebus Sabbatis euidentèr rapidius transit, quàm alijs sex diebus.

Peruenitur hinc ad satis altum montem, propè Tripolim ciuitatem, in qua ad præsens plures Christiani Catholicæ fidei habitant iugo infidelium nimis oppressi. [Sidenote: Sur, vel Tyrus.] Ex hoc loco sibi deliberet peregrinus, quem sibi maris portum accipiat ad repatriandum, videlicet Beruth, an Sur vel Tyrum.

Postremò sciendum, quod terra promissionis in totali longitudine sui à Dan qui est sub Libano vsque ad Berseba in Austrum continet circiter centum, et

80. leucas Lombardicas, et ab Hierico in totali latitudine circiter 60. Notandum, Dan est viculus in quarto à Pennea de Miliario euntibus, contra Septentrionem: vsque hodiè sic vocatur terminus Iudeæ, contra Septentrionem est etiam et fons Ior, de quo et Iordanis fluuius erumpens alterum sortitus nomen Ior. Termini Iudeæ terræ à Bersabe incipiunt vsque ad Dan, qui vsque Peneaden terminatur, Ieronimus.

CAPVT. 21.

De secta detestabili Saracenorum et eorum fide.

[Sidenote: Diligentia Mandevillu.] Iam restat vt de secta Saracenorum aliquid scribam vel compendiosè, secundum quòd cum ijs frequentèr, colloquendo audiui, et liber Mahometi, quem Alcaron, vel Mesahaf, vel Harmè vocant, ijs præcipit, sicut illum sæpè inspexi, et studiosè perlegi.

[Sidenote: Fides Saracenorum.] Credunt itaque Saraceni in Deum creatorem coeli et terræ, qui fecit omnia in ijs contenta, et sine quo nihil est factum. Et expectant diem nouissimum iudicij, in quo mali cum corpore et anima descensuri sunt in infernum perpetuò cruciandi, et boni equidem cum anima et corpore intraturi Paradisum foelicitatis æternæ. Et hæc quidem fides poenè inest omnium mortalium nationibus, lingua et ratione vtentibus. Verumtamen de qualitate Paradisi est magna diuersitas inter credentes.

Nam et Saraceni et Pagani, et omnes sectæ præter Iudæos et baptizatos Christianos sentiunt bonorum Paradisum fore terrestrem illum de quo fuit expulsus Adam propter inobedientiam protoplaustus: qui (vt putant) fluit, vel tunct fluet pluribus riuis lactis et mellis, et vbi in domibus et mansionibus nobiliter iuxta meritum vniuscuiusque ædificatur auro, et argento et gemmis, perfruentur omnibus corporalibus delicijs, in oblectatione animæ æternaliter sine fine. Ille ergò qui fide sanctæ Trinitatis carent, et Christum qui est vera lux ignorant, in tenebris ambulant. Iudæi vero et omnes baptizati rectè sentiunt Paradisum coelestem et spiritualem, vbi quilibet secundum meritum Diuinitati vnietur, per cognitionem, et amorem. Attamen Iudæi quod contra Scripturas suas sanctæ Trinitati contradicunt, et Christo obloquuntur, qui est vera via, nesciunt quo vadunt. De baptizatis autem, qui firmiter fidem Catholicam in humilitate cordis sub Ecclesiæ præceptis seruauerunt, hi soli filij sunt lucis, et in via veniendi ad coelestem Paradisum quem Christus verbo prædicauit, et ad quem corpore et anima, videntibus discipulis, de facto conscendit.

Credunt etiam Saraceni, omnia esse vera, quæ Deus ore prophetarum est locutus, sed in diuersitate, quia nesciunt specificari, imo specificanti contradicerent defacili, vel negarent. Inter omnes prophetas ponunt quatuor excellentiores, quorum supremum et excellentissimum fatentur Iesum Mariæ Virginis filium, quem et asserunt, sermonem, vel loquelam, vel spiritum Dei, et pronunciatorem sententiarum Dei, in iudicio generali futuro, et missum à Deo ad Christianos docendos.

Secundo loco Abrahamum dicunt fuisse verum Dei cultorem, et amicum.

Tertium dant Mosi locum tanquam prolocutori Dei Misso specialiter, ad instruendos Iudæos.

Quartum volant esse Mahomet, sanctum, et verum Dei nuncium ad seipsos missum, cum lege diuina in dicto libro plene contenta. Tenent itaque indubitate, quod beata Maria Iesum peperit, et concepit virgo manens intacta, ac libentèr loqui audiunt de incarnatione in ipsa facta per annunciationem Gabrielis Archangeli. Nam et Alcharon eorum dicit, ad salutationem Angeli virginem expauisse, quod tunc erat in partibus Galileæ incantator, Turquis nomine, qui per susceptam sibi formam Angeli plures virgines deflorauerat, et beatam Virginem conuenisse Angelum, an esset Turquis. Refert quoque eam peperisse sub palma Arbore, vbi habebatur præsepe bouis, et asinæ, et illic præ confusione puerperij, et verecundia ac dolore, fuisse in proximo desperatam, et infantulum in consolationem matris dixisse, mater ne timeas, Deus in te effudit secreta ad saluationem Mundi. Hæc et his similia multa ibi scribuntur figmenta, et isti plura inter se narrando componunt, quæ hoc loco ventilanda non sunt.

Et dicit liber Iesum sanctissimum omnium Prophetarum fuisse veracem in dictis et factis, benignum, pium, iustum, et ab omni vitio penitus alienum: Sanctum quoque Ioannem Euangelistam post prædictos Prophetas fuisse alijs Sanctiorem, cuius et Euangelium fatentur esse plenum salutari, ac veraci doctrina, et ipsum Sanctum Ioannem illuminasse cæcos, leprosos mundasse, suscitasse mortuos, et in coelum volasse viuentem. Erat enim (prout dicit) plus quàm Propheta, et absque omni peccato, contradicente eodem de seipso, si dixerimus quòd peccatum non habemus, veritas in nobis non est: vnde et si quando Sarraceni tenent scriptum Euangelij Sancti Ioannis, aut illud beati Lucæ, missus est Angelus Gabriel, eleuant ambabus manibus pro reuerentia super caput et super oculos id ponentes, et osculantur quàm sæpè cum summa deuotione. Nonnulli etiam eorum in Græco, aut Latino literati consueuerunt cum deuotione cordis id lectitare.

Idem liber dicit Iudæos perfidos fuisse, quod Iesu eis primùm misso a Deo, et multa miracula facienti credere noluerunt, quodque per ipsum tota gens Iudæorum fuit dignè decepta, et meritò illusa hoc modo. Iesus in hora dum Iudas eum pro signo traditionis osculabatur, posuit per Metamorphosin figuram suam, in ipsum Iudam, sícque Iudæi in ambiguo lumine nocturni temporis, pro Iesu Iudam capientes, ligantes, trahentes, deridentes, in fine crucifixerunt, putantes se omnia facere Iesu, qui protinus capto et ligato Iuda, viuus ascendit in cælum, descensurus iterum viuus ad iudicium in die finali.

Et addit, Iudæos falsissimè vsque hodie nos Christianos suo mendacio decipere, quo dícunt se Iesu crucifixisse quem non tetegerunt. Hinc errorem tenent Sarraceni obstinati: et quoddam argumentum inire conantur. Nam si Deus (aiunt) permisisset Iesum, innocentem, et iustum ita miserabiliter occidi, censuram suæ summæ iustitiæ minuisset. [Sidenote: Conuersio Saracenorum non desperanda.] Sed cùm ipsi, vt supradictum est, in tenebris ambulant, idcircò ignorantes Dei iustitiam, statuere volunt iustitiam, imo iniustitiam quam fabricant in corde suo, quia nos de cruce Christi scriptum nouimus, benedictum est lignum per quod fit iustitia. Isti tamen quod in aliquibus appropinquant veræ fidei, multi quandoque eorum inuenti sunt conuersi, et plures adhuc de facili conuerterentur, si haberunt prædicatores, sincerè eis verbum tractantes, quippe cùm iam fateantur legum Mahometi quandoque defecturam, sicut nunc perijt lex Iudæorum, et legem Christianorum vsque in finem seculi permansuram.

CAPVT 22.

De vita, et nomine Mahometi.

Promisi in superioribus aliquid narrare de vita Mahometi legislatoris Sarracenorum, prout vidi in scriptis, vel audiui in partibus illis. Itaque Macho, siue Machon, vtrum in secunda syllaba scribatur N, litera, vel non idem refert: et si tertia syllaba addatur, et dicatur Machomet, vel etiam quarta, Machometus, nihil differt, quòd semper idem nomen representat. Ipsi tamen illum sæpiùs nominant Machon. Putatur autem istum Mahomet habuisse generationis ortum de Ismael Abrahæ filio naturali de concubina Agar, vnde et vsque hodie quidam Sarracenorum dicuntur Ismaelitæ, alij Agarení: sed et quidam Moabitæ, et Ammonitæ, à duobus Loth filijs Moab et Amon, genitis per incestum de proprijs filiabus.

[Sidenote: Tempus Natiuitatis Mahometi.] Hic verò Machon, circa annum incarnationis Domini sexcentissimum natus, in Arabia pauper erat gratis pascens camelos, et interdum sequens Mercatores in Aegyptum fordellos illorum proprio collo deferens pro mercede. Et quoniam tunc temporis tota Aegyptus erat Christianæ fidei, didicit aliquid de fide nostra, quod diuertere solebat ad cellulam Heremitæ commorantis in deserto. [Sidenote: Fabulæ Saracenorum.] Et quodammodo fabulantur Sarraceni, quod illo quandoque ingrediente cellulam, cellulæ ostium mutatum in ianuam valdè patentem, velut ante palatium, et gloriantur hoc primum miraculum. Qui ex tunc conquerendo sibi pecunias, et discendo seculi actus diues est effectus, et prudens ab omnibus reputatus, in tantum, vt postmodum in terræ gubernatorem Corrozæn, (quæ est vna prouinciarum regni Arabiæ) assumeretur, ac de inde defuncto principe Codige per coniugium illius relictæ in eiusdem prouinciæ principem eleuaretur. Erat autem satis formosus, et valens, et vltra modum in verbis et factis maturus, et principalis, et satis diligebatur à suis, magis tamen metuebatur, et erat epilepticus, nemine tamen sciente. Sed tandem ab vxore comperto contristabatur, se tali morbido nuptam, qui versutus fefellit, et consolabatur moestam figmento mendacij excogitati, dicens sanctum Dei Archangelum Gabrielem ad colloquendum et inspirandum sibi, quædam arcana et diuina interdum venire, et pro virtute aut claritate veniente se subito cadere et iacere ad intendendum inspirationem.

[Sidenote: Incrementum authoritatis Mahometi.] Post hoc autem, mortuo etiam Rege Arabiæ, tanta egit per simulationem sanctitatis, per donorum effusionem, et copiam promissionum, quod electus est et assumptus, in totias Arabiæ Regem.

[Sidenote: Tempus promulgationis Alcharani.] Confirmato igitur Mahometo in regnationis suæ maiestate suprema, transactis à conceptione Domini nostri Iesu Christi annis solaribus 612. in die Iouis feria quinta Hebdomadæ promulgauit præfatum detestandæ legis suæ librum, plenum perfidiæ et erroris, et à subditis tempore vitæ suæ seruari coegit, qui et vsque hodie in tanto æuo, et tot populis non sine iusto Dei iudicio colitur et seruatur, quamuis miserabile, et miserandum videtur, quod tot animæ in illo perduntur. Erat quoque tempore regni eius et alius Heremita in deserto Arabiæ, quem etiam quasi pro deuotione frequentare solebat, ducens secum aliquos de principibus et famlia. Super quo plures eorum attediati tractabant occidere Heremitan. [Sidenote: Occasio vina, interdicendi Sarracenis.] Accedit tandem vna noctium, vt rex Heremitam et seipsum inebriaret, et inter loquendum ambo consopiti dormirent. Et ecce habita occasione comites gladio de latere Regis clam extracto Heremitam interfecerunt, iterum clam condentes cruentum gladium in vagina: ac ille euigilans virum videns occisum, magno furore succensus imposuit familiæ factum, volens omnes per iustitiam condemnari ad mortem. Cumque coram iudicibus et sapientibus ageretur, hi omnes pari concordia, simili voce, et vno ore testabantur tam diuisim quam coniunctim, Regem in ebrietate sua hominem occidisse, quamuis fortassis esset facti oblitus. Et in plenariam rei probationem, dixerunt ipsum reposuisse mucronem in loculo nudum intersum, sed calido cruore madentem. Quo ita inuento, ac tantis rex obrutus testificationibus nimiùm erubuit, plenè obmutuit, et confusus recessit. Et ob hoc omnibus diebus suis vina bibere renunciauit: et in lege sua à cunctis bibi vetuit, ac vniuersis bibentibus, colentibus, et vendentibus maledixit. Cuius maledictio couertatur in caput eius, et in verticem ipsius iniquitas eius descendat, cum de vino scriptum constet, quòd Deum et homines lætificet. [Sidenote: Potus Sarracenorum.] Igitur de eo Sarraceni in sua superstitione deuoti vinum non bibunt, quanquam plures eorum quòd timent in publico non verentur in secreto.

Est autem communis potus eorum dulcis, delectabilis, et nutritiuus de Casaniel confectus, de qua et Saccarum fieri solet.

[Sidenote: Alias Mecca.] Mahometus iste post mortem suam pessimam (mors enim peccatorum pessima) conditus fuit honorificè in capsa, ditissimo auro, et argento, et saxis perornata in vna ciuitate regni sui Arabiæ, vbi et pro sancto, et vero Dei nuncio incepit deuotè coli à suis per annos ducentos sexaginta, atque ex tunc circa annum Domini nongentissimum cum veneratione multa cadauer eius translatum est, in digniorem ciuitatem dictam Merchuel Iachrib, vbi iam longe lateque pro maximo sanctorum, à cordibus à diabolica fraude deceptis colitur, requiritur et adoratur.

[Sidenote: Oregus a Templarijs proditus.] In ipsius translatione ipsa ciuitas restaurabatur, et firmabatur multò honorificentiùs, et fortiùs destructione sua, quæ per Carolum magnum Regem Franciæ antea fuit plenè annihilata, dum Ogerus dux Danorum præfatus in ea tenebatur captiuus, quem Templarij ad filios Brehir Regis Sarracenorum cum traditione vendiderant, eò quòd ipse Ogerus dictum Brehir in proelio occiderat, iuxta Lugdunum Franciæ ciuitatem. Et si quando nationis alterius quis ad legem conuertitur Sarracenorum, dum a flamine eorum recipiendus est, dicit et facit eum Dei nuncium, et repetit sic: Lællech ella alla Mahomet zoyzel alla heth: quod valet tantum: Non est Deus nisi vnus, et Mahomet fuit eius nuncius.

CAPVT. 23.

De colloquio Authoris cum Soldano.

Finaliter Sarraceni ponunt Iudæos malos, eò quod legem Dei violauerunt sibi missam, et commissam per Mosem. Et à simili probant Christianos malos, quod non seruant legem Euangelij Christi, quam seruandam susceperint. [Sidenote: Error eorum qui putant vnumquemque in sua religione posse beari.] Inest enim ijs falsa persuasio ita vt putent vnumquemque in ea qua natus est secta posse beari, si susceptam seruauerit illibatè: ideoque probant ab opposito se esse bonos, quia, sicut dicunt, obseruant scripta legis præcepta et ceremonias sancti libri sui à Deo sibi transmissi per beatum nuncium suum Mahomet. Vnde et ego non tacebo quid mihi contigit.

Dominus Soldanus quodam die in castro, expulsis omnibus de camera sua, me solùm retinuit secum tanquam pro secreto habendo colloquio. [Sidenote: Colloquium Soldani cum Mandeuillo.] Consuetum enim est ijs eijcere omnes tempore secretorum: qui diligenter à me interrogauit qualis esset gubernatio vitæ in terra nostra, breuiter respondebam, bona, per Dei gratiam, qui recepto hoc verbo dixit ita non esse. [Sidenote: Reprehensio Sacerdotum.] Sacerdotes (inquit) vestri, qui seipsos exhibere deberent alijs in exemplum, in malis iacent actibus, parùm curant de Templi seruitio:

habitu et studijs se conformant mundo: se inebriant vino, continentiam infringentes, cum fraude negotiantes, ac praua principibus consilia ingerentes. [Sidenote: Reprehensio vulgi iustissima.] Communis quoque populus, dum festus diebus intendere deberent deuotioni in templo, currit in hortis, in spectaculis, in tabernis vsque ad crapulam, et ebrietatem, et pinguia manducans et bibens, ac in bestiarum morem, luxuriam prauam exercens. [Sidenote: Vestimentorum varietas reprehensa.] In vsura, dolo, rapina, furto, detractione, mendacio et periurio viuunt plures eorum euidenter, ac si qui talia non agant, vt fatui reputantur, et pro nimia cordis superbia nesciunt ad libitum excogitare, qualiter se velint habere, mutando sibi indumenta, nunc longa, nunc curta nimis, quandoque ampla, quandoque stricta vltra modum, vt in his singulis appareant derisi potiùs quam vestiti: pileos quoque, calceos, caligas, corrigias sibi fabricante exquisitas, cùm etiam è contra deberent secundùm Christi sui doctrinam simplices, Deo deuoti, humiles, veraces, inuicem diligentes, inuicem concordantes, et inluriam de facili remittentes. Scimus etiam eos propter peccata sua perdidisse hanc terram optimam quam tenemus, nec timemus eam amittere, quamdiu se taliter gubernant. Attamen non dubitamus, quin in futurum per meliorem vitæ conuersationem merebuntur de nostris eam manibus recuperare.

Ad hoc ego vltra confusus et stupefactus, nequiui inuenire responsum; verebar enim obloqui veritati, quamuis ab Infidelis ore prolatæ, et vultu præ rubore demisso percunctatus sum, Domine, salua reuerentia, qualiter potestis ita plenè hoc noscere? De hominibus (ait) meis interdum mitto ad modum Mercatorum per terras, et regiones Christianorum, cum Balsamo, gemmis, sericis, ac aromatibus, ac per illos singula exploro, tam de statu Imperatoris, ac Pontificum, Principum, ac Sacerdotum, quàm Prælatorum, nec non æquora, prouincias, ac distinctiones earum.

Igitur peracta collocutione nostra satis producta, egressos principes in cameram reuocauit, ex quibus quatuor de maioribus iuxta nos aduocans, fecit eos expressè ac debitè, per singulas diuisiones in lingua Gallicana destinguere per partes, et singuarum nomina partium, omnem regionem terræ Angliæ, ac alias Christianorum terras multas, acsi inter nostros fuissent nati, vel multo tempore conuersati.

Nam et ipsum Soldanum audiui cum ijs bene et directè loquentem idioma Francorum. Itaque in omnibus his mente consternatus obmutui, cogitans, et dolens de peccatis singulis, rem taliter se habere.

Nunc piè igitur (rogo) consideremus, et corde attendamus, quantæ sit confusionis, et qualis opprobrij, dum Christiani nominis inimici nobis nostra exprobrant crimina. [Sidenote: Insignis Mandeuilli peroratio.] Et student quilibet in melius emendare, quatenus (Deo propitio) possit in breui tempore, hæc, de qua loquimur, terra Deo delecta, hæc sacrosancta terra, hæc filijs Dei promissa, nobis Dei adoptiuis restitui: vel certè, quod magis exorandum est, ipsi Sarraceni ad fidem Catholicam, et Christianam obedientiam, Ecclesiæ filijs aggregari, vt simul omnes per Dominum nostrum Iesum Christum consubstantialem Dei filium perueniamus ad coelestem Paradisum.

Explicit prima pars huius operis.

The English Version.

Betheleem is a litylle cytee, long and narwe and well walled, and in eche syde enclosed with gode dyches; and it was wont to ben cleped Effrata; as Holy Writt seythe, *Ecce audivimus cum in Effrata*; that is to seye, *Lo, we herde him in Effrata*. And toward the est ende of the cytee, is a fulle fair chirche and a gracyouse; and it hathe many toures, pynacles and corneres, fulle stronge and curiously made: and with in that chirche ben 44 pyleres of marble, grete and faire. And betwene the cytee and the chirche in the felde floridus; that is to seyne, the feld florisched: for als moche as a fayre mayden was blamed with wrong, and sclaundred, that sche hadde don fornycacioun; for whiche cause sche was demed to the dethe, and to be brent in that place, to the whiche sche was ladd. And as the fyre began to brenne about hire, sche made hire preyeres to oure Lord, that als wissely as sche was not gylty of that synne, that he wold helpe hire, and make it to be knowen to alle men, of his mercyfulle grace. And whan sche hadde thus seyd, sche entred in to the fuyer: and anon was the fuyr quenched and oute: and the brondes that weren brennynge, becomen rede roseres; and the brondes that weren not kyndled, becomen white roseres, fulle of roses. And theise weren the first roseres and roses, both white and rede, that evere ony man saughe. And thus was this mayden saved be the grace of God. And therfore is that feld clept the feld of God florysscht: for it was fulle of roses. Also besyde the queer of the chirche, at the right syde, as men comen dounward 16 greces, [Footnote: Steps.] is the place where oure Lord was born, that is fulle welle dyghte of marble, and fulle richely peynted with gold, sylver, azure, and other coloures. And 3 paas besyde, is the crybbe of the ox and the asse. And besyde that, is the place where the sterre fell, that ladde the 3 kynges, Jaspar, Melchior and Balthazar: but men of Grece clepen hem thus, Galgalathe, Malgalathe and Saraphie: and the Jewes clepen in this manere, in Ebrew, Appelius, Amerrius and Damasus. Theise 3 kynges offreden to oure Lord, gold, ensence and myrre: and thei metten to gedre, thorghe myracle of God; for thei metten to gedre in a cytee in Ynde, that Men clepen Cassak, that is 53 journeyes fro Betheleem; and thei weren at Betheleem the 13 day. And that was the 4 day aftre that thei hadden seyn the sterre, whan they metten in that cytee: and thus thei weren in 9 dayes, fro that cytee at Betheleem; and that was gret myracle. Also undre the cloystre of the chirche, be 18 degrees, at the righte syde, is the charnelle of the innocentes, where here bones lyzn. And before the place where oure Lord was born, is the tombe of Seynt Jerome, that was a preest and a cardynalle, that translatede the Bible and the psaultere from Ebrew in to Latyn: and witheoute the mynstre; is the chayere that he satt in, whan he translated it. And faste besyde that chirche, a 60 fedme, [Footnote: Fathom.] is a chirche of Seynt Nicholas, where oure Lady rested hire, aftre sche was lyghted of oure Lord. And for as meche as sche had to meche mylk in hire pappes, that greved hire, sche mylked hem on the rede stones of marble; so that the traces may zit be sene in the stones alle whyte. And zee schulle undrestonde, that alle that duellen in Betheleem ben Cristene men. And there ben fayre vynes about the cytee, and gret plentee of wyn, that the Cristene men han don let make. But the Sarazines ne tylen not no vynes, ne thei drynken no wyn. For here bokes of here lawe, that Makomete betoke hem, whiche thei clepen here Alkaron, and sume clepen it Mesaphe; and in another langage it is cleped Harme; and the same boke forbedethe hem to drinke wyn. For in that boke, Machomete cursed alle tho that drynken wyn, and alle hem that sellen it. For sum men seye, that he sloughe ones an heremyte in his dronkenesse, that he loved ful wel: and therefore he cursed wyn, and hem that drynken it. But his curs be turned in to his owne hed; as Holy Wrytt seythe; *Et in verticem ipsius iniquitas ejus descendet*; that is for to seye, *Hi wykkednesse schalle turne and falle in his owne heed*. And also the Sarazines bryngen forthe no pigges, nor thei eten no swynes flessche: for thei seye, it is brother to man, and it was forboden be the olde lawe: and thei holden hem alle accursed that eten there of. Also in the lond of Palestyne and in the lond of Egypt, thei eten but lytille or non of flessche of veel or of beef; but he be so old, that he may no more travayle for elde; for it is forbode: and for because the have but fewe of hem, therfore thei norisschen hem, for to ere here londes. In this cytee of Betheleem was David the kyng born: and he hadde 60 wyfes; and the firste wyf hihte Michol: and also he hadde 300 lemmannes.

An fro Betheleem unto Jerusalem nys but 2 myle. And in the weye to Jerusalem, half a myle fro Betheleem is a chirche, where the aungel seyde to the scheppardes, of the birthe of Crist. And in that weye is the tombe of Rachelle, that was Josephes modre, the patriarke; and sche dyede anon, aftre that sche was delyvered of hire sone Beniamyn; and there sche was buryed of Jacob hire husbonde: and he leet setten 12 grete stones on here, in tokene that sche had born 12 children. [Footnote: Rachel had only two children, but twelve grandchildren.] In the same weye, half myle fro Jerusalem, appered the sterre to the 3 kynges. In that weye also ben manye chirches of Cristen men, be the whiche men gon towardes the cytee of Jerusalem.

Of the Pilgrimages in Jerusalem and of the Holy Places thereaboute.

[Sidenote: Cap. VII.] After for to speke of Jerusalem, the holy cytee, zee schulle undirstonde, that it stont fulle faire betwene hilles: and there ben no ryveres ne welles; but watre comethe be condyte from Ebron. And zee schulle undirstonde, that Jerusalem of olde tyme, unto the tyme of Melchisedeche, was cleped Jebus; and aftre it was clept Salem, unto the tyme of Kyng David, that putte theise 2 names to gidere, and cleped it Jebusalem; and aftre that Kyng Salomon cleped it Jerosoloyme: and aftre that, men cleped it Jerusalem; and so it is cleped zit. And aboute Jerusalem is the kyngdom of Surrye: and there besyde is the lond of Palestyne: and besyde it is Ascolone: and besyde that is the lond of Maritaine. But Jerusalem is in the lond of Judee; and it is clept Jude, for that Judas Machabeus was kyng of that contree; and it marchethe estward to the kyngdom of Arabye; on the southe syde, to the lond of Egipt; and on the west syde, to the grete see; on the north syde, towarde the kyngdom of Surrye, and to the See of Cypre. In Jerusalem was wont to be a patriark, and erchebysshoppes and bisshoppes abouten in the contree. Abouten Jerusalem ben theise cytees: Ebron, at 7 myle; Jerico, at 6 myle; Bersabee, at 8 myle; Ascalon, at 17 myle; Jaff, at 16 myle; Ramatha, at 3 myle; and Betheleem, at 2 myle. And a 2 myle trom Betheleem, toward the sowthe, is the chirche of Seynt Karitot, that was abbot there; for whom thei maden meche Doel [Footnote: Mourning.] amonges the monkes, whan he scholde dye; and zit thei ben in moornynge, in the wise that thei maden here lamentacioun for him the firste tyme: and it is fulle gret pytee to beholde.

This contree and lond of Jerusalem hathe ben in many dyverse naciounes hondes: and often therfore hathe the contree suffred meche tribulacioun, for the synne of the people, that duellen there. For that contree hathe ben in the hondes of alle nacyouns: that is to seyne, of Jewes, of Chananees, Assiryenes, Perses, Medoynes, Macedoynes, of Grekes, Romaynes, of Cristene men, of Sarazines, Barbaryenes, Turkes, Tartaryenes, and of manye othere dyverse nacyouns. For God wole not, that it be longe in the hondes of trytoures ne of synneres, be thei Cristene or othere. And now have the hethene men holden that lond in here hondes 40 zeere and more: but thei schulle not holde it longe, zif God wole.

And zee schulle undirstond, that whan men comen to Jerusalem, here first pilgrymage is to the Chirche of the Holy Sepulcre, where oure Lord was buryed, that is with oute the cytee, on the northe syde: but it is now enclosed in, with the toun walle. And there is a fulle fayr chirche, alle rownd, and open above, and covered with leed. And on the west syde is a fair tour and an highe, for belles, strongly made. And in the myddes of the chirche is a tabernacle, as it were a lytylle hows, made with a low lytylle dore: and that tabernacle is made in manere of half a compass, righte curiousely and richely made, of gold and azure and othere riche coloures, fulle nobelyche made. And in the righte syde of that tabernacle is the sepulcre of oure Lord. And the tabernacle is 8 fote longe, and 5 fote wyde, and 11 fote in heighte. And it is not longe sithen the sepulcre was alle open, that men myghte kisse it and touche it. But for pilgrymes that comen thidre, peyned hem to breke the ston in peces or in poudre, therfore the Soudan hathe do make a walle aboute the sepulcre, that no man may towche it. But in the left syde of the walle of the tabernacle is well the heighte of a man, a gret ston to the quantytee of a mannes hed, that was of the holy sepulcre: and that ston kissen the pilgrymes, that comen thidre. In that tabernacle ben no wyndowes: but it is alle made lighte with lampes, that hangen before the sepulcre. And there is a lampe, that hongethe before the sepulcre, that brennethe lighte: and on the Gode Fryday it gothe out be him self; and lyghtith azen be him self at that oure, that oure Lorde roos fro dethe to lyve. Also within the chirche, at the righte syde, besyde the queer of the chirche, is the Mount of Calvarye, where oure Lord was don on the Cros: and it is a roche of white colour, and a lytille medled with red: and the Cros was set in a morteys, in the same roche: and on that roche dropped the woundes of our Lord, whan he was payned on the Crosse; and that is cleped Golgatha. And men gon up to that Golgotha be degrees: and in the place of that morteys was Adames hed founden, aftre Noes flode; in tokene that the synnes of Adam scholde ben boughte in that same place. And upon that roche made Abraham sacrifice to oure Lord. And there is an awtere: and before that awtere lyzn Godefray de Boleyne and Bawdewyn, and othere Cristene kynges of Jerusalem; And there nyghe, where our Lord was crucyfied, is this written in Greek, [Greek: Ho Theos Basileus hæmon pro aionon eirgasato aotærian en meso tæs gæs.] that is to seyne, in Latyn, *Deus Rex noster ante secula operatus est salutem, in medio terræ*; that is to seye, *Gode oure Kyng, before the worldes, hathe wroughte hele in myddis of the erthe.* And also on that roche, where the Cros was sett, is writen with in the roche theise, wordes; [Greek: Ho eideis esti basis tæs pisteos holæs tou kosmou touton.] that is to seyne in Latyn, *Quod vides, est fundamentum totius Fidei hujus Mundi*; that is to seyne, *That thou seest, is ground of alle the feythe of this world.* And zee schulle undirstonde, that whan oure Lord was don upon the Cros, he was 33 zere and 3 moneths of elde. And the prophecye of David seythe thus: *Quadraginta annis proximus fui generationi huic*; that is to seye, *fourty zeer was I neighebore to this kynrede.* And thus scholde it seme, that the prophecyes ne were not trewe: but thei ben bothe trewe: for in old tyme men maden a zeer of 10 moneths; of the whiche Marche was the firste, and Decembre was the laste. But Gayus, that was Emperour of Rome, putten theise 2 monethes there to, Janyver and Feverer; and ordeyned the zeer of 12 monethes; that is to seye, 365 dayes, with oute lepe zeer, aftre the propre cours of the sonne. And therfore, aftre cowntynge of 10 monethes of the zeer, de dyede in the

40 zeer; as the prophete seyde; and aftre the zeer of 12 monethes, he was of age 33 zeer and 3 monethes. Also with in the Mount Calvarie, on the right side, is an awtere, where the piler lyzthe, that oure Lord Jesu was bounden to, whan he was scourged. And there besyde ben 4 pileres of ston, that alle weys droppen watre: and sum men seyn, that thei wepen for our Lordes dethe. And nyghe that awtier is a place undre erthe, 42 degrees of depnesse, where the holy croys was founden, be the wytt of Seynte Elyne, undir a roche, where the Jewes had hidde it. And that was the verray croys assayed: for thei founden 3 crosses; on of oure Lord, and 2 of the 2 theves: and Seynte Elyne preved hem on a ded body, that aros from dethe to lyve, whan it was leyed on it that oure Lord dyed on. And there by in the walle is the place where the 4 nayles of oure Lord weren hidd: for he had 2 in his hondes, and 2 in his feet: and of on of theise, the Emperour of Costantynoble made a brydille to his hors, to bere him in batayle: and thorghe vertue there of, he overcam his enemyes, and wan alle the lond of Asye the lesse; that is to seye, Turkye, Ermonye the lasse and the more; and from Surrye to Jerusalem, from Arabye to Persie, from Mesopotayme to the kyngdom of Halappee, from Egypt the highe and the lowe, and all the othere kyngdomes, unto the Depe of Ethiope, and into Ynde the lesse, that then was Cristene. And there were in that tyme many gode holy men and holy heremytes; of whom the book of fadres lyfes spekethe: and thei ben now in Paynemes and Sarazines honds. But whan God alle myghty wole, righte als the londes weren lost thorghe synne of Cristene men, so schulle thei ben wonnen azen be Cristen men thorghe help of God. And in myddes of that chirche is a compas, in the whiche Joseph of Aramathie leyde the body of oure Lord, whan he had taken him down of the cross: and there he wassched the woundes of oure Lord: and that compas, seye men, is the myddes of the world. And in the Chirche of the Sepulchre, on the north syde, is the place where oure Lord was put in presoun; (for he was in presoun in many places) and there is a partye of the Cheyne that he was bounden with: and there he appered first to Marie Magdaleyne, whan he was rysen; and sche wende, that he had ben a gardener. In the chirche of Seynt Sepulchre was wont to ben chanouns of the ordre of Seynt Augustyn, and hadden a priour; but the patriark was here sovereygne. And withe oute the dores of the chirche, on the right syde, as men gon upward 18 Greces, seyde oure Lord to his moder, *Mulier, ecce filius tuus*; that is to seye, *Woman, lo thi Sone*. And aftre that, he seyde to John his disciple, *Ecce mater tua*; that is to seyne, *Lo, behold thi modir*. And these wordes he seyde on the cros. And on theise Greces wente oure Lord, whan he bare the crosse on his schuldir. And undir this grees is a chapelle; and in that chapelle syngen prestes, yndyenes; that is to seye, prestes of ynde; noght aftir oure lawe, but aftir here: and alle wey thei maken here sacrement of the awtier, seyenge, *Pater noster*, and othere preyeres there with: with the which preyeres, thei seye the

wordes, that the sacrement is made of. For thei ne knowe not the addiciouns, that many Popes han made; but thei synge with gode devocioun. And there nere, is the place where that oure Lord rested him, whan he was wery, for berynge of the Cros. And zee schulle undirstonde, that before the Chirche of the Sepulcre, is the cytee more feble than in ony othere partie, for the grete playn that is betwene the chirche and the cytee. And toward the est syde, with oute the walles of the cytee, is the Vale of Josaphathe, that touchethe to the walles, as thoughe it were a large dyche. And anen that Vale of Josaphathe, out of the cytee, is the Chirche of Seynt Stevene, where he was stoned to dethe. And there beside, is the gildene zate, that may not ben opened; be the whiche zate, oure Lord entrede on Palmesonday, upon an asse; and the zate opened azenst him, whan he wolde go unto the temple: and zit apperen the steppes of the asses feet, in 3 places of the degrees, that ben of fulle harde ston. And before the chirche of Seynt Sepulcre, toward the southe, a 200 paas, is the gret hospitalle of Seynt John; of the whiche the hospitleres hadde here foundacioun. And with inne the palays of the seke men of that hospitalle ben 124 pileres of ston: and in the walles of the hows, with oute the nombre aboveseyd, there ben 54 pileres, that beren up the hows. And fro that hospitalle, to go toward the est, is a fulle fayr chirche, that is clept *Nostre Dame la Graund*. And than is there another chirche right nyghe, that is clept *Nostre Dame la Latytne*. And there weren Marie Cleophee and Marie Magdaleyne, and teren here heer, whan oure Lord was peyned in the cros.

Of the Temple of oure Lord. Of the Crueltee of Kyng Heroud. Of the Mount
   Syon. Of Probatica Piscina. And of Natatorium Siloe.

[Sidenote: Cap. VIII.] And fro the chirche of the sepulcre, toward the est, at 160 paas, is *Templum Domini*. It is right a feir hows, and it is alle round, and highe, and covered with leed, and it is well paved with white marble: but the Sarazine wole not suffre no Cristene manne Jewes to come there in; for thei seyn, that none so foule synfulle men scholde not come in so holy place: but I cam in there, and in othere places, where I wolde; for I hadde lettres of the Soudan, with his grete seel; and comounly other men han but his signett. In the whiche lettres he comanded of his, specyalle grace, to all his subgettes, to lete me seen alle the places, and to enforme me pleynly alle the mysteries of every place, and to condyte me fro cytee to cytee, zif it were nede, and buxomly to resceyve me and my companye, and for to obeye to alle my requestes resonable, zif thei weren not gretly azen the royalle power, and dignytee of the Soudan or of his lawe. And to othere, that asken him grace, suche as han served him, he ne zevethe not but his signet; the whiche thei make to be born before hem, hangynge on a spere; and the folk of the contree don gret worschipe and reverence to his signett or his seel, and knelen there to, as lowly as wee don to *Corpus Domini*. And zit men don fulle grettere reverence to his lettres. For the admyralle and alle othere lordes, that thei ben schewed to, before or thei resceyve hem, thei knelen doun, and than thei take hem, and putten hem on here hedes, and aftre thei kissen hem, and than thei reden hem, knelynge with gret reverence, and than thei offren hem to do alle, that the berere askethe. And in this *Templum Domini* weren somtyme chanouns reguleres: and thei hadden an abbot, to whom thei weren obedient. And in this temple was Charlemayn, when that the aungelle broughte him the prepuce of oure Lord Jesu Crist, of his circumcisioun: and aftre Kyng Charles leet bryngen it to Parys, in to his chapelle: and aftre that to Chartres. And zee schulle undirstonde, that this is not the temple that Salomon made: for that temple dured not, bat 1102 zeer. For Tytus, Vespasianes sone, Emperour of Rome, had leyd sege aboute Jerusalem, for to discomfyte the Jewes: for thei putten oure Lord to dethe, with outen leve of the Emperour. And whan he hadde wonnen the cytee, he brente the temple and beet it down, and alle the cytee, and toke the Jewes, and dide hem to Dethe, 1100000: and the othere he putte in presoun, and solde hem to servage, 30 for o peny: for thei seyde, thei boughte Jesu for 30 penyes: and he made of hem bettre cheep, whan he zaf 30 for o peny. And aftre that tyme, Julianas Apostate, that was Emperour, zaf leve to the Jewes to make the Temple of Jerusalem: for he hated Cristene men; and zit he was cristned, but he forsoke his law, and becam a renegate. And whan the Jewes hadden made the temple, com an erthe quakeng, and cast it doun (as God wolde) and destroyed alle that thei had made. And aftre that, Adryan, that was Emperour of Rome, and of the lynage of Troye, made Jerusalem azen, and the temple, in the same manere, as Salomon made it. And he wolde not suffre no Jewes to dwelle there, but only Cristene men. For alle thoughe is were so, that hee was not cristned, zet he lovede Cristene men, more than ony other nacioun, saf his owne. This Emperour leet enclose the Chirche of Seynt Sepulcre, and walle it, within the cytee, that before was with oute the cytee, long tyme beforn. And he wolde have chaunged the name of Jerusalem, and have cleped it Elya: but that name lasted not longe. Also zee schulle undirstonde, that the Sarazines don moche reverence to that temple; and thei seyn, that that place is right holy. And whan thei gon in, thei gon barefote, and knelen many tymes. And whanne my felowes and I seyghe that, whan we comen in, wee diden of oure shoon, and camen in barefote, and thoughten that we scholden don as moche worschipe and reverence there to, as ony of the mysbeleevynge men sholde, and as gret compunction in herte to have. This temple is 64 cubytes of wydenesse, and als manye in lengthe; and of heighte it is 120 cubites: and it is with inne, alle aboute, made with pyleres of marble: and in the myddel place of the temple ben manye highe stages, of 14 degrees of heighte, made with gode pyleres alle aboute: and this place the Jewes callen *Sancta Sanctorum*; that is to seye, *holy of halewes*. And in that place comethe no man, saf only here prelate, that makethe here sacrifice. And the folk stonden alle aboute, in diverse stages, aftre thei ben of dignytee or of worschipe; so that thei alle may see the sacrifice. And in that temple ben 4 entrees; and the zates ben of cypresse, wel made and curiousely dight. And with in the est zate, oure Lorde seyde, *Here is Jerusalem.* And in the northsyde of that temple with in the zate, there is a welle; but it rennethe noght; of the whiche Holy Writt spekethe, and seythe, *Vidi aquam egredientem de Templo*; that is to seyne, *I saughe watre come out of the Temple.* And on that other syde of the Temple there is a roche, that men clepen Moriache: but aftre it was clept Bethel; where the arke of God, with relykes of Jewes, weren wont to ben put. That arke or hucche, with the relikes, Tytus ledde with hym to Rome, whan he had scomfyted alle the Jewes. In that arke weren the 10 commandementes, and of Arones zerde, and of Moyses zerde, with the whiche he made the Rede See departen, as it had ben a walle, on the righte syde and on the left syde, whils that the peple of Israel passeden the see drye foot: and with that zerde he smoot the roche; and the watre cam out of it: and with that zerde he dide manye wondres. And there in was a vessel of gold, fulle of manna, and clothinges and ournements and the tabernacle of Aaron, and a tabernacle square of gold, with 12 precyous stones, and a boyst of jasper grene, with 4 figures, and 8 names of oure Lord, and 7 candelstykes of gold, and 12 pottes of gold, and 4 censeres of gold, and an awtier of gold, and 4 lyouns of gold, upon the whiche thei bare cherubyn of gold, l2 spannes long, and the cercle of swannes of Hevene, with a tabernacle of gold, and a table of sylver, and 2 trompes of silver, and 7 barly loves, and alle the othere relikes, that weren before the birthe of oure Lord Jesu Crist. And upon that roche, was Jacob slepynge, when he saughe the aungeles gon up and doun, by a laddre, and he seyd, *Vere locus isse sanctus est, et ego ignorabam*; that is to seyne, *Forsothe this place is holy, and I wiste it nought.* And there an aungel helde Jacob stille, and turned his name, and cleped him Israel. And in that same place, David saughe the aungelle, that smot the folk with a swerd, and put it up blody in the schethe. And in that same roche, was Seynt Symeon, whan he resceyved oure Lord into the Temple. And in this roche he sette him, whan the Jewes wolde a stoned him; and a sterre cam doun, and zaf him light. And upon that roche, prechede our Lord often tyme to the peple; and out of that seyd temple, oure Lord drof the byggeres and the selleres. And upon that roche, oure Lord sette him, whan the Jewes wolde have stoned him; and the roche cleef in two, and in that clevynge was oure Lord hidd; and there cam doun a sterre, and zaf lighte and served him with claretee; and upon that roche, satt oure lady, and lerned hire sawtere; and there our Lord forzaf the womman hire sinnes, that was founden in Avowtrie: and there was oure Lord circumcyded: and there the aungelle schewede tydynges to Zacharie of the birthe of Seynt Baptyst his sone; and there offred first Melchisedeche bred and wyn to oure Lord, in tokene of the sacrement that was to comene; and there felle David preyeng to oure Lord, and to the aungelle, that smot the peple, that he wolde have mercy on him and on the peple; and oure Lorde herde his preyere; and therefore wolde he make the temple in that place: but oure Lord forbade him, be an aungelle, for he had don tresoun, whan he leet sle Urie the worthi knyght, for to have Bersabee his wyf; and therfore all the purveyance, that he hadde ordeyned to make the temple with, he toke it Salomon his sone; and he made it. And he preyed oure Lord, that alle tho that preyeden to him, in that place, with gode herte, that he wolde heren here preyere and graunten it hem, zif thei asked it rightefullyche: and oure Lord graunted it him: and therfore Salomon cleped that temple, the Temple of Conseille and of Help of God. And with oute the zate of that temple is an awtiere, where Jewes werein wont to offren dowves and turtles. And betwene the temple and that awtiere was Zacharie slayn. And upon the pynacle of that temple was oure Lord brought, for to ben tempted of the enemye, the feend. And on the heighte of that pynacle, the Jewes setten Seynt Jame, and casted him down to the erthe, that first was Bisschopp of Jerusalem. And at the entree of that temple, toward the west, is the zate that is clept *Porta speciosa*. And nyghe besyde that temple, upon the right syde, is a chirche covered with leed, that is clept Salomones Scole. And fro that temple, towardes the southe, right nyghe, is the Temple of Salomon, that is righte fair and wel pollisscht. And in that temple duellen the knyghtes of the temple, that weren wont to be clept templeres: and that was the foundacionn of here ordre; so that there duelleden knyghtes; and in *Templo Domini*, chanouns reguleres. Fro that temple toward the est, a 120 paas, in the cornere of the cytee, is the bathe of oure Lord: and in that bathe was wont to come watre fro paradys, and zit it droppethe. And there besyde, is oure ladyes bed. And faste by, is the temple of Seynt Symeon: and with oute the cloyster of the temple, toward the northe, is a fulle faire chirche of Seynte Anne, oure ladyes modre: and there was oure lady conceyved. And before that chirche, is a gret tree, that began to growe the same nyght. And undre that chirche, in goenge doun be 22 degrees, lythe Joachym, oure ladyes fader, in a faire tombe of ston: and there besyde, lay somtyme Seynt Anne his wyf; but Seynt Helyne leet translate hire to Costantynople. And in that chirche is a welle, in manere of a cisterne, that is clept *Probatica Piscina*, that hathe 5 entrees. Into that welle, aungeles weren wont to come from Hevene, and bathen hem with inne: and, what man that first bathed him, aftre the mevynge of the watre, was made hool, of what maner sykenes that he hadde: and there oure Lord heled a man of the palasye, that laye 38 zeer: and oure Lord seyde to him, *Tolle Grabatum tuum & ambula*: that is to seye, *Take thi bed, and go*. And there besyde, was Pylates hows. And faste by, is Kyng Heroudes hows, that leet sle the innocentes.

This Heroude was over moche cursed and cruelle: for first he leet sle his wif, that he lovede righte welle; and for the passynge love, that he hadde to hire, whan he saughe hire ded, he felle in a rage, and oute of his wytt, a gret while; and sithen he cam azen to his wytt: and aftre he leet sle his two sones, that he hadde of that wyf: and aftre that, he leet sle another of his wyfes, and a sone, that he hadde with hire: and aftre that, he leet sle his owne modre: and he wolde have slayn his brother also, but he dyede sodeynly. And aftre he fell into seknesse, and whan he felte, that he scholde dye, he sente aftre his sustre, and aftre alle the lordes of his lond; and whan thei were comen; he leet commande hem to prisoun, and than he seyde to his sustre, he wiste wel, that men of the contree wolde make no sorwe for his dethe; and therefore he made his sustre swere, that sche scholde lete smyte of alle the heds of the lordes, whan he were ded; and than scholde alle the lond make sorwe for his dethe, and else nought: and thus he made his testement. But his sustre fulfilled not his wille: for als sone as he was ded, sche delyvered alle the lordes out of presoun, and lete hem gon, eche lord to his owne; and tolde hem alle the purpos of hire brothers ordynance: and so was this cursed kyng never made sorwe for, as he supposed for to have ben. And zee schulle undirstonde, that in that tyme there weren 3 Heroudes, of gret name and loos for here crueltee. This Heroude, of whiche I have spoken offe, was Heroude Ascalonite: and he that leet beheden seynt John the Baptist, was Heroude Antypa: and he that leet smyte of Seynt James hed, was Heroude Agrippa; and he putte Seynt Peter in presoun.

Also furthermore, in the cytee, is the Chirche of Seynt Savyour; and there is the left arm of John Crisostom, and the more partye of the hed of Seynt Stevene. And on that other syde of the strete, toward the southe, as men gon to Mount Syon, is a chirche of Seynt James, where he was beheded. And fro that chirche, a 120 paas, is the Mount Syon: and there is a faire chirche of oure Lady, where sche dwelled; and there sche dyed. And there was wont to ben an abbot of Chanouns Reguleres. And fro thens, was sche born of the apostles, onto the Vale of Josaphathe. And there is the ston, that the aungelle broughte to oure Lady, fro the Mount of Synay; and it is of that colour, that the roche is of Seynt Kateryne. And there besyde, is the zate, where thorghe oure Ladye wente, whan sche was with childe, whan sche wente to Betheleem. Also at the entree of the Mount Syon, is a chapelle; and in that chapelle is the ston gret and large, with the whiche the sepulcre was covered with, whan Josephe of Aramathie had put oure Lord thereinne: the whiche ston the 3 Maries sawen turnen upward, whan thei comen to the sepulcre, the day of his resurrexioun; and there founden an aungelle, that tolde hem of oure Lordes uprysynge from dethe to lyve. And there also is a ston, in a walle, besyde the zate, of the pyleer, that oure Lord was scourged ate: and there was Annes hows, that was Bishop of the Jewes, in that ryme. And there was oure Lord examyned in the nyght, and scourged and smytten and vylently entreted. And in that same place, Seynt Peter forsoke oure Lord thries, or the cok creew. And there is a party of the table, that he made his souper onne, whan he made his maundee, with his discyples; whan he zaf hem his flesche and his blode, in forme of bred and wyn. And undre that chapelle, 32 degrees, is the place, where oure Lord wossche his disciples feet and zit is the vesselle, where the watre was. And there besyde that same vesselle, was Seynt Stevene buryed. And there is the awtier, where oure Lady herde the aungelles synge messe. And there appered first oure Lord to his disciples, after his resurrexioun, the zates enclosed, and seyde to hem, *Pax vobis*: that is to seye, *Pees to zou*. And on that mount, appered Crist to Seynt Thomas the apostle, and bade him assaye his woundes; and there beleeved he first, and seyde, *Dominus meus et Deus meus*; that is to seye, *my Lord and my God*. In the same chirche, besyde the awteer, weren alle the aposteles on Whytsonday, whan the Holy Gost descended on hem, in lyknesse of fuyr. And there made oure Lord his pask, [Footnote: Pascal feast] with his disciples. And there slept Seynt John the Evaungeliste, upon the breeste of oure Lord Jesu Crist, and saughe slepynge many hevenly prevytees.

Mount Syon is with inne the cytee; and it is a lytille hiere than the other syde of the cytee: and the cytee is strongere on that syde, than on that other syde. For at the foot of the Mount Syon, is a faire castelle and a strong, that the Soudan leet make. In the Mount Syon weren buryed Kyng David and Kyng Salomon, and many othere kynges, Jewes of Jerusalem. And there is the place, where the Jewes wolden han cast up the body of oure Lady, whan the apostles beren the body to ben buryed, in the Vale of Josaphathe. And there is the place, where Seynt Petir wepte fulle tenderly, aftre that he hadde forsaken oure Lord. And a stones cast fro that chapelle, is another chapelle, where oure Lord was jugged: for that tyme, was there Cayphases hows. From that chapelle, to go toward the est, at 140 paas, is a deep cave undre the roche, that is clept the Galylee of oure Lord; where Seynt Petre hidde him, whanne he had forsaken oure Lord. Item, betwene the Mount Syon and the Temple of Salomon, is the place, where oure Lord reysed the mayden, in hire fadres hows. Undre the Mount Syon, toward the Vale of Josaphathe, is a welle, that is clept *Natatorium Siloe*; and there was oure Lord wasshen, aftre his bapteme: and there made oure Lord the blynd man to see. And there was y buryed Ysaye the prophete. Also streghte from Natatorie Siloe, is an ymage of ston, and of olde auncyen werk, that Absalon leet make: and because there of, men clepen it the head of Absalon. And faste by, is zit the tree of eldre, that Judas henge him self upon, for despeyr that he hadde, whan he solde and betrayed oure Lord. And there besyde, was the synagoge, where the bysshoppes of Jewes and the pharyses camen to gidere, and helden here conseille. And there caste

Judas the 30 pens before hem, and seyde, that he hadde synned, betrayenge oure Lord. And there nyghe was the hows of the apostles Philippe and Jacob Alphei. And on that other syde of Mount Syon, toward the southe, bezonde the Vale, a stones cast, is Acheldamache; that is to seye, the Feld of Blood; that was bought for the 30 pens, that oure Lord was sold fore. And in that feld ben many tombes of Cristene men: for there ben manye pilgrymes graven. And there ben many oratories, chapelles and heremytages, where heremytes weren wont to duelle. And toward the est, an 100 pas, is the charnelle of the hospitalle of seynt John, where men weren wont to putte the bones of dede men.

Also fro Jerusalem, toward the west, is a fair chirche, where the tree of the cros grew. And 2 myle fro thens, is a faire chirche; where oure lady mette with Elizabethe, whan thei weren bothe with childe; and seynt John stered in his modres wombe, and made reverence to his Creatour, that he saughe not. And undre the awtier of that chirche, is the place where seynt John was born. And fro that chirche, is a myle to the castelle of Emaux; and there also oure Lord schewed him to 2 of his disciples, aftre His resurrexion. Also on that other syde, 200 pas fro Jerusalem, is a chirche, where was wont to be the cave of the lioun: and undre that chirche, at 30 degrees of depnesse, weren entered 12000 martires, in the tyme of Kyng Cosdroc, that the lyoun mette with alle in a nyghte, be the wille of God. Also fro Jerusalem 2 myle, is the Mount Joye, a fulle fair place and a delicyous: and there lythe Samuel the prophete in a faire tombe: and men clepen it Mount Joye; for it zevethe joye to pilgrymes hertes, be cause that there men seen first Jerusalem. Also betwene Jerusalem and the Mount of Olyvete, is the Vale of Josaphathe, undre the walles of the cytee, as I have seyd before: and in the myddes of the vale, is a lytille ryvere, that men clepen Torrens Cedron; and aboven it, over thwart, lay a tre, (that the cros was made offe) that men zeden over onne: and faste by it is a litylle pytt in the erthe, where the foot of the pileer is zit entered; and there was oure Lord first scourged: for he was scourged and vileynsly entreted in many places. Also in the myddel place of the vale of Josaphathe, is the chirche of oure lady: and it is of 43 degrees, undre the erthe, unto the sepulchre oure lady. And oure lady was of age, when sche dyed, 72 zeer. And beside the sepulchre of oure lady, is an awtier, where oure Lord forzaf seynt Petir all his synnes. And fro thens, toward the west, undre an awtere, is a welle, that comethe out of the ryvere of Paradys. And witethe wel, that that chirche is fulle lowe in the erthe; and sum is alle with inne the erthe. But I suppose wel, that it was not so founded: but for because that Jerusalem hathe often tyme ben destroyed, and the walles abated and beten doun and tombled in to the vale, and that thei han ben so filled azen, and the ground enhaunced; and for that skylle, is the chirche so lowe with in the erthe: and natheles men seyn there comounly, that the erthe hathe so ben cloven, sythe the tyme, that oure

Lady was there buryed: and zit men seyn there, that it wexethe and growethe every day, with outen dowte. In that chirche were wont to ben blake monkes, that hadden hire abbot. And besyde that chirche, is a chapelle, besyde the roche, that highte Gethesamany: and there was oure Lord kyssed of Judas; and there was he taken of the Jewes; and there laft oure Lord his disciples, whan he wente to preye before his passioun, whan he preyed and seyde, *Pater, si fieri potest, transeat a me calix iste*; that is to seye, *Fadre, zif it may be, do lete this chalys go fro me*. And whan he cam azen to his disciples, he fond hem slepynge. And in the roche, with inne the chapelle, zit apperen the fyngres of oure Lordes hond, whan he putte hem in the roche, whan the Jewes wolden have taken him. And fro thens a stones cast, toward the southe, is anothere chapelle, where oure Lord swette droppes of blood. And there righte nyghe, is the tombe of Kyng Josaphathe; of whom the vale berethe the name. This Josaphathe was kyng of that contree, and was converted by an heremyte, that was a worthi man, and dide moche gode. And fro thens a bowe drawghte, towards the south, is the chirche, where Seynt James and Zacharie the prophete weren buryed. And above the vale, is the Mount of Olyvete: and it is cleped so, for the plentee of olyves, that growen there. That mount is more highe than the cytee of Jerusalem is: and therfore may men, upon that mount, see manye of the stretes of the cytee. And between that mount and the cytee, is not but the vale of Josaphathe, that is not fulle large. And fro that mount, steighe oure Lord Jesu Crist to Hevene, upon ascencioun day: and zit there schewethe the schapp of his left foot, in the ston. And there is a chirche, where was wont to be an abbot and chanouns reguleres. And a lytylle thens, 28 pas, is a chapelle, and there in is the ston, on the whiche oure Lord sat, whan he prechede the 8 blessynges, and seyde thus: *Beati pauperes spiritu*: and there he taughte his disciples the *Pater noster*; and wrote with his finger in a ston. And there nyghe is a chirche of Seynte Marie Egipcyane; and there sche lythe in a tombe. And fro then toward the est, a 3 bow schote, is Bethfagee; to the whiche oure Lord sente Seynt Peter and Seynt James, for to feche the asse, upon Palme Sonday, and rode upon that asse to Jerusalem. And in comynge doun fro the Mount of Olyvete, toward the est, is a castelle, that is cleped Bethanye: and there dwelte Symon leprous, and there herberwed oure Lord; and aftre, he was baptized of the Apostles, and was clept Julian, and was made bisschoppe: and this is the same Julyan, that men clepe to for gede herberghgage; for oure Lord herberwed with him, in his hows. And in that hous, oure Lord forzaf Marie Magdaleyne hire synnes; there sche whassched his feet with hire teres, and wyped hem with hire heer. And there served seynt Martha, oure Lord. There oure Lord reysed Lazar fro dethe to lyve, that was ded 4 dayes and stank, that was brother to Marie Magdaleyne and to Martha. And there duelte also Marie Cleophe. That castelle is wel a myle long fro Jerusalem. Also in comynge doun fro the

Mount of Olyvete, is the place where oure Lord wepte upon Jerusalem. And there besyde is the place, where oure lady appered to seynt Thomas the Apostle, aftre hire assumptioun, and zaf him hire Gyrdylle. And right nyghe is the ston, where oure Lord often tyme sat upon, whan he prechede: and upon that same schalle he sytte, at the day of doom; righte as him self seyde.

Also aftre the Mount of Olyvete, is the Mount of Galilee: there assembleden the apostles, whan Marie Magdaleyne cam, and tolde hem of Cristes uprisynge. And there, betwene the Mount Olyvete and the Mount Galilee, is a chirche, where the aungel seyde to our lady, of hire dethe. Also fro Bethanye to Jerico, was somtyme a lityylle Cytee: but it is now alle destroyed; and now is there but a lityylle village. That cytee tok Josue, be myracle of God and commandement of the aungel, and destroyed it and cursed it, and alle hem that bylled it azen. Of that citee was Zacheus the dwerf, that clomb up in to the Sycomour Tre, for to see oure Lord; be cause he was so litille, he myghte not seen Him for the peple. And of that cytee was Raab the comoun womman, that ascaped allone, with hem of hire lynage; and sche often tyme refressched and fed the messageres of Israel, and kepte hem from many grete periles of dethe: and therfore sche hadde gode reward; as Holy Writt seythe: *Qui accipit prophetam in nomine meo, mercedem prophetæ accipiet*; that is to seye, *He that takethe a prophete in my name, he schalle take mede of the prophete*: and so had sche; for sche prophecyed to the messageres, seyenge, *Novi quod Dominus tradet vobis Terram hanc*; that is to seye, *I wot wel, that oure Lord schal betake zou this Lond*: and so he dide. And after Salomon, Naasones sone, wedded hire; and fro that tyme was sche a worthi womman, and served God wel. Also from Betanye gon men to flom [Footnote: River,—Latin, *flumen*.] Jordan, by a mountayne, and thorghe desert; and it is nyghe a day jorneye fro Bethanye, toward the est, to a gret hille, where oure Lord fasted 40 dayes. Upon that hille, the enemy of helle bare our Lord, and tempted him, and seyde; *Dic ut lapides isti panes fiant*; that is to seye, *Sey, that theise stones be made loves*. In that place, upon the hille, was wont to ben a faire chirche; but it is alle destroyed, so that there is now but an hermytage, that a maner of Cristene men holden, that ben cleped Georgyenes: for Seynt George converted hem. Upon that hille duelte Abraham a gret while: and therfore men clepen it, Abrahames gardyn. And betwene the hille and this gardyn rennethe a lytille broke of watre, that was wont to ben byttre; but be the blessyng of Helisee the prophete, it becam swete and gode to drynke. And at the foot of this hille, toward the playn, is a grete welle, that entrethe in to flom Jordan. Fro that hille to Jerico, that I spak of before, is but a myle, in goynge toward flom Jordan. Also as men gon to Jerico, sat the blynde man, cryenge, *Jesu, fili David, miserere mei*; that is to seye, *Jesu, Davides sone, have mercy on me*: and anon he hadde his sighte. Also 2 myle fro Jerico is flom Jordan: and an half myle more nyghe, is a faire chirche of Seynt John the Baptist; where he baptised oure Lord: and there besyde, is the hous of Jeremye the prophete.

Of the dede See; and of the Flom Jordan. Of the Hed of Seynt John the Baptist; and of the Usages of the Samaritanes.

[Sidenote: Cap. IX.] And fro Jerico, a 3 myle, is the dede See. Aboute that See growethe moche alom and of alkatram. [Footnote: Brimstone.] Betwene Jerico and that see is the lond of Dengadde; and there was wont to growe the bawme; but men make drawe the braunches there of, and beren hem to ben graffed at Babiloyne; and zit men clepen hem vynes of Gaddy. At a cost of that see, as men gon from Arabe, is the mount of the Moabytes; where there is a cave, that men clepen Karua. Upon that hille, ladde Balak the sone of Booz, Balaam the prest, for to curse the peple of Israel. That dede See departethe the lond of Ynde and of Arabye; and that see lastethe from Soara unto Arabye. The watre of that see is fulle bytter and salt: and ziff the erthe were made moyst and weet with that watre, it wolde nevere bere fruyt. And the erthe and the lond chaungeth often his colour. And it castethe out of the watre a thing that men clepen aspalt; also gret peces, as the gretnesse of an hors, every day, and on alle sydes. And fro Jerusalem to that see, is 200 furlonges. That see is in lengthe 580 furlonges, and in brede 150 furlonges: and it is clept the dede see, for it rennethe nought. but is evere unmevable. And nouther manne, best, ne no thing that berethe lif in him, ne may not dyen in that see: and that hathe ben proved manye tymes, be men that han disserved to ben dede, that han ben cast there inne, and left there inne 3 dayes or 4, and thei ne myghte never dye ther inne: for it resceyvethe no thing with inne him, that berethe lif. And no man may drynken of the watre, for bytternesse. And zif a man caste iren there in, it wole flete aboven. And zif men caste a fedre there in, it wole synke to the botme: and theise ben thinges azenst kynde. And also the cytees there weren lost, be cause of synne. And there besyden growen trees, that beren fulle faire apples, and faire of colour to beholde; but whoso brekethe hem or cuttethe hem in two, he schalle fynde with in hem coles and cyndres; in tokene that, be wratthe of God, the cytees and the lond weren brente and sonken into helle. Sum men clepen that see, Lake Dalfetidee; summe, the Flom of Develes; and summe, the flom that is ever stynkynge. And in to that see sonken the 5 cytees, be wratthe of God; that is to seyne, Sodom, Gomorre, Aldama, Seboym and Segor, for the abhomynable synne of sodomye, that regned in hem. But Segor, be the preyer of Lothe, was saved and kept a gret while: for it was sett upon an hille; and zit schewethe therof sum party, above the watre: and men may see the walles, when it is fayr wedre and cleer. In that cytee Lothe dwelte, a lytylle while; and there was he made dronken of his doughtres, and lay with hem, and engendred of hem Moab and Amon. And the cause whi his doughtres made him dronken, and for to ly by him, was this; because thei sawghe no man aboute hem, but only here fadre: and therfore thei trowed, that God had destroyed alle the world, as he hadde don the cytees; as he hadde don before, be Noes flood. And therfore thei wolde lye with here fadre, for to have issue, and for to replenysschen the world azen with peple, to restore the world azen be hem: for thei trowed, that ther had ben no mo men in alle the world. And zif here fadre had not ben dronken, he hadde not y leye with hem. And the hille aboven Segor, men cleped it thanne Edom: and aftre men cleped it Seyr, and aftre Ydumea. Also at the righte syde of that dede See, dwellethe zit the wife of Lothe, in lyknesse of a salt ston; fur that schee loked behinde hire, whan the cytees sonken into helle. This Lothe was Araammes sone, that was brother to Abraham. And Sarra Abrahames wife, and Melcha Nachors wif, weren sustren to the seyd Lothe. And the same Sarra was of elde 90 zeer, when Ysaac hire sone was goten on hire. And Abraham hadde another sone Ysmael, that he gat upon Agar his chambrere. And when Ysaac his sone was 8 dayes olde, Abraham his fadre leet him ben circumcyded, and Ysmael with him, that was 14 zeer old: wherfore the Jewes, that comen of Ysaacces lyne, ben circumcyded the 8 day; and the Sarrazines, that comen of Ysmaeles lyne, ben circumcyded whan thei ben 14 zeer of age.

And zee schulle undirstonde, that with in the dede See rennethe the Flom Jordan, and there it dyethe; for it rennethe no furthermore: and that is a place, that is a myle fro the Chirche of seynt John the Baptist, toward the West, a lytille benethe the place, where that christene men bathen hem comounly. And a myle from Flom Jordan, is the Ryvere of Jabothe, the whiche Jacob passed over, whan he cam fro Mesopotayme. This Flom Jordan is no great ryvere; but it is plenteous of gode fissche; and it cometh out of the hille of Lyban be 2 welles, that ben cleped Jor and Dan: and of tho 2 Welles hath it the name. And it passethe be a lake, that is clept Maron; and aftre it passethe by the See of Tyberye, and passethe undre the hilles of Gelboe: and there is a full faire vale, bothe on that o syde and on that other of the same ryvere. And men gon the hilles of Lyban, alle in lengthe, onto the desert of Pharan. And tho hilles departen the kyngdom of Surrye and the contree of Phenesie. And upon tho hilles growen trees of cedre, that ben fulle hye, and thei beren longe apples, and als grete as a mannes heved. And also this Flom Jordan departeth the lond of Galilee, and the lond of Ydumye and the lond of Betron: and that rennethe undre erthe a grete weye, unto a fayre playn and a gret, that is clept Meldan, in Sarmoyz; that is to seye, feyre or markett in here langage; be cause that there is often feyres in that pleyn. And there becomethe the watre gret and large. And that playn is the tombe of Job. And in that Flom Jordan above-seyd, was oure Lorde baptized of seynt John; and the voys of God the Fadre was herd seyenge. *Hic est Filius meus dilectus, &c.*; that is to seye, *This is my beloved sone, in the whiche I am well plesed; herethe hym.* And the Holy Gost alyghte upon hym, in lyknesse of a colver: and so at his baptizynge, was alle the hool trynytee. And thorghe that Flom passeden the children of Israel, alle drye feet: and thei putten stones there in the myddel place, in tokene of the myracle, that the watre withdrowghe him so. Also in that Flom Jordan, Naaman of Syrie bathed him; that was fulle riche, but he was meselle: [Footnote: Leprous.] and there anon he toke his hele. Abouten the Flom Jordan ben manye chirches, where that manye cristene men dwelleden. And nyghe therto is the cytee of Hay, that Josue assayled and toke. Also beyonde the Flom Jordan, is the Vale of Mambre; and that is a fulle fair vale. Also upon the hille, that I spak of before, where oure Lord fasted 40 dayes, a 2 myle long from Galilee, is a faire hille and an highe; where the enemye, the fend, bare oure Lord, the thridde tyme, to tempte him, and schewede him alle the regiouns of the world, and seyde, *Hic omnia tibi dabo, si cadens adoraveris me;* that is to seyne, *All this schalle I ʒeve the, ʒif thou falle and worschipe me.*

Also fro the dede See, to gon estward out of the marches of the Holy Lond, that is clept the Lond of Promyssioun, is a strong castelle and a fair, in an hille, that is clept Carak, en Sarmoyz; that is to seyne, Ryally. That castle let make kyng Baldwyn, (that was Kyng of France) whan he had conquered that lond; and putte it in to cristene mennes hondes, for to kepe that contree. And for that cause, was it clept the Mownt rialle. And undre it there is a town, that hight Sobachie: and there alle abowte dwellen cristene men, undre trybute. Fro thens gon men to Nazarethe, of the whiche oure Lord berethe the surname. And fro thens, there is 3 journeyes to Jerusalem: and men gon be the provynce of Galylee, be Ramatha, be Sothym and be the highe hille of Effraim; where Elchana and Anna, the modre of Samuelle the prophete, dwelleden. There was born this prophete: and aftre his dethe, he was buryed at Mount Joye, as I have seyd you before. And than gon men to Sylo; where the arke of God with the relikes weren kept longe tyme, undre Ely the prophete. There made the peple of Ebron sacrifice to oure Lord: and ther thei yolden up here avowes: and there spak God first to Samuelle, and schewed him the mutacioun of ordre of presthode, and the misterie of the sacrament. And right nyghe, on the left syde, is Gabaon and Rama and Beniamyn; of the whiche holy writt spekethe offe. And aftre men gon to Sychem, sumtyme clept Sychar; and that is in the provynce of Samaritanes; and there is a fulle fair vale and a fructuouse, and there is a fair cytee and a gode, that men clepen Neople. And from thens is a jorneye to Jerusalem. And there is the welle, where oure Lord spak to the woman of Samaritan. And there was wont to ben a chirche; but it is beten doun. Besyde that welle, Kyng Roboas let make 2 calveren of gold, and made hem to ben worschipt, and put that on at Dan, and that other at Betelle. And a myle fro Sychar, is the cytee of Deluze. And in that cytee dwelte Abraham, a certeyn tyme. Sychem is a 10 myle fro Jerusalem, and it is clept Neople; that is, for to seyne, the newe cytee. And nyghe besyde is the tombe of Josephe the sone of Jacob, that governed Egypt: for the Jewes baren his bones from Egypt, and buryed hem there. And thidre gon the Jewes oftentyme in pilgrimage, with gret devocioun. In that cytee was Dyne Jacobes doughter ravysscht; for whom hire bretheren slowen many persones, and diden many harmes to the cytee. And there besyde, is the hille of Garasoun, where the Samaritanes maken here sacrifice: in that hille wolde Abraham have sacrificed his sone Ysaac. And there besyde is the vale of Dotaym: and there is the cisterne, where Josephe was cast in of his bretheren, which thei solden; and that is a 2 myle fro Sychar. From thens gon men to Samarye, that men clepen now Sebast; and that is the chief cytee of that contree: and it sytt betwene the hille of Aygnes, as Jerusalem dothe. In that cytee was the syttinges of the 12 tribes of Israel: but the cytee is not now so gret, as it was wont to be. There was buryed seynt John the Baptist, betwene 2 prophetes, Helyseus and Abdyan: but he was beheded in the castelle of Macharyme, besyde the Dede See: and aftre he was translated of his disciples, and buryed at Samarie: and there let Julianas Apostata dyggen him up, and let brennen his bones; (for he was that time Emperour) and let wyndwe [Footnote: Blow away.] the ashes in the wynd. But the fynger, that schewed oure Lord, seyenge, *Ecce Agnus Dei*; that is to seyne, *Lo the Lamb of God*: that nolde nevere brenne, but is alle hol: that fynger leet seynte Tecle the holy virgyne be born in to the hill of Sebast; and there maken men gret feste. In that place was wont to ben a faire chirche; and many othere there weren; but thei ben alle beten doun. There was wont to ben the heed of seynt John Baptist, enclosed in the walle; but the Emperour Theodosie let drawe it out, and fond it wrapped in a litille clothe, alle blody; and so he leet it to be born to Costantynoble: and zit at Costantynoble is the hyndre partye of the heed: and the for partie of the heed, til undre the chyn, is at Rome, undre the chirche of seynt Silvestre, where ben nonnes of an hundred ordres; and it is zit alle broylly, as thoughe it were half brent: for the Emperour Julianus aboyeseyd, of his cursednesse and malice, let brennen that partie with the other bones; and zit it schewethe: and this thing hathe ben preved, both be popes and by emperours. And the Jowes benethe, that holden to the Chyn, and a partie of the assches, and the platere, that the hed was leyd in, whan it was smyten of, is at Gene: and the Geneweyes maken of it gret feste; and so don the Sarazynes also. And sum men seyn; that the heed of seynt John is at Amyas, in Picardye: and other men seyn, that it is the heed of seynt John the Bysschop. I wot nere, but God knowethe: but in what wyse than men worschipen it, the blessed seynt John holt him a payd.

From this cytee of Sebast unto Jerusalem, is 12 myle. And betwene the hilles of that contree, there is a welle, that 4 sithes in the zeer chaungethe his colour; sometyme grene, sometyme reed, sometyme cleer, and sometyme trouble; and men clepen that welle Job. And the folk of that contree, that men clepen Samaritanes, weren converted and baptized by the apostles; but thei holden not wel here doctryne; and alle weys thei holden lawes by hem self, varyenge from cristene men, from Sarrazines, Jewes and Paynemes. And the Samaritanes leeven well in o Godi: and thei seyn wel, that there is but only o God, that alle formed, and alle schalle deme: and thei holden the Bible aftre the lettre: and thei usen the psawtere, as the Jewes don: and thei seyn, that thei ben the righte sones of God: and among alle other folk, thei seyn that thei ben best beloved of God; and that to hem belongethe the heritage, that God behighte to hise beloved children: and thei han also dyverse clothinge and schapp, to loken on, than other folk han; for thei wrappen here hedes in red linnene cloth, in difference from othere. And the Sarazines wrappen here hedes in white lynnene clothe. And the Cristene men, that duellen in the contree, wrappen hem in blew of Ynde; and the Jewes in zelow clothe. In that contree duellen manye of the Jewes, payenge tribute, as Cristene men don. And zif zee wil knowe the lettres, that the Jewes usen, as thei clepem hem, in manner of here *A. B. C. Alephe, Bethe, Gymel, Delethe, He, Vau, Zay, Cy, Thet, Joht, Kapho, Lampd [sic— KTH], Mem, Num, Samethe, Ey, Fhee, Sade, Cophe, Resch, Son, Tau.*

Of the Province of Galilee, and where Antecrist schalle be born; Of Nazarethe. Of the Age of oure Lady. Of the Day of Doom; and of the Customes of Jacobites, Surryenes; and of the Usages of Gcorgyenes.

[Sidenote: Chap. IX.] From this contree of the Samaritanes, that I have spoken of before, gon men to the playnes of Galilee. And men leven the hilles, on that o partye. And Galilee is on of the provynces of the Holy Land: and in that provynce is the cytee of Naym and Capharnaum and Chorosaym and Bethsayde. In this Bethseyde was Seynt Petre and Seynt Andrew borne. And thens, a 4 myle, is Chorosaym: and 5 myle fro Chorosaym, is the cytee of Cedar, of the psautre spekethe: *Et habitavi cum habitantibus Cedar*; that is for to seye, *And I have dwelled with the dwellynge men in Cedar*. In Chorosaym schalle Antecrist be born, as sum men seyn; and other men seyn, he schalle be born in Babyloyne: for the prophete seyth; *De Babilonia Coluber exiet, qui totum mundum devorabit*; that is to seyne, *Out of Babiloyne schal come a worm, that schal devouren alle the world.* This Antecrist schal be norysscht in Bethsayda, and he schal regne in Capharnaum: and therfore seythe Holy Writt: *Ve tibi, Chorosaym: ve tibi, Bethsayda: ve tibi, Capharnaum*; that is to seye, *Wo be to the, Chorosaym; wo to the, Bethsayda: wo to the, Capharnaum.* And alle theise townes ben in the lond of Galilee. And also, the cane of Galilee is 4 myle fro Nazarethe: of that cytee was Simon Chananeus, and his wif Canee; of the whiche the holy evaungelist spekethe off: there dide oure Lord the first myracle at the wedyng, whan he turned water in to wyn. And in the ende of Galilee, at the hilles, was the arke of God taken; and on that other syde is the Mownt Hender or Hermon. And there aboute gothe the Broke of Cison: and there besyde, Barache, that was Abymeleche sone, with Delbore the prophetisse, overcam the Oost of Ydumea, whan Cysera the kyng was slayn of Gebelle, the wif of Aber; and chaced beyonde the Flom Jordan, be strengthe of sword, Zeb and Zebec and Salmana; and there he slowghe him. Also a 5 myle fro Naym, is the cytee of Jezreel, that sometyme was clept Zarym; of the which cytee Jezabel the cursed queen was lady and queen, that toke awey the vyne of Nabaothe, be hire strengthe. Faste by that cytee, is the Feld Magede, in the whiche the Kyng Joras was slayn of the Kyng of Samarie, and aftre was translated and buryed in the Mount Syon. And a myle fro Jezrael ben the Hilles of Gelboe, where Saul and Jonathas that weren so faire, dyeden: wherfore David cursed hem, as holy writt seythe; *Montes Gelboe, nec Ros nec Pluvia, &c.*; that is to seye, *Zee hilles of Gelboe, nouther Dew ne Reyne com upon you*. And a myle fro the hilles of Gelboe, toward the est, is the cytee of Cyrople, that was clept before Bethsayn. And upon the walles of that cytee was the hed of Saul honged.

After gon men be the hille, besyde the pleynes of Galylee, unto Nazarethe, where was wont to ben a gret cytee and fair: but now there is not, but a lytille village, and houses a brood here and there. And it is not walled; and it sytt in a litille valeye, and there ben hilles alle aboute. There was our lady born: but sche was goten at Jerusalem. And be cause that oure lady was born at Nazarethe, therefore bare our Lord his surname of that town. There toke Josephe our lady to wyf, when sche was 14 zeere of age: and there Gabrielle grette our lady, seyenge, *Ave Gratia plena, Dominus tecum*; that is to seyne, *Heyl fulle of Grace, oure Lord is with the*. And this Salutacioun was don in a place of a gret awteer of a faire chirche, that was wont to be somtyme: but it is now alle downe; and men han made a lityle resceyt, besyde a pylere of that chirche, for to resceyve the offrynges of Pilgrymes. And the Sarrazines kepen that place fulle derely, for the profyte that thei han there offe: and thei ben fulle wykked Sarrazines and cruelle, and more dispytous than in ony other place, and han destroyed alle the chirches. There nyghe is Gabrielles Welle, where oure Lord was wont to bathe Him, whan He was yong: and fro that welle bare he watre often tyme to his modre: and in that well sche wossche often tyme the clowtes of hire sone Jesu Crist. And fro Jerusalem unto thidre, is 3 journeyes. At Nazarathe was our Lord norisscht. Nazarethe is als meche to seye, as flour of the gardyn: and be gode skylle may it ben clept flour; for there was norisscht the flour of lyf, that was Crist Jesu. And 2 myle fro Nazarethe, it the cytee of Sephor, be the weye, that gothe from Nazerethe to Acon. And an half myle fro Nazarethe, is the lepe of oure Lorde: for the Jewes ladden him upon an highe roche, for to make him lepe doun, and have slayn him: but Jesu passed amonges hem, and lepte upon another roche; and zit ben the steppes of his feet sene in the roche, where he allyghte. And therfore seyn sum men, whan thei dreden hem of thefes, on ony weye, or of enemyes; *Jesus autem transiens per medium illorum ibet*; that is to seyne, *Jesus forsothe passynge be the myddes of hem, he wente*: in tokene and mynde, that oure Lord passed thorghe out the Jewes crueltee, and scaped safly fro hem: so surely mowe men passen the perile of thefes. And than sey men 2 vers of the psautre, 3 sithes: *Irruat super eos formido et pavor in magnitudine Brachii tui, Domine, Fiant inmobiles, quasi Lapis, donec pertranseat populus tuus, Domine; donec pertranseat populus tuus iste, quem possedisti*. And thanne may men passe with outen perile. And zee schulle undirstonde, that oure lady hadde child, whan sche was 15 zeere old: and sche was conversant with hire sone 33 zeer and 3 monethes; And aftre the passioun of oure Lord, sche lyvede 24 zeer.

Also fro Nazarethe, men gon to the Mount Thabor; and that is a 4 myle: and it is a fulle faire hille, and well highe, where was wont to ben a toun and many chirches; but thei ben alle destroyed; but zit there is a place, that men clepen the scole of God, where he was wont to teche his disciples, and tolde hem the prevytees of hevene. And at the foot of that hille, Melchisedeche, that was Kyng of Salem, in the turnynge of that hille, mette Abraham in comynge azen from the batoylle, whan he had slayn Abymeleche: and this Melchisedeche was bothe kyng and prest of Salem, that now is cleped Jerusalem. In that hille Thabor, oure Lord transfigured him before seynt Petre, seynt John and seynt Jame; and there they sawghe gostly Moyses and Elye the prophetes besyde hem: and therefore seyde seynt Petre, *Domine, bonum est nos hic esse; faciamus tria Tabernacula*; that is to seye, *Lorde, it is gode for us to ben here; make we here 3 dwellying places*. And there herd thei a voys of the fadir, that seye, *Hic est filius meus dilectus, in quo mihi bene complacui*. And oure Lord defended hem, that thei scholde not telle that avisioun, til that he were rysen from dethe to lyf. In that hille and in that same place, at the day of doom, 4 aungeles, with 4 trompes, schulle blowen and reysen alle men, that hadden suffred dethe, sithe that the world was formed, from dethe to lyve; and schnlle comen in body and soule in juggement; before the face of oure Lord, in the Vale of Josaphate. And the doom schalle ben on Estre Day, suche tyme as oure Lord aroos: and the dom schalle begynne, suche houre as oure Lord descended, to helle and dispoyled it; for at such houre schal he dispoyle the world, and lede his chosene to blisse; and the othere schalle be condempne to perpetuelle peynes: and thanne schalle every man have aftir his dissert, outher gode or evylle; but zif the mercy of God passe his rightewisnesse.

Also a myle from Mount Thabor, is the Mount Heremaon; and there was the cytee of Naym. Before the zate of that cytee, reysed oure Lord the wydewes sone, that had no mo children. Also 3 myle fro Nazarethe, is the

Castelle Saffra; of the whiche, the sones of Zebedee and the sones of Alphee weren. Also a 7 myle fro Nazarethe is the Mount Kayn; andl andre that is a welle, and besyde that welle, Lameche Noees fadre sloughe Kaym with an arwe. For this Kaym wente thorghe breres and bosshes, as a wylde best; and he had lyved fro the tyme of Adam his fadir, unto the tynme of Noe; and so he lyvode nyghe to 2000 zeer. And this Lameche was alle blynd for elde.

Fro Saffra, men gothe to the see of Galylee and to the cytee of Tyberye, that sytt upon the same see. And alle be it, that men clepen it a see, zit is it nouther see ne arm of the see: for it is but a stank of fresche watir, that is in lengthe 100 furlonges; and of brede 40 furlonges; and hathe with in him gret plentee of fissche, and rennethe in to Flom Jordan. The cytee it not fulle gret, but it hathe gode bathes with in him. And there; as the Flom Jordan partethe fro the see of Galilee, is a gret brigge, where men passen from the lond of promyssioun, to the lond of Baazan and the lond of Gerrasentz, that ben about the Flom Jordan, and the begynnynge of the see of Tyberie. And fro thens may men go to Damask, in 3 dayes, be the kyngdom of Traconye; the whiche kyngdom lastethe fro mount Heremon to the see of Galilee, or to the see of Tyberie, or to the see of Jenazarethe; and alle is o see, and this the stank that I have told zou; but it chaungethe thus the name, for the names of the cytees that sytten besyde hem. Upon that see, went oure Lord drye feet; and there he toke up seynt Peter, when he began to drenche with in the see, and seyde to him, *Modice Fidei, quare dubitasti?* And aftre his resurrexioun, oure Lord appered on that see, to his disciples, and bad hem fyssche, and filled alle the nett fulle of gret fisshes. In that see rowed oure Lord often tyme; and there he called to him, seynt Peter, seynt Andrew, seynt James and seynt John, the sones of Zebedee. In that cytee of Tyberie, is the table, upon the whiche oure Lord eete upon, with his disciples, aftre his resurrexioun; and thei knewen him in brekynge of bred, as the gospelle seythe; *Et cognoverunt cum in fractione Panis*. And nyghe that cytee of Tyberie, is the hille, where oure Lord fedde 5 thousand persones, with 5 barly loves and 2 fisshes. In that cytee, a man cast an brennynge dart in wratthe aftir oure Lord, and the hed smot in to the eerthe, and wax grene, and it growed to a gret tree; and zit it growethe, and the bark there of is alle lyk coles. Also in the hed of that See of Galilee, toward the Septemtryon, is a strong castelle and an highe, that highte Saphor: and fast besyde it, is Capharnaum: with in the lond of Promyssioun, is not so strong a castelle: and there is a gode toun benethe, that is clept also Saphor. In that castel, seynt Anne our ladyes modre was born. And there benethe was Centurioes hous. That contree is clept the Galilee of Folk, that weren taken to tribute of Sabulon, and of Neptalym. And in azen comynge fro that castelle, a 30 myle, is the cytee of Dan, that somtyme was clept Belynas, or Cesaire Philippon, that sytt at the foot of the

Mount of Lyban, where the Flom Jordan begynnethe. There begynnethe the lond of Promyssioun, and durethe unto Bersabee, in lengthe, in goynge toward the northe in to the southe; and it conteynethe well a 180 myles: and of brede, that is to seye, fro Jericho unto Jaffe, and that conteynethe a 40 myle of Lombardye, or of our contree, that ben also lytylle myles. Theise ben not myles of Gascoyne, ne of the provynce of Almayne, where ben gret myles. And wite zee welle, that the lond of Promyssioun is in Sirye. For the reme of Sirye durethe fro the desertes of Arabye, unto Cecyle, and that is Ermonye the grete, that is to seyne, fro the southe to the northe: and fro the est to the west, it durethe fro the grete desertes of Arabye onto the West See. But in the reme of Syrie, is the kyngdom of Judee, and many other provynces, as Palestyne, Galilee, litylle Cilicye, and many othere. In that contree and other contrees bezonde, thei han a custom, whan thei schulle usen werre, and whan men holden sege abbouten cytee or castelle, and thei with innen dur not senden out messagers with lettres, from lord to lord, for to aske sokour, thei maken here letters and bynden hem to the nekke of a colver, and leten the colver flee; and the colveren ben so taughte, that threi fleen with tho lettres to the verry place, that men wolde sende hem to. For the colveres ben norysscht in tho places, where thei ben sent to; and thei senden hem thus, for to beren here lettres. And the colveres retournen azen, where as thei ben norisscht; and so thei doe comounly.

MANDEVILLE'S VOYAGES

PART II.

Secunda pars.

CAPVT. 24.

Persuasio ad non credentes terrarum diuersitates per orben terræ.

Mirabilis Deus mirabilia propter semetipsum creauit, vt scilicet ab intellectualibus creaturis suis intelligeretur, et per hoc diligeretur, atque in hoc ipse creator, et creatura se mutuo fruerentur. Mirabilis est ergo Deus maximè in illo, quòd ipse solus sufficit sibi: et mirabilis in altis Dominus, hoc est, in coelo et in coelestibus: sed et mirabilis in terris, et in terrestribus: tamen si verum indicauerimus, nihil est mirabile, quod mirum videri non debet, si ille qui omnipotens est, fecit quæcunque voluit in coelo et in terra. Sed ecce dum nobis contingit videre rem quam priùs non vidimus, miràtur noster animus, non quòd simpliciter mirum est, sed quod nobis id mirum et nouum. Deus vnus, simplex quidem est, vt creaturæ coelestes quò Deo magis de propinquo sunt eò simpliciores existunt. Terrestres autem quòd in situ remotiori sint, idcircò magis diuersæ, magis contrariæ inter se sunt.

[Sidenote: Reprehensio incredulorum qui nihil credunt, nisi quod domi viderint.] Ergo quicunque sapiens est non stupet animo, dum in terrenis respicit res varias, et diuersas, vel dum diuersa contingunt, seu inueníuntur in partibus terræ diuersis: sed qui intellectum super sensum non eleuant, et magis credunt oculo suo corporeo, quàm spirituali, et qui nunquam à natiuitatis suæ loco recesserunt, isti vix volunt credere, seu possunt alijs vera narrantibus de mundi diuersitatibus.

Attamen tales, si vellent, de facili videre possint suum errorem. Quia quicunque natus in vna ciuitate, vel patria, si tantummodo moueat se ad proximam ciuitatem, inueniet ibi procul dubio aliquam differentiam, vel diuersitatem in idiomate linguæ, vel in modo loquendi, in moribus hominum, in occupationibus, in legibus, in consuetudinibus, vel etiam in agrorom fructibus, in arborum frugibus, seu in his quæ gignuntur in terra, in aere, et in aquis.

Si ergo aliqualiter inueniri possit differentia in proximo, quanto maior sit distantia, tanto maior differentia æstimandi est in remoto, vel in remotiori, seu remotissimo loco. Vnde ego, quia in præcedente parte tractatus narrare coepi aliqua, quæ in his, et in peregrinatione mea vsque in terram promissionis sanctam vidi, de quibus etiam potest, et poterit constare multis, qui in partibus nostris eadem peregrinatione me præcesserunt, et secuti sunt, procedam in describendo aliqua illorum, quæ vidi et percepi in deambulatione mea, qua peragraui multas alias terras, et perlegi multas vndas, vsque in multorum hoc tempus annorum, et propter insipientes, et discredentes non tacebo. Sed nec propter credentes nec sapientes satis mouebor; tamen vt diuersa Dei opera qui respicere non possunt oculo, saltem legant, vel audiant ex hoc scripto. Pauca vtique vidí horum quæ sunt, sed pauca horum quæ vidi, narrabo.

CAPVT. 25.

De Armenia, Persia, et Amazonia.

De regionibus quæ Iudeæ contiguantur, scilicet Arabia, Aegypto et Syria, statui modicum vltra narrare, relinquens hunc locum narrandi alijs peregrinis. Et festinans ad terras remotiores, Armeniam minorem, non per singulas ciuitates, sed celeriter transiens, vidi à remotis amplum cástrum vocatum Dei espoyer de quo mihi sustinui dici, quod sit vastum, et à nemine, habitatum, nisi à fantastica quadam Domina, seruante in medio maioris aulæ super perticam, volucrem rapacem, quæ dicitur Latinè accipiter, vel huiusmodi: quam auem, si aliquis hominum ingrediens se custodire peruigil absque vlla somnolentia per septem continuos dies et noctes posset, ipsa Domina in fine facti apparens concederet illi quantamcunque faceret petitionem terræ, commodi, vel honoris, sed si obdormiret, periret. Huic tamen dicto parùm curaui accommodare aurem, nisi quod communiter dicebatur, in bene transacto tempore prædicta fuisse tentata per duas personas, vnum Regem, et alterum Pastorem. Et Regi quidem quod indebitam fecit petitionem, vile successit negotium, pastori peroptimè successit negotium.

In Armenia maiori, est magna et bona ciuitas Artyron ad dietam prope fluuium Euphratem. Et sunt ibi duo montes euecti valdè, vnus Sabissatele, alter Ararath, quorum vltimus habet per anfractius, et periodos per ascensum viæ, ferè 7. leucas, et quasi omni tempore est plenus niue.

In illo loco fertur quicuisse Arca diluuii, cuius vnicus asser monstratur, in Ecclesia Monachorum ad montis pedem habitantium; attamem nullus hominum pro frigore nimio attentare præsumit ascensum.

Est autem et ibi ciuitas Landania, de qua nonnulli dicunt quòd Noe illam fundauerat, et ciuitas magna Hany, in qua tempore Christianorum mille habebantur Ecclesiæ.

In illa Armenia sub Imperio Persiæ est famosa ciuitas Tauris, vbi de mercimonijs ponderalibus fit inestimabilis mercatura. Hinc ad decem diates ad Orientem habeatur ciuitas Zadona, in ea Imperator Persarum moratur, et est in eodem imperio ciuitas valdè magna Cassach, quæ recto itinere dicitur store ab Hierosolymis 55. dietis. Geth ciuitas imperialis, et melior totius Persiæ in hac terra noscitur esse, cum tamen Carnaa sit satis maior.

Circa fines Persiæ in terra Sennaar, est illa quæ olim dicebatur Babylonia, nec apparet ibi aliquid, quàm ruinæ grandis et vetustæ cuitatis, quæ ab hominibus est deserta, sed à Draconibus inhabitata, et alijs animalibus, et volucribus venenosis. Hanc terram tenet Imperator Persarum, vt suprà dixi. Etiam intra fines Persiæ, est terra, vbi sanctus Iob patiens morabatur, quæ modo dicitur terra Sues, in cuius montanis inuenitur Manna, quod venditur in Apothecis. Hunc terræ Sues contiguatur Chaldæa, quæ non est magna, quamuis nobilis regio habeatur. Et ab ista intratur Amazonia.

Amazonia est modica insula, quam absquæ viris sofæ regunt et inhabitant mulieres: cuius rei prima causa hæc fuit.

Olim cum insula communiter a viris, et mulieribus habitabatur, Rex eius dictus Colopius cum omnibus nobilibus suis in bello contra Regnum Scithiæ occisus fuit. Audientes igitur nobilium vxores ipsius insulæ se viduatas, super his, in doloroso furore animi ad plures congressiones occiderunt et fugauerunt omnes aliarum mulierum maritos, ne scilicet sua ingennitas subiaceret voluntati, et potestati plebis. Et tandem post reformatam inter se pacem mulieres inito consilio statuerum se solas absque viris dominari in terra, atque ex tunc sumi sibi regimen per certam electionis formam quæ robusta, agilis, sapiens, iuuenis, ac valens apparet in armis.

Sciendum tamen est, extra hanc insulam flumen esse, et alias modicas insulas, quarum vna dicitur Carmagite, de quibus licitum est ijs accessire viros, et amasios bis in anno, ita vt nulla moram trahat septem dierum naturalium sub poena indubitata occisionis. Infantem masculum nutrire licet quoadusque per se comedat et gradiatur, tunc transmittendus est in domum paternam. Generosæ natæ puellæ aufertur ignito cultro vber sinistrum pro scuto gerendo, degeneri dextrum, ad sagittandum de arcu Turco.

Regina cum consiliariis et officialibus suis regit sapienter et benè terràm, et seruat omnes sibi sub districta obedientia, per leges, et poenas, et amendas conscriptas. Et cum circumiacentium insularum Reges contra se ad inuicem proeliari solent, tunc Regina Amazoniæ cum suis Nobilibus ab vna parte pro magno stipendio vocari solet in adiutorium, vbi et inuentæ sunt sapientes in consilijs, probæ in armis, acres in conflictibus, et in omnibus Curiæ actibus bene valentes.

CAPVT. 26.

De Aethiopia, et Diamantibus, et de infima India.

Aethiopia consistit à terra Chaldeorum in Austrum, quæ distinguitur in Orientalem Aethiopiam, et ['and' in source text—KTH] Meridionalem, quarum prima in illis partibus vocatur Cush, propter hominum nigredinem, altera Mauritania. [Sidenote: Mauritania. Regnum Saba.] Et est ibi Regnum Saba, de quo legitur, quod Regi Salomoni Regis Arabum, et Saba, dona et tributa adduxerunt. Eòque Regina Saba venit à finibus, hoc est, à longinquis terræ partibus audire sapientiam Salomonis. Omnes in Aethiopia aquæ in fluuijs et riparijs, et fontibus sapiunt Sal, propter nimium calorem. [Sidenote: Plinius.] Est ibi vnus aquæ fons ita de nocte calidus, vt nemo in eo sustineat manum, et ita de die frigidus, vt bibi vix possit.

Generaliter isti de Mauritania Aethiopes comedunt parum, de facili inebriantur, fluxum ventris patiuntur nec diu viuunt.

[Sidenote: India triplex.] De Aethiopia intratur in Indiam, mediam, nam triplex est videlicet infima, quæ in quibusdam suis partibus est nimis frigida ad inhabitandum: Media quæ satis temperata est, et superior, quæ nimis calida. In India infima propter continuum et graue frigus generatur christallum de aqua per gelu, sicut quidam asserunt. Sed certum est ibi haberi rupes christalli, et in illis gigni optimos Diamantes, quos lingua illius vocant Hamefht. [Sic. 'Hamese' in English version below—KTH.]

Est autem diamas paruus præciosus lapis, magnæ virtutis, sicut pleniùs describitur in lapidariis. Quidam inueniuntur in magnitudine pisi, vel etiam piso minores: alii ad quantitatem fabæ, sed nullus maior auellana, vel nuce. Et dicitur de eo in partibus illis quod si hic qui portat sit continens, et sobrius reddit illum magnanimum et audacem, et iuuat in causis iustis certantem, conseruat substantias corporales, aufert praua somnia, depellit prauorum spirituum illusiones, sortilegia, et incantationes, ac valet contra lunaticam passionem, vt dæmonis obsessionem, et venenosum quod illi appropinquauerit exsudat, et exhumescit.

Optimi Diamantes de India assimulantur in colore multum christallo, sed sunt aliquantulum magis citrini, et pro sui duritie poliri non possunt. Inueniuntur autem ibi nonnulli subnigri ad colorem violæ: Alii nascuntur in Arabia nigri, et tenuiores prædictis, alii in Macedonia, et quidam in Cypro, sed in mineriis auri, dum prima massa in minutias confringitur, interdum reperíuntur. Sciendum enim est, sæpè plures simul crescere, nec non generant, et concipiunt inuicem de rore coeli, quemadmodum et Margaritæ: quod ego pluries tentans, accepi de rupe cespitem cum diamante masculo, et femella, plantans in pratello, et frequentans, focillans madefeci de rore Maii. Et ecce in breui, paruulus ex iis gignebatur, nascebatur, et adolescebat ad debitam quantitatem: fiunt verò omnes per naturam cum pluribus angulis vt trium vel quatuor, aut quinque laterum, et nonnulli cum lateribus senis. E contra omnes margaritæ nascuntur in forma sphærica, seu rotunda.

Et notandum quòd mercatores, pro diamantibus frequenter aliud vendunt: Nam solet commixtio fieri de christallo Crochee, de Saphiro, de Lonpes Citrino, de lapide Yri, et de paruis petris ex murium nidis. Probatio veri diamantis haberi potest his modis.

Primò si ita inuenitur tener, vt se poliri dimittat non est verus.

Item si de eo non potest scindi vitrum cristallum, non est verus.

Item accipe paruum quantitatis lapidem Adamantem, qui solet sibi attrahere acum et ferrum, et pone verum diamantem, super adamantem, túncque si ministraueris adamanti acum, videbis adamantem operari nihil, vero diamante præsente, dum tamen adamas non sit diamante maior.

Item si cultellum laminæ tenuis, habentem in manubrio inclusum vel alligatum verum diamantem in mensa vel assere erexeris, protinus vt ipsi venenum appropinquabit, stabit tremulans atque sudans. Et notandum, quòd per luxuriosum, seu gulosum qui ferret diamantem amitteret virtutem ad tempus.

Terra Indiæ appellatur ab Indo ibi currente fluuio, cuius anguillæ inueniuntur quandoque vltra 20. pedes in longitudine. In media India transitur per multas insulas vsque ad mare Oceanum, in insulam Ormuz, vbi Mercatores Venetiæ sæpè tendunt, sed viri, qui assueti non sunt tantum sustinere calorem, ne exeant perpendicula de corporibus propè ad genua, ibi se contra hoc debitè inuoluunt, et ligant, nec audent ibi transire nauibus ferrum continentibus, ne teneantur de rupibus adamantum.

Hic in aliquibus Aethiopiæ partibus habitant publicè, inhonestorum vtriusque sexus hominum consuetudinem inhonestam gerentes, et in æstu meridiano refrigerandi causa exeunt circa ciuitatem ad riparias iacere, et discurrere nudis prorsus corporibus omni pudore reiecto, ex quo procul dubio inhonesta vitia sequuntur.

Est et non longè ab ista insula regio seu insula Caua vel Chaua, quæ à primo statu multùm est minorata per mare. Hi sunt infidelissimi Paganorum. Nam quidam adorant Solem, alij Lunam, ignem, aquam, et terram, arborem, vel serpentem, vel cui de mane primò obuiant. Ibi magni mures, quos nos dicimus rattas, sunt in quantitate paruorum canum. Et quoniam per cattos capi non possunt, capiuntur per canes maiores.

Corpora mortuorum non sepeliuntur ibi, nec cadauera quælibet bestiarum operiuntur, quòd ad aeris æstum carnes in breui tempore consumuntur, nam et tota insula consistit sub zona torrida. Inde transiri potest per mare in Indiam superiorem, sine maiorem, videlicet Imperium Presbyteri Ioannis ad portum ciuitatis Zarke, quæ est elegans et bona satis. In ea habitant plurimi Catholicæ fidei Christiani: et habentur plurimæ Abbatiæ religiosorum, quas olim Dux Danorum Ogerus constituit, vnde et vsque nunc dicuntur Ecclesiæ Dani, atque ex hoc nauigari potest in terram Lombe.

CAPVT. 27.

De foresto Piperis, et fonte iuuentutis.

Regio seu insula dicta Lombe, spatiosa quidem est, continens forestum dictum aliàs Tombar, longum per dietas 18. In orbe vniuerso non noscimus crescere piper, præterquàm in hoc foresto. In quo et habetur duæ, ciuitates, vna Flandrina, (et illa ciuitas inhabitata est à Iudæis, et Christianis, inter quos sæpè magna seditio oritur) altera Singlant: quas quondam Danus fertur fundasse Ogerus, vocans vnam Flandrinam, nomine auiæ suæ ex parte patris sui, alteram Florentam nomine auiæ ex parte matris suæ, quæ mutato nomine nunc vocatur Singlant.

Sciendum est autem, piper ibi crescere in hunc modum: sicut nos plantamus vites aut quercus arbores robustas, vt vitis cum fructibus se spargat, vt supportetur per ramos, sic coluntur arbusta piperis ad arbores foresti, et sparguntur per ramos, et dependent fructus vt botri. Et venit in eodem arbusto triplex piper in anno.

Primum est quod vocatur longum piper, et venit priusquam nascuntur folia in arbustis, quemadmodum nos in arbore videmus corylo in hyeme ante folia præcedere quasdam caudulas longas, quo circa initium vindemiato, nascuntur cum foliis botri piperis viridis ad similitudinem paruarum vuarum. Quod quidem circa tempus Iulii in eadem viriditate vindemiatum in æstu feruido siccatur ad Solem, vt accipiat nigredinem, et rugarum contractionem.

Posteà exurgit piper album in granis minoribus, et in abundantia satis minori, quo tanquam preciosiori vtuntur in partibus illis et rarò vendunt ad partes istas.

Primum piper appellatur Sorbotyn, secundum Fulful, tertium verò Bauos.

Sunt autem per nemus istud fera animalia, et venenosa, sicut parui serpentes, colubri, et huiusmodi, de quibus nescio quis famam diffundit per nostras partes, quod vindemiatores piperis tales vermes fugant per ignem: sed non est ita, imò vngunt brachia manus, tibias, et pedes cum quodam succo herbæ dictæ Limonse, à quo cito diffugit omne venenum.

In huius foresti capite sub monte Polembo, est ciuitas dicta Bolemba, et sub eodem monte fons qui dicitur Iuuentutis. Aqua huius fontis reddit odorem et saporem quasi de omni genere aromatum, nam singulis penè horis immutat odorem, et saporem. Et quisquis per aliquos dies potat ieiuno stomacho sanatur in breui tempore, à quacunque interiori infirmitate, languore duntaxat mortis excepto: et sanè illorum qui propè sunt, et frequenter bibunt apparet per totum vitæ tempus mira iuuentus. Ego autem ter vel quater bibi, quamobrem et vsque hodiè arbitror potius me corporaliter valere. Putatur enim fons ille immediatè per poros subterraneos eliquari de fonte paradisi terrestris, ita quòd nulla via decurrentium super terram fluentium vitietur. In ista etiam regione, et in insulis circumquaque crescit gingiber valdè bonum, vnde et mercatores sæpè ibi tendunt de Venetia pro emendo pipere et gingibere. Gentes verò huius insulæ peruersæ et stollidissimæ sunt superstitionis adorantes bouem tanquam animal beatissimum, propter eius simplicitatem mansuetudinem, patientiam, et vtilitatem.

Multitudo cuiuslibet ciuitatis vel uillæ vnum specialem nutrit bouem, quem postquam laborauit in aratro per sex annos immolant manducantes pariter cum maxima solemnitate. Et quicunque inde minimam minutiam comedit, reputat se sanctificatum totum.

Porro apud Regem tenetur bos singularis, cuius custos diligentissimè vrinam in uase aureo accipit simpliciter, et de fimo in vase consimili: et quotidie venit summus eorum prælatus quem dicunt Archiprotoplaustum, offert personaliter in prædictis preciosis vasis, Domino Regi de bouis vrina et fimo, atque in vrina, quam appellant Gaul, tingens manus, defricit, et perungit Regis pectus et frontem, deinde similiter de fimo in multa cordis attentione, ad finem vt possint assequi quatuor virtutes bouis præfati.

Post regem cum reuerentia accedunt, et vnguntur Barones, principes, et post ipsos cæteri ordinati quicúnque attingere possint, putantes se sanctificari per rem penitus non valentem, imo nimis foetidam, et inhostem.

Præterea populi isti colunt Idola facta ad medium in forma humana, et ad medium in forma bouis. In quibus permissione Dei per eorum perfidiam maligni spiritus habitant dantes de interrogatis responsa. Et hijs Idolis offerunt infinita donari aquandoque, et sacrificant interdum proprios infantes, ipsorum sanguine Idola respergentes.

Dum hic maritus moritur, vxor comburitur cum marito, nisi de illo habeat sobolem cum quo viuere solet, et vilet. Quæ sibi eligit cum prole superuiuere, non habebitur de cætero fide digna.

Attamen in simili causa, si vir non vult cremari cum vxore mortua, non minuit ei honorem.

Et forte vinum nascitur ibi: quod mulieres bibunt, et non viri, vt sic mulieribus crescant barbæ, sed mulieribus raduntur, et viris minime.

CAPVT. 28.

De Ecclesia et corpore Saneti Thomæ Apostoli.

Hinc Meridiem pluribus exactis Insulis per viam decem dietarum venitur in Regnum Mabron. Illic in ciuitate Calamiæ, seruatur in magno templo corpus beatissimi Thomæ Apostoli Domini nostri Iesu Christi in capsa honorificata. In quo loco et martirizatus fuit, licet dicunt quidam, quod in Edissa ciuitate. Iste populus non est multum tempus transactum, quin fuit totus in fidei religione, sed nunc est ad pessimos Gentilium ritus peruersus, nec attendit, nec veneratur relliquias sancti corporis Apostoli ibidem contentas, quamuis ijs euidens, ac vtile, et mirificum præstare solebat beneficium, quod infra narrabo.

Per certas historias habetur Ducem Danorum Ogerum conquisiuisse has terras, et in exaltatione sanctarum Apostoli relliquiarum fecisse fieri præfatam spectactilem Ecclesiam, ac intra, eum reponi in nobilissimo loculo gemmis auro, argentoque decenter ornato Sanctum corpus, ac deinde post annorum tempus trecentorum Assyrios abstulisse feretrum cum ipso corpore sancto in Edissam ciuitatem Mesopotamiæ, in qua et fuit martyrizatus secundum quosdam, rursumque post sexaginta et tres annos recuperatum corpus in suam fuisse Ecclesiam restitutum, videlicet in Calamia, atque in eiusdem recuperationis signum certum dimiserunt isti, et dimittunt extra feretri loculum dependere brachium dextrum, cum manu quæ tetigisse creditur pia resurgentis vulnera Christi.

Eadem quoque manus solet vsque hodie suæ veræ poenitentiæ tale manifestere miraculum vt dum partes quælibet litigantes velint vtræque suas causas iuramento confirmare, conscriptis hinc inde causis ponantur ambæ cartulæ in Apostili manu. Quæ cuntis [Footnote: Interea dum exirent, Monachi suos dolos potuerunt exercere.] exeuntibus Ecclesiam protinus sub vnius horæ tempore reiecta longius falsitate, veritatem sibi reseruat: sed nunc sicut dicere coepi isti populi huic beneficio Dei ingrati, et diabolica illusione excæcati mirabiliter paganizant.

Nam et in hac ipsa beati Thomæ Ecclesia statuerunt multa miræ magnitudinis simulachra, ex quibus vnum quod maius est multo alijs apparet sedens homo in alto solio adoperto aureis sericis, et lapidibus præciosis, habensque ad collum suspensa pro ornatu multa cinctoria præciose gemmis, et auro contexta. Ad hoc autem Idolum adorandum confluunt peregrini à remotis partibus, et propinquis, in satis maiori copia, et valdè feruentiori deuotione quàm Christiani, ad sanctum Iacobum in Galizia quia multi eorum per totum peregrinationis iter, non audent erigere palpebras oculorum, ne forte propter hoc deuotio intermittatur.

Alij de propè venientes superaddunt labori itinerandi, vt ad tertium vel ad quartum passum semper cadant in genibus. Nonnulli quoque demoniaca inspiratione semetipsos per viam peregrinationis lanceolis, et cultellis nunc minoribus, nunc maioribus sauciant vulneribus per singula corporis loca, et dum ante Idolum perueniunt, excisum frustum de carne propria proijciunt ad Idolum pro offerenda, ac plagis durioribus se castigant, et quandoque spontaneè penitus se occidunt: in solemnitatibus verò, sicut in dedicatione, et sicut in thronizatione simulachrorum, fit conuentis populi, quasi totius Regni. Et ducitur cum processione maius Idolum per circuitum ciuitatis, in curru preciosissimo, modis omnibus perornato, et præcedunt in numero magno puellæ cantantes binæ, et binæ ordinatissimè, succeditque pluralitas Musicorum cum instrumentis varijs simphonizantes, quos continuè subsequitur currus, cuius lateribus coniungit se peregrinorum exercitus, qui et venerunt de remotis.

Ibique cernitur miserabilis actus vltra modum. Nam aliqui victi vltrà modum diabolica deuotione proijciunt se sub rotis currus præcedentis, vt frangantur sibi crura, brachia, latera, dorsa, nec non et colla in reuerentiam Dei sui (vt dicunt) a quo remunerationem sperant, venire ad Paradisum terrestrem.

Et post processionem postquam statuerunt Idolum in templo suo loco, multiplicatur coram simulachris numerus sæpè plangentium, et occidentium vltrà quam credi sit facile. Ita quod quandoque in illa vnica solemnitate inueniuntur ducenta corpora, vel plura occisorum. Et adstantes propinqui amici talium diaboli martyrum, eum magna musicorum melodia decantantes in sua lingua offerunt. Idolis corpora ac demum accenso rogo omnia corpora comburunt in honorem Idolurum, assumentes sibi singuli aliquid de ossibus aut cineribus pro reliquiis, quas putant sibi valituras contra quælibet infortunia, et tempestates. Et habetur ante templum aquæ lacus, velut seruatorium piscium, in quo proijcit populus largissimè suas oblationes, argentum, aurum, gemmas, cyphos, et similia, quibus ministri certis temporibus exhibentes prouident Ecclesiæ, ac simulachro, ac sibi ipsis abundantèr. Quoddam fabulosum scriptum exiuit per partes nostras, quod in prædicta processione circumferatur cumpheretro corpus beati Thomæ, qui et in fine processionis populu compopulo communicaret proprijs manibus de Eucharistæ sacramento, sed non est ita, et nunquam fuit.

CAPVT. 29.

De Iaua, et quibusdam aiijs meridionalibus Insulis, et de farina, melle et piscibus Ogeri Ducis Danorum.

Inde vlterius procedendo in Austrum per multas et mirabiles terras quinquaginta duarum diætarum spacio, habetur magna Insula Lamori. Illic omnes nudi incedunt, et ferè omnia sunt singulis communia, nec vtuntur priuatis clauibus siue seris, imo et omnes mulieres sunt communes omnibus et singulis viris, dummodo violentia non inferatur: Sed et peior est ijs consuetudo, quòd libentèr comedunt teneras carnes humanas: vnde et negotiatores adferunt eis crassos infantes venales: quod si non satis pingues afferuntur, eos saginant sicut nos vitulum, siue porcum.

Hic apparet in bona altitudine polus Antarcticus, et incipit modò apparere in alta Lybia, ita quod in alta Æthiopia eleuatur octodecim gradibus, prout ipse prohaui Astrolabio.

Ad meridiem terræ Lamori est Insula bona, Sumebor, cuius gentes reputant se nobiliores alijs, signantes se in facie certo cauterio. Isti semper guerras geerunt contra præfatus gentes nudas de Lamory.

Ad modicam inde destantiam habetur Insula Rotonigo abundans in bonis pluribus: sed et in Austrum sequuntur aliæ plures regiones et Insulæ, de quibes prolixum narrare fuisset.

Et est valde grandis regio Iaua, habens in circuitu ambitum leucarum duarum millium. Huius rex est valdè potens, et imperans septem insularum vicinarum regibus. Terra ista est populosa valdè, et crescunt in ea species, et abundantia gingiberis, canella, gariofoli, nuces muscata, et mastix cum aromatibus multis. Sed et quod ibi nascatur vinum, non habent: aurum et argentum est ibi in copia immensa, quòd patet in regis Iauæ palatio, cuius palatij nobilitas non est facilè scribenda.

Cuncti gradus ascendentes ad palatij aulas, et aularum cameras, et ad thalamos Camerarum sunt solidi de argento vel auro, sed et omnis stratura pauimentorum in alijs habetur ad similitudinem scacarij, vnam quadratam argenti, alteram auri, laminis valdè crassis, et in ipsis pauimentis, sunt exsculpta gesta, et historiæ diuersæ. In principali verò aula, est plenariè expressa Dani Ducis Ogeri historia, à natiuitate ipsius, quousque in Franciam fantasticè dicatur reuersus, cum tempore Caroli magni regis Franciæ, ipse Ogerus armata manu conquisiuit Christianitati ferè omnes partes transmarinas à Ierosolymis vsque ad arbores solis et Lunæ, ac propè paradisum terrestrem.

Pro hac Regione Iaua, (quæ tangit fines Imperij Tartariæ) sibi subiuganda, Imperator Grand Can multoties pugnauit, sed nunquam valuit expugnare. Hinc per mare venitur ad regnum Thalamassæ, [Footnote: Vel Tholomassi.] quòd et Panchon [Footnote: Vel Paten.] dicitur, in quo habetur magnus numerus bonarum ciuitatum. Intra hanc Insulam, quatuor sunt genera arborum, de quarum vna accipitur farina ad panem, de secunda mel, de tertia vinum, et de quarta pessimum venenum. Extrabitur autem farina de suis arboribus isto modo.

Certo tempore anni percutitur stipes arboris vndique propè terram cum securi, et cortex in locis pluribus vulneratur, de quibus recipitur liquor spissus, qui desiccatus ad solis æstum et contritus reddit farinam albam, ac si de frumento esset confectus, attamen hic panis non est triticei saporis, sed alterius valdè boni.

Simili modo de suis arboribus mel elicitur, et vinum liquitur: excepto quod illa non sicut gramina prima desiccantur. Fertur quoque ibidem, extractionem huius farinæ, mellis, et vini, per Angelum primitus fuisse ostensam prædicto Danorum Duci, illic fame cum suo exercitu laboranti.

Contra venenum quod de quarto arboris genere stillat, solum est intoxicato remedium, vt de proprio fimo per puram aquam distemperato bibat.

Et est in hac Insula quoddam mare mortuum, velut lacus foetidus, cuius in plerísque locis fundus, humano ingenio non valet attingi: miræ magnitudinis arundines crescunt super hunc lacum, in altitudine cedrorum aut abietum pedum ducentorum, ita vt viginti socij mecum nequiuimus vnius caput iacentis arundinis subleuare de terra. Minores etiam arundines nascuntur ad fluuii ripam, habentes in terra radices longitudinis trecentorum cubitorum aut plurium, Ad quarum nodos radicum, inueniuntur gemmæ preciosæ, de quibus expertum est, siquis vnam habuerit in pugno suo, ferrum corpori suo non nocebit: vnde si quis ibi pugnans, petat aduersarium, ac inimicum hac gemma munitum aggreditur eum cum fustibus non ferratis.

De hac intratur in Insulam Calanoch, [Marginal note: Vel Alcnak.] magnam et refertam bonorum omnium. Rex eius potens est multum, et licitum est ei, quandocunque, et quibuslibet in regno vti mulieribus, de quibus interdum magnum numerum tenet puerorum. Mille quadringentos habere solet ad præliandum elephantes, quos sibi nutriunt villani per regnum. Elephantes vocant verkes.

In littore maris miraculosè veniunt ibi semel in anno, per tres continuos dies, quasi de omni genere piscium marinorum, in maxima abundantia: et præbent se omnibus liberè capiendos ad manum. Nam et ego ipse cepi quamplures. Vnde notandum, quod eodem tempore anni quo super dicta extrahitur farina, mel, et vinum, conueniunt in hoc isti pisces: qua ambo mirabilia fecit vno tempore Deus olim producere suo Ogero, quæ et in memoria illius, vsque nunc, singulis annis innouantur.

Et sunt in hoc territorio testudines terribilis quantitatis, fitque de maioribus Regi ac nobilibus delicatus ac preciosus cibus: mentior, si non quasdam ibidem viderim testudinum conchas, in quarum vna se tres homines occultarent, suntque omnes multum albi coloris.

Si hic vir vxoratus moritur, sepelitur et vxor vna cum eo, quatenus, sicut ibi credunt, habeant eam statim sociam in seculo altero.

The English version.

And zee schulte undirstonde, that amonges the Sarazines, o part and other, duellen many Cristene men, of many maneres and dyverse names; and alle ben baptized, and han dyverse lawes and dyverse customes: but alle beleven in God the Fadir and the Sone and the Holy Gost: but alle weys fayle thei, in somme articles of oure feythe. Some of theise ben clept Jacobytes: for seynt Jame converted hem, and seynt John baptized hem. They seyn, that a man schal maken his confessioun only to God, and not to a man: for only to Him, scholde man zelden him gylty of alle, that he hathe mys don. Ne

God ordeyned not, ne never devysed, ne the prophete nouther, that a man scholde schryven him to another, (as thei seyn) but only to God: as Moyses writethe in the Bible, and as David seythe in the Psawtre boke; *Confitebor tibi, Domine, in toto Corde meo*: and, *Delictum meum tibi cognitum feci*: and, *Deus meus es tu, et confitebor tibi*; and, *Quoniam cogitatio hominis confitebitur tibi*; &c. Fot thei knowen alle the bible, and the psautere: and therfore allegge thei so the lettre: but thei alleggen not the aucthoritees thus in Latyn, but in here langage, fulle appertely; and seyn wel, that David and othere prophetes seyn it. Natheles seynt Austyn and seynt Gregory seyn thus: Augustinus; *Qui scelera sua cogitat, et conversus fuerit, veniam sibi credat.* Gregorious; *Dominus potius mentem quam verba respicit.* And seynt Hillary seythe; *Longorum temporum crimina, in ictu Oculi pereunt, si Cordis nata fuerit compunctio.* And for suche auctoritees, thei seyn, that only to God schalle a man knouleche his defautes, zeldynge him self gylty, and cryenge him mercy, and behotynge to him to amende him self. And therfore whan thei wil schryven hem, thei taken fyre, and sette it besyde hem, and casten therin poudre of frank encens; and in the smoke therof, thei schryven hem to God, and cryen him mercy. But sothe it is, that this confessioun was first and kyndely: but seynt Petre the apostle, and thei that camen aftre him, han ordeynd to make here confessioun to man; and be gode resoun: for thei perceyveden wel, that no syknesse was curable, by gode medycyne to leye therto, but zif men knewen the nature of the maladye. And also no man may zeven covenable medicyne, but zif he knowe the qualitee of the dede. For o synne may be grettere in o man than in another, and in o place and in o tyme than in another: and therfore it behovethe him, that he knowe the kynde of the dede, and thereupon to zeven him penance.

There ben othere, that ben clept Surienes; and thei holden the beleeve amonges us, and of hem of Grece. And thei usen alle berdes, as men of Grece don: and thei make the sacrament of therf bred: and in here langage, thei usen lettres of Sarrazines; but aftre the misterie of Holy chirche, thei usen lettres of Grece; and thei maken here confessioun, right as the Jacobytes don.

There ben othere, that men clepen Georgyenes, that seynt George converted; and him thei worschipen, more than ony other seynt; and to him thei cryen for help: and thei camen out of the reme of George. Theise folk usen crounes schaven. The clerkes han rounde crounes, and the lewed men han crownes alle square: and thei holden Cristene lawe, as don thei of Grece; of whom I have spoken of before.

Othere there ben, that men clepen Cristene men of Gyrdynge: for thei ben alle gyrt aboven. And ther ben othere, that men clepen Nestoryenes; and summe Arryenes, sume Nubyenes, sume of Grees, same of Ynde, and sume of Prestre Johnes Lond. And alle theise han manye articles of oure feythe, and to othere thei ben varyaunt. And of here variance, were to longe to telle; and go I wil leve, as for the tyme, with outen more spekynge of hem.

Of the Cytee of Damasce. Of 3 Weyes to Jerusalem; on be Londe and be See; another more be Londe than be See; and the thridde Weye to Jerusalem, alle be Londe.

[Sidenote: Chap. XI] Now aftre that I have told zou sum partye of folk, in the contrees before, now wille I turnen azen to my weye, for to turnen azen to this half. Thanne whoso wil go fro the lond of Galilee, of that that I have spoke, for to come azen on this half, men comen azen be Damasce, that is a fulle fayre cytee, and fulle noble, and fulle of alle merchandises, and a 3 journeyes long fro the see, and a 5 journeyes fro Jerusalem. But upon camaylles, mules, hors, dromedaries and other bestes, men caryen here merciandise thidre: and thidre comethe marchauntes with merchandise be see, from Yndee, Persee, Caldee, Ermonye, and of manye othere kyngdomes. This cytee founded Helizeus Damascus, that was Zoman and Despenser of Abraham, before that Ysaac was born: for he thoughte for to have ben Abrahames heir: and he named the toun aftre his surname Damasce. And in that place, where Damasc was founded, Kaym sloughe Abel his brother. And besyde Damasc is the Mount Seyr. In that cytee of Damasce, ther is gret plentee of welles: and with in the cytee and with oute, ben many fayre gardynes, and of dyverse frutes. Non other citee is not lyche in comparisoun to it of faire gardynes, and of faire desportes. The cytee is gret and fulle of peple, and wel walled with double walles. And there ben manye phisicyens. And seint Poul him self was there a physicyen, for to kepen mennes bodies in hele, before he was converted: and aftre that, he was phisicien of soules. And seynt Luke the Evaungelist was Disciple of seynt Poul, for to lerne phisik; and many othere. For seynt Poul held thanne scole of phisik. And neere besyde Damasce, was he converted: and aftre his conversionn, he duelte in that cytee 3 dayes, with outen sight, and with outen mete or drinke. And in tho 3 dayes he was ravisscht to hevene, and there he saughe many prevytees of oure Lord. And faste besyde Damasce, is the Castelle of Arkes, that is bothe fair and strong. From Damasce, men comen azen, be oure Lady of Sardenak, that is a 5 myle on this half Damasce; and it is sytt upon a roche, and it is a fulle faire place, and it semethe a castelle; for there was wont to ben a castelle; but it is now a fulle faire chirche. And there with inne, ben monkes and nonnes Cristene. And there is a vowt, undre the chirche, where that Cristene men duellen also: and thei han many gode vynes. And in the chirche, behynde the high awtere, in the walle, is a table of black wode, on the whiche somtyme was depeynted an ymage of oure Lady, that turnethe into flesche; but now the ymage schewethe but litille: but evermore thorewe the grace of God that table droppeth as hyt were of olyve. And there is a vessel of marbre, undre the table, to resseyve the oyle, thare of thay yeven unto pylgrymes: for it heleth of many sykenesses. And he that kepeth it clanly a yere, aftre that yere, hyt turneth yn to flesche and bloode.

By twyne the cytee of Darke and the cytee of Raphane, ys a ryvere, that men clepen Sabatorye. For on the Saturday, hyt renneth faste; and alle the wooke elles, hyt stondeth stylle, and renneth nouzt or lytel. And there ys a nother ryvere, that upon the nyzt freseth wondur faste; and uppon the day, ys noon frost sene. And so gon men by a cytee, that men clepen Beruche. And thare men gon un to the see, that schal goon un to Cypre. And thay aryve at Porte de Sure or of Tyrye; and than un to Cypre. Or elles men mowen gon from the Porte of Tyrye ryzt welle, and com not yn to Cypre; and aryve at som haven of Grece; and thanne comen men un to theis countrees, by weyes, that I have spoken of by fore.

Now have I tolde you of wayes, by the whyche men gon ferrest and longest; as by Babyloyne and Mounte Synay and other places many, thorewe the whyche londes, men turne azen to the lande of promyssyoun. Now wul y telle the ryzt way to Jerusalem. For som men wyl nouzt passe hyt, som for thay have nouzt despence of hem, for they have noon companye, and other many causes reasonables. And thare fore I telle you schorttely, how a man may goon with lytel costage and schortte tyme. A man that cometh from the londes of the weste, he goth thorewe Fraunce, Borgoyne and Lumbardye, and to Venys and to Geen, or to som other havene of the marches, and taketh a schyppe thare, and gon by see to the Isle of Gryffle; and so aryveth hem yn Grece or in Port Myroche or Valon or Duras, or at som other havene, and gon to londe, for to reste hem; and gon ayen to the see, and aryves in Cypre; and cometh nouzt yn the Ile of Roodes; and aryves at Famegoste, that ys the chefe havene of Cypre, or elles at Lamatoun. And thenne ynto the schyp ayen, and by syde the havene of Tyre, and come nouzt to lande; and so passeth he by alle the havens of that coast, until he come to Jaffe, that ys the neyest haven unto Jerusalem: for it is seven and twenty myle. And from Jaffe men goon to the cytee of Rames: and that ys but lytel thenne, and hyt is a fayre cytee. And by syde Rames, ys a fayre churche of oure Lady, whare oure Lord schewede hym to oure Lady, in thys lykenesse, that he tokeneth the Trynyte. And thare fast by, ys a churche of Seynt George, whare that hys heed was smyten of. And thanne un to the Castel Emaus; and thanne unto Mounte Joye: and from thenne, pylgrymes mowen fyrste se un to Jerusalem. And thanne un to Mount Modeyn: and thanne unto Jerusalem. And at the Mount Modeyn lythe the prophete Machabee. And overe Ramatha, ys the town of Douke; where of Amos the goude prophete was.

A nother way. For alse moche as many men ne may not suffre the savour of the see, but hadden lever to gon by londe, they that hyt be more payne; a man schal soo goon un to on of the havenes of Lumbardye, als Venys or an other; and he schal passe yn to Grece, thorwe Port Moroche, or an other; and so he schal gon un to Constantynople. And he schal so passe the wature, that ys cleped the Brace of Seynt George, that ys an arm of the see. And from thens he schal cum un to Pulveralle; and sythen un to the Castelle of Cynople. And from thens schal he gon unto Capadose, that ys a grete countree, whare that ben many grete hylles. And he schal gon thorewe Turkye, and unto the cytee of Nyke, the whyche they wonne from the Emperoure of Constantynople. And hyt is a fayre cytee, and wounder wel walled: and thare ys a ryvere, that men clepen the laye: and thare men goon by the Alpes of Aryoprynant, and by the Valez of Mallebrynez, and eke the Vale of Ernax; and so un to Anthyoche the lesse, that sytteth on the Ryehay. And there aboute ben many goude hylles and fayre, and many fayre woodes, and eke wylde beestes.

And he that wylle goon by an other way, he mote goon by the playnes of Romayne, costynge the Romayne see. Uppon that cost, ys a woundur fayre castelle, that men clepen Florathe. And whanne that a man ys oute of that ylke hylles, men passen thenne thorewe a cytee, that ys called Maryoche and Arteyse, whare that ys a grete brygge upon a ryvere of Ferne, that men clepen Fassar: and hyt ys a grete ryvere, berynge schyppes. And by syde the cytee of Damas, ys a ryvere that cometh from the mounteyne of Lybane, that men hyt callen Albane. Atte passynge of this ryvere, seynt Eustache loste hys two sones, whanne that he hadde lost hys wyffe. And yt gooth thorewe the playne of Arthadoe; and so un to the Reed See. And so men moten goon un to the cytee of phenne, and so un to the cytee of Ferne. And Antyoche ys a ful fayre cytee and wel walled. For hyt ys two myle longe and eche pylere of the brygge thare ys a goud toure. And thys ys the beest cytee of the kyngdom of Surrye. And from Antyoche, men moten so forth goon un to the cytee of Lacuthe; and thanne un to Geble; and thanne un tyl Tourtous: and thare by ys the lande of Cambre, whare that ys a stronge castelle, that men clepen Maubeke. And from Tourtouse men goon up to Thryple, uppon the see. And uppon the see, men goon unto Deres; and thare ben two weyes un to Jerusalem: Uppon the lyfte way, men goon fyrst un to Damas, by Flome Jordane: uppon the ryzt syde, men goon thorewe the lande of Flagam, and so un to the cytee of Cayphas: of the whiche Cayphas was Lord: and som clepeth hyt the castelle Pellerynez: And from thens ys foure dayes journeyes un to Jerusalem and they goon thorewe Cesarye Phylyppum and Jaffe and Ramys and Emaux, and so unto Jerusalem.

Now have I told yow som of the wayes, by the land, and eke by water, how that men mowen goon unto Jerusalem: they that hyt be so, that there been many other wayes, that men goon by, aftur countrees, that thay comen fram, nevere the lasse they turne alle un tylle an ende. Yet is thare a way, alle by lande, un to Jerusalem, and pass noon see; that ys from Fraunce or Flaundres; but that way ys fulle lange and perylous, of grete travayle; and thare fore fewe goon that ylke way. And who so gooth that, he mote goon thorewe Almayn and Pruys; and so un to Tartarye. This Tartarye ys holden of the great Chan, of whom y schal speke more afterwarde. For thydur lasteth hys Lordschup. And the Lordes of Tartarye yeldeth unto the grete Chan trybute. Thys ys a ful ille lande, and a sondye, and wel lytel fruyt beryng. For thare groweth lytel goude of corne or wyn, ne benes ne pese: but beestes ben thare y nowe, and that ful grete plente. And thare ete thay nought but flesche with outen brede; and thay soupe the brothe there of: and also thay drynke the mylk. And alle manere of wylde beestes they eten, houndes, cattes, ratouns, and alle othere wylde bestes. And thei have no wode, or elle lytylle. And therfore thei warmen and sethen here mete with hors dong and cow dong, and of other bestes dryed azenst the sonne. And princes and othere eten not, but ones in the day; and that but lytille. And thei ben righte foule folk and of evyl kynde. And in somer, be alle the contrees, fallen many tempestes and many hydouse thondres and leytes, and slen meche peple and bestes also, fulle often tyme. And sodeynly is there passynge hete, and sodeynly also passynge cold. And it is the foulest contree, and the most cursed, and the porest, that men knowen. And here prince, that governethe that contree, that thei clepen Batho, duellethe at the cytee of Orda. And treuly no gode man scholde not duellen in that contre. For the lond and the contree is not worthi houndes to dwelle inne. It were a gode contree to sowen inne thristelle and breres and broom and thornes; and for no other thing is it not good. Natheless there is gode londe in sum place; but it is pure litille, as men seyn. I have not ben in that contree, ne be tho weyes: but I have ben at other londes, that marchen to tho contrees; and in the lond of Russye, and in the lond of Nyflan, and in the reme of Crako, and of Letto, and in the reme of Daresten, and in manye other places, that marchen to the costes: but I wente never be that weye to Jerusalem; wherfore I may not wel telle zou the manere. But zif this matiere plese to ony worthi man, that hathe gon be that weye, he may telle it, zif him lyke; to that entent, that tho that wole go by that weye, and maken here viage be tho costes, mowen knowen what weye is there. For no man may passe be that weye godely, but in time of wyntir, for the perilous watres, and wykkede mareyes that ben in tho contrees; that no man may passe, but zif it be strong frost, and snowe aboven. For zif the snow ne were, men myght not gon upon the yse, ne hors ne carre nouther. And it is wel a 3 journeys of suche weye, to passe from Prusse to the lond of Sarazin habitable. And it behovethe to the Cristene men, that schulle werre azen hem every zeer, to bere here vitaylles with hem: for thei schulle fynde there no good. And than most thei let carye here vitaylle upon the yse, with carres that have no wheeles, that thei clepen scleyes. And als longe as here vitaylles lasten, thei may abide there, but no longer. For there schulle they fynde no wight that will selle hem ony vitaille or ony thing. And whan the spyes seen ony Cristene men comen upon hem, thei rennen to the townes, and cryen with a lowd voys, Kerra, Kerra, Kerra; and than anon thei armen hem and assemblen hem to gydere.

And zee schulle undirstonde, that it fresethe more strongly in tho contrees than on this half; and therefore hathe every man stewes in his hous, and in tho stewes thei eten and don here occupatiouns, alle that they may. For that is at the northe parties, that men clepen the septentrionelle, where it is alle only cold. For the sonne is but lytille or non toward tho contreyes: and therefore in the Septentryon, that is verry northe, is the lond so cold, that no man may duelle there: and in the contrarye, toward the southe, it is so hoot, that no man ne may duelle there: because that the sonne, whan he is upon the southe, castethe his bemes alle streghte upon that partye.

Of the Customes of Sarasines, and of hire Lawe; and how the Soudan arresond me, Auctour of this Book. And of the begynnynge of Machomete.

[Sidenote: Cap. XII.] Now because that I have spoken of Sarazines and of here contree, now zif zee wil knowe a party of here lawe and of here beleve, I schalle telle zou, aftre that here book, that is clept Alkaron, tellethe. And sum men clepen that book Meshaf: and sum men clepen it Harme, aftre the dyverse langages of the contree. The whiche book Machamete toke hem. In the whiche boke, among other thinges, is written, as I have often tyme seen and radd, that the gode shulle gon to paradys, and the evele to helle: and that beleven alle Sarazines. And zif a man aske hem, what paradys thei menen; thei seyn, to paradys, that is a place of delytes, where men schulle fynde alle maner of frutes, in alle cesouns, and ryveres rennynge of mylk and hony, and of wyn, and of swete watre; and that thei schulle have faire houses and noble, every man aftre his dissert, made of precyous stones, and of gold, and of sylver; and that every man schalle have 80 wyfes, alle maydenes; and he schalle have ado every day with hem, and zit he schalle fynden hem alle weys maydenes. Also thei beleeven and speken gladly of the Virgine Marie and of the Incarnacioun. And thei seyn, that Marye was taughte of the angel; and that Gabrielle seyde to hire, that sche was forchosen from the begynnynge of the world; and that he schewed to hire the incarnacioun of Jesu Crist; and that sche conceyved and bare child, mayden: and that wytnessethe here boke. And they seyn also, that Jesu Crist spak als sone as he was born; and that he was an holy prophete and a trewe, in woord and dede, and meke and pytous and rightefulle and with outen ony vyce. And thei seyn also, that whan the angel schewed the Incarnacioun of Crist unto Marie, sche was zong, and had gret drede. For there was thanne an enchantour in the contree, that deled with wycche craft, that men clepten Taknia, that he his enchauntementes cowde make him in lyknesse of an angel, and wente often tymes and lay with maydenes: and therfore Marie dredde, lest it hadde ben Taknia, that cam for to desceyve the maydenes. And therfore sche conjured the angel, that he scholde telle hire, zif it were he or no. And the angel answerde and seyde, that sche scholde have no drede of him: for he was verry messager of Jesu Crist. Also here book seythe, that whan that sche had childed undre a palme tree, sche had gret schame, that sche hadde a child; and sche grette, and seyde, that sche wolde that sche hadde ben ded. And anon the child spak to hire and comforted hire, and seyde, Modir, ne dismaye the noughte; for God hathe hidd in the his prevytees, for the salvacioun of the world. And in othere many places seythe here Alkaron, that Jesu Crist spak als sone as he was born. And that book seythe also, that Jesu was sent from God alle myghty, for to ben myrour and ensample and tokne to alle men. And the Alkaron seythe also of the day of doom, how God schal come to deme alle maner of folk; and the gode he schalle drawen on his syde, and putte hem into blisse; and the wykkede he schal condempne to the peynes of helle. And amonges alle prophetes, Jesu was the most excellent and the moste worthi, next God; and that he made the Gospelles, in the whiche is gode doctryne and helefulle, fulle of charitee and sothefastnesse, and trewe prechinge to hem that beleeven in God; and that he was a verry prophete, and more than a prophete; and lyved withouten synne, and zaf syghte to the blynde, and helede the lepres, and reysed dede men, and steyghe to hevene. And whan thei mowe holden the boke of the Gospelles of oure Lord written, and namely, *Missus est Angelus Gabriel*; that Gospel, thei seyn, tho that ben lettred, often tymes in here orisouns, and thei kissen it and worschipen it, with gret devocioun. Thei fasten an hool monethe in the zeer, and eten noughts but be nyghte, and thei kepen hem fro here wyfes alle that monethe: but the seke men be not constreyned to that fast. Also this book spekethe of Jewes; and seythe, that thei ben cursed; for thei wolde not beleven, that Jesu Crist was comen of God; and that thei lyeden falsely on Marie and on hire sone Jesu Crist, seyenge that thei hadden crucyfyed Jesu the sone of Marie: for he was nevere crucyfyed, as thei seyn; but that God made him to stye up to him with outen dethe, and with outen anoye: but he transfigured his lyknesse into Judas Scariothe, and him crucyfyden the Jewes, and wenden that it had ben Jesus: but Jesus steyge to hevenes alle quyk; and therfore thei seyn, that the Cristene men erren and han no gode knowleche of this, and that thei beleeven folyly and falsly, that Jesu Crist was crucyfyed. And they seyn zit, that and he had ben crucyfyed, that God had don azen his righteswisnesse, for to suffre Jesu Crist, that was innocent, to ben put upon the Cros, with outen gylt. And in this article thei seyn, that wee faylen, and that the gret rightewisnesse of God ne myghte not suffre so gret a wrong. And in this, faylethe here feythe. For thei knoulechen wel, that the werkes of Jesu Crist ben gode, and his wordes and his dedes and his doctryne by his Gospelles, weren trewe and his meracles also trewe; and the blessed Virgine Marie is good, and holy mayden, before and aftre the birthe of Jesu Crist; and that alle tho, that beleven perfitely in God, schul ben saved. And because that thei gon so nye oure feythe, thei ben lyghtly converted to Cristene lawe, whan men prechen hem and schewe hem distynctly the lawe of Jesu Crist, and tellen hem of the prophecyes. And also thei seyn, that thei knownen wel, be the prophecyes, that the lawe of Machomete schalle faylen, as the lawe of the Jewes dide, and that the lawe of Cristine peple schalle laste to the day of doom. And zif ony man aske hem, what is here beleeve; thei answeren thus, and in this forme, Wee beleven God formyour of hevene and of erthe and of alle othere things, that he made. And we beleven of the day of doom, and that every man schalle have his meryte, aftre he hathe disserved. And we beleve it for sothe, alle that God hathe seyd be the mouthes of his prophetes. Also Machomet commanded in his Alkaron, that every man scholde have 2 wyfes or 3 or 4; but now thei taken unto 9, and of lemmanes als manye as he may susteyne. And zif ony of here wyfes mys beren hem azenst hire husbonde, he may caste hire out of his house; and departe from him, and take another: but he schalle departe with hire his godes. Also whan men speken to hem, of the Fadre and of the Sone and of the Holy Gost, thei seyn, that thei ben 3 persones; but not o God. For here Alkaron spekethe not of the Trynyte. But thei seyn wel, that God hathe speche, and elle where he dowmb; and God hathe also a Spirit, thei knowen wel, for elle thei seyn, he were not in lyve. And whan men speken to hem of the Incarnacioun, how that be the word of the angel, God sente his wysdom in to erthe, and enumbred him in the Virgyne Marie: and be the Woord of God, schulle the dede ben reysed, at the day of doom; thei seyn, that it is sothe, and that the Woord of God hathe gret strengthe. And thei seyn, that whoso knew not the Woord of God, he scholde not knowe God. And thei seyn also, that Jesu Crist is the Woord of God; and so seythe here Alkaron, where it seythe, that the angel spak to Marie and seyde, Marie, God schalle preche the Gospel be the woord of his mowthe, and his name schalle be clept Jesu Crist. And thei seyn also, that Abraham was frend to God, and that Moyses was famileer spekere with God; and Jesu Crist was the Woord and the Spirit of God; and that Machomete was right messager of God. And thei seyh, that of theise 4, Jesu was the most worthi and the most excellent and the most gret; so that thei han many gode articles of oure feythe, alle be it that thei have no parfite lawe and feythe, as Cristene men han; and therfore ben thei lightly converted; and namely, tho that undirstonden the Scriptures and the prophecyes. For thei han Gospelles and the prophecyes and the Byble, writen in here langage. Wherfore thei conne meche of Holy Wrytt, but thei undirstonde it not, but aftre the lettre:

and so don the Jewes; for thei undirstonde not the lettre gostly, but bodyly; and therfore ben thei repreved of the wise, that gostly understonden it. And therfore seythe seynt Poul; *Litera occidit; Spiritus vivificat*. Also the Sarazines seyn, that the Jewes ben cursed: for thei han defouled the lawe, that God sente hem be Moyses. And the Cristene ben cursed also, as thei seyn: for their kepen not the commandementes and the preceptes of the Gospelle, that Jesu Crist taughte hem. And therfore I schalle telle zou, what the Soudan tolde me uppn a day, in his chambre. He leet voyden out of his chambre alle manner of men, lordes aad othere: for he wolde speke with me in conseille. And there he asked me, how the Cristene men governed hem in oure contree. And I seyde him, righte wel: thonked be God. And he seyde me, treulyche, nay: for zee Cristene men ne recthen righte noghte how untrewly to serve God. Ze scholde zeven ensample to the lewed peple, for to do wel; and zee zeven hem ensample to don evylle. For the comownes, upon festyfulle dayes, whan thei scholden gon to chirche to serve God, than gon thei to tavernes, and ben there in glotony, alle the day and alle nyghte, and eten and drynken, as bestes that have no resoun, and wite not whan thei have y now. And also the Cristene men enforcen hem, in alle maneres that thei mowen, for to fighte, and for to desceyven that on that other. And there with alle thei ben so proude, that thei knowen not how to ben clothed; now long, now schort, now streyt, now large, now swerded, now daggered, and in alle manere gyses. Thei scholden ben symple, meke and trewe, and fulle of almes dede, as Jhesu was, in whom thei trowe: but thei ben alle the contrarie, and evere enclyned to the evylle, and to don evylle. And thei ben so coveytous, that for a lytylle sylyer, thei sellen here doughtres, here sustres and here owne wyfes, to putten hem to leccherie. And on with drawethe the wif of another; and non of hem holdethe feythe to another; but thei defoulen here lawe, that Jhesu Crist betook hem to kepe, for here salvacioun. And thus for here synnes, han thei lost alle this lond, that wee holden. For, for hire synnes there God hathe taken hem in to oure hondes, noghte only be strengthe of our self, but for here synnes. For wee knowen wel in verry sothe, that whan zee serve God, God wil hepe zou: and whan he is with zou, no man may be azenst you. And that knowe we wel, be oure prophecyes, that Cristene men schulle wynnen azen this lond out of oure hondes, whan thei serven God more devoutly. But als longe als thei ben of foule and of unclene lyvynge, (as thei ben now) wee have no drede of hem, in no kynde: for here God wil not helpen hem in no wise. And than I asked him, how he knew the state of Cristene men. And he answered me, that he knew alle the state of the comounes also, be his messangeres, that he sente to alle londes, in manere as thei weren marchauntes of precyous stones, of clothes of gold and of othere things; for to knowen the manere of every contree amonges Cristene men. And than he leet clepe in alle the lordes, that he made voyden first out of his chambre; and there he schewed me 4, that weren grete lordes in the contree, that tolden me of my contree, and of many othere Cristene contrees, als wel as thei had ben of the same contree: and thei spak Frensche righte wel; and the Sowdan also, where of I had gret marvaylle. Alas! that it is gret sclaundre to oure feythe and to oure lawe, whan folk that ben with outen lawe, schulle repreven us and undernemen us of oure synnes. And thei that scholden ben converted to Crist and to the lawe of Jhesu, be oure gode ensamples and be oure acceptable lif to God, and so converted to the lawe of Jhesu Crist, ben thorghe oure wykkednesse and evylle lyvynge, fer fro us and straungeres fro the holy and verry beleeve, schulle thus appelen us and holden us for wykkede lyveres and cursed. And treuly thei sey sothe. For the Sarazines ben gode and feythfulle. For thei kepen entierly the commaundement of the holy book Alkaron, that God sente hem be his messager Machomet; to the whiche, as thei seyne, seynt Gabrielle the aungel often tyme tolde the wille of God. And zee schulle undirstonde, that Machamote was born in Arabye, that was first a pore knave, that kept cameles, that wenten with marchantes fur marchandize; and so befelle, that he wente with the marchandes in to Egipt: and thei weren than Cristene, in tho partyes. And at the desertes of Arabye, he wente in to a chapelle, where a Eremyte duelte. And when he entred in to the chapelle, that was but a lytille and a low thing, and had but a lityl dore and a low, than the entree began to wexe so gret and so large and so highe, as thoughe it had ben of a gret mynstre, or the zate of a paleys. And this was the firste myracle, the Sarazins seyn, that Machomete dide in his zouthe. Aftre began he for to wexe wyse and riche; and he was a gret astronomer: and aftre he was governour and prince of the lond of Cozrodane; and he governed it fully wisely, in suche manere, that whan the prince was ded, he toke the lady to wyfe, that highte Gadridge. And Machomete felle often in the grete sikenesse, that men callen the fallynge evylle: wherfore the lady was fulle sorry, that evere sche toke him to husbonde. But Machomete made hire to beleeve, that alle tymes, whan he felle so, Gabriel the angel cam for to speke with him; and for the gret lighte and brightnesse of the angelle, he myghte not susteyne him fro fallynge. And therfore the Sarazines seyn, that Gabriel cam often to speke with him. This Machomete regned in Arabye, the zeer of oure Lord Jhesu Crist 610; and was of the generacioun of Ysmael, that was Abrahames sone, that he gat upon Agar his chamberere. And therfere ther ben Sarazines, that ben clept Ismaelytenes; and summe Agaryenes, of Agar: and the othere propurly ben clept, Sarrazines, of Sarra: and summe ben clept Moabytes, and summe Amonytes; fro the 2 sones of Lothe, Moab and Amon, that he begat on his doughtres, that weren aftirward grete erthely princes. And also Machomete loved wel a gode heremyte, that duelled in the desertes, a myle fro Mount Synay, in the weye that men gon fro Arabye toward Caldee, and toward

Ynde, o day journey fro the See, where the marchauntes of Yenyse comen often for marchandise. And so often wente Machomete to this heremyte, that alle his men weren wrothe: for he wolde gladly here this heremyte preche, and make his men wake alle nyghte: and therfore his men thoughten to putte the heremyte to dethe: and so it befelle upon a nyght, that Machomete was dronken of gode wyn, and he felle on slepe; and his men toke Machometes swerd out of his schethe, whils he slepte, and there with thei slowghe this heremyte: and putten his swerd alle blody in his schethe azen. And at morwe, whan he fond the heremyte ded, he was fulle sory and wrothe, and wolde have don his men to dethe: but they alle with on accord seyd, that he him self had slayn him, when he was dronken, and schewed him his swerd alle blody: and he trowed, that thei hadden seyd sothe. And than he cursed the wyn, and alle tho that drynken it. And therfore Sarrazines, that be devout, drynken nevere no wyn: but sume drynken it prevyly. For zif thei dronken it openly, thei scholde ben repreved. But thei drynken gode beverage and swete and norysshynge, that is made of galamelle: and that is that men maken sugar of, that is of righte gode savour: and it is gode for the breest. Also it befallethe sumtyme, that Cristene men becomen Sarazines, outher for povertee, or for symplenesse, or else for here owne wykkednesse. And therfore the archiflamyn or the flamyn, as oure erchebisshop or bisshopp, whan he receyvethe hem, seythe thus, *La ellec, Sila. Machomete rores alla*; that is to seye, *There is no God but on, and Machomete his messager.*

Of the Londes of Albanye, and of Libye. Of the Wisshinges, for Wacchinge of the Sperhauk; and of Noes Schippe.

[Sidenote: Cap. XIII.] Now sithe I have told zou beforn of the Holy Lond, and of that contree abouten, and of many weyes for to go to that lond, and to the Mount Synay, and of Babyloyne the more and the lesse, and to other places, that I have spoken beforn; now is tyme, zif it lyke zou, for to telle zou of the marches and iles, and dyverse bestes, and of dyverse folk bezond theise marches. For in tho contrees bezonden, ben many dyverse contrees, and many grete kyngdomes; that ben departed be the 4 flodes, that comen from Paradys terrestre. For Mesopotayme and the Kyngdom of Caldee and Arabye, ben betwene the 2 ryveres of Tygre and of Eufrates. And the kyngdom of Mede and of Persye, ben betwene the ryveres of Nile and of Tigres. And the kyngdom of Syrie, where of I have spoken beforn, and Palestyne and Phenycie, ben betwene Eufrates and the See Medyterrane: the whiche see durethe in lengthe, fro Mayrok, upon the See of Spayne, unto the grete See; so that it lastethe bezonde Costantynople 3040 myles of Lombardye. And toward the see occyan in Ynde, is the kyngdom of Shithie, that is alle closed with hilles. And aftre undre Schithie, and fro the See of Caspie, unto the Flom Thainy, is Amazoyne, that is the lond of femynye, where that no man is, but only alle wommen. And aftre is Albanye, a fulle grete reme. And it is clept Albanye, because the folk ben whitere there, than in other marches there abouten. And in that contree ben so gret houndes and so stronge, that thei assaylen lyouns, and sleu hem. And thanne aftre is Hircanye, Bactrye, Hiberye, and many other kyngdomes. And betwene the Rede See and the see occyan, toward the southe, is the kyngdom of Ethiope, and of Lybye the hyere. The which lond of Lybye, (that is to seyne Libye the lowe) that begynnethe at the See of Spayne, fro thens where the Pyleres of Hercules ben, and durethe unto aneyntes Egipt and towards Ethiope. In that contree of Libye, is the see more highe than the lond; and it semethe that it wolde covere the erthe, and natheles zit it passethe not his markes. And men seen in that contre a mountayne, to the whiche no man comethe. In this lond of Libye, whoso turnethe toward the est, the schadewe of him self is on the right syde: and here in oure contree, the schadwe is on the left syde. In that See of Libye, is no fissche: for thei mowe not lyve ne dure, for the gret hete of the sonne; because that the watre is evermore boyllynge, for the gret hete. And many othere londes there ben, that it were to long to tellen or to nombren: but of sum parties I schal speke more pleynly here aftre.

Whoso wil thanne gon toward Tarterie, toward Persie, toward Caldee, and toward Ynde, he most entre the see, at Gene or at Venyse or at sum other havene, that I have told zou before. And than passe men the see, and arryven at Trapazond, that is a gode cytee; and it was wont to ben the havene of Pountz. There is the havene of persanes and of medaynes and of the marches there bezonde. In that cytee lythe Seynt Athanasie, that was Bishopp of Alisandre, that made the Psalm *Quicunque vult*. This Athanasius was a gret Doctour of Dyvynytee: and because that he preched and spak so depely of Dyvynytee and of the Godhede, he was accused to the Pope of Rome, that he was an Heretyk. Wherfore the Pope sente aftre hym, and putte him in presoun: and whils he was in presoun, he made that Psalm, and sente it to the Pope, and seyde: that zif he were an heretyk, that was that heresie; for that, he seyde, was his beleeve. And whan the Pope saughe it, and had examyned it, that it was parfite and gode, and verryly oure feythe and oure beleeve, he made him to ben delyvered out of presoun, and commanded that Psalm to ben seyd every day at Pryme: and so he held Athanasie a gode man. But he wolde nevere go to his bisshopriche azen, because that thei accused him of heresye. Trapazond was wont to ben holden of the Emperour of Costantynople: but a gret man, that he sente for to kepe the contree azenst the Turkes, usurped the lond, and helde it to himself, and cleped him Emperour of Trapazond.

And from thens, men gon thorghe litille Ermonye. And in that contree is an old castelle, that stont upon a roche, the whiche is cleped the Castelle of the

Sparrehawk, that is bezonde the cytee of Layays, beside the town of Pharsipee, that belongethe to the lordschipe of Cruk; that is a riche lord and a gode Cristene man; where men fynden a sparehauk upon a perche righte fair, and righte wel made; and a fayre lady of fayrye, that kepethe it. And who that wil wake that sparhauk, 7 dayes and 7 nyghtes, and as sum men seyn, 3 dayes and 3 nyghtes, with outen companye, and with outen sleep, that faire lady schal zeven him, whan he hathe don, the first wyssche, that he wil wyssche, of erthely thinges: and that hathe been proved often-tymes. And o tyme befelle, that a kyng of Ermonye, that was a worthi knyght and doughty man and a noble prince, woke that hauk som tyme: and at the ende of 7 dayes and 7 nyghtes, the lady cam to him, and bad him wisschen: for he had wel disserved it. And he answerde, that he was gret Lord y now, and wel in pees, and hadde y nowghe of worldly ricchesse: and therfore he wolde wisshe non other thing, but the body of that faire lady, to have it at his wille. And sche answerde him, that he knew not what he asked; and seyde, that he was a fool, to desire that he myghte not have; for sche seyde, that he scholde not aske, but erthely thing: for sche was non erthely thing, but a gostly thing. And the kyng seyde, that he ne wolde asken non other thing. And the lady answerde, sythe that I may not withdrawe zou fro zoure lewed corage, I schal zeve zou with outen wysschinge, and to alle hem that schulle com of you. Sire kyng, zee schulle have werre withouten pees, and alle weys to the 9 degree, zee schulle ben in subjeccioun to zoure enemyes; and zee schulle ben nedy of alle godes. And nevere sithen, nouther the kyng of Ermoyne, ne the contree, weren never in pees, ne thei hadden never sithen plentee of godes; and thei han ben sithen alle weyes undre tribute of the Sarrazines. Also the sone of a pore man woke that hauke, and wisshed that he myghte cheve wel, and to ben happy to merchandise. And the lady graunted him. And he becaam the most riche and the most famouse marchaunt, that myghte ben on see or on erthe. And he becam so riche, that he knew not the 1000 part of that he hadde: and he was wysere, in wisschynge, than was the king. Also a knyght of the temple wooke there; and wyssched a purs evere more fulle of gold: and the lady graunted him. But sche seyde him, that he had asked the destruccioun of here ordre; for the trust and the affiance of that purs, and for the grete pryde, that they scholde haven: and so it was. And therfore loke, he kepe him wel, that schalle wake: for zif he slepe, he is lost, that nevere man schalle seen him more. This is not the righte weye for to go to the parties, that I have nempned before; but for to see the merveyle, that I have spoken of.

And therfore who so wil go right weye, men gon fro Trapazond toward Ermonye the gret, unto a cytee that is clept Artyroun, that was wont to ben a gode cytee and a plentyous; but the Turkes han gretly wasted it. There aboute growethe no wyn ne fruyt, but litylle or elle non. In this lond, is the erthe more highe than in ony other; and that makethe gret cold. And there hen many gode watres, and gode welles, that comen undre erthe, fro the flom of paradys, that is clept Eufrates, that is a jorneye besyde that cytee. And that ryvere comethe towardes Ynde, undre erthe, and restorethe into the lond of Altazar. And so passe men be this Ermonie, and entren the see of Persie. Fro that cytee of Artyroun go men to an hille, that is clept Sabissocolle. And there besyde is another hille, that men clepen Ararathe: but the Jewes clepen it Taneez; where Noes schipp rested, and zit is upon that montayne: and men may seen it a ferr, in cleer wedre: and that montayne is wel a 7 myle highe. And sum men seyn, that thei han seen and touched the schipp; and put here fyngeres in the parties, where the feend went out, whan that Noe seyde *Benedicite*. But thei that seyn suche wordes, seyn here wille: for a man may not gon up the montayne, for gret plentee of snow that is alle wayes on that montayne, nouther somer ne wynter: so that no man may gon up there; ne never man dide, sithe the tyme of Noe; saf a monk, that, be the grace of God, brought on of the plankes doun: that zit is in the mynstere, at the foot of the montayne. And besyde is the cytee of Dayne, that Noe founded. And faste by is the cytee of Any, in the whiche were 1000 chirches. But upon that montayne, to gon up, this monk had gret desire; and so upon a day, he wente up: and whan he was upward the 3 part of the montayne, he was so wery, that he myghte no ferthere, and so he rested him, and felle o slepe; and whan he awook, he fonde him self lyggynge at the foot of the montayne. And than he preyede devoutly to God, that he wolde vouche saf to suffre him gon up. And an angelle cam to him, and seyde, that he scholde gon up; and so he dide. And sithe that tyme never non. Wherfore men scholde not beleeve such woordes.

Fro that montayne go men to the cytee of Thauriso, that was wont to ben clept Taxis, that is a fulle fair cytee, and a gret, and on of the beste, that is in the world, for marchandise: and it is in the lond of the Emperour of Persie. And men seyn, that the Emperour takethe more gode, in that cytee, for custom of marchandise than dothe the ricchest Cristene kyng of alle his reme, that livethe. For the tolle and the custom of his marchantes is with outen estymacioun to ben nombred. Beside that cytee, is a hille of salt; and of that salt, every man takethe what he will, for to salte with, to his nede. There duellen many Cristene men, undir tribute of Sarrazines. And fro that cytee, men passen be many townes and castelles, in goynge toward Ynde, unto the cytee of Sadonye, that is a 10 journeyes fro Thauriso; and it is a fulle noble cytee and a gret. And there duellethe the Emperour of Persie, in somer: for the contree is cold y now. And there ben gode ryveres, berynge schippes. Aftre go men the weye toward Ynde, be many iorneyes, and be many contreyes, unto the cytee, that is clept Cassak, that is a fulle noble cytee, and a plentyous of cornes and wynes, and of alle other godes. This is the cytee, where the 3 kynges metten to gedre, whan thei wenten to sechen oure Lord in Bethtem, to worschipe him, and to presente him with gold, ensence, and myrre. And it is from that cytee to Bethleem 53 iourneyes. Fro that cytee, men gon to another cytee, that is clept Bethe, that is a iourneye fro the see, that men clepen the gravely see. That is the best cytee, that the Emperour of Persie hathe, in alle his lond. And thei clepen it there Chardabago; and others clepen it Vapa. And the Paynemes seyn, that no Cristene man may not longe duelle, ne enduren with the lif, in that cytee: but dyen with in schort tyme; and no man knowethe not the cause. Aftre gon men, be many cytees and townes, and grete contrees, that it were to longe to telle, unto the cytee of Cornaa, that was wont to be so gret, that the walles abouten holden 25 myle aboute. The walks schewen zit: but it is not alle enhabited. From Cornaa, go men be many londes, and many cytees and townes, unto the lond of Job: and there endethe the lond of the Emperour of Persie.

Of the Lond of Job; and of his Age. Of the Aray of men of Caldee. Of the Lond where Wommen duellen with outen companye of men. Of the knouleche and vertues of the verray Dyamant.

[Sidenote: Chap. XIV.] Aftre the departynge fro Cornaa, men entren in to the lond of Job, that is a fulle faire contree, and a plentyous of alle godes. And men clepen that lond the lond of Sweze. In that lond is the cytee of Theman. Job was a Payneem, and he was Are of Gosre his sone, and held that lond, as prynce of that contree and he was so riche, that he knew not the hundred part of his godes. And alle thoughe he were a Payneem, natheless he served wel God, aftre his lawe: and oure Lord toke his service to his plesance. And whan he felle in poverte, he was 78 zeer of age. And aftre, whan God had preved his pacyence, and that it was so gret, he broughte him azen to richesse, and to hiere estate than he was before. And aftre that he was kyng of Ydumye, aftre Kyng Esau. And whan he was kyng, he was clept Jobab. And in that kyngdom, he lyvede aftre 170 zere: and so he was of age, whan he dyede, 248 zeer. In that lond of Job, there nys no defaute of no thing, that is nedefulle to mannes body. There ben hilles, where men getten gret plentee of manna, in gretter habundance, than in ony other contree. This manna is clept bred of aungelles; and it is a white thing, that is fulle swete and righte delicyous, and more swete than hony or sugre; and it comethe of the dew of hevene that fallethe upon the herbes, in that contree; and it congelethe and becomethe alle white and swete: and men putten it in medicynes for rich men, to make the wombe lax, and to purge evylle blood: for it clensethe the blode, and puttethe out malencoyle. This lond of Job marchethe to the kyngdom of Caldee. This lond of Caldee is fulle gret: and the langage of that contree is more gret in sownynge, that it is in other parties bezonde the see. Men passen to go bezond, be the Tour of Babiloyne the grete: of the whiche I have told zou before, where that alle the langages weren first chaunged. And that is a 4 jorneyes fro Caldee. In that reme, ben faire men, and thei gon fulle nobely arrayed in clothes of gold, or frayed and apparayled with grete perles and precyous stones, fulle nobely: and the wommen ben righte foule and evylle arrayed; and thei gon alle bare fote, and clothed in evylle garnementes, large and wyde, but thei ben schorte to the knees; and longe sleves doun to the feet, lyche a monkes frokke; and here sleves ben hongyng aboute here schuldres: and thei ben blake women, foule and hidouse; and treuly as foule as thei ben, als evele thei ben. In that kyngdom of Caldee, in a cytee, that is cleped Hur, duelled Thare, Abrahames fadre: and there was Abraham born: and that was in that tyme, that Nunus was Kyng of Babiloyne, of Arabye and of Egypt. This Nunus made the cytee of Nynyvee, the whiche that Noe had begonne before: and be cause that Nunus performed it, he cleped it Nynyve, aftre his owne name. Ther lythe Thobye the prophete, of whom Holy Writt spekethe offe. And fro that cytee of Hur Abraham departed, be the commandement of God, fro thens, aftre the dethe of his fadre; and ladde with him Sarra his wife and Lothe his brotheres sone, because that he hadde no child. And thei wenten to duelle in the lond of Chanaan, in a place, that is clept Sychem. And this Lothe was he, that was saved, whan Sodom and Gomorre and the othere cytees weren brent and sonken doun to helle; where that the dede see is now, as I have told zou before. In that lond of Caldee, thei han here propre langages, and here propre lettres.

Besyde the lond of Caldee, is the lond of Amazoyne. And in that reme is alle wommen, and no man; noght, as summe men seyn, that men mowe not lyve there, but for because that the wommen will not suffre no men amonges hem, to ben here Sovereynes. For sum tyme, ther was a kyng in that contrey; and men maryed, as in other contreyes: and so befelle, that the kyng had werre, with hem of Sithie; the whiche kyng highte Colopeus, that was slayn in bataylle, and alle the gode blood of his reme. And whan the queen and alle the othere noble ladyes sawen, that thei weren alle wydewes, and that alle the rialle blood was lost, thei armed hem, and as creatures out of wytt, thei slowen alle the men of the contrey, that weren laft. For thei wolden, that alle the wommen weren wydewes, as the queen and thei weren. And fro that tyme hiderwardes, thei nevere wolden suffren man to dwelle amonges hem, lenger than 7 dayes and 7 nyghtes; ne that no child that were male, scholde duelle amonges hem, longer than he were noryscht; and thanne sente to his fader. And whan thei wil have ony companye of man, than thei drawen hem towardes the londes marchynge next to hem: and than thei have loves, that usen hem; and thei duellen with hem an 8 dayes or 10; and thanne gon hom azen. And zif thei have ony knave child, thei kepen it a certeyn tyme, and than senden it to the fadir, whan he can gon allone, and eten be him self; or elle thei sleen it: and zif it be a femele, thei don away that on pappe, with an hote hiren; and zif it be a womman of gret lynage, thei don awey the left pappe, that thes may the better beren a scheeld: and zif it be a woman of symple blood, thei don awey the ryght pappe, for to scheeen [sic—KTH] with bowe Turkeys: for thei schote wel with bowes. In that lond thei have a Queen, that governethe alle that lond: and alle thei ben obeyssant to hire. And alweys thei maken here queen by eleccioun, that is most worthy in armes. For thei ben right gode werryoures, and wyse, noble and worthi. And thei gon often tyme in sowd, to help of other kynges in here werres, for gold and sylver, as othere sowdyoures don: and thei meyntenen hem self right vygouresly. This lond of Amazoyne is an Yle, alle enviround with the see, saf in 2 places, where ben 2 entrees. And bezond that watir, duellen the men, that ben here paramoures, and hire loves, where thei gon to solacen hem, whan thei wole. Besyde Amazoyne, is the lond of Tarmegyte, that is a gret contree and a fulle delectable: and for the godnesse of the contree, kyng Alisandre leet first make there the cytee of Alisandre; and zit he made 12 cytees of the same name: but that cytee is now clept Celsite. And fro that other cost of caldee, to ward the southe, is Ethiope, a gret contree, that strecchethe to the ende of Egypt. Ethiope is departed in 2 princypalle parties; and that is, in the est partie and in the meridionelle partie: the whiche partie meridionelle is clept Moretane. And the folk of that contree ben blake y now, and more blake than in the tother partie; and thei ben clept Mowres. In that partie is a welle, that in the day it is so cold, that no man may drynke there offe; and in the nyght it so hoot, that no man may suffre his hond there in. And bezonde that partie, toward the southe, to passe by the see occean, is a gret lond and a gret contrey: but men may not duelle there, for the fervent brennynge of the sonne; so is it passvnge hoot in that contrey. In Ethiope alle the ryveres and alle the watres ben trouble, and thei ben somdelle salte, for the gret hete that is there. And the folk of that contree ben lyghtly dronken, and han but litille appetyt to mete: and thei han comounly the flux of the wombe: and thei lyven not longe. In Ethiope ben manye dyverse folk: and Ethiope is clept Cusis. In that contree ben folk, that han but o foot: and thei gon so fast, that it is marvaylle: and the foot is so large, that it schadewethe alle the body azen the sonne, whanne thei wole lye and reste hem. In Ethiope, whan the children ben zonge and lytille, thei ben alle zelowe: and whan that thei wexen of age, that zalownesse turnethe to ben alle blak. In Ethiope is the cytee of Saba; and the lond, of the whiche on of the 3 kynges, that presented oure Lord in Bethleem was kyng offe.

Fro Ethiope men gon to Ynde, be manye dyverse contreyes. And men clepen the highe Ynde, Emlak. And Ynde is devyded in 3 princypalle parties; that is, the more, that is a fulle hoot contree; and Ynde the lesse, that is a fulle atempree contrey, that strecchethe to the lond of Mede; and the 3 part toward the Septentrion, is fulle cold; so that for pure cold and contynuelle frost, the watre becomethe cristalle. And upon tho roches of cristalle, growen the gode dyamandes, that ben of trouble colour. Zallow cristalle drawethe colour lyke oylle. And thei ben so harde, that no man may pollysche hem: and men clepen hem dyamandes in that contree, and Hamese in another contree. Othere dyamandes men fynden in Arabye, that ben not so gode; and thei ben more broun and more tendre. And other dyamandes also men fynden in the ile of Cipre, that ben zit more tendre; and hem men may wel pollische. And in the lond of Macedoyne men fynden dyamaundes also. But the beste and the most precyouse ben in Ynde. And men fynden many tymes harde dyamandes in a masse, that comethe out of Gold, whan men puren it and fynen it out of the myne; whan men breken that masse in smale peces. And sum tyme it happenethe, that men fynden summe as grete as a pese, and summe lasse; and thei ben als harde as tho of Ynde. And alle be it that men fynden gode dyamandes in Ynde, zit natheles men fynden hem more comounly upon the roches in the see, and upon hilles where the myne of gold is. And thei growen many to gedre, on lytille, another gret. And ther ben summe of the gretness of a bene, and summe als gret as an haselle note. And thei ben square and poynted of here owne kynde, bothe aboven and benethen, with outen worchinge of mannes hond. And the growen to gedre, male and femele. And thei ben norysscht with the dew of hevene. And thei engendren comounly, and bryngen forthe smale children, that multiplyen and growen alle the zeer. I have often tymes assayed, that zif a man kepe hem with a litylle of the roche, and wete hem with May dew ofte sithes, thei schulle growe everyche zeer; and the smale wole wexen grete. For righte as the fyn perle congelethe and wexethe gret of the dew of hevene, righte so dothe the verray dyamand: and righte as the perl of his owne kynde takethe roundnesse, righte so the dyamand, be vertue of God, takethe squarenesse. And men schalle bere the dyamaund on his left syde: for it is of grettere vertue thanne, than on the righte syde. For the strengthe of here growynge is toward the Northe; that is the left syde of the world; and the left parte of man is, whan he turnethe his face toward the est. And zif zou lyke to knowe the vertues of the dyamand, (as men may fynde in the lapidarye, that many men knowen noght) I schalle telle zou: as thei bezonde the see seyn and affermen, of whom alle science and alle philosophie comethe from. He that berethe the diamand upon him, it zevethe him hardynesse and manhode, and it kepethe the lemes of his body hole. It zevethe him victorye of his enemyes, in plee and in werre; zif his cause be rightefulle: and it kepethe him that berethe it, in gode wytt; and it kepethe him fro strif and riot, fro sorwes and from enchauntementes and from fantasyes and illusiouns of wykked spirites. And zif ony cursed wycche or enchauntour wolde bewycche him, that berethe the dyamand; alle that sorwe and myschance schalle turne to him self, thorghe vertu of that ston. And also no wylde best dar assaylle the man, that berethe it on him. Also the dyamand scholde ben zoven frely, with outen coveytynge and with outen byggynge: and than it is of grettere vertu. And it makethe a man more strong and more sad azenst his enemyes. And it helethe him that is lunatyk, and hem that the fend pursuethe or travaylethe. And zif venym or poysoun be broughte in presence of the dyamand, anon it begynnethe to wexe moyst and for to swete. There ben also dyamandes in Ynde, that ben cept violastres; (for here colour is liche vyolet, or more browne than violettes) that ben fulle harde and fulle precyous; but zit sum men love not hem so wel as the othere: but in sothe to me, I wolde loven hem als moche as the othere; for I have seen hem assayed. Also there is an other maner of dyamandes, that ben als white as cristalle; but thei ben a lityll more trouble: and thei ben gode and of gret vertue, and alle thei ben square and poynted of here owne kynde. And summe ben 6 squared, summe 4 squared, and summe 3, as nature schapethe hem. And therefore whan grete lordes and knyghtes gon to seche worschipe in armes, thei beren gladly the dyamaund upon hem.

I schal speke a litille more of the dyamandes, alle thoughe I tarye my matere for a tyme, to the ende that thei that knowen hem not, be not disceyved be gabberes, that gon be the contree, that sellen hem. For whoso wil bye the dyamande, it is needefulle to him, that he knowe hem; be cause that men counterfeten hem often of cristalle, that is zalow; and of saphires of cytryne colour, that is zalow also; and of the saphire loupe, and of many other stones. But I telle zou, theise contrefetes ben not so harde; and also the poyntes wil breken lightly, and men may easily pollische hem. But summe werkmen, for malice, will not pollische hem, to that entent, to maken men beleve, that thei may not ben pollischt. But men may assaye hem in this manere; first schere with hem or write with hem in saphires, in cristalle or in other precious stones. Aftre that men taken the ademand, that is the schipmannes ston, that drawethe the nedle to him, and men leyn the dyamand upon the ademand, and leyn the nedle before the ademand; and zif the dyamand be gode and vertuous, the ademande drawethe not the nedle to him, while the dyamand is there present. And this is the preef, that thei bezonde the see maken. Natheles it befallethe often tyme, that the gode dyamande losethe his vertue, be synne and for incontynence of him, that berethe it: and thanne it is nedfulle to make it to recoveren his vertue azen, or elle it is of litille value.

Of the customs of Yles abouten Ynde. Of the differences betwixt Ydoles and Simulacres. Of 3 maner growing of Peper upon a Tree. Of the welle, that chaungethe his odour, every hour of the day: and that is mervaylle.

[Sidenote: Cap. XV.] In Ynde ben fulle manye dyverse contrees: and it is cleped Ynde, for a flom, that rennethe thorghe out the contree, that is clept Ynde. In that flomme men fynden eles of 30 fote long and more. And the folk that duellen nyghe that watre, ben of evylle colour, grene and zalow. In Ynde and abouten Ynde, ben mo than 5000 iles, gode and grete, that men duellen in, with outen tho that ben inhabitable, and with outen othere smale iles. In every ile, is gret plentee of cytees and of townes and of folk, with outen nombre. For men of Ynde han this condicioun of kynde, that thei nevere gon out of here owne contree: and therfore is ther gret multitude of peple: but thei ben not sterynge ne mevable, be cause that thei ben in the firste clymat, that is of Saturne. And Saturne is sloughe and litille mevynge: for he taryethe to make his turn be the 12 signes, 30 zeer; and the mone passethe thorghe the 12 signes in o monethe. And for because that Saturne is of so late sterynge, therfore the folk of that contree, that ben undre his clymat, han of kynde no wille for to meve ne stere to seche strange places. And in oure contree is alle the contrarie. For wee ben in the sevenethe climat, that is of the mone. And the mone is of lyghtly mevynge; and the mone is planete of weye: and for that skylle, it zevethe us wille of kynde, for to meve lyghtly, and for to go dyverse weyes, and to sechen strange thinges and other dyversitees of the world. For the mone envyrounethe the erthe more hastyly than ony othere planete.

Also men gon thorghe Ynde be many dyverse contrees, to the grete see occean. And aftre men fynden there an ile, that is clept Crues: and thidre comen marchantes of Venyse and Gene and of other marches, for to byen marchandyses. But there is so grete hete in tho marches, and namely in that ile, that for the grete distresse of the hete, mennes ballokkes hangen doun to here knees, for the gret dissolucioun of the body. And men of that contree, that knowen the manere, lat bynde hem up, or elle myghte thei not lyve; and anoynt hem with oynementes made therfore, to holde hem up. In that contree and in Ethiope and in many other contrees, the folk lyggen alle naked in ryveres and watres, men and wommen to gedre, fro undurne of the day, tille it be passed the noon. And thei lyen alle in the watre, saf the visage, for the gret hete that there is. And the wommen haven no schame of the men; but lyen alle to gidre, syde to syde, tille the hete be past. There may men see many foule figure assembled, and namely nyghe the gode townes. In that ile ben schippes with outen nayles of iren or bonds, for the roches of the Ademandes: for thei ben alle fulle there aboute in that see, that it is merveyle to speken of. And zif a schipp passed be tho marches, that hadde outher iren bondes or iren nayles, anon he scholde ben perisscht. For the Ademand, of his kynde, drawethe the iren to him: and so wolde it drawe to him the schipp, because of the iren: that he scholde never departen fro it, ne never go thens.

Fro that ile, men gon be see to another ile, that is clept Chana, where is gret plentee of corn and wyn: and it was wont to ben a gret ile, and a gret havene and a good; but the see hathe gretly wasted it and overcomen it The kyng of that contree was wont to ben so strong and so myghty, that he helde werre azenst King Alisandre. The folk of that contree han a dyvers lawe: for summe of hem, worschipe the sonne, summe the mone, summe the fuyr, summe trees, summe serpentes, or the first thing that thei meeten at morwen: and summe worschipen symulacres, and summe Ydoles. But betwene symulacres and ydoles, is a gret difference. For symulacres ben ymages made aftre lyknesse of men or of wommen, or of the sonne or of the mone, or of ony best, or of ony kyndely thing: and ydoles, is an ymage made of lewed wille of a man, that man may not fynden among kyndely thinges; as an ymage, that hathe 4 hedes, on of a man, another of an hors, or of an ox, or of sum other best, that no man hathe seyn aftre kyndely disposicioun. And thei that worschipen symulacres, thei worschipen hem for sum worthi man, that was sum tyme, as Hercules and many othere, that diden many marvayles in here tyme. For thei seyn wel, that thei be not goddes: for thei knowen wel, that there is a God of kynde, that made alle thinges; the which is in hevene. But thei knowen wel, that this may not do the marvayles that he made, but zif it had ben be the specyalle zifte of God: and therfore thei seyn, that he was wel with God. And for be cause that he was so wel with God, therfore the worschipe him. And so seyn thei of the sonne; be cause that he chaungethe the tyme and zevethe hete and norisschethe alle thinges upon erthe; and for it is of so gret profite, thei knowe wel, that that myghte not be, but that God lovethe it more than ony other thing. And for that skylle, God hath zoven it more gret vertue in the world: therfore it is gode resoun, as thei seyn, to don it worschipe and reverence. And so seyn thei, that maken here resounes, of othere planetes; and of the fuyr also, because it is so profitable. And of Ydoles, thei seyn also, that the ox is the moste holy best, that is in erthe, and most pacyent and more profitable than ony other. For he dothe good y now, and he dothe non evylle. And thei knowen wel, that it may not be with outen specyalle grace of God; and therfore maken thei here God, of an ox the on part, and the other halfondelle of a man: because that man is the most noble creature in erthe; and also for he hathe lordschipe aboven alle bestes: therfore make thei the halfendel of ydole of a man upwardes, and the tother half of an ox dounwardes: and of serpentes and of other bestes, and dyverse thinges, that thei worschipen, that thei meten first at morwe. And thei worschipen also specyally alle tho that thei han gode meetynge of; and whan thei speden wel in here iorneye, aftre here meetynge; and namely suche as thei han preved and assayed be experience of longe tyme. For thei seyn, that thilke gode meetynge ne may not come, but of the grace of God. And therefore thei maken ymages lyche to tho thinges, that thei han beleeve inne, for to beholden hem and worschipen hem first at morwe, or thei meeten ony contrarious thinges. And there ben also sum Cristene men, that seyn, that summe bestes han gode meetynge, that is to seye, for to meete with hem first at morwe; and summe bestes wykked metynge: and that thei han preved ofte tyme, that the hare hathe fulle evylle meetynge, and swy, and many othere bestes. And the sparhauk and other foules of raveyne, whan thei fleen aftre here praye, and take it before men of armes, it is a gode signe: and zif he fayle of takynge his praye, it is an evylle sygne. And also to suche folk, it is an evylle meetynge of ravenes. In theise thinges and in suche othere, ther ben many folk, that beleeven; because it happenethe so often tyme to falle, aftre here fantasyes. And also ther ben men y nowe, that han no beleve in hem. And sithe that Cristene men han suche beleeve, that ben enformed and taughte alle day, be holy doctryne, where inne thei schold beleeve, it is no marvaylle thanne, that the Paynemes, that han no gode doctryne, but only of here nature, beleeven more largely, for here symplenesse. And treuly I have seen of Paynemes and Sarazines, that men clepen Augurynes, that whan wee ryden in armes in dyverse contrees, upon oure enemyes, be the flyenge of foules, thei wolde telle us the prenosticaciouns of thinges that felle aftre: and so thei diden fulle often tymes, and profreden here hedes to wedde, but zif it wolde falle as thei seyden. But natheles ther fore scholde noght a man putten his beleeve in suche thinges: but always han fulle trust and beleeve in God oure Sovereyn Lord. This ile of Chana, the Sarazines han wonnen and holden. In that ile ben many lyouns, and many othere wylde bestes. And there ben rattes in that ile, als gret as houndes here: and men taken hem with grete mastyfes: for cattes may not take hem. In this ile and many othere, men berye not no dede men: for the hete is there so gret, that in a lityle tyme the flesche wil consume fro the bones.

Fro thens, men gon be see toward Ynde the more, to a cytee that men clepen Sarche, that is a fair cytee and a gode; and there duellen many Cristene men of gode feythe: and ther ben manye religious men, and namely of Mendynantes. Aftre gon men be see, to the lond of Lomb. In that lond growethe the peper, in the forest that men clepen Combar; and it growethe nowhere elle in alle the world, but in that forest: and that dureth wel an 18 iourneyes in lengthe. In the forest ben 2 gode cytees; that on highte Fladrine, and that other Zinglantz. And in every of hem, duellen Cristene men, and Jewes, gret plentee. For it is a gode contree and a plenteyous: but there is over meche passynge hete. And zee schulle undirstonde, that the peper growethe, in maner as dothe a wylde vyne, that is planted faste by the trees of that wode, for to susteynen it by, as dothe the vyne. And the fruyt thereof hangethe in manere as reysynges. And the tree is so thikke charged, that it semethe that it wolde breke: and whan it is ripe, it is all grene as it were ivy beryes; and than men kytten hem, as men don the vynes, and than thei putten it upon an owven, and there it waxethe blak and crisp. And there is 3 maner of peper, all upon o tree; long peper, blak peper, and white peper. The long peper men clepen sorbotyn; and the blak peper is clept fulfulle, and the white peper is clept bano. The long peper comethe first, whanthe lef begynhethe to come; and it is lyche the chattes of Haselle, that comethe before the lef, and it hangethe lowe. And aftre comethe the blake with the lef, in manere of clustres of reysinges, alle grene: and whan men han gadred it, than comethe the white, that is somdelle lasse than the blake; and of that men bryngen but litille into this contree; for thei bezonden with holden it for hem self, be cause it is betere and more attempree in kynde, than the blake: and therfore is ther not so gret plentee as of the blake. In that contree ben manye manere of serpentes and of other vermyn, for the gret hete of the contree and of the peper. And summe men seyn, that whan thei will gadre the peper, thei maken fuyr, and brennen aboute, to make the serpentes and cokedrilles to flee. But save here grace of alle that seyn so. For zif thei brenten abouten the trees, that beren, the peper scholden ben brent, and it wolde dryen up alle the vertue, as of ony other thing: and han thei diden hemself moche harm; and thei scholde nevere quenchen the fuyr. But thus thei don; thei anoynten here hondes and here feet with a juyce made of snayles and of othere thinges, made therfore; of the whiche the serpentes and the venymous bestes haten and dreden the savour: and that makethe hem flee before hem, because of the smelle; and than thei gadren it seurly ynow.

Also toward the heed of that forest, is the cytee of Polombe. And above the cytee is a grete mountayne, that also is clept Polombe: and of that mount, the cytee hathe his name. And at the foot of that mount, is a fayr welle and a gret, that hathe odour and savour of alle spices; and at every hour of the day, he chaungethe his odour and his savour diversely. And whoso drynkethe 3 tymes fasting of that watre of that welle, he is hool of of alle maner sykenesse, that he hathe. And thei that duellen there and drynken often of that welle, thei nevere han sekenesse, and thei semen alle weys zonge. I have dronken there of 3 or 4 sithes; and zit, me thinkethe, I fare the better. Sum men clepen it the Welle of Zouthe: for thei that often drynken there of, semen alle weys zongly, and lyven with outen sykenesse. And men seyn, that that welle comethe out of paradys; and therfore it is so vertuous. Be alle that contree growethe gode gyngevere: and therfore thidre gon the marchauntes for spicerye. In that lond men worschipen the ox, for his symplenesse and for his mekenesse, and for the profite that comethe of him. And thei seyn, that he is the holyest best in erthe. For hem semethe, that whoso evere be meke and paycyent, he is holy and profitable: for thanne thei seyn, he hathe alle vertues in him. Thei maken the ox to laboure 6 zeer or 7, and than thei ete him. And the kyng of the contree hathe alle wey an ox with him: and he that kepethe him, hathe every day grete fees, and kepethe every day his dong and his uryne in 2 vessells of gold, and bryngen it before here prelate, that thei clepen archiprotopapaton; and he berethe it before the kyng, and makethe there over a gret blessynge; and than the kyng wetethe his hondes there, in that thei clepen gaul, and anyntethe his front and his brest: and aftre he frotethe him with the dong and with the uryne with gret reverence, for to ben fulfilt of vertues of the ox, and made holy be the vertue of that holy thing, that nought is worthe. And whan the kyng hathe don, thanne don the lordes; and aftre hem here mynystres and other men, zif thei may have ony remenant. In that contree thei maken ydoles, half man, half ox; and in tho ydoles, eville spirites speken and zeven answere to men, of what is asked hem. Before theise ydoles, men sleen here children many tymes, and spryngen the blood upon the ydoles; and so thei maken here sacrifise. And whan ony man dyethe in the contree, thei brennen his body in name of penance, to that entent, that he suffre no peyne in erthe, to ben eten of wormes. And zif his wif have no child, thei brenne hire with him; and seyn, that it is resoun, that sche make him companye in that other world, as sche did in this. But and sche have children with him, thei leten hire lyve with hem, to brynge hem up, zif sche wole. And zif that sche love more to lyve with here children, than for to dye with hire husbonde, men holden hire for fals and cursed; ne schee schalle never ben loved ne trusted of the peple. And zif the womman dye before the husbonde, men brennen him with hire, zif that he wole; and zif he wil not, no man constreynethe him thereto; but he may wedde another tyme with outen blame and repreef. In that contree growen manye stronge vynes: and the wommen drynken wyn, and men not: and the wommen schaven hire berdes, and the men not.

Of the Domes made be seynt Thomas. Of Devocyoun and Sacrifice made to Ydoles there, in the Cytee of Calamye; and of the processioun in goynge aboute the Cytee.

[Sidenote: Cap. XVI.] From that contree men passen be many marches, toward a contree, a 10 iourneyes thens, that is clept Mabaron: and it is a gret kyngdom, and it hathe many faire cytees and townes. In that kyngdom lithe the body of Seynt Thomas the apostle, in flesche and bon, in a faire tombe, in the cytee of Calamyee: for there he was martyred and buryed. But men of Assirie beeren his bodye in to mesopatayme, in to the cytee of Edisse: and aftre, he was broughte thidre azen. And the arm and the hoond, (that he putte in oure Lordes syde, whan he appered to him, aftre his resurrexioun, and seyde to him, *Noli esse incredulus, sed fidelis*) is zit lyggynge in a vesselle with outen the tombe. And be that hond thei maken alle here juggementes, in the contree, whoso hathe righte or wrong. For whan ther is ony dissentioun betwene 2 partyes, and every of hem meyntenethe his cause, and seyth, that his cause is rightfulle, and that other seythe the contrarye, thanne bothe partyes writen here causes in 2 billes, and putten hem in the hond of seynt Thomas; and anon he castethe awey the bille of the wrong cause, and holdethe stille the bille with the righte cause. And therfore men comen from fer contrees to have juggement of doutable causes: and other juggement usen thei non there. Also the chirche, where seynt Thomas lythe, is bothe gret and fair, and alle fulle of grete simulacres: and tho ben grete ymages, that thei clepen here goddes; of the whiche, the leste is als gret as 2 men. And among theise othere, there is a gret ymage, more than ony of the othere, that is alle covered with fyn gold and precyous stones and riche perles: and that ydole is the god of false Cristene, that han reneyed hire feythe. And it syttethe in a chayere of gold, fulle nobely arrayed; and he hathe aboute his necke large gyrdles, wroughte of gold and precyous stones and perles. And this chirche is fulle richely wroughte, and alle over gylt with inne. And to that ydole gon men on pylgrimage, als comounly and with als gret devocioun, as Cristene men gon to seynt James, or other holy pilgrimages. And many folk that comen fro fer londes, to seche that ydole, for the gret devocyoun that thei han, thei loken nevere upward, but evere more down to the erthe, for drede to see ony thing aboute hem, that scholde lette hem of here devocyoun. And summe ther ben, that gon on pilgrimage to this ydole, that beren knyfes in hire hondes, that ben made fulle kene and scharpe; and alle weyes, as thei gon, thei smyten hem self in here armes and in here legges and in here thyes, with many hydouse woundes; and so thei scheden here blood, for love of that ydole. And thei seyn that he is blessed and holy, that dyethe so for love of his God. And othere there ben, that leden hire children, for to sle, to make sacrifise to that ydole; and aftre thei han slayn hem, thei spryngen the blood upon the ydole. And summe ther ben, that comme fro ferr, and in goynge toward this ydole, at every thrydde pas, that thei gon fro here hows, thei knelen; and so contynuen tille thei come thidre: and whan thei comen there, thei taken ensense and other aromatyk thinges of noble smelle, and sensen the ydole, as we wolde don here Goddes precyouse body. And so comen folk to worschipe this ydole, sum fro an hundred myle, and summe fro many mo. And before the mynstre of this ydole, is a vyvere, in rmaner of a gret lake, fulle of watre: and there in pilgrymes casten gold and sylver, perles and precyous stones, with outen nombre, in stede of offrynges. And whan the mynystres of that chirche neden to maken ony reparacyoun of the chirche or of ony of the ydoles, thei taken gold and silver, perles and precyous stones out of the vyvere, to quyten the costages of suche thing as thei maken or reparen; so that no thing is fawty, but anon it schalle ben amended. And zee schulle undirstonde, that whan grete festes and solempnytees of that ydole, as the dedicacioun of the chirche, and the thronynge of the ydole bethe, alle the contree aboute meten there to gidere; and thei setten this ydole upon a chare with gret reverence, wel arrayed with clothes of gold, of riche clothes of Tartarye, of Camacca, and other precyous clothes; and thei leden him aboute the cytee with gret solempnytee. And before the chare, gon first in processioun alle the maydenes of the contree, 2 and 2 to gidere, fulle ordynatly. And aftre tho maydenes, gon the pilgrymes. And summe of hem falle doun undre the wheles of the chare, and lat the chare gon over hem; so that thei ben dede anon. And summe han here armes or here lymes alle to broken, and summe the sydes: and alle this don thei for love of hire god, in gret devocioun. And he thinkethe, that the more peyne and the more tribulacioun, that thei suffren for love of here god, the more ioye thei schulle have in another world. And schortly to seye zou; thei suffren so grete peynes and so harde martyrdomes, for love of here ydole, that a Cristene man, I trowe, durst not taken upon him the tenthe part of the peyne, for love of oure Lord Jhesu Crist. And aftre, I seye zou, before the chare, gon alle the mynstrelles of the contrey, with outen nombre, with dyverse instrumentes; and thei maken alle the melodye, that thei cone. And whan thei han gon alle aboute the cytee, thanne thei retournen azen to the mynstre, and putten the ydole azen in to his place. And thanne, for the love and in worschipe of that ydole, and for the reverence of the feste, thei slen himself, a 200 or 300 persones, with scharpe knyfes, of the whiche thei bryngen the bodyes before the ydole; and than thei seyn, that tho ben seyntes, because that thei slowen hemself of here owne gode wille, for love of here ydole. And as men here, that hadde an holy seynt of his kyn, wolde thinke, that it were to hem an highe worschipe, right so hem thinkethe there. And as men here devoutly wolde writen holy seyntes lyfes and here myracles, and sewen for here canonizaciouns, righte so don thei there, for hem that sleen hem self wilfully, for love of here ydole; and seyn, that thei ben gloriouse martyres and seyntes, and putten hem in here wrytynges and letanyes, and avaunten hem gretly on to another of here holy kynnesmen; that so becomen seyntes; and seyn, I have mo holy seyntes in my kynrede, than thou in thin. And the custome also there is this, that whan thei that han such devocioun and entent, for to sle him self, for love of his god, thei senden for alle here frendes, and han gret plentee of mynstrelle, and thei gon before the ydole ledynge him, that wil sle himself for such devocioun, betwene hem with gret reverence. And he alle naked hath a ful scharp knyf in his hond, and he cuttethe a gret pece of his flesche and castethe it in the face of his ydole, seyenge his orysounes, recommendynge him to his god: and than he smytethe himself, and makethe grete woundes and depe here and there, tille he falle doun ded. And than his frendes presenten his body to the ydole: and than thei seyn, syngynge, Holy God, behold what thi trewe servant hath don for the; he hathe forsaken his wif and his children and his ricchesse and alle the godes of the worlde and his owne lyf, for the love of the, and to make the sacrifise of his flesche and of his blode. Wherfore, Holy God, putte him among thi beste belovede seyntes in thi blisse of paradys: for he hathe well disserved it. And than thei maken a gret fuyr, and brennen the body: and thanne everyche of his frendes taken a quantyte of the assches, and kepen hem in stede of relykes, and seyn, that it is a holy thing. And thei have no drede of no perile, whils thei han tho holy assches upon hem. And thei putten his name in here letanyes, as a seynt.

Of the evylle Customs used in the Yle of Lamary: and how the Erthe and the
> See ben of round Forme and schapp, be pref of the Sterre, that is clept Antartyk, that is fix in the Southe.

[Sidenote: Chap. XVII.] Fro that contree go men be the see occean, and be many dyverse yles, and be many contrees, that were to longe for to telle of. And a 52 iorneyes fro this lond, that I have spoken of, there is another lond, that is fulle gret, that men clepen Lamary. In that lond is fulle gret hete: and the custom there is such, that men and wommen gon alle naked. And thei scornen, whan thei seen ony strange folk goynge clothed. And thei seyn, that God made Adam and Eve alle naked; and that no man scholde schame, that is of kyndely nature. And thei seyn, that thei that ben clothed ben folk of another world, or thei ben folk, that trowen not in God. And thei seyn, that thei beleeven in God, that formede the world, and that made Adam and Eve, and alle other thinges. And thei wedden there no wyfes: for all the wommen there ben commoun, and thei forsake no man. And thei seyn, thei synnen, zif thei refusen ony man: and so God commannded to Adam and Eve, and to alle that comen of him, whan he seyde, *Crescite et multiplicamini, et replete terram.* And therfore may no man in that contree seyn, this is my wyf: ne no womman may seye, this is myn husbonde. And whan thei han children, thei may zeven hem to what man thei wole, that hathe companyed with hem. And also all the lond is comoun: for alle that a man holdethe o zeer, another man hathe it another zeer. And every man takethe what part that him lykthe. And also alle the godes of the lond ben comoun, cornes and alle other thinges: for no thing there is clept in clos, ne no thing there is undur lok; and every man there takethe what he wole, with outen ony contradiccioun: and als riche is o man there, as is another. But in that contree, there is a cursed custom: for thei eten more gladly mannes flesche, than ony other flesche: and zit is that contree habundant of flesche, of fissche, of cornes, of gold and sylver, and of alle other godes. Thidre gone Marchauntes, and bryngen with hem children, to selle to hem of the contree, and thei byzen hem: and zif thei ben fatte, thei eten hem anon; and zif thei ben lene, thei feden hem, tille thei ben fatte, and thanne thei eten hem: and thei seyn, that it is the best flesche and the swettest of alle the world. In that lond, ne in many othere bezonde that, no man may see the sterre transmontane, that is clept the sterre of the see, that is unmevable, and that is toward the northe, that we clepen the lode sterre. But men seen another steere, the contrarie to him, that is toward the south, that is clept Antartyk. And right as the schip men taken here avys here, and governe hem be the lode sterre, right so don schip men bezonde the parties, be the sterre of the southe, the whiche sterre apperethe not to us. And this sterre, that is toward the north, that wee clepen the lode sterre, ne apperethe not to hem. For whiche cause, men may wel perceyve, that the lond and the see ben of rownde schapp and forme. For the partie of the firmament schewethe in o contree, that schewethe not in another contree. And men may well preven be experience and sotyle compassement of wytt, that zif a man fond passages be schippes, that wolde go to serchen the world, MEN MYGHTE GO BE SCHIPPE ALLE ABOUTE THE WORLD, and aboven and benethen. The whiche thing I prove thus, aftre that I have seyn. For I have ben toward the parties of Braban, and beholden the astrolabre, that the sterre that is clept the Transmontayne, is 53 degrees highe. And more forthere in Almayne and Bewme, it hathe 58 degrees. And more forthe toward the parties septemtrioneles, it is 62 degrees of heghte, and certeyn mynutes. For I my self have mesured it by the astrolabre. Now schulle ze knowe, that azen the Transmontayne, is the tother sterre, that is clept Antartyke; as I have seyd before. And tho 2 sterres ne meeven nevere. And be hem turnethe alle the firmament, righte as dothe a wheel, that turnethe be his axille tree; so that tho sterres beren the firmament in 2 egalle parties; so that it hathe als mochel aboven, as it hathe benethen. Aftre this, I have gon toward the parties meridionales, that is toward the southe: and I have founden, that in Lybye, men seen first the sterre Antartyk. And so fer I have gon more forthe in tho contrees, that I have founde that sterre more highe; so that toward the highe Lybye, it is 18 degrees of heghte, and certeyn minutes (of the whiche, 60 minutes maken a degree). After goynge be see and be londe, toward this contree, of that I have spoke, and to other yles and londes bezonde that contree, I have founden the sterre Antartyk of 33 degrees of heghte, and mo mynutes. And zif I hadde had companye and schippynge, for to go more bezonde, I trowe wel in certeyn, that wee scholde have seen alle the roundnesse of the firmament alle aboute. For as I have seyd zou be forn, the half of the firmament is betwene tho 2 sterres: the whiche halfondelle I have seyn. And of the tother halfondelle, I have seyn toward the north, undre Transmontane 62 degrees and 10 mynutes; and toward the partie meridionalle, I have seen undre the Antartyk 33 degrees and 16 mynutes: and thanne the halfondelle of the firmament in alle, ne holdethe not but 180 degrees. And of tho 180, I have seen 62 on that o part, and 33 on that other part, that ben 95 degrees, and nyghe the halfondelle of a degree; and so there ne faylethe but that I have seen alle the firmament, saf 84 degrees and the halfondelle of a degree; and that is not the fourthe part of the firmament. For the 4 partie of the roundnesse of the firmament holt 90 degrees: so there faylethe but 5 degrees and an half, of the fourthe partie. And also I have seen the 3 parties of alle the roundnesse of the firmament, and more zit 5 degrees and an half. Be the which I seye zou certeynly, that men may envirowne alle the erthe of alle the world, as wel undre as aboven, and turnen azen to his contree, that hadde companye and schippynge and conduyt: and alle weyes he scholde fynde men, londes, and yles, als wel as in this contree. For zee wyten welle, that thei that ben toward the Antartyk, thei ben streghte, feet azen feet of hem, that dwellen undre the transmontane; als wel as wee and thei that dwellyn undre us, ben feet azenst feet. For alle the parties of see and of lond han here appositees, habitable or trepassables, and thei of this half and bezond half. And wytethe wel, that aftre that, that I may parceyve and comprehend, the londes of Pestre John, Emperour of Ynde, ben undre us. For in goynge from Scotland or from England toward Jerusalem, men gon upward alweys. For oure lond is in the lowe partie of the erthe, toward the west: and the lond of Prestre John is the lowe partie of the erthe, toward the est: and thei han there the day, whan wee have the nyghte, and also highe to the contrarie, thei han the nyghte, whan wee han the day. For the erthe and the see ben of round form and schapp, as I have seyd beforn. And that that men gon upward to o cost, men gon dounward to another cost. Also zee have herd me seye, that Jerusalem is in the myddes of the world; and that may men preven and schewen there, be a spere, that is pighte in to the erthe, upon the hour of mydday, whan it is equenoxium, that schewethe no schadwe on no syde. And that it scholde ben in the myddes of the world, David wytnessethe it in the psautre, where he seythe, *Des operatus est salutem in medie Terre.* Thanne thei that parten fro the parties of the west, for to go toward Jerusalem, als many iorneyes as thei gon upward for to go thidre, in als many iorneyes may thei gon fro Jerusalem unto other confynyes of the superficialtie of the erthe bezonde. And whan men gon bezonde tho iourneyes, toward Ynde and to the foreyn yles, alle is envyronynge the roundnesse of this erthe and of the see, undre oure contrees on this half. And therfore hathe it befallen many tymes of o thing, that I have herd cownted, whan I was zong; how a worthi man departed somtyme from oure contrees, for to go serche the world. And so he passed Ynde, and the yles bezonde Ynde, where ben mo than 5000 yles: and so longe he wente be see and lond, and so enviround the world be many seysons, that he fond an yle, where he herde speke his owne langage, callynge an oxen in the plowghe, suche wordes as men speken to bestes in his owne contree: whereof he hadde gret mervayle: for he knewe not how it myghte be. But I seye, that he had gon so longe, be londe and be see, that he had envyround alle the erthe, that he was comen azen envirounynge, that is to seye, goynge aboute, unto his owne marches, zif he wolde have passed forthe, til he had founden his contree and his owne knouleche. Bur he turned azen from thens, from whens he was come fro; and so he loste moche peynefulle labour, as him self seyde, a gret while aftre, that he was comen hom. For it befelle aftre, that he wente in to Norweye; and there tempest of the see toke him; and he arryved in an yle; and whan he was in that yle, he knew wel, that it was the yle, where he had herd speke his owne langage before, and the callynge of the oxen at the plowghe: and that was possible thinge. But how it semethe to symplemen unlerned, that men ne mowe not go undre the erthe, and also that men scholde falle toward the hevene, from undre! But that may not be, upon lesse, than wee mowe falle toward hevene, fro the erthe, where wee ben. For fro what partie of the erthe, that men duelle, outher aboven or benethen, it semethe alweys to hem that duellen, that thei gon more righte than ony other folk. And righte as it semethe to us, that thei ben undre us, righte so it semethe hem, that wee ben undre hem. For zif a man myghte falle fro the erthe unto the firmament: be grettere resoun, the erthe and the see, that ben so grete and so hevy, scholde fallen to the firmament: but that may not be: and therfore seithe oure Lord God, *Non timeas me, qui suspendi Terram ex nichilo?* And alle be it that it be possible thing, that men may so envyrone alle the world, natheles of a 1000 persones, on ne myghte not happen to returnen in to his contree. For, for the gretnesse of the erthe and of the see, men may go be a 1000 and a 1000 other weyes, that no man cowde redye him perfitely toward the parties that he cam fro, but zif it were be aventure and happ, or be the grace of God. For the erthe is fulle large and fulle gret, and holt in roundnesse and aboute envyroun, be aboven and be benethen 20425 myles, aftre the opynyoun of the olde wise astronomeres. And here seyenges I repreve noughte. But aftre my lytylle wytt, it semethe me, savynge here reverence, that it is more. And for to have bettere understondynge, I seye thus, Be ther ymagyned a figure, that hathe a gret compas, and aboute the poynt of the gret compas, that is clept the centre, be made another litille compas: then aftre, be the gret compas devised be lines in manye parties; and that alle the lynes meeten at the centre; so that in as many parties, as the grete compas schal be departed, in als manye schalle be departed the litille, that is aboute the centre, alle be it that the spaces ben lesse. Now thanne, be the gret compas represented for the firmament, and the litille compas represented for the erthe. Now thanne the firmament is devysed, be astronomeres, in 12 signes; and every signe is devysed in 30 degrees, that is 360 degrees, that the firmament hathe aboven. Also, be the erthe devysed in als many parties as the firmament; and lat every partye answere to a degree of the firmament: and wytethe it wel, that aftre the auctoures of astronomye, 700 fulonges of erthe answeren to a degree of the firmament; and tho ben 87 myles and 4 furlonges. Now be that here multiplyed by 360 sithes; and than thei ben 31500 myles, every of 8 furlonges, aftre myles of oure contree. So moche hathe the erthe in roundnesse, and of heght enviroun, aftre myn opynyoun and myn undirstondynge. And zee schulle undirstonde, that aftre the opynyoun of olde wise philosophres and astronomeres, oure contree ne Irelond ne Wales ne Scotlond ne Norweye ne the other yles costynge to hem, ne ben not in the superficialte cownted aboven the erthe: as it schewethe be alle the bokes of astronomye. For the superficialtee of the erthe is departed in 7 parties, for the 7 planetes: and tho parties ben clept clymates. And oure parties be not of the 7 clymates; for thei ben descendynge toward the west. And also these yles of Ynde, which beth even azenst us, beth noght reckned in the climates; for thei ben azenst us, that ben in the lowe contree. And the 7 clymates strecchen hem envyrounynge the world.

Of the Palays of the Kyng of the Yle of Java. Of the Trees, that beren Mele, Hony, Wyn and Venym; and of othere Mervayilles and Customes, used in the Yles marchinge thereabouten.

[Sidenote: Cap. XVIII.] Besyde that yle that I have spoken of, there is another yle, that is clept Sumobor, that is a gret yle: and the kyng thereof is righte myghty. The folk of that yle maken hem alweys to ben marked in the visage with an hote yren, bothe men and wommen, for gret noblesse, for to ben knowen from other folk. For thei holden hem self most noble and most worthi of alle the world. And thei han werre alle weys with the folk that gon alle naked. And faste besyde is another yle, that is clept Betemga, that is a gode yle and a plentyfous. And many other yles ben there about; where ther ben many of dyverse folk: of the whiche it were to longe to speke of alle.

But fast besyde that yle, for to passe be see, is a gret yle a gret contree, that men clepen Java: and it is nyghe 2000 myle in circuyt. And the kyng of that contree is a fulle gret lord and a ryche and a myghty, and hathe undre him 7 other kynges of 7 other yles abouten hym. This yle is fulle wel inhabyted, and fulle wel manned. There growen alle maner of spicerie, more plentyfous liche than in ony other contree; as of gyngevere, clowegylofres, canelle, zedewalle, notemuges and maces. And wytethe wel, that the notemuge berethe the maces. For righte as the note of the haselle hathe an husk with outen, that the note is closed in, til it be ripe, and aftre fallethe out; righte so it is of the notemuge and of the maces. Manye other spices and many other godes growen in that yle. For of alle thing is there plenty, saf only of wyn: but there is gold and silver gret plentee. And the kyng of that contree hathe a paleys fulle noble and fulle marveyllous, and more riche than ony in the world. For alle the degrez to gon up into halles and chambres, ben on of gold, another of sylver. And also the pavmentes of halles and chambres ben alle square, on of gold and another of sylver: and alle the walles with inne ben covered with gold and sylver, in fyn plates: and in tho plates ben stories and batayles of knyghtes enleved. And the crounes and the cercles abouten here hedes ben made of precious stones and riche perles and grete. And the halles and the chambres of the palays ben alle covered with inne with gold and sylver: so that no man wolde trowe the richesse of that palays, but he had seen it. And witethe wel, that the kyng of that yle is so myghty, that he hathe many tymes overcomen the grete Cane of Cathay in bataylle, that is the most gret emperour that is undre the firmament, outher bezonde the see or on this half. For thei han had often tyme werre betwene hem, be cause that the grete cane wolde constreynen him to holden his lond of him: but that other at alle tymes defendethe him wel azenst him.

Aftre that yle, in goynge be see, men fynden another yle, gode and gret, that men clepen Pathen, that is a gret kyngdom, fulle of faire cytees and fulle of townes. In that lond growen trees, that beren mele, wherof men maken gode bred and white, and of gode savour; and it semethe as it were of whete, but it is not allynges of suche savour. And there ben other trees, that beren hony, gode and swete: and other trees, that beren venym; azenst the whiche there is no medicyne but on; and that is to taken here propre leves, and stampe hem and tempere hem with watre, and then drynke it: and elle he schalle dye; for triacle will not avaylle, ne non other medicyne. Of this venym, the Jewes had let seche of on of here frendes, for to empoysone alle Cristiantee, as I have herd hem seye in here confessioun, before here dyenge. But thanked be alle myghty God, thei fayleden of hire purpos: but alle weys thei maken gret mortalitee of people. And other trees there ben also, that beren wyn of noble sentement. And zif zou like to here how the mele comethe out of the trees, I shalle seye zou. Men hewen the trees with an hatchet, alle aboute the fote of the tree, tille that the bark be parted in many parties; and than comethe out ther of a thikke lykour, the whiche thei resceyven in vesselles, and dryen it at the hete of the sonne; and than thei han it to a mylle to grynde; and it becomethe faire mele and white. And the hony and the wyn and the venym ben drawen out of other trees, in the same manere, and put in veselles for to kepe. In that yle is a ded see, that is a lake, that hathe no ground. And zif ony thing falle in to that lake, it schalle nevere comen up azen. In that lake growen redes, that ben cannes, that thei clepen thaby, that ben 30 fadme long. And of theise canes men maken faire houses. And ther ben other canes, that ben not so longe, that growen neer the lond, and han so longe rotes, that duren wel a 4 quartres of a furlong or more; and at the knottes of tho rotes, men fynden precious stones, that han gret vertues: and he that berethe ony of hem upon him, yren ne steel ne may not hurt him, ne drawe no blood upon him: and therfore thei that han tho stones upon hem, fighten fulle hardyly, bothe on see and lond: for men may not harmen hem on no partye. And therfore thei that knowen the manere, and schulle fighten with hem, thei schoten to hem arwes and quarrelles with outen yren or steel; and so thei hurten hem and sleen hem. And also of tho cannes, thei maken houses and schippes and other thinges; as wee han here, makynge houses and schippes of oke or of ony other trees. And deme no man, that I seye it, but for a truffulle: for I have seen of the cannes with myn owne eyzen fulle many tymes lyggynge upon the ryvere of that lake: of the whiche, 20 of oure felowes ne myghten not liften up ne beren on to the erthe.

Aftre this yle, men gon be see to another yle, that is clept Calonak: and it is a fair lond and a plentifous of godes. And the kyng of that contrey hath als many wyfes as he wole; for he makethe serche alle the contree, to geten him the fairest maydens that may ben founde, and makethe hem to ben broughte before him; and he takethe on o nyght, and another another nyght, and so forthe contynuelle sewyng; so that he hath a 1000 wyfes or mo. And he liggethe never but o nyght with on of hem, and another nyght with another, but zif that on happene to ben more lusty to his plesance than another. And therfore the kyng getethe fully many children; sum tyme an 100, sum tyme an 200, and sum tyme mo. And he hathe also into a 14000 olifauntz or mo, that he makethe for to ben brought up amonges his vileynes, be alle his townes. For in cas that he had ony werre azenst any other kyng aboute him, thanne he makethe certeyn men of armes for to gon up in to the castelles of tree, made for the werre, that craftily ben sett up on the olifantes bakkes, for to fyghten azen hire enemyes: and so don other kynges there aboute. For the maner of werre is not there, as it is here or in other contrees; ne the ordinance of werre nouther. And men clepen the olifantes, warkes.

And in that yle there is a gret marvayle, more to speke of than in ony other partie of the world. For alle manere of fisschen, that ben there in the see abouten hem, comen ones in the zeer, eche manere of dyverse fisschen, on maner of kynde aftre other; and thei casten hem self to the see banke of that yle, so gret plentee and multitude, that no man may unnethe see but fissche; and there thei abyden 3 dayes: and every man of the contree takethe of hem, als many as him lykethe: And aftre, that maner of fissche, after the thridde day, departethe and gothe into the see. And aftre hem, comen another multitude of fyssche of another kynde, and don in the same maner as the firste diden other 3 dayes. And aftre hem, another; tille alle the dyverse maner of fisschen han ben there, and that men han taken of hem, that hem lykethe. And no man knowethe the cause wherfore it may ben. But thei of the contree seyn, that it is for to do reverence to here kyng, that is the most worthi kyng, that is in the world, as thei seyn; because that he fulfillethe the comandement, that God bad to Adam and Eve, whan God seyde, *Crescite et multplicamini et replete terram*. And for because that he multipliethe so the world with children, therfore God sendethe him so the fissches of dyverse kyndes, of alle that ben in the see, to taken at his wille, for him and alle his peple. And therfore alle the fissches of the see comen, to maken him homage, as the most noble and excellent kyng of the world, and that is best beloved with God, als thei seyn. I knowe not the resoun, whi it is; but God knowethe. But this, me semethe, is the moste marveylle, that evere I saughe. For this mervaylle is azenst kynde, and not with kynde, that the fissches, that han fredom to enviroun alle the costes of the see, at here owne list, comen of hire owne wille to profren hem to the dethe, with outen constreynynge of man: and therfore I am syker, that this may not ben, with outen a gret tokene.

There ben also in that contree a kynde of snayles, that ben so grete, that many persones may loggen hem in here schelles, as men wolde done in a litylle hous. And other snayles there ben, that ben fulle grete, but not so huge as the other. And of theise snayles, and of gret white wormes, that han blake hedes, that ben als grete as a mannes thighe, and somme lesse, as grete wormes that men fynden there in wodes, men maken vyaunde rialle, for the kyng and for other grete lordes. And zif a man, that is maryed, dye in that contree, men buryen his wif with him all quyk. For men seyn there, that it is resoun, that sche make him companye in that other world, as sche did in this.

CAPVT. 30.

De Regnis Cynocephalorum, et alijs Insulis.

Per mare oceanum potest hinc veniri in Insulam Kaffa: [Marginal note: Vel Caffeles.] quicunque ibi infirmari videtur ad mortem, suspenditur ad arborem, antequam moriatur, vt non ab immundis terræ vermibus, sed a coeli auibus, quas reputant Dei Angelos, comedatur.

In alia insula faciunt suos infirmos ante mortem ab eductis in hoc magnis canibus strangulari, manducantes in conuiuio carnes pro optimo ferculo venationis.

Interpositis quoque multis Insulis, de quibus subticeo gratia breuitatis, habetur Insula Mylke, [Marginal note: Vel Mekke.] et hij videntur omnium hominum crudelissimi; Nam quilibet particularitèr pro leui et modica stimulatione, vulnerat, sauciat, et occidit, proximum, vicinum et amicum: Et si quando dissidentes contigerit concordari, non habebitur pax rata, nisi quisque de alterius sanguine biberit bonum haustum.

Hinc nauigando per multas et diuersas Insulas, qui in singulas intrare, et moram trahere voluerit, stupenda multa videbit, et poterit venire in Insulam Tracoide. [Marginal Note: Vel Traceda.]

Illic sunt homines àbsque vllo ingenio penitus bestiales, serpentibus, vermibusque vescentes, nec inuicem loquentes, sed conceptus suos signis et indicijs ostendentes. Diligunt preciosos lapides tantummodo pulchritudinis gratia, non causa virtutis: et super omnes vnum diligunt lapidem habentem 60. colorum varietates, qui et Tracoides vocatur propter ipsos.

Intratur hinc per Oceanum in regionem Niconoram, vel Nacumeram, habentem in circuitu spacium mille leucarum: omnes ibi geniti homines habent capita ad formam canum, vnde et in Græco Cynocephali dicuntur. Isti etiam incedunt nudis corporibus, excepto parui panniculi operimento, secretiora loca et posteriora retro tegente. Rationabiles tamen multum sunt hij, et plurimum virtuosi, ac de omni forefacto rigidam iustitiam exercentes. Sunt statura elegantes, robusti corpore, in prælijs lanceam cum tergia lata gerentes, viriliterque, et prudentèr pugnantes. Omnes pro deo adorant bouem, vnde et quilibet in fronte argenteam seu auream similitudinem bouis defert, et si quem viuum in prælio ceperint, sine vlla miseratione manducant.

Rex multum est diues et potens, ac deuotus in superstitione. Nam circa collum gestat trecentas orientales margaritas, quibus quotidiè antè commestionem orationes suas colligit, quemadmodum nos colligimus, Pater noster, etc. Ac præterea portat ad collum [Marginal note: Siue carbunculum.] rubetum orientalem, nobilem, purum, pulchrum, resplendentem, et summè preciosum, ad longitudinem pedis humani, quem habet diligentèr seruare, quod dum eo caret non tenetur pro Rege.

Pro isto carbunculo Grand Can Imperator, per ingenium, per insidias, per precium, et per prælium sæpè laborauit, sed nihil profecit. Post istam apparet insula Syllan, habens leucas de circuitu 80. quæ paucos habet homines propter multitudinem draconum, serpentum, crocodilorum in ea. Sunt autem crocodili speciales serpentes, coloris virgulati de croceo et nigro, cum quatuor cruribus, et tibijs et latis pedum vngulis. Aliqui horum habent longitudinem quínque tensarum, aut citrà, qui dum tendunt per arenosa relinquunt signum semitæ, acsi sit ibi tractus grandis arboris truncus.

Item in hac insula habetur nons altus, et in sui vertice satis altus et distentus et magnus aquæ lacus, de quo et stulti homines fabulantur, quòd primi parentes post eiectionem suam, illam aquam primò lacrymauerunt. In huius fundo lacus nascuntur margaritæ, et habentur semper lapides preciosi. Solentque pauperes terræ, accepta à Rege licentia, semel in anno ingredi, ac piscari gemmas, qui intrantes vngunt se succo Lymonsæ, contra hirudines, colubros, et serpentes. Sed et de lacu effluit riuulus per montis descensum, in quo nonnunquam margaritæ inueniuntur, et gemmæ: dicunt etiam ibi nullum venenatum animal nocere aduenis.

Ibi videntur leones albi in mira magnitudine boum nostrorum, et multæ diuersæ bestiæ, et aues, bestiolæ, et auiculæ aliarum specierum quàm in partibus istis. Nam ibi et in nonnullis alijs insulis vidi vnum mirum, de quo prius vix credidissem narranti, videlicet anates cum duobus capitibus.

Et sciatis quòd tam hic quam alibi mare apparet satis altius suo littore, imo qui a remotis aspicit videt suspensum quasi ad nubes. Et de hoc admiratus fuissem, nisi quod scriptum sciui mirabiles elationes maris.

CAPVT. 31.

De multis alijs Insulis Meridionalibus, de quibus et Plinius, et Munsterus.

Versus meridien hinc legendo per mare, inuenitur regio speciosa nomine Doudin: [Marginal note: Vel Doudeia.] cuius rex imperat seu principatur 54. regibus in circuitu insularum.

Dum quis hic infirmatur tendit proximus ad Idolum sciscitans an morietur, et si respondit non, addit et dicere medicinam qua curabitur: si autem responderit moriturum, statim conuocatis amicis occiditur, et cum symphonia, et solemnitate comedunt eius carnes, ossa tantummodò sepelientes. In Insulis verò circumiacentibus, habentur incredibilitèr diuersæ gentes. Nam vna habet homines enormis magnitudinis, cum solo in medio frontis oculo, qui absque vllo condimento manducant carnes et pisces.

Alia Insula habet homines aspectu deformes, nihil autem colli aut capitis ostendentes, vnde et Acephali nuncupantur: oculos autem habent ante ad scapulas, et in loco pectoris os apertum ad formam ferri, quo nostri caballi frænantur.

In alia Insula sunt gentes planis faciebus absque eleuatione nasorum, et palpebratum cum paruis foraminibus oculorum, et scissura modica oris. Et in alia gentes cum superiore oris labio ita lato et amplo, vt, dum velint, totam faciem de illo tegant.

Alia generat homines paruæ saturæ cum oris foramine sic paruo, vt per fistulas alimentum, et potum sumant, et quoniam carent lingua et dentibus, monstrant per naturalia signa conceptus. Et aliqui sunt homines debitæ quidem staturæ, et formæ, nisi quòd habent pedes equinos, quibus ita sunt præpetes, vt syluestres bestias capiant, quas comedunt, et manducant.

In alia homines sunt toti pilosi et hispidi, vsu simiarum manibus et pedibus ambulantes, et ad arbores reptantes, qui quamuis non loquuntur, apparent rationabiles, qui regem habent, et rectores.

Et in alia omnes sunt claudi, qui quamuis pedes habeant, tamen ambulant super genua multum ridiculosè, imò miserabiliter, vt de passu in passum videantur casuri in terrem. Et in quadam, sexum tam masculinum, quàm foeminieum habentes, qui dum masculino vtuntur generant, dum foeminino, impregnantur et pariunt. Atque, in compendio multa concludam, in singulis 54. insularum inueniuntur homines, forma, statura, actibus et moribus singulis ab inuicem differentes, de quibus potest fieri descriptio, quam pertranseo gratia breuitatis, et causa incredulitatis fortè quorundum audientium.

In istis autem meridionalibus partibus apparebat mihi eleuatio poli Antarctici 33. graduum, cum 16. minutis. Et sciendum quod in Bohemia, similitèr in Anglia eleuatur polus Arcticus 52. gradibus vel citra: Et in partibus magis septentrionalibus, vbi sunt Scoti 62. gradibus cum quatuor minutis. Ex quo patet respiciendo ad latitudinem coeli, quæ est de polo ad polum, quod itineratio mea fuit per quartum Horizontis spheræ terræ et vltra, per quinque gradus, cum 20. minutis. Cum ergò secundum Astrologos, totus terræ circuitus sit 31500. milliarium, octo stadijs pro milliario computatis, et septinginta stadia respondeant ad vnum gradum, quod patet ad latitudinem terræ, perambulaui 66733. stadia cum vno tertio, quæ faciunt 4170. leucas Geometricas cum dimidia vel propè.

CAPVT. 32.

De bona Regione Man chus. [Footnote: Mangi.]

Cum igitur tot et talsa in istis Insulis vidimus monstra (quæ si explicarem scribendo vix à legentibus omnia crederentur) non curauimus vlterius procedere sub polo australi, ne in maiora pericula incideremus: sed proptèr auditam et inuisam nobis famositatem potentiæ, nobilitatis, et gloriæ Imperatoris Tartarorum, vertebam faciem cum socijs nauigare magis versus Orientem. Cumque per multas diætas sustinuissemus multa pericula maris, peruenimus in Regnum Manchus, [Marginal Note: Vel Mangi.] quod est in confinibus superioris Indiæ, et iungitur ab vna parte Tartariæ. Hæc Regio Manchus, pro sui quantitate reputatur melior, delectabilior, et omnium bonorum abundantior de cunctis ibi propè Regionibus. Nam et homines bestiæ, et volucres maiores et corpulentiores sunt alijs, et præ vbertate vix inuenirentur in vna ciuitate decem mendici. Formosi sunt viri, sed feminæ formosiores. Sed viri loco barbæ, habent perpaucos pilos, rigidos, et longos ab vtraque oris parte, quemadmodum nostros videmus cattos habere.

Prima quam ingrediebaumer ciuitàs est Lachori, [Marginal Note: Siue Lateryn.] distans vna dieta à mari, et mirabamur, et gauisi sumus nos inuenisse integram ciuitatem Christianæ fidei. Nam et maior pars Regni credit in Christum.

Ibi habetur in leui precio copia rerum omnium, et præcipuè victualium: vnum genus est ibi serpentum in abundantia quod manducant ad omne conuiuium, et nisi pro finali ferculo ministraretur de illis serpentibus, conuiuium quàm modicum diceretur.

Suntque per hoc regnum pleræque ciuitates et Ecclesiæ, et relligiones, quas instituit dux Ogerus, quia hoc est vnum de quindecim regnis quæ quæsiuit, sicut infra dicetur.

Illic sunt elegantes albæ gallinæ, quæ non vestiuntur plumis vt nostræ, sed optima lana. Canes aquatici, quos nos lutras nominamus, sunt ibi multi edomiti, quòd quoties mittuntur in flumen, exportant domino piscem.

Ab hoc loco per aliquas diætas, venitur ad huius regionis maximam vrbem Cansay, hoc est dicere ciuitatem coeli, imo de vniuerso orbe terrarum putatur hæc maxima Ciuitatum; nam eius circuitus 50. leucis est mensus, nec est facile dicere, quàm, compressè a quamplurimis populis inhabitatur. Hæc sedet in lacu maris, quemadmodum, et Venetiæ: et habentur in ea plures quàm mille ducenti pontes, et in quolibet turres miræ magnitudinis, ac fortitudinis, munitæ peruigíli custodia, et pro vrbe tuenda contra Imperatorem Grand Can.

Multi sunt ibi Christiani, et multæ Religiones Christianorum, sed et de ordinibus Minorum, et prædicatorum, qui tamen ibi non mendicant; est magna pluralitas ex diuersis nationibus Mercatorum. Per Regionem nascitur vinum valdè bonum, quod appellatur Bigon. Et ad leucam extra ciuitatem, Abbatia magna est, non de religione Christiana sed Pagana: et in ea forrestum, siue hortus magnus vndíque circumclusus, consitus arboribus, et arbustis, in cuius etiam medio mons, altus simul et latus, habens hortum vbi solum inhabitant bestiolæ mirabiles, sicut Simiæ, marmotæ, Lanbon, papiones, foreti et huiusmodi ad varia et multa genera, et ad numerum infinitum.

Omni autem die post refectionem conuentus Abbatiæ, qui est valdè monachosus, deferuntur reliquiæ ciborum cum magno additamento, in vasis auro lucentibus ad hunc hortum: et ad sonitum campanæ argenteæ, quam Eleemosynarius manu gestat descendentes, et occurrentes de bestiolis duo millia aut plures sese componunt residere ad circulum more pauperum mendicorum, et traditur singulis per seruos aliquid de his cibarijs, ac denuò audita campana segregando recurrunt: Cumque nos tanquam redarguentes, diceremus, cur hæc non darentur egenis, responderunt, illic pauperes non habentur, quod si inuenirentur, potius tamen dari deberent bestiolis. Habet enim eorum perfidia, et Paganissimus, animas nobilium hominum post mortem ingredi corpora nobilium bestiarum, et animas ignobilium corpora bestiarum ignobilium et vilium, ad luenda videlicet crimina, donec peracta poenitentia transeant in Paradisum: ideoque nutriunt, prout dicunt, has nobiliores bestias, siue bestiolas, quòd a quibusdam nobilibus fundabatur in principio hæc Abbatia. Multa sunt alia mira in hac ciuitate, de quibus sciatis, quod non omnia vobis recitabo.

CAPVT. 33.

De Pygmæis, et de itinere vsque in prouinciam Cathay.

Eundo per Regionem eandem à dicta ciuitate Cansay, ad sex dietas venitur ad nobilem vrbem Tylenso, [Marginal Note: Vel Chezolo.] cuius muri per circuitum tendunt ad spacium 20. leucarum: [Marginal Note: Vel Miliarium.] et sunt 60. petrini pontes, quibus nullos memini pulchriores.

In ista fuit prima sedes regni Mangi, nec immeritò, cum sit munita, delectabilis, et abundans omnibus bonis, ac deinde in predicta Cansay, nunc autem tenetur in quadam alia ciuitate.

Nota, quilibet ignis soluit quolibet anno vnum balis pro tributo, quod valet vnum florenum cum dimidio, sed omnes famuli de domo vna pro vno igne computantur: summa ignium tributalium, octies centum millia. Reliqui verò Christiani mercatores, in isto vico non computantur. Copia est ibi victualium.

Quatuor fratres minores vnum potentem conuertebant apud quem hospitabar, et qui duxit me ad Abbatiam istam, ibi vidi scilicet quod hic narratur.

Ad fines itaque regni Mangi transitur grandis fluuius de Dylay, [Marginal note: Vel de Delay.] maius flumen mundi, vbi strictius est continet septem miliaria Odericus: cuius alueus in loco districtiori continet quatuor leucas. Et ex hoc in breui temporis spacio intratur Imperium Tartarorum, sequendo fluuium vsque in terram Pygmeorum, per cuius medium transit.

Hij Pygmei sunt homines statura breues ad longitudinem nostri brachij, seu trium manuum expansarum. Tam mares quam feminæ formosæ et gratiosæ, et viuunt communiter ad annos sex vel septem: si qui pertingunt ad octo, mire putantur senectutis. Ad dimidiam anni ætatem nubere possunt, in secundo anno parturiunt: rationalis sunt, et sensati iuxta ætatem pusillam, ac satis ingeniosi ad opera de serico, et de lana arboris. Frequentèr præliantur contra aues grandes patriæ, exercitibus congregatis hinc inde, et fit strages vtrimque. Hæc gens tam parua optimè operatur sericum et bombycem. Isti Pygmei venerunt mihi obuiam chorizando. Non laborant terram, prædia, seu vineas, sed morantur inter eos nostræ quantitatis homines, qui eos incolunt, sicut serui, quos et Pygmæi sæpè derident, quia sunt ipsis maiores: et quod ipse non cesso mirari dum dicti homines in illa terra generant vel pariunt, non crescit proles supra Pygmæi staturam: Insula non est protensa, sed fortè 12. ciuitatum. Quarum vna est grandis, et bene munita, et quam Grand Can facit cum fortibus armaturis curiosè seruari, contra regem Mangi.

Hinc proceditur per Imperium Grand Can, ad multas ciuitates, et villas morum mirabiliter diuersorum, vsque in regnum Iamchan, quod est vnum de 12. prouincijs maximis, quibus distinguitur totum Imperium Tartarorum.

Nobilior ciuitas huius Regni seu Prouinciæ dicitur Iamchan, abundans mercimonijs, et diuitijs infinitis, et multa præstans proprio Regi tributa, quoniam sicut illi de ciuitate fatentur, valet annuè regi quinquaginta milia cuman florenorum auri.

Nota. In Iamchan ciuitate est conuentus fratrum minorum: in hac sunt tres Ecclesiæ Monasteriorum: reditus simul ascendit ad 12. cuman. Odericus dixit, Vnus cuman est decem millium. Summa tributi annui, quinquaginta milia millium Florenorum. In illis namque partibus magnus numerorum summas estimant per cuman, numerum 10. millium qui et in Flamingo dicitur laste.

Ad quinque leucas ab hac ciuitate est alia dicta Meke, in qua fiunt de quodam albissimi genere ligni naues maxtimæ cum aulis et thalamis, ac multis ædificijs, tanquam Palatium tellure fundatum.

Inde per idem regnum ad viam octo dietarum per aquam dulcem, multas per ciuitates, et bonas villas, venimus Laucherim, [Marginal note: Siue Lanterin.] (Odericus appellat Leuyim,) vrbem formosam opumque magnarum, sitam super flumen magnum Cacameran. [Marginal note: Vel Caremoron.] Hoc flumen transit per medium Cathay, cui aqua infert damnum, quando nimis inundat, sicut palus in Ferraria, Mogus in Herbipoli: et illud sequentes intrauimus principalem prouinciam Imperij Tartariæ, dictam Cathay Calay: et ista prouincia est multum distenta, ac plena ciuitatibus, et oppidis bonis, et magnis omnibusque referta mercimonijs, maximè sericosis operibus, et aromaticis speciebus.

Nauigando per dictum flumen versus Orientem, et itinerando per hanc Cathay prouinciam ad multas dietas per plurimas vrbes et villas, venitur in ciuitatem Sugarmago, [Marginal note: Engarmago.] abundantiorem omnibus in mercemoniis antedictis, quando sericum est hic vilissimum: quadragintæ libræ habentur ibi pro decem florenis.

Ab hac ciuitate, multis ciuitatibtus peregratis versus Orientem, veni ad ciuitatem Cambalu, quæ est antiqua in prouincia Cathay: Hanc postquam Tartari ceperunt, ad dimidium miliare fecerunt vnam ciuitatem nomine Caydo, et habet duodecim portas, et à porta in portam duo sunt grossa miliaria Lombardica, spacium inter medium istarum ciuitatum habitatoribus plenum est, et circuitus cuiuslibet istarum ambit 60. miliaria Lombardica, quæ faciunt octo Teutonica.

In hac ciuitate Cambalu residet Imperator Magnus Can, Rex Regum terrestrium, et Dominus Dominorum terrestrium. Atque indè vlterius in Orientem intratur vetus vrbs Caydo, vbi communiter tenet suam sedem Imperialem Grand Can in suo palatio. Ambitus autem vrbis Caydo, est viginti ferè leucarum, duodecim habens portas à se distantes ampliùs quàm stadia 24.

The English Version.

From that contree, men gon be the see occean, be an yle that is clept Caffolos. Men of that contree, whan here frendes ben seke, thei hangen hem
upon trees; and seyn, that it is bettre, that briddes, that ben angeles of God, eten hem, than the foule wormes of the erthe.

From that yle men gon to another yle, where the folk ben of fulle cursed kynde: for thei norysschen grete dogges, and techen hem to strangle here frendes, whan thei ben syke: for thei wil noughte, that thei dyen of kyndely dethe: for thei seyn, that thei scholde suffren to gret peyne, zif thei abyden to dyen be hem self, as nature wolde: and whan thei ben thus enstrangled, thei eten here flesche, in stede of venysoun.

Aftreward men gon be many yles be see, unto an yle, that men clepen Milke: and there is a fulle cursed peple: for thei delyten in ne thing more, than for to fighten and to sle men. And thei drynken gladlyest mannes blood, the whiche thei clepen dieu. And the mo men that a man may slee, the more worschipe he hathe amonges hem. And zif 2 persones ben at debate, and peraventure ben accorded be here frendes or be sumn of here alliance, it behovethe that every of hem, that schulle ben accorded, drynke of otheres blood: and elle the accord ne the alliance is noghte worthe, ne it schalle not be ne repref to him to breke the alliance and the accord, but zif every of hem drynke of otheres blood.

And from that yle, men gon be see, from yle to yle, unto an yle, that is clept Tracoda; where the folk of that contree ben as bestes and unresonable, and duellen in caves, that thei maken in the erthe; for thei have no wytt to maken hem houses. And whan thei seen ony man passynge thorghe here contrees, thei hyden hem in here caves. And thei eten flesche of serpentes; and thei eten but litille, and thei speken nought; but thei hissen, as serpentes don. And thei sette no prys be no richesse, but only of a precyous ston, that is amonges hem, that is of 60 coloures. And for the name of the yle, thei clepen it Tracodon. And thei loven more that ston, than ony thing elle: and zit thei knowe not the vertue thereof: but thei coveyten it and loven it only for the beautee.

Aftre that yle, men gon be the see occean, be many yles, unto an yle, that is clept Nacumera; that is a gret yle and good and fayr: and it is in kompas aboute, more than a 1000 myle. And alle the men and wommen of that yle han houndes hedes: and thei ben clept Cynocephali: and thei ben fulle resonable and of gode undirstondynge, saf that thei worschipen an ox for here god. And also everyche of hem berethe an ox of gold or of sylver in his forhed, in tokene that thei loven wel here god. And thei gon alle naked, saf a litylle clout, that thei coveren with here knees and hire membres. Thei ben grete folk and wel fyghtynge; and thei han a gret targe, that coverethe alle the body, and a spere in here hond to fighte with. And zif thei taken ony man in bataylle, anon thei eten him. The kyng of that yle is fulle riche and fulle myghty, and righte devout aftre his lawe: and he hathe abouten his nekke 360 perles oryent, gode and grete, and knotted, as Pater Nostres here of amber. And in maner as wee seyn oure Pater Noster and oure Ave Maria, cowntyng the Pater Nosters, right so this kyng seythe every day devoutly 300 preyeres to his god, or that he ete: and he berethe also aboute his nekke a rubye oryent, noble and fyn, that is a fote of lengthe, and fyve fyngres large. And whan thei chesen here kyng, thei taken him that rubye, to beren in his hond, and so thei leden him rydynge alle abouten the cytee. And fro thens fromward, thei ben alle obeyssant to him. And that rubye he schalle bere alle wey aboute his nekke: for zif he hadde not that rubye upon him, men wolde not holden him for kyng. The grete Cane of Cathay hathe gretly coveted that rubye; but he myghte never han it, for werre ne for no maner of godes. This kyng is so rightfulle and of equytee in his doomes, that men may go sykerlyche thorghe out alle his contree, and bere with him what him list, that no man schalle ben hardy to robben hem: and zif he were, the kyng wolde iustifyed anon.

Fro this lond men gon to another yle, that is clept Silha: and it is welle a 800 myles aboute. In that lond is fulle mochelle waste; for it is fulle of serpentes, of dragouns and of cokadrilles; that no man dar duelle there. Theise cocodrilles ben serpentes, zalowe and rayed aboven, and han 4 feet and schorte thyes and grete nayles, as clees or talouns; and there ben somme that han 5 fadme in lengthe, and summe of 6 and of 8, and of 10: and whan thei gon be places, that ben gravelly, it semethe as thoughe men hadde drawen a gret tree thorghe the gravelly place. And there ben also many wylde bestes, and namelyche of olyfauntes. In that yle is a gret mountayne; and in mydd place of the mount, is a gret lake in a fulle faire pleyne, and there is a gret plentee of watre. And thei of the contree seyn, that Adam and Eve wepten upon that mount an 100 zeer, whan thei weren dryven out of Paradys. And that watre, thei seyn, is of here teres: for so moche watre thei wepten, that made the forseyde lake. And in the botme of that lake, men fynden many precious stones and grete perles. In that lake growen many reedes and grete cannes; and there with inne ben many cocodrilles and serpentes and grete watre leches. And the kyng of that contree, ones every zeer, zevethe leve to pore men to gon in to the lake, to gadre hem precyous stones and perles, be weye of alemesse, for the love of God, that made Adam. And alle the zeer, men fynde y nowe. And for the vermyn, that is with inne, thei anoynte here armes and here thyes and legges with an oynement, made of a thing that is clept lymons, that is a manere of fruyt, lyche smale pesen: and thanne have thei no drede of no cocodrilles, ne of non other venymous vermyn. This watre rennethe, flowynge and ebbynge, be a syde of the mountayne: and in that ryver men fynden precious stones and perles, gret plentee. And men of that yle seyn comounly, that the serpentes and the wilde bestes of that contree ne will not don non harm, ne touchen with evylle, no strange man, that entrethe into that contree, but only to men that ben born of the same contree. In that contree and othere there abouten, there ben wylde gees, that han 2 hedes: and there ben lyouns alle white, and als grete as oxen, and many other dyverse bestes, and foules also, that be not seyn amonges us. And witethe wel, that in that contree and in othere yles there abouten, the see is to highe, that it semethe as though it henge at the clowdes, and that it wolde covere alle the world: and that is gret mervaylle, that it myghte be so, saf only the wille of God, that the eyr susteynethe it. And therfore seyth David in the Psautere, *Mirabiles elationes Maris.*

How men knowen be the Ydole, zif the sike schalle dye or non. Of folk of dyverse schap and merveylously disfigured: And of the Monkes, that zeven hire releef to Babewynes, Apes and Marmesettes and to other Bestes.

[Sidenote: Cap. XIX.] From that yle, in goynge be see, toward the southe, is another gret yle, that is clept Dondun. In that yle ben folk of dyverse kyndes; so that the fadre etethe the sone, the sone the fadre, the husbonde the wif, and the wif the husbonde. And zif it so befall, that the fadre or modre or ony of here frendes ben seke, anon the son gothe to the prest of here law, and preyethe him to aske the ydole, zif his fadre or modre or frend schalle dye on that evylle or non. And than the prest and the sone gone to gydere before the ydole, and knelen fulle devoutly, and asken of the ydole here demande. And zif the devylle, that is with inne, answere, that he schalle lyve, thei kepen him wel: and zif he seye, that he schalle dye, then the prest gothe with the sonne, with the wif of him that is seeke, and thei putten here hondes upon his mouthe, and stoppon his brethe, and so thei sleen him. And aftre that, thei choppen alle the body in smale peces, and preyen alle his frendes to comen and eten of him, that is ded: and thei senden for alle the mynstralle of the contree, and maken a solempne feste. And whan thei han eten the flessche, thei taken the bones, and buryen hem, and syngen and maken gret melodye. And alle tho that ben of his kyn, or pretenden hem to ben his frendes, and thei come not to that feste, thei ben repreved for evere and schamed, and maken gret doel; for nevere aftre schulle thei ben holden as frendes. And thei seyn also, that men eten here flesche, for to delyveren hem out of peyne. For zif the wormes of the erthe eten hem, the soule scholde suffre gret peyne, as thei seyn; and namely, whan the flesche is tendre and megre, thanne seyn here frendes, that thei don gret synne, to leten hem have so long langure, to suffre so moche peyne, with oute resoun. And whan thei fynde the flessche fatte, than thei seyn, that it is wel don, to senden him sone to paradys; and that thei have not suffred him to longe, to endure in peyne. The kyng of this yle is a ful gret lord and a myghty; and hathe undre him 54 grete yles, that zeven tribute to him: and in everyche of theise yles, is a kyng crowned, and alle ben obeyssant to that kyng. And he hathe in tho yles many diverse folk. In one of theise yles ben folk of gret stature, as Geauntes; and thei ben hidouse for to loke upon; and thei han but on eye, and that is in the myddylle of the front; and thei eten no thing but raw flessche and raw fyssche.

And in another yle, toward the southe, duellen folk of foule suture and of cursed kynde, that han no hedes: and here eyen ben in here scholdres.

And in another yle ben folk, that han the face all platt, alle pleyn, with outen nese and with outen mouthe: but thei han 2 smale holes alle round, in stede of hire eyen: and hire mouthe is plait also, with outen lippes.

And in another yle ben folk of foul fasceon and schapp, that han the lippe above the mouthe so gret, that whan thei slepen in the sonne, thei keveren alle the face with that lippe.

And in another yle, ther ben litylle folk, as dwerghes; and thei ben to so meche as the pygmeyes, and thei han no mouthe, but in stede of hire mouthe, thei han a lytylle round hole: and whan thei schulle eten or drynken, thei taken thorghe a pipe or a penne or suche a thing, and sowken it in: for thei han no tonge; and therfore thei speke not, but thei maken a maner of hissynge, as a neddre doth, and thei maken signes on to another, as monkes don; be the whiche, every of hem undirstondethe other.

And in another yle ben folk, that han gret eres and longe, that hangen doun to here knees.

And in another yle ben folk, that han hors feet; and thei ben stronge and myghty and swift renneres; for thei taken wyld bestes with rennyng, and eten hem.

And in another yle ben folk, that gon upon hire hondes and hire feet, as bestes: and thei ben alle skynned and fedred, and thei wolde lepen als lightly in to trees, and fro tree to tree, as it were squyrelles or apes.

And in another yle ben folk that ben bothe man and womman: and thei han kynde of that on and of that other; and thei han but o pappe on the o syde, and on that other non: and thei han membres of generacioun of man and womman; and thei usen bothe, whan hem list, ones that on, and another tyme that other: and thei geten children, whan thei usen the membre of man; and thei bere children, whan thei usen the membre of womman.

And in another yle ben folk, that gon alle weyes upon here knees, ful merveylously; and at every pas that thei gon, it semethe that thei wolde falle: and thei han in every foot, 8 toes.

Many other dyverse folk of dyverse nature ben there in other yles abouten, of the whiche it were to longe to telle: and therfore I passe over schortly.

From theise yles, in passynge be the see occean toward the est, be many iourneyes, men fynden a gret contree and a gret kyngdom, that men clepen Mancy: and that is in Ynde the more: and it is the beste lond, and on of the fairest, that may be in alle the world, and the most delectable, and the most plentifous of all godes, that is in power of man. In that lond duellen many Cristene men and Sarrazynes: for it is a gode contree and a gret. And there ben there inne mo than 2000 grete cytees and riche, with outen other grete townes. And there is more plentee of peple there, than in ony other partie of Ynde; for the bountee of the contree. In that contree is no nedy man, ne none that gothe on beggynge. And thei ben fulle faire folk: but thei ben all pale. And the men han thynne berdes and fewe heres; but thei ben longe: but unethe hathe ony man passynge 50 heres in his berd; and on heer sitt here, another there, as the berd of a lyberd or of a catt. In that lond ben many fairere wommen, than in ony other contree bezonde the see: and therfore men clepen that lond Albanye; because that the folk ben whyte. And the chief cytee of that contree is clept Latoryn; and it is a iourneye from the see: and it is moche more than Parys. In that cytee is a gret ryvere, berynge schippes, that gon to alle the costes in the see. No cytee of the world is so wel stored of schippes, as is that. And alle tho of the cytee and of the contree worschipen ydoles. In that contree ben double sithes more briddes than ben here. There ben white gees, rede aboute the nekke, and thei han a gret crest, as a cokkes comb upon hire hedes: and thei ben meche more there, than thei ben here; and men byen hem there alle quykke, right gret chepe. And there is gret plentee of neddres, of whom men maken grete festes, and eten hem at grete sollempnytees. And he that makethe there a feste, be it nevere so costifous, and he have no neddres, he hathe no thanke for his travaylle.

Many gode cytees there ben in that contree, and men han gret plentee and gret chep of alle wynes and vitailles. In that contree ben manye chirches of religious men, and of here lawe: and in tho chirches been ydoles, als grete as geauntes. And to theise ydoles thei zeven to ete, at grete festyfulle dayes, in this manere. Thei bryngen before hem mete alle soden, als hoot as thei comen fro the fuyr, and thei leten the smoke gon up towardes the ydoles; and than thei seyn, that the ydoles han eten; and than the religious men eten the mete aftrewardes. In that contree been white hennes withouten fetheres: but thei beren white wolle, as scheep don here. In that contree, wommen that ben unmaryed, thei han tokenes on hire hedes, lyche coronales, to ben knowen for unmaryed. Also in that contree, ther ben bestes, taughte of men to gon in to watres, in to ryveres and in to depe stankes, for to take fysche; the whiche best is but lytille, and men clepen hem loyres. And whan men casten hem in to the watre, anon thei bringen up gret fissches, als manye as men wold. And zif men wil have mo, thei cast hem in azen, and thei bryngen up als many as men list to have.

And fro that cytee, passynge many iourneyes, is another cytee, on of the grettest of the world, that men clepen Cassay; that is to seyne, the Cytee of Hevene. That cytee is well a 50 myle aboute, and it is strongliche enhabyted with peple, in so moche that in on house men maken 10 housholdes. In that cytee ben 12 princypalle zates; and before every zate, a 3 myle or a 4 myle in lengthe, is a gret toun, or a gret cytee. That cytee sytt upon a gret lake on the see; as dothe Venyse. And in that cytee ben mo than 12000 brigges: and upon every brigge, ben stronge toures and gode; in the whiche duellen the wardeynes, for to kepen the cytee fro the gret Cane. And on that o part of the cytee, rennethe a gret ryvere alle along the cytee. And there duellen Cristene men, and many marchauntes and other folk of dyverse natyouns: be cause that the lond is so gode and so plentifous. And there growethe fulle gode wyn, that men clepen Bigon, that is fulle myghty and gentylle in drynkynge. This is a cytee ryalle, where the Kyng of Mancy was wont to duelle: and there duellen many religious men, as it were of the order of freres: for thei ben mendyfauntes.

From that cytee, men gon be watre, solacynge and disportynge hem, tille thei come to an abbey of monkes, that is faste bye, that ben gode religious men, after here feythe and lawe. In that abbeye is a gret gardyn and a fair, where ben many trees of dyverse manere of frutes: and in this gardyn, is a lytille hille, fulle of delectable trees. In that hille and in that gardyn, ben many dyverse bestes, as of apes, marmozettes, babewynes, and many other dyverse bestes. And every day, whan the covent of this abbeye hathe eten, the awmener let bere the releef to the gardyn, and he smytethe on the gardyn zate with a clyket of sylver, that he holdethe in his hond, and anon alle the bestes of the hille and of dyverse places of the gardyn, comen out, a 3000 or a 4000; and thei comen in gyse of pore men: and men zeven hem the releef, in faire vesselles of sylver, clene over gylt. And whan thei han eten, the monk smytethe eft sones on the gardyn zate with the clyket; and than anon alle the bestes retornen azen to here places, that thei come fro. And thei seyn, that theise bestes ben soules of worthi men, that resemblen in lyknesse of the bestes, that ben faire: and therfore thei zeve hem mete, for the love of God. And the other bestes that ben foule, they seyn, ben soules of pore men and of rude comouns. And thus thei beleeven, and no man may putte hem out of this opynyoun. Theise bestes aboveseyd, thei let taken, whan thei ben zonge, and norisschen hem so with almesse; als manye, as thei may fynde. And I asked hem, zif it had not ben better, to have zoven that releef to pore men, rathere than to the bestes. And thei answerde me and seyde, that thei hadde no pore men amonges hem, in that contree: and thoughe it had ben so, that pore men had ben among hem, zit were it gretter almesse, to zeven it to tho soules, that don there here penance. Many other marveylles ben in that cytee and in the contree there aboute, that were to long to telle zou.

Fro that cytee, go men be the contree a 6 iourneyes, to another cytee, that men clepen Chilenfo: of the whiche cytee, the walles ben 20 myle aboute. In that cytee ben 60 brigges of ston, so faire, that no man may see fairere. In that cytee was the firste sege of the Kyng of Mancy: for it is a faire cytee, and plenteeyous of alle godes.

Aftre passe men overthwart a gret ryvere, that men clepen Dalay: and that is the grettest ryvere of fressche water, that is in the world. For there, as it is most narow, it is more than a myle of brede. And thanne entren men azen into the lond of the grete Chane. That ryvere gothe thorghe the lond of Pigmaus: where that the folk ben of litylle stature, that ben but 3 span long: and thei ben right faire and gentylle, aftre here quantytees, bothe the men and the wommen. And thei maryen hem, whan thei ben half zere of age, and geten children. And thei lyven not, but 6 zeer or 7 at the moste. And he that lyvethe 8 zeer men holden him there righte passynge old. Theise men ben the beste worcheres of gold, sylver, cotoun, sylk, and of alle suche thinges, of ony other, that be in the world. And thei han often tymes werre with the briddes of the contree, that thei taken and eten. This litylle folk nouther labouren in londes ne in vynes. But thei han grete men amonges hem, of oure stature, that tylen the lond, and labouren amonges the vynes for hem. And of tho men of oure stature, han thei als grete skorne and wondre, as we wolde have among us of geauntes, zif thei weren amonges us. There is a gode cytee, amonges othere, where there is duellynge gret plentee of tho lytylle folk: and it is a gret cytee and a faire, and the men ben grete, that duellen amonges hem: but whan thei geten ony children, thei ben als litylle as the pygmeyes: and therfore thei ben alle, for the moste part, alle pygmeyes; for the nature of the lond is suche. The grete Cane let kepe this cytee fulle wel: for it is his. And alle be it, that the pygmeyes ben lytylle, zit thei ben fulle resonable, aftre here age, and connen bothen wytt and gode and malice, y now.

Fro that cytee, gon men be the contree, be many cytees and many townes, unto a cytee, that men clepen Jamchay: and it is a noble cytee and a riche, and of gret profite to the lord: and thidre go men to sechen marchandise of alle manere of thing. That cytee is fulle moche worthe zerly to the lord of the contree. For he hathe every zere to rente of that cytee (as thei of the cytee seyn) 50000 cumantz of floreyns of gold: for thei cownten there alle be cumanz: and every cumant is 10000 floryns of gold. Now may men wel rekene, how moche that it amountethe. The kyng of that contree is fulle myghty: and zit he is undre the grete Cane. And the gret Cane hathe undre him 12 such provynces. In that contree, in the gode townes, is a gode custom. For whoso wille make a feste to ony of his frendes, there ben certeyn innes in every gode toum; and he that wil make the feste, wil seye to the hostellere, arraye for me, to morwe, a gode dyner, for so many folk; and tellethe him the nombre; and devysethe him the viaundes: and he seythe also, thus moche I wil dispende, and no more. And anon the hostellere arrayethe for him, so faire and so wel and so honestly, that ther schalle lakke no thing. And it schalle be don sunnere, and with lasse cost, than and a man made it in his owne hous.

And a 5 myle fro that cytee, toward the hed of the ryvere of Dalay, is another cytee, that men clepen Menke. In that cytee is strong navye of schippes; and alle ben white as snow, of the kynde of the trees, that thei ben made offe. And thei ben fulle grete schippes, and faire, and wel ordeyned, and made with halles and chambres, and other eysementes, as thoughe it were on the lond.

Fro thens go men be many townes and many cytees, thorghe the contree, unto a cytee, that men clepen Lanteryne: and it is an 8 iourneyes from the cytee aboveseyd. This cytee sitt upon a faire ryvere, gret and brood, that men clepen Caramaron. This ryvere passethe thorghe out Cathay: and it dothe often tyme harm, and that fulle gret, whan it is over gret.

Of the grete Chane of Chatay. Of the Rialtee of his Palays, and how he sitt at Mete; and of the grete nombre of Officeres, that serven hym.

[Sidenote: Cap. XX.] Chatay is a gret contree and a faire, noble and riche, and fulle of marchauntes. Thidre gon marchaundes alle zeres, for to sechen spices and alle manere of marchandises, more comounly than in ony other partye. And zee schulle undirstonde, that marchaundes, that comen fro Gene or fro Venyse or fro Romanye, or other partyes of Lombardye, thei gon be see and be lond 11 monethes, or 12, or more sum tyme, or thei may come to the yle of Cathay, that is the princypalle regyoun of alle partyes bezonde; and it is of the grete Cane.

Fro Cathay go men toward the est, be many iourneyes: and than men fynden a gode cytee, betwene theise othere, that men clepen Sugarmago. That cytee is on of the beste stored of sylk and other marchandises, that is in the world. Aftre go men zit to another old cytee, toward the est: and it is in the provynce of Cathay. And besyde that cytee, the men of Tartarye han let make another cytee, that is clept Caydon; and it hathe 12 zates: and betwene the two zates, there is alle weyes a gret myle; so that the 2 cytees, that is to seyne, the olde and the newe, han in circuyt more than 20 myle.

CAPVT. 34.

De pallatio Imperatoris Grand Can.

Palatium Imperatoris Grand Can, quod est in Caydo ciuitate, continet in circuitu proprij muralis vltrà duas leucas, et sunt in eo aulæ quàm plures, in forma nobiles, et in materia nobiliores. Aula autem sedis, quæ est maxime cæterarum, habet intrinsecus pro sui sustentatione 24. aereas columnas factas opere fusorio, de auro puro, et omnes parietes ab intus opertas pellibus quorundam animalium, quæ vocantur Pantheres: hæ sanguinei sunt coloris, et ita remicantes, vt Sole desuper relucente; vix oculus valeat humanus sufferre splendorem, tantæque fragantiæ, vt illi approximare non posset aer infectus, vnde et ista opertura parietum appreciatur super tegmen aurearum laminarum.

Namque stultorum aliqui Paganorum huiusmodi adorant animalia propter colorum, odorumque virtutem. Proposui retrahere calamum à describenda nobilitate, gubernatione et ministrantium frequentia, atque Imperatoris magnificentia: attamen quia coepi ego, propter incredulos, et nescios, ac inerudibiles, non dimittam in toto. Quicunque enim nihil credunt, nihil sciunt, neque erudiri possunt, Scriptura testante, si non credideritis non intelligetis. Dico ergo, et verè dico, quòd in huius aulæ capite sit thronus, vel sedes Imperialis, excelsus et eminens in ascensu graduum quamplurium, in quo residere solet in plenaria maiestate, in cuius throni toto corpore nihil apparet minùs nobile, auro, margaritis, gemmis, et lapidibus preciosis. Singuli gradus sunt de singulis, ac inter se diuersis magnis lapidibus, vtpote primus de Hæmatisto, alius de Sardio, et alius de Chrysolito, et sic vsque ad supremum gradum, qui singuli ad formam cuiusque gradus sunt circumfusi, et clusorio opere firmati, auro solido, et nihilominùs per superficiem auri, distinctè seminati, firmitèrque inclusi lapilli cari, cum orientalibus Margaritis, summitas autem cum ferculo residentiæ in nobilitate excisionis, et fabrifactura operis tam diuersa est, et mira, vt paruitatem mei ingenij excedat, quamobrem et ei cedo, vlteriusque procedo.

Ad Imperatoris sinistram gradu vno bassior, est sedes suæ primæ coniugis, tota de iaspidibus auro circumfusis, et in superficie aulæ distinctæ gemmulæ cum granellis eodem schemate, et similiter de iaspide. Sed adhuc submissior vno gradu est sedes coniugis secundæ, nec non et sub illa vxoris tertiæ. Nam tres proprias secum habet vxores, Odericus dicit, istas duas concubinas. Itémque resident sub tertia coniuge nobiles mulieres de Imperatoris progenie, iuxta illustriam vniuscuiusque.

Et notandum, quòd per totam patriam singulæ mulieres maritatæ, vt intelligantur maritis subiectæ, et vt discernantur à solutis, gestant in capitis summitate similitudinem pedis viri, longitudinis brachij et dimidij, quadam leui materia operatam: videlicet nobiles de sericosis operibus pannorum, seu alijs raris et pulchris pannis, et preciosis lapillis, et ignobiles iuxta statum suum de materia communiori.

Ad dextram verò sedentis Imperatoris vno gradu submissus residet primogenitus eius filius, et sub ipso ordinatè in consimilibus sedibus nobiles proximi de cognitione Imperiali.

Item super thronum et desuper ante ipsius throni locum, tanquam pro celato seu operimento in throno residentium, et eorum ministrantium, est extensa similitudo vitis operata in palmitibus, et pampinis, de auro puro ad extensionem cubitorum quadraginta, per quadrum, atque per eam dependentes botri vuarum de gemmis, et granellis quinque colorum, quorum albi sunt de christallo et beryllo, et iriscrocei de topazio et fuluo christallo, rubei de rubetorum granis, corallo, et alibandinis, virides de Smaragdis, pyropis, et chrysolytis, nigri, de onichinis, gagetis, et gerateris.

Tempore prandij in hac aula, Imperator et Imperatrices, et quisque de prædictis, habet mensam sibi solam, quarum vilior præualet thesauro grandi.

In solennitatibus ponitur mensa Imperatori de exquisito electro, seu de auro examinato, distincta diamantibus, et nobis ignotis in comparabilibus gemmis, quandóque de christallo perspicuo, seu croceo, circumclusa auro cum gemmis: quandóque de Hæmatisto, quandóque de ebore candido, vel rubicundo: interdum de ligno artificiosè combinato, quod descendit per flumina de Paradiso. Idem dicit Odericus.

His mensis astant Barones, et Principes pro vasallis attentè in suis officijs ministrantes, quorum nec vnus emittere verbum aliqua præsumit audacia, nisi Imperatore annuente, vel ad illum loquente, illis duntaxat exceptis, qui certis interspatijs canunt, aut recitant de principum gestis.

Et notandum, quando in hoc solio Maiestatis diebus solennibus residet Imperator, subsidere ad pedes eius notarios quatuor, qui omne quod Dominus loquitur, singuli ponunt in scriptis: nam quodcunque tunc ex ore illius egreditur, necesse est esse, vel effici, nec valet item ipse verbum suum mutare, nec reuocare, nisi magno consilio conuocato.

Vniuersa vtensilia quibus in solennitate ad has seruitur mensas, sunt de nobilibus petris auro reclusis, Cyphi de Smaragdis, vel Saphyris, topasijs, pyropis, siue gryophis: et priuatioribus diebus, de auro probato etiam in cameris, et cubiculis, nec reputatur ibi claritas argenti, nisi pro pilarijs, columnis, gradibus, et pauimentis.

Istius autem ostia aulæ, dum in ea residet, aut deambulat Imperator, multi Barones ingressum seruant intentè, et ne limen tangatur, quod hoc haberent pro augurio, et benè verberaretur, quia Imperatore præsente, nemo nisi adductus in quacunque camera, vel habitatione intromittitur, donec interrogatus iusserit Imperator.

Latitudinem huius Basilicæ æstimo ad spatium de meis pedibus centum et longitudinem vltrà quatuor centum. In cubiculo autem Regis dormitorio, constat vnus pillarius, seu columna de auro solido et carbunculus conclusus in illo longitudinis pedis vnius, totum habitaculum de nocte perfundens lumine claro. Hic prout ego notaui, non est plenè rubeus, sed subrufus, quasi coloris Hæmatistini. Porrò in vna aularum, circà medium palatii, est alius excelsus ascensus, Odericus dicit pigma, super quem dum placet, stat, vel residet Imperator, ditissimè etiam operatus, ex auro, gemmis, baccis, margaritis, et lapidibus raris, et in quatuor angulis, imagines quatuor serpentum de auro puro.

Huius per tria latera dependent retia seu cortinæ de cordulis sericis, in quibus ad singulos nodos, grossa margarita habetur innexa, quibus cortinis tegitur officina: in eius concauitate tenetur tumba quadrata, in qua conueniunt conductus omnium potuum, qui bibuntur in Curia, et innumera vasorum genera, quibus potus omnibus ministratur.

Præstereà, iuxta palatii ambitum, habetur grandis parci spaciamentum, diuersi generis arboribus repletum, fructus ferentibus varios, et nobis inuisos, et in parte media, aula super excelsum collem de tam mira et pulchra structura, vt eius nobilitas de facili ad præsens, non possit describi. Et vndique, par collis gyrum aquæ fossatum profundum, et latum vltrà quod pons vnicus ducit ad collem. Atque ex duobus montis lateribus, stagnum cum diuersorum copia piscium, et volucrum indomitarum, vt aucarum, anatum, cignorum, ciconiarum, ardearum, et collectorum in magna pluralitate, nec non et per parcum, multæ syluestres bestiæ, et bestiolæ quatenùs per aulæ fenestras possit Dominus pro solatio respicere volucrum aucupationes, bestiarum venationes, et piscium captiones.

Et hoc proculdubio sciendum, quòd in nostris partibus rara sint oppida cum pluribus mansionibus, quàm in isto palatio continentur.

Tota æstate moratur in India terra frigidissima, in hyeme in Cambalu. Odericus.

Præter palatium hoc in Caydo, habet Imperator similitèr tria: vnum in ciuitate Sadus, versus Septentrionem, vbi competens est frigus, ibi moratur in æstate. Cambalu, vbi competens calor, ibi moratur hyeme. Tertium in ciuitate Iongh, in quo et in isto Caydo, vt sæpiùs seruat sedem, eò quòd in istis est aer magis temperatus, quamuis semper calidus videtur Nostratibus.

The English Version.

In this cytee is the Sege of the grete Cane in a fulle gret palays, and the most passynge fair in alle the world: of the whiche the walles ben in circuyt more than 2 myle: and within the walles, it is alle fulle of other palays. And in the gardyn of the grete palays, there is a gret hille, upon the whiche there is another palays; and it is the most fair and the most riche, that ony man may devyse. And all aboute the palays and the hille, ben many trees, berynge many dyverse frutes. And alle aboute that hille, ben dyches grete and depe: and besyde hem, ben grete vyneres, on that o part and on that other. And there is a fulle fair brigge to passe over the dyches. And in theise vyneres, ben so many wylde gees and gandres and wylde dokes and swannes and heirouns, that it is with outen nombre. And alle aboute theise dyches and vyneres, is the grete gardyn, fulle of wylde bestes; so that, whan the gret Cane wil have ony desport on that, to taken ony of tho wylde bestes or of the foules, he wil lete chace hem and taken hem at the wyndowes, with outen goynge out of his chambre. This palays, where his sege is, is bothe gret and passynge fair. And with in the palays, in the halle, there ben 24 pyleres of fyn gold: and alle the walles ben covered with inne, of rede skynnes of bestes, that men clepen panteres; that ben faire bestes, and well smellyng: so that for the swete odour of tho skynnes, non evylle ayr may entre in to the palays. Tho skynnes ben als rede as blode, and thei schynen so brighte azen the sonne, that unethes no man may beholden hem. And many folk worschipen tho bestes, whan thei meeten hem first at morwe, for here gret vertue and for the gode smelle that thei han: and tho skynnes thei preysen more than thoughe thei were plate of fyn gold. And in the myddes of this palays is the mountour for the grete Cane, that is alle wrought of gold and of precyous stones and grete perles: and at 4 corneres of the mountour, been 4 serpentes of gold: and alle aboute ther is y made large nettes of sylk, and gold and grete perles hangynge alle aboute the mountour. And undre the mountour, ben condytes of beverage, that thei drynken in the emperours court. And besyde the condytes, ben many vesselles of gold, be the whiche, thei that ben of houshold, drynken at the condyt. And the halle of the palays is fulle nobelyche arrayed, and fulle merveylleousely atyred on all parteys, in alle thinges, that men apparayle with ony halle. And first, at the chief of the halle, is the emperours throne, fulle highe, where he syttethe at the mete: and that is of fyn precyouse stones, bordured alle aboute with pured gold and precyous stones and grete perles. And the grees, that he gothe up to the table, ben of precyous stones, medled with gold. And at the left syde of the emperoures sege, is the sege of his firste wif, o degree lowere than the emperour: and it is of jaspere, bordured with gold and preciouse stones. And the sege of his seconde wif is also another sege, more lowere than his firste wif: and it is also of jaspere, bordured with gold, as that other is. And the sege of the thridde wif is also more lowe, be a degree, than the seconde wif. For he hathe alweys 3 wifes with him, where that evere he be. And aftre his wyfes, on the same syde, sytten the ladyes of his lynage, zit lowere, aftre that thei ben of estate. And alle tho that ben maryed, han a countrefete, made lyche a mannes foot, upon here hedes, a cubyte long, alle wrought with grete perles, fyne and oryent, and aboven, made with pecokes fedres and of other schynynge fedres; and that stont upon here hedes, like a crest, in tokene that thei ben undre mannes fote and undre subiectioun of man. And thei that ben unmaryed, han none suche. And aftre, at the right syde of the Emperour, first syttethe his eldest sone, that schalle regne aftre him: and he syttethe also o degree lowere than the emperour, in suche manere of seges, as don the emperesses. And aftre him, sytten other grete lordes of his lynage, every of hem a Degree lowere than other, as thei ben of estate. And the emperour hathe his table allone be him self, that is of gold, and of precious stones, or of cristalle, bordured with gold, and fulle of precious stones or of amatystes or of lignum aloes, that comethe out of paradys, or of ivory, bounden or bordured with gold. And everyche of his wyfes hathe also hire table be hire self. And his eldest sone, and the other lordes also, and the ladyes, and alle that sitten with the emperour, han tables allone be hem self, fulle riche. And there nys no table, but that it is worthe an huge tresour of gode. And undre the emperoures table, sitten 4 clerkes, that writen alle, that the emperour seythe, be it good, be it evylle. For alle that he seythe, moste ben holden; for he may not chaungen his word, ne revoke it. At grete solempne festes, before the emperoures table, men bryngen grete tables of gold, and there on ben pecokes of gold, and many other maner of dyverse foules, alle of gold, and richely wrought and enameled; and men maken hem dauncen and syngen, clappynge here wenges to gydere, and maken gret noyse: and where it be by craft or be nygromancye, I wot nere; but it is a gode sight to beholde, and a fair; and it is gret marvayle how it may be. But I have the lasse marvaylle, be cause that thei ben the moste sotyle men in alle sciences and in alle craftes, that ben in the world. For of sotyltee and of malice and of fercastynge, thei passen alle men undre hevene. And therfore thei seyn hem self, that thei seen with 2 eyen; and the Cristene men see but with on: be cause that thei ben more sotylle than thei. For alle other naciouns, thei seyn, ben but blynde in conynge and worchynge in comparisoun to hem. I did gret besynesse, for to have lerned that craft: but the maistre tolde me, that he had made a vow to his God, to teche it to no creature, but only to his eldeste sone. Also above the emperours table and the othere tables, and aboven a gret partie in the halle, is a vyne, made of fyn gold: and it spredethe alle aboute the halle; and it hath many clustres of grapes, somme white, somme grene, summe zalowe and somme rede and somme blake, alle of precious stones: the white ben of cristalle and of berylle and of iris; the zalowe ben of topazes; the rede ben of rubies, and of grenaz and of alabraundynes; the grene ben of emeraudes, of perydos and of crisolytes; and the blake ben of onichez and garantez. And thei ben alle so propurlyche made, that it semethe a verry vyne, berynge kyndely grapes. And before the emperoures table, stonden grete lordes, and riche barouns and othere, that serven the emperour at the mete. And no man is so hardy, to speke a word, but zif the emperour speke to him; but zif it be mynstrelles, that syngen songes, and tellen gestes or other desportes, to solace with the emperour. And alle the vesselle, that men ben served with, in the halle or in chambres, ben of precious stones; and specially at grete tables; outher of jaspre or of cristalle or of amatystez or of fyn gold. And the cuppes ben of emeraudez and of saphires or of topazes, of perydoz, and of many other precyouse stones. Vesselle of sylver is there non: for thei telle no prys there of, to make no vesselle offe: but thei maken ther of grecynges and pileres and pawmentes, to halles and chambres. And before the halle dore, stonden manye barounes, and knyghtes clene armed, to kepe that no man entre, but zif it be the wille or the commandement of the emperour, or but zif thei ben servauntes or mynstralle of the houshold: and other non is not so hardy, to neighen nye the halle dore.

CAPVT. 35.

De quatuor solennitatibus, quas Magnus Can celebrat in anno.

Sciatis quòd ego, meíque sodales, pro fama magnificentiæ huius Imperatoris, tradidimus nos stipendiarios esse in guerris, contra Regem Mangi prænominatum. Et fuimus apud ipsum 15. mensibus, et certè inuenimus multò maiorem partem hominum, in mediam partem nobis non fuisse relatam: hominum (exceptis custodibus bestiarum et volucrum,) qui intra palatium certa gerunt ministeria est numerus decem cuman.

Nota. Traxi moram in Cambalu tribus annis: fratres nostri locum habent in Curia sua specialiter, et festis diebus statutis dant benedictionem, Odericus. Et quoniam Imperator habet satis plures quàm decem mille Elephantes edomitos, et velut vltrà numerum alias bestias, (quarum quædam tenentur in caueis, stabulis mirabilibus, vel catenis) nec non et aues rapaces, et accipitres, falcones, ostrones, gryfandos gentiles, Laueroys, et Satyros, sed et auiculas loquentes, et papingos, et similes, aliásque cantantes: reputatur numerus hominum de istis curam et laborem gerentium, vltrà sex cuman, et prættereà iugiter ad Curiam equites cum plenarijs armaturis, quinque cuman, et de peditibus cum præliandi armaturis, cuman decem. Sed et omnes de natione quacunque mundi venientes, qui petunt describi pro Curia recipiuntur. Sic enim iussit Imperator.

Habet et medicos Paganos viginti, et totidem Physicos, atque sine his Medicos Christianos ducentos, et totidem Physicos, quoniam iste Grand

Can maiorem gerit confidentiam in Medicis Christianis, quàm in suæ propriæ nationis medicis.

Hoc ergò firmiter scias, quod de Curia Regis accipiunt necessaria sua iugitèr vltrà triginta cuman hominum, præter expensas animalium et volucrum, cùm tamen in festis maioribus sint homines propè in duplo tanti. Nec valet hic dominus defectum vllum pati pecuniæ, eò quòd in terra sua non currit moneta de argento, vel auro, alióue metallo, sed tantùm de corio vel papyro: horum enim forma denariorum signo Imperatoris impressorum preciatur minoris aut maioris valoris, secundum diuersitatem impressionis, qui per visitationem, detriti vel rupti, cùm ad Regis thesaurarios deferuntur, protinùs dantur pro illis noui.

Quatèr in anno celebrat Imperator festiuitates solennes.

Primam de die propriæ Natiuitatis.

Secundam de die suæ primæ præsentationis in eorum Templo, quod appellant
Moseath, vbi et fit ijs, nescio quod genus circumcisionis.

Tertiam in thronizatione sui Idoli in Templo.

Quartam de die quo Idolum cepit dare responsum, seu facere diabolica mira. Plures enim in anno non tenet solennitates, nisi si quando nuptias filij aut filiæ celebrat.

Itaque in istis solennitatibus est populi multitudo absque numero, omnes tamen in ordine debito, et singuli intendentes proprio ministerio, nam ad hoc ordinandum, et disponendum, electa sunt quatuor Baronum nobilium genera, ex quibus nonnulli sunt Reges, et alij Equites potentes, Duces, et Marchiones, omnes induti holosericis, quibus inserti cum certa disseminatione sunt vbique preciosi lapides, miræ virtutis, et aurifigia speciosa, vt si quis in his partibus vnum de talibus haberet mutatorijs, dici non posset pauper imò prædiues. Et habet quodlibet millenariorum in his vestibus colorem sibi proprium: primum viridem, secundum vermiculum, tertium croceum, quartum purpureum, seu indicum. Ergo in die solenni, dum de mane Maiestatis thronum conscenderit, veniunt se præsentari hoc modo Regi.

Ante primum millenarium procedit copiosa symphonia dulcis chordarum, sicut de violis, cytharis, lyris, et psalterijs, non autem de tubis aut tympanis: et præcedunt Baronis per transuersum Aulæ coram residente Domino ordinatè bini, et bini sub silentio, ferentes ambabus manibus ante pectus tabulam de Iaspide, ebore, christallo, pyropo, vel Hæmatisto, et ante faciem throni inclinant se Imperatori profundè.

Illísque pertranseuntibus, succedit simili modo millenarius secundus, et tertius, atque quartus, nec auditur à quoquam vnicum verbum. Hac præsentatione cum debita maturitate perfecta, resident in basso à latere throni ad proprias mensas, multi Philosophi, seu Artistæ, sicut de Astronomia, Geomantia, Pyromantia, Hydromantia, Chiromantia, Necromantia, auguriis, ac aruspiciis, et huiusmodi, tenentes coram instrumenta suæ artis, alii Astrolabium, et Sphæras de auro, alii in aureis vasis arenam, prunas ardentes, aquam, vinum, oleum, et caluarias mortuorum, loquentes et respondentes, nec non de auro horologia ad minùs duo: et ad cunctas horas secundum cursum horologiorum innuunt Philosophi seruis sibi ad hoc deputatis, vt faciant præstari auditum per aulam, quorum vnus aut duo conscendentes scallum, alta voce proclamant, audite, auscultate, et omnibus intendentibus dicit Philosophorum vnus: Quilibet nunc faciat reuerentiam Imperatori, qui est filius Dei excelsi, Dominus et superior omnium Dominorum Mundi, quia ecce hæc est hora. Et mox singuli in aula inclinato corpore et capite se inclinant maiestati manentes accliui, donec idem philosophus dicat, leuate. Atque protinùs super hoc factum, Musici suis instrumentis, suauem personant melodiam.

Posteà ad aliquantam moram simili modo dicit alias philosophorum, minimus digitus in aure: et ecce hoc omnes faciunt, donec dicat, sufficit: sic in aliam horam, seu moram dicit, manus vestra super os, et posteà manus super caput. Atque in hunc modum iuxta temporis cursum imponunt facienda signa diuersa. Innuunt in eis latere magna mysteria, et quodlibet horum factorum melodia terminat Musicorum. Et sciatis me quandoque in tempore opportuno ab eis interrogasse de his signis, qui responderunt quòd inclinare caput Domino ad illius horæ momentum, foret confirmatio omnibus diebus vitæ suæ, ad obediendum ipsi et fidelitatem obseruandam imperio, nec posse corrumpi promissionibus siue donis, quódque digitum in auricula imponere, obturatio est auditus contra omnia Imperatori, et Imperio contraria. Et sic de singulis factis singula mysteria confingentes decipiunt audientes: horum itaque fraudulento ingenio, iste Grand Can festiuatus, non nisi ad talium iudicium parari permittit cibaria, aut fieri indumenta pro suo corpore.

Dura autem est visum Curiæ gubernatoribus satis de prædictis auditum, faciunt proclamatores silentium imperari, et incipit fieri offerenda Imperatori hoc modo. Intrant omnes qui sunt de cognatione Imperatoris Barones adornati nobilissimè pro cuiusque decentia balteis, et indumentis, quorum primus cum resonante symphonia præmittit ad oblationem quotquot valet de dextrarijs albis, et inclinans ante thronum pertransit, atque per eundem modum singuli Baronum offerentes aliquid dignum iocale inclinant transeuntes, silentio firmè seruato. Post hos intrantes simili modo prælati et Abbates, de iurisdictionibus et religionibus Paganorum offerunt singuli pro suo statu se reuerentèr inclinantes maiestati, et maior prælatorum benedicit Regi, et suis ac Curiæ quadam suæ legis oratione.

Deinde introducuntur elephantes, leones, pardi, simiæ, marmotæ, et diuersæ bestiæ, quarum ductores singuli transeuntes inclinant reuerenter, et intentè. Postremò afferuntur aquilæ, struthiones, gryphandi, accipitres, et papingi, cum diuersis auibus et auiculis, nec non serpentes ac pisces, quorum portitores inclinant profundè, quoniam dicunt omnes terrenas creaturas debere adorationem Imperatori Grand Can filio Dei excelsi: et his perfectis,

Musicæ Camenæ persoluunt debita plenè.

Nos igitur intendamus hoc loco quæso quomodo veraciter Pagani in tenebris ambulant: diabolica inuolutione mens eorum obtenebrata non videt quomodò, cùm Imperator sit homo mortalis nuper natus, et similiter sicut illi infirmitate circundatus, atque in breui cum ipsis moriturus, quem etiam non dubitant sub Deo, clamant eum non Deum, sed Dei filium, vbi vtique prorsus ignorant illum non esse laudandum, nec adorandum, sed eum non intendunt alium filium, filium increatum et connaturalem, qui et ipsos et eum creauit, solum superlaudabilem in secula.

Et hoc alto corde considerantes, laudemus, adoremus, glorificemus, et superexaltemus totis viribus Deum, qui nos filios lucis esse voluit, et salutis, nasci, baptizari, educari, erudiri sub sinceritate fidei Christianæ, excluso schismate et errore, atque sub instituto sacrosanctæ matris Ecclesiæ, in qua sola penè ab omni circumferentia orbis terræ fides, quæ saluat, et per dilectionem operatur nunc remansit.

Et oremus instantèr pro ipsis Paganis, vt agnita veritatis luce videre possint quò ambulant, vt perueniant ad Iesum Christuro coæqualem Dei filium, atque in ipso, et per ipsum laudare et adorare solum vnum verum Deum.

CAPVT. 36.

De ludis et præstigijs in suo festo, et de suo comitatu.

Celebrato post hoc prandio satis morosè, quia nunquam est vltrà semel edendum in die, de quo et eius administratione nunc longum est scribere, adsunt gesticulatores, mira visu, suauiáque auditu pedibus, manibus, brachijs, humeris, capitibus, et toto corpore, ac ad singulos gestus, correspondentes debito vocis sono. Et semper finem horum mirabilium cantilena subsequitur musicorum. Ex hoc ioculatores præstò sunt, et Magi, qui suis incantationibus præstant præstigia multa.

Imprimis faciunt videri Solem et Lunam, oriendo, descendendo consuetum diei intra Basilicam peragere cursum, cum tanta nimietate splendoris, vt vix se inuicem homines valeant recognoscere præ fulgore, dicentes et mentientes, Solem et Lunam coeli hanc mittere reuerentiam Imperatori.

Hinc pari ludo comparent speciosæ puellæ ducere semitas et choreas, nobili gestu nobilissimum ferre poculum lactis equarum in aureis vasis, de quo, ponentes se in genibus, tradunt potum dominis et dominabus.

Tunc portantur et milites in equis, et armis quoque pleni atque parati, qui feruentibus sonipedibus se inuicem cuspidibus ad fragorem magnum configentes lanceas comminuunt, et fragmenta per mensas, et pauimenta discurrunt. Ac deindè fantasticè venantur per aulam, cum canibus et papionibus, ad ceruos, lupos, vrsos, et apros, ad lepores, et marmotas. Quæ singula cùm ad horam pascant vana delectatione sensus corporeos, miseriam tamen inserunt piæ menti, quòd tot et tanti homines, neglecta prorsus animi salute, his diabolicis operationibus se dederunt in toto. Nam certò non ita sine dæmonum consolatione et familiaritate præmissa confingi dicerem.

Nota: à Cambalu ad viginti dietas, est pulchrum nemus girans octo dietas in circuitu, in quo sunt omnia genera animalium: custodes habet circa eum. Triennio vel quadriennio visitat illud Imperator, et cum multa gente nemus circumdat, canes emittuntur et aues, cum multo clamore, et feras congregant in medio nemoris, ad planiciem sibi sitam. Tunc Imperator priùs iacit quinque sagittas, posteà alij: tunc Imperator dicit, Eya, hoc est, mina bestijs, et sicut quilibet capit sagittam suam signatam, percussam, aliis recedentibus ad sua loca. Odericus.

Prætereà ante Imperatoris mensam eriguntur tabulæ latæ aureæ cum sculptis, ac si viuerent, imaginibus gallorum, pauonum ac diuersarum volucrum artificiosè, quas præstigiator facit pro libitu sine apprehensione manus ire, tripudiare, chorizare, tremere, compugnare, bibere, manducare, sed et cantare: quod quidem inter cætera mihi videbatur mirabilius et aspectu delectabilius. Nullus istud plenè intueri potuit, nisi qui erat in throno vel circa: et me oportet hoc loco fateri stultitiam propriam, quòd hac delectatione tractus, magnam adhibui apud Artistam diligentiam, verbis blandis, et quibuscunque munusculis, ac melioribus promissis, quod de tali mihi traderet artem, qui sagax simul et fallax imprimis, spem meam trahebat sponsionum funibus: sed at vltimum penitùs abscindebat, dicens se vouisse Deo immortali, ne cuiquam doceret nisi proprio filio seniori, ac per hoc me Deus ab illo malo conseruauit inuitum, et gratias nunc reddentem.

Certum est illic homines esse subtiles ad quasdam humanas artes, et ingeniosos ad fraudes super omnes, quas noui mundi partes, vnde et inter se dicunt prouerbium, se solos videre duobus oculis, et Christianos vno, cæteros autem homines cæcos: sed mentitur iniquitas sibi, quoniam ipsi vident solo oculo terrena et transitoria, et nos Christiani duobus, quia cum terrenis videmus spiritualia, et mansura: percussit enim Naas, [Marginal

Note: I Sam. 11. 2.] id est, humani generis hostis cum illis fœdus, vt erueret omnibus oculos dextros, scilicet spirituales.

Cùm itaque narrata de præmissis debeant sufficere, quando Imperator Grand Can de vno quatuor palatiorum ad aliud transire velit, vel fortè gratia visitationis aut ardui negotii per Imperium de Regno ad Regnum tendit per comitatus, quatuor exercitibus antè et retrò, et ex ambobus lateribus.

Primus exercitus præcedit personam Regis per vnam de suis dietis, vt semper in hospitium de quo recessit exercitus Rex intret nocte sequenti, et est hic primus comitatus descriptus, et statutus de numero quinquaginta cuman virorum, hoc est, quingentorum millium, sempérque præuisum, et prouisum est, vt inueniant necessaria in locis, vbi habent quiescere, vel tardare siue in hospitiis, siue in tentoriis.

Secundus et tertius comitatus sunt eiusdem numeri virorum cum primo, quorum vnus ad dextram tendit Imperatoris, alius ad sinistrum in distantia ab ipso ad trium vel duarum leucarum.

Quartus autem qui maior est omnibus, subsequitur Imperatorem quasi ad spatium iactus balistæ. Et ad hoc sciendum est, quòd personæ horum comitatuum sunt sigillatim, et summatim omnes descriptæ, vt dum vna moritur vel recedit, protinùs alia inscribatur, et numerus non minuatur. Ipse verò Imperator tendit residens in cella seu camera ædificata super currum grandem forma, fortem robore, nobilem in structura, est cella de ligno Aloes optimi odoris, et parietes cellæ operti in quibusdam locis laminis aureis, quæ et ipsæ distinguuntur gemmis variis, et margaritis.

Est autem currus quatuor rotarum duntaxat, quem trahunt quatuor Elephantes ad hoc curiosè instructi, cum quatuor hippis albis equæ doctis et ipsi cooperti ditissimis tegumentis, ac præter aurigas nobiliter indutos, qui currum cautissimè ducunt, adsunt et quatuor de maioribus palatii Dominis, indè ad vehiculum habentes iugem curam, de minatione eius, et ne vltimo exercitu appropriet infra iactum (vt dixi) sagittæ. Ipse autem interdum pro sodalitate iubet secum ascendere quam vult personam, sed minimè vltra duos. In cellæ quoque culmine, quod aperiri valet et claudi, astant in pertica quatuor grifandi, vel ostiones. Odericus: duodecim Girfalcones, vt si fortè Imperator in ære aquilam, vulturum, ardeam, vel collectorem cerneret, citò dimitteret istorum duas aut plures ad aucupandum.

Nota, per Dromedarios, et cursores, et veloces, qui de hospitio ad hospitium permutantur, scit de remotis noua. Cursor enim appropinquans cornu sonat, et tunc alius præparat, et vlteriùs currit. Odericus. Sciendumque tam primogenitum Regis, quàm singulas de tribus vxoribus ducere similem apparatum in itinerando post ipsum; scilicet cum quatuor comitatibus, antè, et retrò, et à lateribus, sed in valdè minori numero personarum pro placito, et in singulis curribus sequentibus se inuicem per vnam dietam.

Præmissa omnia sic fiunt, dum Imperatori tendendum est remotè, aliàs autem minuuntur, et distinguuntur comitatus, iuxta quod decet, vt nonnunquam omnes Imperatores etiam cum filio simul tendant, cum vna comitatuum distinctione. Transeunte autem sic Imperatore per ciuitates et villas quilibet ante fores proprias præparato igne iactat poluerem aromata redolentem, stans genibus flexis ad reuerentiam illi. Et sciatis vbi propè transitum illius habentur Christianæ Abbatiæ, quas olim constituit Dux Ogerus, exeunt obuiam illi in processione cum vexillis, et sancta cruce, et aqua benedicta, et thuribulo, hymnum, Veni Creator spiritus decantantes.

Nota: Ego semel cum Episcopo nostro, et alijs fratribus, uimus obuiam per duas dietas, et portaui thuribulum. Odericus. Quos ipse à remotis videns, consueuit ad se appellare, et ad crucem suum galeatum deponere, ac reuerentèr nudo capite inclinare: et prælatus dicens super cum aliquam orationem signat cruce, et aqua benedicta aspergit. Et quoniam necesse est, vt quisque extraneus ante Regem apparens, offerat ei aliquid, prælatus in disco præsentat ei fructus, et poma, vel pyra, et hoc in numero nouenario, (ratio ponitur primo capitullo proximo, quod iste numerus est plus cæteris acceptus,) de quibus Imperator vnum sibi sumens, reliqua tradit Dominis præsentibus: quo facto habent relligiosi recedere citò, ne opprimantur multitudine populi subsequentis.

Præfatum Domini galeatum, est ita intextum auro, diamantibus, gemmunculis, et orientalibus margaritis, granellis, et dubletis, et prædiues in materia et artificio, vt ei non sit æquandus magni in partibus istis Regis thesaurus. Item sicut hæc fiunt transeunti Imperatori, fiunt et Imperatricibus, et filio seniori.

The English Version.

And zee schulle undirstonde, that my felawes and I, with oure zomen, we serveden this emperour, and weren his soudyoures, 15 monethes, azenst the Kyng of Mancy, that held werre azenst him. And the cause was, for we hadden gret lust to see his noblelesse and the estat of his court and alle his governance, to write zif it were suche, as wee herde seye, that it was. And treuly, we fond it more noble and more excellent and ricchere and more marveyllous, than ever we herde speke offe; in so moche, that we wolde never han leved it, had wee not seen it. For I trowe, that no man wolde beleve the noblesse, the ricchesse, ne the multytude of folk that ben in his court, but he had seen it. For it is not there, as it is here. For the lordes here han folk of certeyn nombre, als thei may suffise: but the grete Chane hathe every day folke at his costages and expenses, as with outen nombre. But the ordynance, ne the expenses in mete and drynk, ne the honestee ne the clennesse, is not so arrayed there, as it is here: for alle the comouns there eten withouten clothe upon here knees; and thei eten alle maner of flessche, and lityll of bred. And aftre mete, thei wypen here hondes upon here skyrtes: and thei eten not but ones a day. But the estat of lordes is fulle gret and riche and noble. And alle be it, that sum men wil not trow me; but holden it for fable, to telle hem the noblesse of his persone and of his estate and of his court and of the gret multytude of folk, that he holt, natheles I schalle seye zou, a partye of him and of his folk, aftre that I have seen, the manere and the ordynance, fulle many a tyme. And whoso that wole, may leve me, zif he wille; and who so wille not, may chuse. For I wot wel, zif ony man hathe ben in tho contrees bezonde, thoughe he have not ben in the place, where the grete Chane duellethe, he schalle here speke of him so meche merveylouse thing, that he schalle not trowe it lightly: and treuly, no more did I my self, til I saughe it. And tho that han ben in tho contrees and in the gret Canes houshold, knowen wel, that I seye sothe. And therfore I wille not spare, for hem that knowe not, ne beleve not, but that that thei seen, for to telle zou a partie of him and of his estate, that he holt, whan he gothe from contree to contree, and whan he makethe solempne festes.

CAPVT. 37.

Qua de causa dicitur Grand Gan.

Si placet audire, dicam cur hic Imperator sit appellatus Grand Can. Audieram ego in partibus Ierosolymorum hunc esse sic dictum, à filio Noe, Cham: sed in terra Cathay accepi et aliam, et meram huius rei veritatem. Nam et scribendo hæc duo nomina habent differentiam, quòd filius Noe Cham scribitur quatuor elementis, quorum vltimum est M. et iste Can tribus tantùm, quorum vltimum est N.

Post annos Christi 1100. illa prima Tartaria (de qua suprà scripsi in prima parte, capitulo quinto) fuit nimis oppressa seruitute sub Regibus circumiacentium sibi nationum. Quandò autem Deo placuit, maiores illius Tartariæ eleuauerunt de seipsis sibi Regem dictum Guis Can, cui et promiserunt subiectissimam obedientiam.

Idem cùm esset prudens strenuus 12. viriles habens filios, debellauit cum ijs et populo suo, et vicit, ac subiecit cunctos in circuitu Reges, quibus terra indebitè diù subiacuerat. Quin etiam apparente sibi in visione Angelo Dei velut milite in albo equo, et candidis armis, et hortante se, vt transiret Alpes, per montem Beliam, [Marginal note: Vel Belgiam.] et per brachium maris, ad terram Cathay, et ad alias illic plurimas regiones transiuit, et coepit com filijs suis aliquas ex illis debellare, et subijcere, Deo in omnibus adiuuante patentèr. Et quoniam in equo albo ei Angelus apparuit, qui etiam antè passum prædicti maris nouem orationes Deo facere iussit, ideò successores vsque hodiè diligunt equos albos, et nouenarium numerum habent præ cæteris in gratia. Dumque Guis Can morti præ senio appropinquaret, conuocatos ante se filios hortabatur, et mouebat exemplo 12. telorum in simul colligatorum, quæ à nullo filiorum paritèr frangi potuerant, sed dissoluta vnumquodque per se facilè frangebatur, sic filij (inquit) dilectissimi, si per concordiam vos inuicèm dilexeritis, et vixeritis seniori fratri obedientes, confido in Deo iuxta promissionem mihi ab Angelo factam, quòd omnem latissimam istam terram, et optimam illius imperio subijcietis, quod et post patris discessum strenuissimè, ac fidelissimè (Deo sibi prosperante) perfecerunt. Et quia cum proprijs nominibus habebant cognomen Can, primogenitus pro differentia obtinuit nomen Grand Can, id est, Magnus Can, videlicet suprà cæteros fratres, qui sibi in omnibus obediebant.

Itaque iste secundus Imperator vocabatur Ochoto Can.

Post quem filius eius regnauit dictus Guican.

Quartus autem, qui Mango Can baptizabatur, permansitque fidelis Christianus, qui etiam misso magno exercitu cum fratre suo Hallaon in partes Arabiæ et Aegypti mandauit destrui in toto Mahometi superstitionem, et terram poni in manibus Christianorum. Et fratre procedente, accepit rumores de fratris sui Imperatoris morte inopinata, quapropter et redijt negotio imperfecto.

Quintus Cobilacan, qui etiam fuit Christianus, et regnauit 42. annis, et ædificauit magnam ciuitatem Iong, maiorem satis vrbe Roma, in qua et continetur valdè nobile palatium Imperiale. Hinc vsque hodie omnes successores paganismo foedantur.

Tempore autem meò erat nomen Imperatoris Echian Can, et primogenitus eius Cosuecan, præter quem et alios filios habuit 12. de quorum nominibus conscribendis non est curæ presentis.

Prima vxorum suorum vocabatur Serochan, quæ et est filia Præsbyteri Ioannis scilicet Imperatoris Indiæ.

Secunda Verouchan.

Tertia Caranthcan.

Istis duobus Imperatoribus non creditur inueniri maior Dominus sub firmamento Coeli.

In literis quæ huius Imperatoris Tartariæ scribuntur nomine ponitur semper iste Titulus. Can filius Dei excelsi, omnium vniuersam terram colentium summus Imperator, et Dominus Dominantium omnium.

Circumferentia magni sui sigilli, continet hoc scriptum.

Deus in Coelo, Can super terram, eius fortitudo. Omnium hominum Imperatoris sigillum.

Sciendum quoque quod quamuis populi ibi dicuntur, et sunt Pagani, tamen et rex et omnes credunt in Deum immortalem, et omnipotentem, et iurant per ipsum appellantes, Yroga, id est, Deum Naturæ. Sed nihilominus colunt et adorant idola, et simulachra aurea, et argentea, lapidea, lignea, filtria, lanea, et linea.

The English Version.

Wherefore he is clept the grete Chane. Of the Style of his Lettres, and of the Superscripcioun abowten his grete Sealle, and his pryvee Sealle.

[Sidenote: Chap. XXI.] First I schalle seye zou, whi he was clept the gret Chane. Zee schulle undirstonde, that alle the world was destroyed by Noes flood, saf only Noe and his wif and his children. Noe had 3 sones, Sem, Cham and Japhethe. This Cham was he that saughe his fadres prevy membres naked, whan he slepte, and scorned hem and schewed hem with his finger, to his brethren, in scornynge wise: and ther fore he was cursed of God. And Japhethe turned his face away, and covered hem. Theise 3 bretheren had cesoun in alle the lond: and this Cham, for his crueltee, toke the gretter and the beste partie, toward the est, that is clept Asye: and Sem toke Affryk: and Japhethe toke Europe. And therfore is alle the erthe departed in theise 3 parties, be theise 3 bretheren. Cham was the grettest, and the most myghty: and of him camen mo generaciouns, than of the othere. And of his sone Chuse, was engendred Nembrothe the geaunt, that was the firste kyng, that ever was in the world: and he began the foundacion of the Tour of Babyloyne. And that tyme, the fendes of helle camen many tymes, and leyen with the wommen of his generacioun, and engendered on hem dyverse folk, as monstres, and folk disfigured, summe with outen hedes, summe with gret eres, summe with on eye, summe geauntes, summ with hors feet, and many other dyverse schapp, azenst kynde. And of that generacioun of Cham, ben comen the Paynemes, and dyverse folk, that ben in yles of the see, be alle Ynde. And for als moche as he was the moste myghty, and no man myghte withstonde him, he cleped himself the sone of God, and sovereyn of alle the world. And for this Cham, this emperour clepeth him Cham and sovereyn of all the world. And of the generacioun of Sem, ben comen the Sarrazines, And of the generacioun of Japhethe, is comen the peple of Israel. And thoughe that wee duellen in Europe, this is the opynyoun, that the Syryenes and the Samaritanes, han amonges hem; and that thei told me, before that I wente toward Ynde: but I fond it otherwise. Natheles the sothe is this, that Tartarynes and thei that duellen in the grete Asye, thei camen of Cham. But the emperour of Cathay clepeth him not Cham, but Can: and I schalle telle zou how. It is but lityllle more but 8 score zeer, that alle Tartarye was in subiectioun and in servage to othere nacyouns abouten: for thei weren but bestyalle folk, and diden no thing but kepten bestes, and lad hem to pastures. But among hem, thei hadden 7 princypalle nacyouns, that weren soveraynes of hem alle: of the whiche, the firste nacyoun or lynage was clept Tartar; and that is the most noble and the most preysed. The seconde lynage is clept Tanghot; the thridde Eurache; the 4 Valair; the 5 Semoche; the 6 Megly; the 7 Coboghe. Now befelle it so, that of the firste lynage succeeded an old worthi man, that was not riche, that hadde to name Changuys. This man lay upon a nyght in his bed, and he sawhe in a visioun, that there cam before him a knyght armed alle in white, and he satt upon a white hors, and seyd to him, Can, slepest thou? The inmortalle God hathe sent me to the; and it is his wille, that thou go to the 7 lynages, and seye to hem, that thou schalt ben here emperour. For thou schalt conquere the londs and the contrees, that ben abouten: and thei that marchen upon zou, schulle ben undre zoure subieccioun, as zee han ben undre hires: for that is Goddes wille inmortalle. And whan he cam at morwe, Changuys roos, and wente to the 7 lynages, and tolde hem how the white knyght had seyd. And thei scorned him, and seyden, that he was a fool; and so he departed fro hem alle aschamed. And the nyght sewynge, this white knyght cam to the 7 lynages, and commaunded hem, on Goddes behalve inmortalle, that thei scholde make this Changuys here emperour; and thei scholde ben out of subieccioun; and thei scholde holden alle other regiounes aboute hem in here servage, as thei had ben to hem beforn. And on the morwe, thei chosen him to ben here emperour: and thei setten him upon a blak fertre; and aftre that, thei liften him op with gret solempnytee, and thei setten him in a chayer of gold, and diden hym alle maner of reverence; and thei cleped him, Chan, as the white knyght called him. And whan he was thus chosen, he wolde assayen, zif he myghte trust in hem or non, and whether thei wolde ben obeyssant to him or non. And thanne he made many statutes and ordinances, that thei clepen *Ysya Chan*. The first statute was, that thei scholde beleeven and obeyen in God inmortalle, that is allemyghty, that wolde casten hem out of servage; and at alle tymes clepe to him for help, in tyme of nede. The tother statute was, that alle maner of men that myghte beren armes, scholden ben nombred: and to every 10 scholde ben a maystre, and to every 100 a maystre, and to every 1000 a maystre, and to every 10000 a maystre. Aftre he commanded to the princypales of the 7 lynages, that thei scholde leven and forsaken alle that thei hadden in godes and heritage; and fro thens forthe to holden hem payd, of that that he wolde zeve hem of his grace. And thei diden so anon. Aftre he commanded to the princypales of the 7 lynages, that every of hem scholde brynge his eldest sone before him, and with here owne handes smyten of here hedes, with outen taryenge. And anon his commandement was performed. And whan the Chane saghe, that thei made non obstacle to performen his commandement, thanne he thoughte wel, that he myghte trusten in hem, and commanded hem anon to make hem redy, and to sewen his banere. And aftre this, Chane putt in subieccioun alle the londes aboute him. Aftreward it befelle upon a day, that the Cane rood with a fewe meynee, for to beholde the strengthe of the contree, that he had wonnen: and so befelle, that a gret multytude of his enemyes metten with hem; and for to zeven gode ensample of hardynesse to his peeple, he was the firste that faughte, and in the myddes of his enemyes encountred; and there he was cast from his hors, and his hors slayn. And whan his folk saughe him at the erthe, thei weren alle abasscht, and wenden he had ben ded, and flowen everych one; and hire enemyes aftre, and chaced hem: but thei wiste not, that the emperour was there. And whan thei weren comen azen fro the chace, thei wenten and soughten the wodes, zif ony of hem had ben hid in the thikke of the wodes: and manye thei founden and slowen hem anon. So it happend, that as thei wenten serchinge, toward the place that the emperour was, thei saughe an owle sittynge upon a tree aboven hym; and than thei seyden amonges hem, that there was no man, be cause that thei saughe that brid there: and to thei wenten hire wey; and thus escaped the emperour from dethe. And thanne he wente prevylly, alle be nyghte, tille he cam to his folk, that weren fulle glad of his comynge, and maden grete thankynges to God immortalle, and to that bryd, be whom here lord was saved. And therfore princypally aboven alle foules of world, thei worschipen the owle: and whan thei han ony of here fedres, thei kepen hem fulle precyously, in stede of relykes, and beren hem upon here hedes with gret reverence: and thei holden hem self blessed and saf from alle periles, while that thei han hem upon hem; and therfore thei beren here fedres upon here hedes. Aftre alle this the Cane ordeyned him, and assembled his peple, and wente upon hem that hadden assayled hym before, and destroyed hem, and put hem in subieccioun and servage. And whan he had wonnen and putt alle the londes and contrees, on this half the Mount Belyan, in subieccioun, the whyte knyght cam to him azen in his sleep, and seyde to him, Chan, the wille of God immortalle is, that thou passe the Mount Belyan; and thou schalt wynne the lond, and thou schalt putten many nacyouns in subieccioun: and for thou schalt fynde no gode passage for to go toward that contree, go to the Mount Belyan, that is upon the see, and knele there 9 tymes toward the est, in the worschipe of God immortalle; and he schal schewe the weye to passe by. And the Chane dide so. And anon the see, that touched and was fast to the mount, began to withdrawe him, and schewed fair weye of 9 fote brede large; and so he passed with his folk, and wan the lond of Cathay, that is the grettest kyngdom of the world. And for the 9 knelynges, and for the 9 fote of weye, the Chane and alle the men of Tartarye han the nombre of 9 in gret reverence. And therfore who that wole make the Chane ony present, be it of hors, be it of bryddes, or of arwes, or bowes, or of frute, or of ony other thing, alweys he most make it of the nombre of 9. And so thanne ben the presentes of grettere plesance to him, and more benygnely he wil resceyven hem, than though he were presented with an 100 or 200. For hym semethe the nombre of 9 so holy, be cause the messagre of God immortalle devised it. Also whan the Chane of Cathay hadde wonen the contree of Cathay, and put in subieccioun and undre fote many contrees abouten, he felle seek. And whan he felte wel, that he scholde dye, he seyde to his 12 sones, that everyche of hem scholde brynge him on of his arewes; and so thei diden anon. And thanne he commanded, that men scholde bynden hem to gedre, in 3 places; and than he toke hem to his eldest sone, and bad him breke hem alle to gedre. And he enforced hem with alle his myght to breken hem: but he ne myghte not. And than the Chane bad his seconde sone to breke hem; and so schortly too alle, eche aftre other: but non of hem myght breke hem. And than be bad the zongest sone dissevere everyche from other, and breken everyche be him self: and so he dide. And than seyde the Chane to his eldest sone, and to alle the othere, Wherfore myght zee not breke hem? And thei answereden, that thei myght not, be cause that thei weren bounden to gydre. And wherfore, quothe he, hathe zoure litylle zongest brother broken hem? Because, quothe thei, that thei weren departed eche from other. And thanne seyde the Chane, My sones, quoth he, treuly thus wil it faren be zou. For als longe as zee ben bounden to gedere, in 3 places, that is to seyne, in love, in trouthe and in gode accord, no man schalle ben of powere to greve zou; but and zee ben disevered fro theise 3 places, that zoure on helpe not zoure other, zee schulle be destroyed and brought to nought: and zif eche of zou love other, and helpe othere, ze schulle be lordes and sovereynes of alle othere. And whan he hadde made his ordynances, he dyed. And thanne after hym, regned Ecchecha Cane his eldest sone. And his othere bretheren wenten to wynnen hem many contrees and kyngdomes, unto the lond of Pruysse and of Rossye, and made hem to ben cleped Chane: but thei weren all obeyssant to hire eldre brother: and therfore was he clept grete Chane. Aftre Ecchecha, regned Guyo Chane: and aftre him, Mango Chan, that was a gode Cristene man, and baptized, and zaf lettres of perpetuelle pes to alle Cristene men, and sente his brother Halaon with gret multytude of folk, for to wynnen the Holy Lond, and for to put it in to Cristene mennes hondes, and for to destroye Machametes lawe, and for to take the Calyphee of Baldak, that was emperour and lord of alle the Sarazines. And whan this Calyphee was taken, men fownden him of so highe worschipe, that in alle the remenant of the world, ne myghte a man fynde a more reverent man, ne highere in worschippe. And then Halaon made him come before him, and seyde to hym: Why, quoth be, haddest thow not taken with the mo sowdyoures, and men y nowe, for a lytille quantytee of thresour, for to defende the and thi contree, that art so habundant of tresore and so high in alle worschipe? And the Calyphee answered him, For he wel trowede, that he hadde y nowe of his owne propre men. And than seyde Halaon, Thou were as a god of the Sarazines: and it is convenyent to a god, to ete no mete, that is mortalle; and therfore thou schalt not ete, but precyous stones, riche perles, and tresour, that thou lovest so moche. And then he commanded him to presoun, and alle his tresoure aboute him; and so he dyed for hungre, and threst. And than aftre this, Halaon wan alle the lond of promyssioun, and putte it in to Cristene mennes hondes. But the grete Chane his brother dyede; and that was gret sorwe and losse to alle Cristen men.

Aftre Mango Chan, regned Coblya Chan, that was also a Cristene man: and he regnede 42 zere. He founded the grete cytee Izonge in Cathay, that is a gret del more than Rome.

The tother gret Chane, that cam aftre him, becam a Payneme, and alle the other aftre him.

The kyngdom of Cathay is the grettest reme of the world. And also the gret Chan is the most myghty emperour of the world, and the grettest lord undre the firmament; and so he clepethe him in his lettres, right thus, *Chan, filius Dei excelsi, omnium universam Terram colentium summus Imperatur, et Dominus omnium Dominantium.* And the lettre of his grete seel, writen abouten, is this, *Deus in Celo, Chan super Terram, ejus fortitudo. Omnium hominum Imperatoris Sigillum.* And the superscripcioun aboute his lityle seel is this, *Dei Fortitudo omnium hominum. Imperatoris Sigillum.* And alle be it that thei be not cristned, zit natheles the emperour and alle the Tarterynes beleeven in God immortalle. And whan thei wille manacen ony man thanne thei seyn, God knowethe wel, that I schalle do the suche a thing, and tellethe his menace. And thus have zee herd, whi he is clept the grete Chane.

Of the governance of the grete Chanes Court, and whan he makethe solempne Festes. Of his Philosophres. And of his Array, whan he riddethe be the contre.

[Sidenote: Cap. XXIII.] Now schalle I telle zou the governance of the court of the grete chane, whan he makethe solempne festes: and that is princypally 4 tymes in the zeer. The firste feste is of his byrthe: that other is of his presentacioun in here temple, that thei clepen here Moscache, where thei maken a manere of circumsicioun: and the tother 2 festes ben of his ydoles. The firste feste of the ydole is, whan he is first put in to hire temple and throned. The tother feste is, whan the ydole begynnethe first to speke or to worche myracles. Mo ben there not of solempne festes, but zif he marye ony of his children. Now undirstondethe, that at every of theise festes, he hathe gret multytude of peple, well ordeyned and wel arrayed, be thousandes, be hundredes and be tenthes. And every man knowethe wel, what servyse he schalle do. And every man zevethe so gode hede and so gode attendance to his servyse, that no man fyndethe no defaute. And there ben first ordeyned 4000 baronnes myghty and riche, for to gouerne and to make ordynance for the feste, and for to serve the emperour. And theise solempne festes ben made with outen, in hales and tentes made of clothes of gold and of tartaries, fulle nobely. And alle tho barouns han crounes of gold upon hire hedes, fulle noble and riche, fulle of precious stones and grete perles oryent. And thei ben alle clothed in clothes of gold or of tartaries or of camokas, so richely and so perfytly, that no man in the world can amenden it, ne better devisen it. And alle tho robes ben orfrayed alle abouten, and dubbed fulle of precious stones and of grete oryent perles, fulle richely. And thei may wel do so; for clothes of gold and of sylk ben gretter chep there a gret del, than ben clothes of wolle. And theise 4000 barouns ben devised in 4 companyes: and every thousand is clothed in clothes alle of o colour; and that so wel arrayed and so richely, that it is marveyle to beholde. The firste thousand, that is of Dukes, of Erles, of Marquyses and of Amyralles, alle clothed in clothes of gold, with tysseux of grene silk, and bordured with gold, fulle of preciouse stones, in maner as I have seyd before. The secounde thousand is alle clothed in clothes dyapred of red silk, alle wroughte with gold, and the orfrayes sett fulle of gret perl and precious stones, fulle nobely wroughte. The 3 thousand is clothed in clothes of silk, of purpre of Ynde. And the 4 thousand is in clothes of zalow. And alle hire clothes ben so nobely and so richely wroughte with gold and precious stones and riche perles, that zif a man of this contree hadde but only on of hire robes, he myghte wel seye, that he sholde nevere be pore. For the gold and the precious stones and the grete oryent perles ben of gretter value, on this half the see, than thei ben bezond the see, in tho contrees. And whan thei ben thus apparaylled, thei gon 2 and 2 togedre, fulle ordynatly before the emperour, withouten speche of ony woord, saf only enclynynge to him. And everyche of hem berethe a tablett of jaspere or of ivory or of cristalle; and the mynstralle goynge before hem, sownyng here instrumentes of dyverse melodye. And whan the firste thousand is thus passed, and hathe made his mostre, he withdrawethe him on that o syde. And than entrethe that other secunde thousand, and dothe right so, in the same manere of array and contenance, as did the firste; and aftre the thridde, and than the fourthe; and non of hem seythe not o word. And at o syde of the emperours table, sitten many philosofres, that ben preved for wise men, in many dyverse scyences; as of astronomye, nigromancye, geomancye, pyromancye, ydromancye, of augurye and of many other scyences. And everyche of hem han before hem astrolabes of gold; sum speres, summe the brayn panne of a ded man, summe vesselles of gold fulle of gravelle or sond, summe vesseles of gold fulle of coles brennynge, sume veselle of gold fulle of watre and of wyn and of oyle, and summe oriloges of gold, mad ful nobely and richely wroughte, and many other maner of instrumentes aftre hire sciences. And at certeyn houres, whan hem thinkethe time, thei seyn to certeyn officeres, that stonden before hem, ordeynd for the tyme, to fulfille hire commaudemenes, Makethe pees. And than seyn the officeres, Now pees lystenethe. And aftre that, seyth another of the philosophres, Every man do reverence, and enclyne to the emperour, that is Goddes sone and soverayn lord of alle the world; for now is tyme. And thanne every man bowethe his hed toward the erthe. And thanne commandethe the same philosophre azen, Stondethe up. And thei don so. And at another hour, seythe another philosophre, Puttethe zoure litille fynger in zoure eres. And anon thei don so. And at another hour, seythe another philosophre, Puttethe zoure honde before zoure mouthe. And anon thei don so. And at another hour, seithe another philosophre, Puttethe zoure honde upon zoure hede. And aftre that, he byddethe hem to don here hond a wey; and thei don so. And so from hour to hour, thei commanden certeyn thinges. And thei seyn, that tho thinges han dyverse significaciouns. And I asked hem prevyly, what tho thinges betokened. And on of the maistres told me, that the bowynge of the hed at that hour betokened this, that alle tho that boweden here hedes, scholden evere more aftre ben obeyssant and trewe to the emperour: and nevere for ziftes, ne for promys in no kynde, ben fals ne traytour unto him for gode ne evylle. And the puttynge of the litylle fynger in the ere, betokenethe, as thei seyn, that none of hem ne schalle not here speke no contrarious thing to the emperour, but that he schalle telle it anon to his conseille, or discovere it to sum men that wille make relacioun to the emperour; thoughe he were his fadre or brother or sone. And so forthe of alle other thtnges, that is don be the philosophres, thei tolde me the causes of many dyverse thinges. And trustethe righte wel in certyn, that no man dothe no thing to the emperour, that belongethe unto him, nouther clothinge, ne bred, ne wyn, ne bathe, ne non other thing, that longethe to hym, but at certeyn houres, that his philosopheres wille devysen. And zif there falle werre in ony syde to the emperour, anon the philosophres comen, and seyn here avys aftre her calculaciouns, and conseylen the emperour of here avys, be here sciences; so that the emperour dothe no thing with outen here conseille. And whan the philosophres han don and perfourmed here commandementes, thanne the mynstralle begynnen to don here mynstralcye, everyche in hire instrumentes, eche aftre other, with alle the melodye that thei can devyse. And whan thei han don a gode while, on of the officers of the emperour gothe up on an highe stage wroughte fulle curyously, and cryethe and seythe with lowde voys, Makethe pees. And than every man is stille. And thanne anon aftre, alle the lordes, that ben of the emperours lynage, nobely arrayed in riche clothes of gold, and ryally apparayled on white stedes, als manye as may wel sewen hem at that tyme, ben redy to maken here presentes to the emperour. And than seythe the styward of the court to the lordes be name, N. of N. and nempnethe first the most enoble and the worthieste be name, and seythe, be zee redy with suche a nombre of white hors, for to serve the emperour, zoure sovereyn lord. And to another lord, he seythe, N. of N. be zee redy with suche a nombre, to serve zoure sovereyn lord. And so another, right so. And to alle the lordes of the emperoures lynage, eche aftre other, as ben of estate. And whan thei ben alle cleped, thei entren eche aftre other, and presentenen the white hors to the emperour; and than gon hire wey. And than aftre, alle the other barouns every of hem zeven hem presentes, or juelle, or sum other thing, aftre that thei ben of estate. And than aftre hem, alle the prelates of hire lawe, and religiouse men and other; and every man zevethe him sum thing. And whan that alle men han thus presented the emperour, the greetest of dignytee of the prelates zevethe hem a blessynge, seyenge an orisoun of hire lawe. And than begynnen the mynstrelle to maken hire mynstralcye, in dyverse instrumentes, with alle the melodye that thei can devyse. And whan thei han don hire craft, than thei bryngen before the emperour, lyouns, libardes and other dyverse bestes; and egles and veutours, and other dyverse foules; and fissches, and serpentes; for to don him reverence. And than comen jogulours and enchauntoures, that don many marvaylles: for thei maken to come in the ayr, the sonne and the mone, be semynge, to every mannes sight. And aftre thei maken the day to come azen, fair and plesant with bright sonne, to every mannes sight. And than thei bryngen in daunces of the faireste damyselles of the world, and richest arrayed. And aftre thei maken to come in, other damyselles, bryngynge coupes of gold, fulle of mylk of dyverse bestes, and zeven drynke to lordes and to ladyes. And than thei make knyghtes to jousten in armes fulle lustyly; and thei rennen to gidre a gret randoum; and thei frusschen to gidere fulle fiercely; and thei breken here speres so rudely, that the tronchouns flen in sprotes and peces alle aboute the halle. And than thei make to come in huntyng, for the hert and for the boor, with houndes rennynge with open mouthe. And many other thinges thei don, be craft of hire enchauntementes; that it is marveyle for to see. And suche pleyes of desport thei make, til the takynge up of the boordes.

This gret Chan hathe fulle gret peple for to serve him, as I have told zou before. For he hathe of mynstralles the nombre of 13 cumanez: but thei abyde not alle weys with hym. For alle the mynstrelle that comen before hym, of what nacyoun that thei ben of, thei ben withholden with him, as of his houshold, and entred in his bokes, as for his owne men. And aftre that, where that evere thei gon, ever more thei cleymen for mynstralle of the grete Chane: and undre that tytle, alle kynges and lordes, cherisschen hem the more with ziftes and alle thing. And therefore he hathe so gret multytude of hem. And he hathe of certeyn men, as thoughe thei were zomen, that kepen bryddes, as ostrycches, gerfacouns, sparehaukes, faukons gentyls, lanyeres, sacres, sacrettes, papyngayes wel spekynge, and briddes syngynge. And also of wylde bestes, as of olifauntz, tame and othere, babewynes, apes, marmesettes, and othere dyverse bestes; the mountance of 15 cumanez of zomen. And of Phisicyens Cristene, he hathe 200. And of leches, that ben Cristene, he hathe 210. And of leches and Phisicyens, that ben Sarrazines 20: but he trustethe more in the Cristene leches, than in the Sarrazines. And his other comoun houshold is with outen nombre: and thei alle han alle necessaries, and alle that hem nedethe, of the emperoures court. And he hathe in his court many barouns, as servytoures, that ben Cristene and converted to gode feythe, be the prechynge of religiouse Cristen men, that dwellen with him: but there ben manye mo, that wil not, that men knowen that thei ben Cristene.

This emperour may dispenden als moche as he wille, with outen estymacioun. For he despendethe not, he makethe no money, but of lether emprented, or of papyre. And of that moneye, is som of gretter prys, and som of lasse prys, aftre the dyversitee of his statutes. And whan that money hathe ronne so longe, that it begynnethe to waste, than men beren it to the emperoures tresorye: and than thei taken newe money for the olde. And that money gothe thorghe out alle the contree, and thorghe out alle his provynces. For there and bezonde hem, thei make no money, nouther of gold nor of sylver. And therfore he may despende y now, and outrageously. And of gold and sylver, that men beren in his contree, he makethe cylours, pyleres and paumentes in his palays, and other dyverse thinges, what him lykethe. This emperour hathe in his chambre, in on of the pyleres of gold, a rubye and a charboncle of half a fote long, that in the nyght zevethe so gret clartee and schynynge, that it is als light as day. And he hathe many other precyous stones, and many other rubyes and charboncles: but tho ben the grettest and the moste precyous.

This emperour duellethe in somer in a cytee, that is toward the northe, that is cleped Saduz: and there is cold y now. And in wyntre, he duellethe in a cytee, that is clept Camaaleche: and that is an hote contree. But the contree, where he duellethe in most comounly, is in Caydo or in Jong, that is a gode contree and a tempree, aftre that the contree is there: but to men of this contree, it were to passyng hoot. And whan this emperour wille ryde from o contree to another, he ordeynethe 4 hostes of his folk; of the whiche, the firste hoost gothe before him, a dayes iourneye. For that hoost schalle ben logged the nyght, where the emperour schalle lygge upon the morwe. And there schalle every man have alle maner of vytaylle and necessaryes, that ben nedefulle, of the emperoures costages. And in this firste hoost is the nombre of peple 50 cumaunez; what of hors, what of fote: of the whiche every cumanez amounten to 10000, as I have told zou before. And another hoost gothe in the right syde of the emperour, nygh half a journeye fro him. And another gothe on the left syde of him, in the same wise. And in every hoost, is as moche multytude of peple, as in the first hoost. And thanne aftre comethe the 4 hoost, that is moche more than ony of the othere, and that gothe behynden him, the mountance of a bowe draught. And every hoost hathe his iourneyes ordeyned in certeyn places, where thei schulle be logged at nyght; and there thei schulle have alle, that hem nedethe. And zif it befalle, that ony of the hoost dye, anon thei putten another in his place; so that the nombre schal evere more ben hool. And zee schulle undirstonde, that the emperour, in his propre persone, rydethe not as othere gret lordes don bezonde; but zif him liste to go prevyly with fewe men, for to ben unknowen. And elle he rytt in a charett with 4 wheles, upon the whiche is made a faire chambre; and it is made of a certeyn wode, that comethe out of paradys terrestre, that men clepen lignum aloes, that the flodes of paradys bryngen out at dyverse cesouns, as I have told zou here beforn. And this chambre is fulle wel smellynge, be cause of the wode, that it is made offe. And alle this chambre is covered with inne of plate of fyn gold, dubbed with precious stones and grete perles. And 4 olifauntz and 4 grete destreres alle white, and covered with riche covertoures ledynge the chariot. And 4 or 5 or 6 of the grettest lordes ryden aboute the charyot, fulle richely arrayed and fulle nobely; so that no man schalle nyghe the charyot, but only tho lordes, but zif that the emperour calle ony man to him, that him list to speke with alle. And above the chambre of this chariot, that the emperour sittethe inne, ben sett upon a perche 4 or 5 or 6 gerfacouns; to that entent, that whan the emperour seethe ony wylde foul, that he may take it at his owne list, and have the desport and the pley of the flight; first with on, and aftre with another: and so he takethe his desport passynge be the contree. And no man rydethe before him of his companye; but alle aftre him. And no man dar not come nyghe the chariot by a bowe draught, but tho lordes only, that ben about him: and alle the hoost cometh fayrely aftre him, in gret multitude. And also suche another charyot, with suche hoostes, ordeynd and arrayd, gon with the empresse, upon another syde, everyche be him self, with 4 hoostes, right as the emperour dide; but not with so gret multytude of peple. And his eldest sone gothe be another weye in another chariot, in the same manere. So that there is betwene hem so gret multitude of folk, that it is marveyle to telle it. And no man scholde trowe the nombre, but he had seen it. And sum tyme it happethe, that whan he wil not go fer; and that it lyke him to have the emperesse and his children with him; than thei gon alle to gydere; and here folk ben alle medled in fere, and devyded in 4 parties only.

Milton Keynes UK
Ingram Content Group UK Ltd.
UKHW030740071024
449371UK00006B/706